Liberal equality

Liberal equality

AMY GUTMANN
PRINCETON UNIVERSITY

CAMBRIDGE UNIVERSITY PRESS
CAMBRIDGE
LONDON   NEW YORK   NEW ROCHELLE
MELBOURNE   SYDNEY

Published by the Press Syndicate of the University of Cambridge
The Pitt Building, Trumpington Street, Cambridge CB2 1RP
32 East 57th Street, New York, NY 10022, USA
296 Beaconsfield Parade, Middle Park, Melbourne 3206, Australia

First published 1980

Printed in the United States of America
Typeset by David E. Seham Assoc., Inc., Metuchen, N.J.
Printed and bound by The Murray Printing Company, Westford, Mass.

Library of Congress Cataloging in Publication Data
Gutmann, Amy.
Liberal equality.
Bibliography: p.
1. Equality.
2. Liberalism. I. Title.
JC575.G87   320.5'1   79–27258
ISBN 0 521 22828 X   hard covers
ISBN 0 521 29665 X   paperback

To the Memory of Kurt Gutmann

CERTAINLY equality will never of itself alone give us a perfect civilisation. But, with such inequality as ours, a perfect civilisation is impossible.

– Matthew Arnold, "Equality"

Contents

Contents

Preface

Having witnessed the enormous concern about inequality in recent years within the United States, we might concur with Tocqueville's observation that citizens within democratic societies are prone to be preoccupied with equality rather than with liberty.[1] Yet only twenty years ago, John Kenneth Galbraith wrote that "few things are more evident in modern social history than the decline of interest in inequality . . . [;] inequality has ceased to preoccupy men's minds."[2] Rather than question whether democratic citizens are "naturally" more preoccupied with liberty or with equality, I want to supply more reasons for citizens of contemporary liberal democratic societies to be concerned with equality, and I want to indicate why that concern should complement, rather than preclude, a concern for individual freedom.

My interest in equality began in a common way: with an intuitive feeling of uneasiness over the extreme poverty and wealth in the United States and Great Britain, the two societies with which I am most familiar. As a student of political theory, I have examined the existing literature on equality. Some of the best works in political philosophy discuss the many meanings and uses of equality as a concept within our language;[3] some of the best in political science measure inequalities of income and wealth within advanced industrial societies and discuss the relative advantages of the measures themselves.[4] The measures of equality told me enough to confirm my belief that many people in liberal democratic societies are quite poor and fewer others very rich. However, empirical theories tell us nothing about which inequalities are most significant or how much inequality is just or unjust. Nor is it sufficiently illuminating of our substantive concerns about equality to explore its meaning as a concept. Equality has so many meanings in our language that it appears to be particularly prone to Tocqueville's indictment of the "abstract terms which abound in democratic languages": "An abstract term is like a box with a false bottom; you may put in it what ideas you please and take them out again

ix

without being noticed."[5] But once one specifies a context, a purpose, and a conceptual framework, the relevant meanings of equality become more limited and the concept of equality takes on an importance for our normative concerns in political philosophy.[6] Therefore, the discussion that follows presupposes a context – specifically that of contemporary liberal democratic societies (I focus exclusively upon the United States and Great Britain); a purpose – justifying a more equal distribution of goods within those societies; and a conceptual framework – that of liberal theory.[7]

Although my concern with equality preceded my education in political theory, teachers, colleagues, and students have enabled me to think about the problem more clearly. Michael Walzer first helped me feel at home as a political theorist in 1969 when I was a college sophomore. Since then he has read, discussed, and criticized my work with the greatest patience and understanding. My intellectual debt to him is very great. Sidney Verba sparked my interest in participation and equality, and encouraged me to undertake my first study of community control. I doubt whether anyone could have forced me to confront skepticism more effectively than has Judith Shklar. I thank her for undermining any degree of intellectual complacency I might once have had. My debt to John Rawls as a teacher and scholar extends even further than is apparent in these pages. I am also extremely grateful to my friend and colleague Dennis Thompson, who judiciously criticized several previous drafts of this manuscript. Huntington Terrill and Bernard Williams have extensively commented upon earlier versions. Terrill impressed upon me the limitations of my argument with regard to problems of international egalitarianism. An ongoing debate with Paul Sigmund while we were jointly teaching an introductory political philosophy course led me to revise my understanding of liberal theory. Although Stephen Holmes read only a small portion of this manuscript, his comments helped me clarify my contextualist claims for liberal egalitarianism. Sheldon Wolin's comments have led me to reconsider several parts of my enterprise, in particular my claims concerning a Kantian basis for liberal egalitarianism. Were I to respond fully to their comments, I would have to write another, much longer book. Nonetheless, this book is better for those criticisms. And I am very grateful for their encouragement.

I am grateful as well to Abigail Erdmann, who enabled me to write this book by providing welcome relief from the problems of liberal equality. Patricia Williams and Janis R. Bolster gave me

Preface

superb editorial advice. June Traube and Richard Hayden also ably assisted me in preparing the manuscript. My greatest appreciation extends to Michael Doyle, for his steadfast support and wisdom. It should be needless to say that, on having received such good counsel, I alone am responsible for what appears below.

Since I began work on this manuscript in 1973, I have received support from the Danforth Foundation, the National Endowment for the Humanities, the American Council of Learned Societies, and Princeton University. I thank all of these institutions for their generosity.

A. G.

Introduction: equality, liberty, and liberal theory

This essay considers both the foundations and the limits of a liberal theory of equality. I begin by examining the working assumptions about human beings that have operated as plausible supports for the distributive arguments made by liberal egalitarians. These views I call the foundations of liberal egalitarianism in part because they are basic to the case for liberal egalitarianism – and fundamental to the egalitarian's case against a more libertarian, laissez-faire, liberalism.

The foundations of liberal egalitarianism consist of two general characterizations of individuals as equal beings. By one view, people are assumed – at least for purposes of political theory – to be similar in their passions: similar in their general capacities for pleasure and pain as well as in their aversions to certain pains and in their desires for certain pleasures. On the second view, all people are judged to be adequately rational beings, with an assumed capacity to create reasonable life plans and to abide by the moral law necessary to maintain a just social order. Late nineteenth- and twentieth-century liberal egalitarians were not the original proponents of these presuppositions of human equality, although I will try to indicate that these assumptions were well suited to their egalitarian purposes.

One can find these assumptions of human equality in two strands of classical liberal theory. The first one might call the eudaemonistic school; it is inhabited by classical utilitarian thinkers such as Bentham and James Mill. The second I shall call the rationalist school; it includes liberal theorists such as Locke and Kant. Although there are many features that distinguish these two groups of thinkers from each other and internally differentiate the theorists of each school, their agreement concerning the existence of some form of human equality is in itself interesting, given later developments within liberal thought. The first chapter of this essay therefore is selectively expository: It is an investigation of the equality assumptions of these classical liberal thinkers. This initial

1

exposition serves to expose the roots and partial supports of subsequent liberal egalitarian arguments.

Two uses of the concept of equality typically enter into discussions of social justice. The first is that of *describing* people as equal *beings.* The second is that of *justifying* a more equal *distribution* of goods, services, and opportunities among those people. I have called the first use of the concept within liberal theory its "equality assumptions," although it should be clear throughout that the assumptions are not meant in any strict sense to suggest that people are identical beings. Perhaps "similarity assumptions" would be more accurate, but that label fails to convey the strength of group identity that these assumptions entail for liberal theory. Claims of human equality convey an author's identification with other members of the species. The political implications of this identification require further, and extensive, specification.

The second use – as an account of principles of distributive justice – transforms the concept of equality into a conception of egalitarianism. A theory is egalitarian if it on the whole recommends a more equal distribution of goods (broadly considered) and opportunities than exists within the society to which it is addressed by the theorist or by the student applying it at a different time. This use is roughly consistent with Felix Oppenheim's definition,[1] although I do not claim that egalitarianism can be completely understood descriptively, because the descriptive definition leaves unspecified the criteria of distribution: Ought we to be concerned about equality of material goods, of treatment, of satisfactions, or of participatory opportunities? Which of these are chosen as criteria for labeling a theory egalitarian must, I believe, be a matter left for further argument. Our use of the terms "egalitarian" and "just" will therefore overlap, because we shall consider egalitarian only those principles that would create a more equal distribution of goods based upon appropriate or relevant criteria.

The egalitarian arguments I discuss and develop into an integrated theory of equality have roots in classical liberal theory. These roots impart strength and stability to the egalitarian argument that I later develop, though they limit its potential for growth. Although I remain an advocate of liberal equality, I hope to make explicit significant theoretical limits to the claims of liberal egalitarianism. One plausible reason for advocating a *liberal* theory of equality is opportunistic: Because the prevailing conception of justice within Anglo-American societies is liberal, liberal egalitarianism may have a greater chance of gaining popular support than does a radical egalitarian theory. But my decision to discuss and develop a liberal theory of equality is more fundamentally based upon the judgment that liberal theory has a greater egalitarian potential than generally has been recognized – greater even than Rawls's explicit arguments in *A Theory of Justice* have led some critics to believe – and that that potential is compatible with the desire to safeguard and expand individual liberty. Having been moved by critics of liberalism, I want to come to terms with liberalism's egalitarian potential.

Like "equality," "liberalism" is a word that is used with great frequency but rarely defined. Yet some definition appears in order, to clarify my argument. My only claim for the following definition is its usefulness in understanding the coherence and limits of liberal thought and its consistency in characterizing as liberal those theories generally associated with the liberal tradition. I take a liberal theory of justice to have the following characteristics:

1. A liberal theory begins by stipulating what constitutes an individual's interests.
2. Among such interests is an interest in liberty: in doing what one chooses without interference from others.
3. A state is then justified if and only if it satisfies the interests of individuals as previously understood.
4. A liberal theory assumes that a state is necessary to regulate the pursuit of individual interests: Those interests are expected to conflict either in themselves (some people seek power over others) or because of conditions of economic scarcity (all peoples' desires for goods cannot be satisfied simultaneously).

From criteria (1) and (3), this definition of liberal theory is a methodological one, specifying liberal theory as a form of methodological individualism.[2] The specific form of methodological individualism liberal theory adopts is normative. Liberal theorists assume that justification of political principles must be grounded upon a preexisting notion of individual interests. This form of methodological individualism does not preclude a belief in the social formation of individual interests. It only entails a rejection of the view that, by sociologically describing the formation of individual interests, one necessarily denies that those interests can be taken as grounds for deriving principles of justice.

Liberal theorists have of course used different principles of aggregation. Utilitarians specify that the satisfaction of interests is to be maximized regardless of whose interests they are, whereas liberal rights theorists argue that all persons' interests are to be protected *equally*. However, the equality assumptions of liberalism

3

have pushed even utilitarian theorists toward an aggregation principle that tends to effect an equal protection of individual interests.

By this definition, liberal theory may accommodate considerable disagreement over the nature of individual interests: People's interests may be said to lie in satisfying their desires (as in Benthamite utilitarianism) or in realizing their rationally determined interests (as in Kant). Hobbes postulates a person's interests to be exclusively *in* his self, whereas the interest of a progressive Millean individual is an interest *of* the self, at least in part, in communal endeavors and in the pursuit of objective truth.

This definition of liberalism is broad, so as to include the wide variety of theories generally associated with the liberal tradition, without, however, subsuming every theory of social justice. Burke's theory is excluded by the second criterion. Burke directed a great deal of his criticism against the view that liberty is among the basic interests of *all* individuals and that the state's role was therefore to secure that liberty for all citizens. Marx's theory is most obviously excluded by the fourth criterion, which stipulates a substantive assumption he did not share with liberal philosophers.[3]

Durkheim creates an interesting problem, because his descriptive argument – that society exists as a sui generis entity molding human nature – did not preclude a normative agreement with liberal theorists that principles of justice ought to be based upon a recognition of individual interests and ought to safeguard individual freedom.[4] Durkheim relativizes liberal individualism to apply only to those societies in which individuals are already conscious of their particular interests as distinct from those defined by the collectivity, societies Durkheim characterizes by their organic solidarity. Liberal theorists ought to acknowledge this strength of Durkheim's theory: that liberal theories of justice have no place, or make little sense, applied to societies Durkheim characterizes by their mechanical solidarity. One might say that such societies – small, undifferentiated, and nonindividualistic – exist in a state of "nonreflective equilibrium." Neither Locke's nor Hobbes's state of nature nor Rawls's original position is a plausible starting point for judging the justice of such societies, because each of these theoretical perspectives presupposes the existence of a society containing individuals with differing conceptions of the good life, who reflect critically both upon their life chances and upon the justice of their society.

Critics are correct in pointing out that classical liberals have made sweepingly universal claims for their theories, as if human interests (and consciousness) have remained constant throughout history and invariable across societal boundaries. Although it is essential that we accept this criticism of classical liberalism, it need not lead us to condemn the entire enterprise of liberal theory. Rather, I suggest that liberal theories of justice must make more modest claims – claims consistent with Durkheim's criticism of the Kantian belief in a noncontingent, preexisting, and universal human nature. Throughout the remainder of this essay, my claims for liberal egalitarianism are contextual: They refer only to its plausibility within the context of industrial societies in which citizens disagree about conceptions of the good life and are capable of critically reflecting upon the justice of their society.

Liberal theorists have not always justified what is conventionally called a liberal state – that is, a state characterized by (1) constitutional government within a legalistic framework, (2) representative democracy, and (3) systems of equal liberty and opportunity. Hobbes is the most prominent example of a liberal theorist who, taking the liberal method of aggregating individual interests as one of his points of departure, does not arrive at the liberal state. Liberalism as a doctrine of the state thus forms a subset within liberal theories. This categorization confirms our intuition that Locke's is the archetypical liberal theory, one that not only is liberal in its method but also explicitly justifies a liberal state.

My preoccupation in this essay will be with a still smaller subset of liberal theories – liberal *egalitarian* thought. But I stipulated at the outset the constraints of theorizing within which liberal egalitarian thought operates, so as to avoid an arbitrary judgment of its limits.

My definition of liberalism is not directly historical, although I have indicated that the force of liberalism as a theory of justice depends upon the historical and social context in which it is applied. But my definition is compatible with a historically based view of liberalism in the Anglo-American tradition. A strictly historical definition of liberalism – as expounded by seventeenth-through nineteenth- (or twentieth-) century theories – might preclude the question I wish to ask about the possibilities for developing a liberal theory beyond its past or present historical forms.

Alternative definitions of liberal theory that are compatible with historically identified forms of liberalism are also possible. The obvious alternatives would define as liberal those theories whose central concern is individual liberty,[5] or those stipulating the need

5

for limited government.[6] My definition overlaps both alternatives. Yet it has the advantage over the first alternative of distinguishing liberal theories from conservative or radical ones that also value individual liberty but define liberty in distinct ways, and consequently put forward distinct arguments about ways of realizing liberty. Suppose we try to separate liberal from other theories by distinguishing between negative and positive freedom. Negative freedom is the absence of interference with one's activities by other men or institutions; positive freedom is the ability to rule oneself by exercising one's highest rational faculties and so to become one's own master. Liberals have traditionally believed that only by allowing people to be free from external interference can we ever know what their self-realization entails. But even Locke's theory is not one of purely negative freedom. Indeed, all plausible liberal theories of freedom are built upon some notion of what constitutes a rational will. All provide us with some understanding of what range of choices we can understand a reasonable individual to have made freely in a particular society. There are thus a series of steps from purely negative to purely positive notions of freedom, rather than a group of liberal theories based upon negative and another group based upon positive freedom, with a slippery slope descending from the latter into a justification of tyrannical government.[7] Nonetheless, a core element of liberal theory is its understanding that freedom is an essential interest of all individuals and that freedom must entail the possibility of *choosing* among a *broad range* of attractive alternatives. There is, however, more to liberalism than this understanding of liberty; there is, for example, also a *method* of arriving at a positive evaluation of negative liberty.

Emphasizing support only for limited government as definitive of liberal theory may also be misleading, because the question one then wants to ask is, *How* limited? Rousseau's and Burke's preferred governments were also limited, and liberal theorists themselves have differed significantly about how limited a just government must be. Their answers to that question have to a significant degree been contingent upon empirical assumptions concerning the effects of expanding governmental power. Once those assumptions are challenged and altered, the same liberal theories can sanction broader governmental powers without any alteration of their basic principles. Less-limited government, of course, need not entail *arbitrary* or undemocratic use of political power. Almost all liberal theorists – along with Rousseau – have condemned arbitrary use of political power. (Even Hobbes attempted, albeit un-

6

successfully, to argue that it would not be in the sovereign's interests to rule by arbitrary decree.)

Because I have stipulated that liberal theorists take the freedom of every individual to be of prima facie value, a reasonable question to ask is whether and how a concern for equality can consistently enter into liberal thought. This is not a question to be answered briefly. But some indication of the direction of my argument may be useful here, because so many theorists have argued or simply assumed that liberty and equality are incompatible.

Let us take the hardest case for a liberal egalitarian. Assume that liberty – understood as freedom to do what one chooses without interference from others – is a right of every individual. Further, assume that there are no other competing individual rights. Even in this simple world of competing individual rights to freedom, it is common and rational to argue that every individual's liberty may justly be constrained by the like liberty of every other. It is rational, given the premise that every individual ought to be considered a moral equal of every other. Now not all individual sacrifices of liberty entail the loss of liberty on an aggregate level – although it is true, as Isaiah Berlin argues, that "if I curtail or lose my freedom . . . and do not thereby materially increase the individual liberty of others, an absolute loss of liberty occurs."[8] Even most libertarian theorists have recognized this simple but important truth: If I, by my actions, deprive other persons of their freedom of choice – for example, by restricting the resources over which their choice can be exercised – then the curtailment of my individual freedom may enhance the individual freedom of others and may therefore be justified. It is his recognition of this that recommends Locke's theory to contemporary liberal egalitarians. Berlin also recognizes that "the freedom of some must at times be curtailed to secure the freedom of others." But why does he believe that there can be no principle regulating such a trade-off, that at best a "practical compromise" can be found?[9]

Perhaps Berlin wants us to consider a society in which a majority of adults do not enjoy the civil and political liberties of a minority. Let us assume that most of the enfranchised minority have never favored extending the suffrage to the disenfranchised. The disenfranchised force (through extralegal actions) the minority to recognize their right to civil and political freedom. Berlin gives us no reason why we should not choose a principle that requires us to maximize liberty, where each person's liberty is counted equally. In this case, temporarily restricting the liberty of the minority maximizes the number of individuals who have liberty both in the short and in the long run. Alternatively, one might argue for a Lockean principle that justifies revolution even by a minority when their rights are systematically violated. Berlin does not provide us with an argument about why he might doubt either of these moral principles, intended to govern cases of injustice. There is a yet more basic principle to govern situations where one individual's freedom of action restricts another's similar freedom. The long-recognized liberal principle is that each person's freedom must be similarly restricted to those actions that do not intrude upon others' comparable freedom.

This reconciliation of liberty and equality is very basic and perhaps too simple. The problem becomes more complex once one recognizes that there are many freedoms to be regulated. In considering each individual as an equal holder of a "package" of freedoms, liberal egalitarians establish a presumption in favor of equalizing all individuals' shares of freedom. Therefore, if unrestricted freedom to own and regulate private property causes some individuals' freedom of speech and association to be severely restricted, a principled argument can be made for limiting private-property rights. The rule of aggregation employed here is one of equalizing liberties among individuals. A blanket refusal to constrain some individual liberties in the name of other liberties or in the name of equalizing individual shares of like liberties prevents any escape from Hobbes's state of nature, unless one assumes that people's desires are naturally harmonious. But on that assumption, we would never have imagined ourselves in a state of nature in the first place. One way in which equality thus enters liberal thought is as a rule of aggregation: a principle of ordering and balancing liberties so that people are permitted to share freedom(s) equally.

Liberty is not the only value recognized by liberal theorists, and we must therefore wonder whether other values conflict with the value of liberty to the extent that, in Berlin's words, only "practical compromises" can be reached. Consider the right to life that Locke recognized along with the rights to liberty and property. Liberal egalitarians want to say that freedom of choice is not very meaningful without a right to those goods necessary to life itself. This step allows us to say that the existence of liberty can be contingent upon providing individuals – who after all exercise choice within a particular society – with what they need in order to enjoy the exercise of their choice among attractive alternatives. Hobbes, Nozick, and less clearly Berlin have refused to take this step, but they have been inconsistent in their refusal to concede Locke's point – that freedom is not a "liberty for every man to do what he lists . . . but a liberty to dispose and order as he lists . . . within the allowance of those laws under which he is, and therein not to be subject to the arbitrary will of another, but freely to follow his own."[10] If liberal theory is characterized by a refusal to admit this meaning of liberty, then Locke fails as a liberal. Rather than surrender our common understanding of Locke as the archetypical liberal, we ought to suspect the test by which he fails.

If it is meaningful to say that the right to nourishment creates the conditions for freedom, and thereby increases individual freedom to follow one's own will, then freedom of human beings from starvation is a form of freedom – freedom to choose or to follow one's life plan – and not simply a verbal disguise for another value. "Everything is what it is," Berlin claims. "Liberty is liberty, not equality or fairness or justice or culture, or human happiness or a quiet conscience."[11] But not everything is just one thing: Freedom from want to pursue other valued ends can also be understood (or defined) as the value of sustenance. Because we cannot fix the meaning of freedom without regard to social context, we cannot conclude that its meaning must never overlap that of other values. Locke's definition makes freedom compatible with those values that provide the context for expanding every individuals' capacities for choice among attractive alternatives. We should not conclude, however, that liberty therefore becomes synonymous with all other values, or even with equality. Berlin is correct in warning us against such definitional imperialism. Nonetheless, freedom can meaningfully be understood in the context of economic scarcity as freedom *from* want, and in the context of international insecurity as freedom *from* fear, to pursue one's own ends.[12] And we can rightly argue that people will have more freedom if the society in which they live restructures its institutions so as to provide more, and more attractive, alternatives among which to choose.

Although even on this contextualist approach, freedom and equality do not become synonymous, their mutual compatibility increases. If one restricts freedom to the Hobbesian definition, then equality and liberty are compatible only in the sense that each individual's freedom is to be counted equally with others'. But once one recognizes that freedom from want or fear is partly constitutive of freedom to do what one chooses with one's life and that individual freedom expands with the creation of more social alternatives among which to choose, then still more egalitarian

9

principles of distribution become preconditions of realizing or, more accurately, increasing the value of liberty. Liberty does not entail a strictly equal distribution of goods, nor does it entail a more equal distribution unless that distribution is a precondition for expanding individual freedom of choice within a given social context. This is precisely what many contemporary liberal egalitarians contend: that an egalitarian principle is thus a prerequisite for realizing freedom from want if, in order to provide every individual with nourishment, material resources must be distributed more equally within our society. As I have indicated, it is not clear what equality as a political value means other than (1) a description of individuals as (in varying ways) equal beings and (2) a principled argument for redistributing goods (material and other) more equally among persons. Yet the *reason* for preferring equality in the second sense is rarely (and never within liberal theory) equality itself. Equality – understood as a preference for a more egalitarian distribution of goods – is "parasitic" upon other values, not least upon liberty.

Berlin warns us against those who would totally destroy the "negative" meaning of liberty by subsuming it under another value – that of realizing one's true, rational, higher, or inner self.[13] It is not that liberals refuse to value self-fulfillment, but that they rightly refuse to call self-fulfilled persons free if they have not *chosen* their fulfillment. To have engaged in a process of choosing who one is or what one has done is an essential part of what it means to be free. One cannot be a free person without continually engaging in processes of choice. Nor can one's actions be free without being subject to one's own choices, however inwardly determined those choice processes are thought to be.

We often decide whether individuals are free by judging whether the alternatives among which they have choices are attractive or reasonable ones, rather than by investigating the internal nature of their decision-making processes. We can acknowledge, therefore, that not every situation in which a person has a choice is a situation of freedom. Choice is a necessary, not a sufficient, condition of individual freedom: The alternatives from which we are able to choose must be reasonable ones, and the situation of choice itself must be one that facilitates, or at least does not stifle, our ability and desire to choose. We say that slaves are not free because in their situation the capacity for effective choice among attractive life plans is stifled. We may also reasonably doubt whether some of the actions of poor people are free – particularly their choice of work, because the range of options available to them is generally very narrow and those that do exist are quite unattractive (or, we might often say, humanly degrading). The relationship between freedom and equality within liberal egalitarian thought that I shall proceed to establish rests upon these two points: (1) that the act of choosing is an essential condition of freedom; and (2) that for our choice to be free we must be able to exercise it within a context that offers us reasonable alternatives among which to choose.

If one simply fixes the meaning of individual liberty as "the ability of an individual to do what he or she chooses at any given moment without the interference of others," every value is, at least in practice, rendered incompatible with complete individual liberty. What I shall argue is that liberty has been and must continue to be understood in relation to those egalitarian principles that *expand* the realm of individual choice and that *create* more valuable alternatives from which individuals can choose their life plans. I could, however, concede at the outset that a right to complete "natural" liberty – as defined by Hobbes – is impossible in any just and liberal state, that liberals value such liberty but not so much as to refuse to sacrifice it (quite readily) to individual peace, prosperity, or happiness. But this concession unnecessarily weakens the liberal egalitarian argument, for it creates the impression that liberty, as *commonly* understood, plays only a minor role within liberal egalitarian (indeed, even within classical liberal) argument, when it plays a large role, a role comfortably supported by that of equality. In charting the development of liberal egalitarianism, we can better understand how the meaning of liberty has expanded and why we can meaningfully assert its compatibility with – indeed, its mutual dependence upon – egalitarian values.

I shall not attempt here to construct or reconstruct deductive proofs of liberal egalitarianism based upon the premises of classical liberal theory. That would be foolhardy; classical liberal theories themselves (contra Hobbes) are not pure deductive systems. Rather, one of the aims of this essay is to show how liberal theory was and might further be extended in egalitarian directions by the addition of new empirical claims about how society can be expected to work, economically and politically. Were one reading of Hobbes correct, that the universals of human nature suffice to deduce the nature of a just state, such changes in liberal theory would be inconceivable.

Even with the addition of empirical claims to the equality assumptions of classical liberal theory, the egalitarian principles and theories I explore do not stand as logically proven or provable systems. Here I plead the case Mill made for the adequacy of arguments that are capable of determining the intellect,[14] with the significant proviso that my arguments are capable of determining the intellect only of those who already share a basic belief in human equality, in our inability to specify objectively the good life, and in the value of individual freedom. In addition, my arguments repeatedly assume that liberal egalitarians must rely upon empirical assessments – particularly concerning the economy and individual psychology – to arrive at principles of justice. These assessments are by no means indisputable, or undisputed. A sympathetic reader may think that this is to concede too much at the outset to critics of liberal egalitarianism. I think not, and not only because a political theorist's task always is to concede the truth as he or she knows it, but also because I believe that the assumptions – empirical and normative – upon which liberal egalitarianism rests are generally stronger and more plausible than those upon which its critics, especially its neo-conservative critics, rest their case.

Now that I have exposed the foundations of liberal egalitarianism in classical liberal theories, my purpose throughout the remainder of this essay is as creative as it is expository. I wish to explore the development of liberal egalitarian theory beginning in the late nineteenth and continuing into the twentieth century. The theorists I shall examine fall within three competing modes of liberal thought: utilitarian, intuitionist, and deontological. All the thinkers I discuss were or are still concerned with questions of the justice of a more equal distribution of freedoms and economic goods than existed or exists within their societies. In examining the limits to their egalitarian arguments, I hope also to shed some additional light upon the limits of their modes of theorizing. Nevertheless, my primary concern is to expound and explain the force of their specific arguments for redistributive justice.

I begin this exploration of the development of liberal egalitarian thought beyond classical liberalism with John Stuart Mill for several reasons. First, although Mill identified his thought with classical utilitarianism, his theory integrates eudaemonism and rationalism to the extent that people appear capable of *rationally choosing* among more and less worthwhile ("higher" and "lower") pleasures. This choice criterion of pleasure significantly distinguishes Mill's thought from that of James Mill and Bentham and is an important factor enabling him to argue for a more equal distribution of participatory opportunities among citizens, all of whom are assumed capable of appreciating and achieving at least a portion of the higher pleasures when given the appropriate opportunities. The opportunities with which Mill appeared most concerned were educational in the broad sense: opportunities for self-development. Political participation was for him an essential component of that opportunity for self-development. This concern with broadening participatory opportunities, and thereby rendering them more nearly equal, is what I take to be the heart and strength of Mill's theory from the perspective of liberal egalitarianism.

The major weakness of Mill's theory from this perspective is its principled indeterminacy on questions of economic distribution. Mill's theory establishes a presumption in favor of laissez-faire, but the strength of that presumption is significantly weakened by the provisos he attached to its sanction in the *Principles of Political Economy*.[15] In *On Liberty*, he admitted that economic exchange, being an other-regarding activity, must in theory be open to the full utilitarian calculation of social costs and benefits.[16] He believed that those calculations would most often result in the justification of a laissez-faire state policy, but the grounds for his belief were to a significant extent empirical, and to that extent, his justification of laissez-faire economics no longer clearly holds.

Not only is the cogency of Mill's support of laissez-faire historically specific, the theoretical basis of his argument is also weak. We are never told how much inequality of distribution is compatible with his goal of human self-development through expanding participatory opportunities. He appears to offer us either a dated historical faith in laissez-faire as a means of maximizing social utility (and spreading the wealth) or a Benthamite calculus of pleasures and pains (already severely complicated by the distinction between higher and lower pleasures). Mill's theory therefore does not sufficiently examine what the relationship should be between his participatory goal, intended to achieve a broader distribution of the higher pleasures, and the nature of economic distribution within a society. Nevertheless, he does succeed in presenting one of the strongest liberal arguments for expanding opportunities for everybody to participate in the economic as well as in the political institutions of society.

Following Mill in the utilitarian tradition are a group of English political thinkers, the Fabians, who compensate for Mill's lack of concern about economic inequality within liberal society. Their greater concern about distributive inequalities is understandable given their historical vantage point: They saw the future of Mill's early laissez-faire policy and concluded that it did not work as he had anticipated. Although staunch critics of liberal society, the Fabians were not critics of liberal theory; they often employed the tools of utilitarian argument to establish a case for equalizing economic benefits among citizens as a means of maximizing social welfare.

The Fabians built their critique of late nineteenth-century British liberal society largely on the grounds of its failure to provide for the very basic needs of each citizen. Once that primary poverty was seen to be well on the way of abolition, the "new" Fabians (by name and political inheritance the descendants of the Fabians) discovered themselves without a clear map of what the future of an egalitarian liberalism should be like. Tawney and G. D. H. Cole, also loose allies of the old Fabians, provided clues for furthering the egalitarian cause after the abolition of primary poverty. Chapter 3 is an attempt to chart the general egalitarian course of this varied group of British thinkers.

In Chapter 4, I turn to two twentieth-century political philosophers whose essays have had a major impact upon contemporary philosophical discussions of equality within Britain and the United States, yet whose method of argument is not directly allied with either classical utilitarian or deontological theories. The deepest roots of the egalitarian arguments of these contemporary theorists are to be found in Aristotle's *Politics*. The more recent intellectual foundations of the "relevant-reason" logic Bernard Williams and Michael Walzer employ can be found in the theory of ordinary-language philosophy. These theorists provide evidence that ordinary-language philosophy need not have conservative political implications, even if its central doctrine is that of conserving meaning in one's inherited language. I wish in Chapter 4 not only to explore the critical potential and limits of this form of egalitarian thought, but also to demonstrate its ties to the equality assumption of liberal theory or, put differently, its essential dependence upon our acceptance of the logic of the particular kind of social life found within liberal Anglo-American societies.

I shall concentrate upon two major problems that emerge within the development of liberal egalitarian thought up to this point. One is raised by the contemporary Fabians, who wonder, without resolving the question, how different values, such as liberty, should be balanced against the value of equality, as reflected for example in the quest for a more equal distribution of goods within society. The Fabians' retreat from equality can be interpreted in part as a result of their failure to find a satisfactory answer to this "priority problem." Bernard Williams and others who use the logic of relevant reasons simply state that the analysis of our language reveals necessary and sufficient conditions for the distribution of health care, legal services, and other goods to people on the basis of need. But they fail to inquire further into *why* this priority in our language has moral force. For these theorists, moral explanation stops at the level of analysis of our language, or of the logic of existing social institutions. Though explanation surely must stop somewhere, those who challenge egalitarianism on grounds of its incomplete explanation of the priority of equality over other values present a legitimate plea for additional moral explanation.

This case is taken up by John Rawls, whose theory of justice provides priority rules intended to balance egalitarian and libertarian concerns. Rawls's contribution to egalitarian argument is on a par with J. S. Mill's, insofar as each theorist attempts to provide us with a complete framework of justice within which we can assess the need for a more equal distribution of goods and for greater participatory opportunities within our society. In Chapter 5, I examine Rawls's contribution to the development of liberal egalitarianism, critically evaluating and revising the priority rules explicitly set out by Rawls.

In Chapter 6, I consider several of the strongest and most representative arguments against liberal egalitarianism. First, I turn to the most cogent arguments against liberal egalitarianism from the left, concentrating on those put forward by C. B. Macpherson. I argue that Macpherson's arguments should be taken as an immanent critique of liberal egalitarianism. Rather than undermining the projects of Mill and Rawls, Macpherson's critique indicates flaws in the present construction of liberal egalitarianism that are capable of being repaired without uprooting the foundations of liberal theory. Similarly, I consider the most recent attack upon liberal egalitarianism from the liberal right, especially that of Robert Nozick in *Anarchy, State and Utopia*. [17] Nozick denies that liberal egalitarian theories, specifically those of Rawls and Williams, are as faithful to the foundations and spirit of classical liberalism as is his libertarian conception of justice. I defend liberal egalitarianism against the libertarian attack by demonstrating its greater completeness, internal coherence, and consistency with classical liberalism.

Liberal egalitarians have traditionally been concerned either with redistributing economic goods or with expanding participatory opportunities within a society. Rarely have both concerns been central to, or adequately integrated within, one egalitarian

15

theory. J. S. Mill, G. D. H. Cole, and Carole Pateman, for example, are clearly "participation theorists." The explicit concerns of the Webbs, Bernard Williams, and John Rawls are overwhelmingly "redistributionist" in nature.[18] Yet some of the greatest tensions within liberal theory and liberal society arise from the apparent conflict between participatory and redistributionist ideals. Within liberal theory, one wants to know whether democratic decision making is always the appropriate procedure for determining what distribution of goods is just within a society. Is democracy a guarantor of just distribution, the best available means to an already predetermined just distribution, or only occasionally and contingently the preferred means to just ends? If democracy does not always guarantee a just distribution of economic goods, is Mill's participatory ideal in any sense undermined by Rawls's argument for the difference principle?

Within contemporary American society we have witnessed this tension between redistributionist and participatory ideals in many arenas. In the field of education, demands for community control may conflict with those of equalizing educational results or opportunity among children in different school districts. In industrial relations, demands for workers' control can be viewed as a challenge to the equitable distribution of income between producers and consumers. Within bureaucracies, participatory democracy may potentially challenge the value of productive efficiency and lines of authority, thereby indirectly calling into question broader redistributionist goals and the ends of "rational" government. In Chapter 7, I attempt a theoretical reconciliation of these two faces of egalitarian justice within the context of ideal theory and explore several of the possible implications of this extended egalitarian vision for recent problems in American society.

An assumption of my method of resolution is that an adequate egalitarian theory can and must unite the redistributive and participatory ideals of egalitarian justice into a single vision, without sacrificing either ideal to the other. At the same time, of course, I risk not satisfying either group of egalitarian theorists entirely. But if in the process of reconciliation I can preserve the fundamental value of both participatory and redistributive ideals, I shall have succeeded in my task. Though the model of egalitarian justice I offer succeeds on these grounds, there undoubtedly exist other modes of reconciliation that remain undiscovered by my method. In addition, many important details of my proposed model of egalitarian justice are left unexamined. Although my own resolution remains undefinitive and incomplete, I hope at least to have made explicit a major problem which has lain relatively dormant within liberal political philosophy and to encourage others to pursue in greater specificity the questions this problem raises for political theory and for contemporary political life. No doubt, were my subject narrower, more precision would be possible. Yet the cost in failing to comprehend the potential egalitarian scope as well as the limits of liberal thought would be great as well.

Chapter 1

The classical liberal foundations

We distinguish modern political theory from ancient and medieval theories of politics by its individualism,[1] which is one of those "isms" that contain many distinct and conflicting ideas "strangely combined and derivative from a variety of dissimilar motives and historic influences."[2] The belief in human equality can be disentangled from the web of individualism, although it is an idea that Steven Lukes rightly argues is basic to the modern doctrine of individualism, equal respect for the human dignity of all people being essential to the realization of individual autonomy, the protection of privacy, and the opportunity for self-development.[3]

But neither individualism nor the more specific belief in human equality has been embraced by all modern thinkers. Saint-Simonian socialists, along with other modern thinkers, expressed disdain for societies that placed the individual citizen at their center and for political theorists whose starting point was a consideration of the interests, desires, or rights of individuals. Burkean conservatives denied that a just state could be conceived on the assumption of human equality: Individuals needed preordained social roles or niches if human dignity – at least the dignity of some humans – was to be preserved.[4] It is only modern *liberal* theorists who overwhelmingly deny previous claims of a natural hierarchy, while contending that a just state must be conceived on the basis of an assumption of human equality. Despite this unifying theme of liberalism, no single postulate of human equality is to be found in classical liberal theory. Rather, there exists a variety of statements concerning human equality, which can be organized into two basic types of equality assumptions. One I call the assumption of equal passions; the other the assumption of equal rationality. Each of these two categories is quite broad and demands explication. In this chapter, we shall explore the nature and role of these equality assumptions in the theories of five classical liberal thinkers: Hobbes, Bentham, James Mill, Locke, and Kant.

To say that classical liberal theories were characterized by assumptions of human equality of course does not imply that classical liberalism was an egalitarian doctrine. Hobbes's theory clearly sanctioned enormous inequalities of power between sovereign and subjects, and Lockean liberalism justified great inequalities in the distribution of property, at least once consent to money was assumed. These political and economic inequalities may have been even greater than those sanctioned by previous hierarchical views of politics. The contribution these classical liberal theorists made to subsequent egalitarian arguments is to be found in their equality assumptions and the principles allied with these assumptions, rather than in the substantive conclusions they reached concerning the correct distribution of goods, services, and political power in their own societies.

By initially separating the basic assumptions of classical liberal theory – and central among these, postulates of human equality – from more contingent empirical claims that have transformed those postulates into inegalitarian principles of justice, we can in the end demonstrate that liberalism and egalitarian justice are not incompatible. Further, if we accept certain plausible empirical claims about contemporary economic and political life, liberalism is more compatible with egalitarian than with inegalitarian principles of justice. The interpretation that follows in this chapter therefore is not meant to illumine the historiographical significance of classical liberal theory, but to exhibit the actual and potential relevance of that theory to subsequent Anglo-American egalitarian thought.

Two strands of classical liberal thought converge in a justification of the minimal liberal state (a state characterized by some form of constitutional government, representative democracy, and a system of equal liberty and opportunity). The two strands are distinguishable by their apparently different assumptions about human equality. One school – typified by the utilitarians Jeremy Bentham and James Mill – views human beings as sharing certain similar passions. As if nerve endings were the most exposed parts of people's characters, Bentham and Mill, examining those endings, conclude that their structure is similar and that they react similarly to certain stimuli, both positive and negative.[5] Hobbes is a precursor of this school of thought: He is a liberal theorist who shares Bentham's and Mill's equality assumptions without justifying a liberal state.

Locke and Kant are the most significant members of the second school. Whereas passions play the politically unifying role for Bentham and Mill, both Locke (in his political writings) and Kant view us as equal in that we share a minimal rational capacity for taking responsibility for our lives and for knowing and obeying the moral law. Bentham and Mill, like Hobbes, begin with a view of people as equal, amoral beings. By nature we are all designed to satisfy our passions. We naturally call good only that which is a means to our own satisfaction.[6] Locke and Kant presuppose that each of us by nature is equipped with a capacity for understanding and accepting principles of justice.[7] At least we are assumed to be equal moral beings until we clearly demonstrate otherwise.

These are the apparent differences on the level of equality assumptions between Bentham and Mill, on the one hand, and Locke and Kant, on the other. By the end of this discussion, the dichotomy between passions and rationality will appear more ambiguous, as neither the assumption of similar passions nor that of a shared rational capacity can stand unsupported by the alternative assumption.[8] We shall stop both to examine this tendency toward integration of equality assumptions and to investigate its epistemological status before moving on to explore the egalitarian uses of these equality assumptions by subsequent liberal thinkers.

EQUAL PASSIONS

Neither Hobbes nor Bentham nor Mill claims the absurd: that all persons are similar in that each experiences the identical emotions (how would we know?), that each desires the same objects (who would we then be?), or that each gains the same satisfactions from identical pursuits (how, given scarcity, could we survive?). Yet although they strenuously deny that we are similar in these respects, Hobbes and Bentham still claim that our passions are similar in one significant respect: We all desire security and have a corresponding aversion to an insecure existence. Our aversion to insecurity for Hobbes is of course of a very specific nature: Our fear of violent death far overrides the political importance of our other passions.[9] This ultimately sets Hobbes's political theory apart from Bentham's and Mill's. But the securing of expectations is a political end shared by each theorist, and an end that has an important role in subsequent arguments for more egalitarian distributive principles than Hobbes, Bentham, or James Mill explicitly sanctioned.

The significance of the passions as a basis for theorizing about justice is the second standard shared by the classical utilitarians.

No preordained or natural hierarchy of the passions is assumed to exist such that if my passions were of more intrinsic worth or my motives more pure than yours, I might be considered superior and entitled to greater consideration on the scales of social justice or to a loftier position in an established social hierarchy. The passions are ranked only on the basis of the satisfaction derived from them; the goodness of motives judged only on the basis of their propensity to produce pleasure or to avert pain:

> With respect to goodness and badness, as it is with everything else that is not itself either pain or pleasure, so is it with motives. If they are good or bad, it is only on account of their effects: good, on account of their tendency to produce pleasure, or avert pain; bad, on account of their tendency to produce pain, or avert pleasure.[10]

Finally, for all three theorists of this school, self-interest is no more than the satisfaction of passions, and happiness is the measure of that satisfaction. Rationality organizes our passions; it engages in scouting and spying expeditions in the service of fulfilling our desires: "For the Thoughts, are to the Desires, as Scouts, and Spies, to range abroad, and find the way to the things Desired. All Stedinesse of the mind's motion, and all quicknesse of the same, proceeding from thence. For . . . to have no Desire, is to be Dead."[11] Bentham and James Mill lead us to a similar self-understanding:

> The understanding is not the source, reason is of itself no spring of action. The understanding is but an instrument in the hand of the will. It is by hopes and fears that the *ends* of action are determined; all that reason does, is to find and determine the *means*.[12]

> The positions which we have already established with regards to human nature, and which we assume as foundations are these: that the actions of men are governed by their wills, and their wills by their desires; that their desires are directed to pleasure and relief from pain as *ends*, and to wealth and power as the principal means; that to the desire of means there is no limit . . .[13]

Reason is therefore not a faculty with its own substantive moral content. In the broadest sense, a person's own interest is the rational ordering of his or her passions at any given moment and over time. Given a society of scarcity and the presence of objects of mutual desire, people's passions will conflict in such a way that their satisfaction will entail asserting power over others. The necessity of creating a state becomes evident, and insofar as the state can prevent or at least moderate the conflicts between people's

21

interests, each person's interest in civil society is likely to be better secured.

Given these shared assumptions, why do Bentham and Mill argue for a representative democracy and Hobbes for an absolute sovereign? Bentham and Mill assume that, other things being equal, each person is the best judge of his or her own interest. Other things are not equal in Hobbes's state of nature: The satisfaction of *one* passion is rationally more important than the satisfaction of the rest. For Hobbes, all people *do* and therefore *should* above all else desire to preserve their lives:

Every man is desirous of what is good for him, and shuns what is evil, but chiefly *the chiefest of natural evils, which is death;* and this he doth, by a certain impulsion of nature, no less than that whereby a stone moves downward.[14]

And forasmuch as necessity of nature maketh men to will and desire *bonum sibi,* that which is good for themselves, and to avoid that which is hurtful; *but most of all that terrible enemy of nature, death,* from whom we expect both the loss of all power, and also the greatest of bodily pains in the losing; it is not against reason that a man doth all he can to preserve his own body and limbes, both from death and pain. And that which is not against reason, men call Right.[15]

Hobbes justifies an absolute monarch on the grounds that he will at least protect this overriding interest of all citizens in avoiding violent death. (At most, he may satisfy another passion Hobbes admits to being universal: the desire for a commodious living.[16] But were Hobbes to emphasize this human interest, the basis for his support of monarchical government would be weaker.) If the satisfaction of one passion is of overwhelming and universal importance, and an agent who can be relied upon to secure that satisfaction for everyone exists, democratic means will be unnecessary – unless political participation is regarded as more than merely the means of satisfying the passions.

Neither Bentham nor James Mill set a value on political participation as an end in itself or as a means to a person's "self-development." (What would "self-development" mean in a Benthamite view of personality?) Nevertheless, because neither Bentham nor Mill shares Hobbes's confidence that one agent can be relied upon to secure everyone's satisfaction, a plausible case for representative democracy emerges from the classical utilitarian view of people as utility maximizers.

Mill argues that as long as people's self-interest is constituted by the desire for power over others or by the desire for scarce objects, representative democracy will be the safest means of governing available. Power, in Mill's as in Hobbes's view, is a good the human desire for which is insatiable. By a natural progression, therefore, kings will become intolerable despots: "Whenever the powers of government are placed in any hands other than those of the community – whether those of one man, of a few, or of several – those principles of human nature imply that those persons will make use of them to defeat the very end for which government exists."[17] As evidence of what may happen without minimal representative democracy, Mill cites the British subjugation of West Indians to slavery.[18] The assumption of self-interest or greed for power does not suffice for Mill to recommend democracy as a means of government, for he must also stipulate that people's interests be *equally* represented. Otherwise an undemocratic form of government might be devised that adequately represented those persons or satisfied those passions judged more valuable than others. Mill thereby dismisses Hobbes's case for monarchical authority by carrying Hobbes's own postulate concerning human nature to a more plausible political conclusion. Yet we should not ignore the intent and implications of Hobbes's individualism for subsequent liberal theory. His theory supplied a potentially egalitarian perspective revised and developed by subsequent liberal theorists, one important tenet of which is that no one need reasonably submit to another's rule unless he benefits and everyone else will do the same.[19]

Having rejected Hobbes's case for legitimizing political authority by a purely formal authorization of sovereignty, why do Bentham and Mill not adopt direct democracy on the Athenian model, especially given their doctrine that pleasures of similar intensity are equally legitimate and worthy of representation?[20] Mill's explicit answer may not be theoretically satisfying, but, contra Hobbes, it reveals that no clear deductive justification of the state exists within liberal theory. All theorists draw their conclusions from a collection of premises, including assumptions concerning human nature as well as debatable empirical claims, a collection bounded by assumptions concerning the parameters within which political theorizing is assumed to operate. Mill took the need for a large-scale society for granted. Unlike Rousseau, he implicitly rejected the critical value of utopia building and therefore concluded that direct democracy is an impracticable means of governance.[21]

Representation becomes the most important means of checking the arbitrary power of government and ensuring equal consider-

ation of interests. The process of checking necessitates the delegation of sufficient power to representatives and an identity of interests between representatives and governed.[22] With the latter
criterion, Mill provided grounds for self-criticism. The forty-six-
year-old Mill argued that the interests of men under forty could
safely be entrusted to their elders and that women's interests were
also safely subsumed under those of their "protectors," men over
forty. But utilitarianism, as John Stuart Mill later recognized, does
not logically entail "older manhood" suffrage.[23] Once one accepts
James Mill's view of the purpose of the state, extending suffrage
requirements only entails noting the inadequacy of his claims
about whose interests require representation.

To the conservative objection that "the people are not capable of
acting agreeably to their interests," Mill has a reply. It is better to
risk being ruled poorly by mistake than by design, because "the
evils which arise from mistake are not incurable; for if the parties
who act contrary to their interest had a proper knowledge of that
interest, they would act well." The notion of *knowing* one's interests enters into Mill's argument here as it must into all utilitarian
argument. He immediately concludes that "what is necessary . . .
is knowledge."[24] People cannot simply and naturally pursue their
pleasures in politics because effective political representation requires knowledge of one's interest – if only because voting is not a
spontaneous act of passion.[25] In general, political acts demand effort without promise of immediate gratification. An act as simple
as voting requires in addition a calculation of individual interest:
a prior understanding of who one is electing and what the nature
of the choice is.[26]

Here is the bridge between the utilitarian and rationalist view of
the individual. Although the work of a rational faculty is limited
for Mill to that of scouting and spying for the passions, some
people's scouts and spies may be better trained than others. And
so knowledge, or at least potential educability, becomes an essential political attribute of citizenship, opening up the possibility for
political inequality. Although Mill's argument suggests an
opinion-leader model of politics, he does not make any institutional recommendations for unequal representation from that
model.[27] The prevailing assumption is that unequal representation is a sure evil, whereas extending suffrage to the ignorant but
educable is not. Suppose, he argues,

the theory of will opposed to interest to be correct: the practical conclusion would be – as there is something of a remedy to the evils arising from
this source, none whatever to the evils arising from the conjunction of

power and sinister interest – to adopt the side which has the remedy, and to do whatever is necessary for obtaining the remedy in its greatest possible strength, and for applying it with the greatest possible efficacy.[28]

Mill's suggested remedy is to employ the "utmost exertions to increase the quantity of knowledge in the body of the community."[29] Education clearly emerges here as one of the most politically relevant institutions within a liberal democracy, second only to the institutions of representative democracy themselves.

Mill's optimism concerning people's educability derives from his conception of knowledge as something that serves rather than transcends natural self-interest. The tasks that a rational faculty must perform are restricted to balancing pleasures and pains – present and future – against each other in order to determine the best course of action. Mill's justification of equal citizenship thus relies upon his estimation both of the equal worth of individual utilities and of the minimal rational capacities of most citizens. His utilitarian scale is of course tipped from the start in favor of democracy, because the assumption that individuals will seek to dominate one another if given the opportunity makes the *risk* of ineffective democratic government well worth taking.[30] After all, the alternative to representative government *ensures* oppression!

Bentham's theory locates more precisely the realm in which representative democracy reigned for classical utilitarianism; for though the argument for equal representation was a strong one, the scope of democratic decision making remained quite restricted in Bentham's theory. Beginning with a premise about individuals' equal capacities for happiness, Bentham lays the moral foundations for the administrative bureaucracy of a liberal state. His arguments reveal that the realm of decision making required for a liberal representative democracy may be very small, depending upon the knowledge available to civil servants. Taken together, Bentham's now familiar rules of thumb – (1) that each individual's utility is to be weighed equally with the others, and (2) that there exists a diminishing marginal utility for any given good – reinforced the case for each person's vote to be counted as one.[31] Yet these two assumptions also made the bureaucrat's tasks practically possible and morally justifiable.

If individual utilities can be known and compared, an impartial observer may be capable of calculating what social distribution will achieve the greatest happiness of the greatest number. Bentham's rules of thumb suggest that, other things being equal, more money to the rich would produce a smaller return to the social store of happiness than more to the poor. These two seemingly innocent assumptions suggest an egalitarian economic policy. But two issues arose within this utilitarian framework, both crucial to an understanding of how far along the road to egalitarian justice utilitarianism took Bentham. One was how to decide on utilitarian grounds which decisions to include within the sphere of democratic decision making and which to authorize to legislative discretion or bureaucratic determination. The second issue Bentham's calculus raised was how to balance the utility of private enterprise against the utility of redistribution. That these are impossible problems to solve "in principle" is, in itself, an important discovery, for it means that Benthamite assumptions may sanction inegalitarian distributive policies in some contexts and egalitarian ones in others.

One answers the first question by determining whether democratic or bureaucratic means will effect the ends sanctioned by the utilitarian pleasure–pain calculus.[32] Benthamite psychology supplies a prima facie case for an equal distribution of goods (assuming the two equality rules). But Bentham's psychology is neutral concerning the means – democratic or bureaucratic – to effect this end. Mill's argument suggests, however, that democratic controls are necessary simply to ensure that bureaucrats (or legislators, as the case may be) do not serve their own, rather than the public's, interests. Democracy therefore becomes a necessary means of controlling the natural egoism of political representatives and civil servants, none of whom can reasonably be considered to be the impartial spectators that a utilitarian would ideally desire.

In Bentham's own theory, democratic participation has no value independent of the limits upon political tyranny that it is expected to effect. However, were participation seen as (in part) a pleasure in itself, or as a means of increasing an individual's future capacity for pleasures, the realm of democracy might be increased, in comparison to that of bureaucratic determination or legislative discretion. John Stuart Mill's revision of classical utilitarian doctrine serves to remind us of this possibility.

The second problem – of balancing the utility of private enterprise against that of redistribution – removes the "other things being equal" clause from the problem of redistribution and thereby enables Bentham to challenge the justice of a strongly redistributive economic policy. Bentham argued that even were the ideal distribution of goods relatively equal – given people's equal capacities for happiness and the rule of diminishing marginal utility – the need for incentives to produce would render the ideal of equal distribution moot. Bentham assumes that people will not work or invest enough if they do not receive the full market return on their production or investment, or at least the full return minus whatever is necessary in taxation for certain collective goods such as defense and a criminal justice system.[33] He never specifies *how much* taxation would render the marginal utility of increased production and investment equal to that of resulting public revenue. He seems to share the prevailing assumption that a society will derive the greatest benefits from a free-market system.[34]

Bentham's own utilitarian calculations thereby placed severe limits upon egalitarian reform, increasing the freedom of private enterprise rather than the realm of democratic decision making. Yet neither the freedom of private enterprise nor that of political choice was considered a *right* inherent in individuals independent of the social results of its exercise. This may be viewed as either an advantage or a disadvantage of classical utilitarianism in relation to egalitarian goals: There are no principled guarantees of equal political rights within the theory, but neither are there principled objections on grounds of individual freedom to restrictions on the scope of private enterprise. Bentham's objection to redistributive goals therefore was contingent upon the elasticity of the supply of goods, services, and savings compared to income; the relative utility of increased investment and production to that of tax dollars at the margin; and the nature of people's passion or dispassion for work. Thus the utilitarian incentive argument against redistribution depends upon, among other things, the nature of available employment; the extent of the disincentives entailed in state provision of goods, services, or income; and the social need for increased production. Because the nature of each of these factors can vary over time, it is not surprising that classical utilitarianism became – in the hands of the Fabians – a framework for justifying more egalitarian principles of justice than either Bentham or James Mill explicitly sanctioned.

EQUAL RATIONALITY

Locke and Kant reject the utilitarian framework of theorizing and focus upon the shared rationality of individuals rather than upon their similar passions. If this dichotomy between passions and rationality is somewhat misleading, as I believe it is, it nevertheless aptly characterizes the distinct emphases and starting points of the utilitarian and rationalist schools of political thought. The presence of a rational faculty, capable of perceiving and acting upon the moral law, is the most politically significant shared attribute of mankind for both Locke and Kant, providing each theorist with an alternative theoretical foundation to utilitarianism for justifying the liberal state.

The equality assumption of Benthamite utilitarianism created the problem of legitimizing passions that were distinctly asocial and perhaps even destructive in their effects, provided those passions were the source of great pleasure to some people. If those passions were productive of greater pain, utilitarian calculations would sanction limiting their exercise. But classical utilitarians implicitly relied upon a notion of what was rational for people to desire, and to what degree, as a means of concluding that certain actions should be punished by the state and other actions encouraged by public policy.

Locke implicitly rejects determining which passions are more worthy of satisfaction than others by assessing the relative quantity of pleasure produced by each. (I am generalizing, of course, from his political writings, not from his *Essay concerning Human Understanding*.) Rational beings share three universal objects of desire: life, liberty, and property. Equal protection of the rights to these universal goods and just compensation and retribution for corresponding infringements of these rights constitute the substantive objects of rational desire vis-à-vis political life:

[All men are naturally in] a state also of equality, wherein all the power and jurisdiction is reciprocal, no one having more than another; there being nothing more evident than that creatures of the same species and rank, promiscuously born to all the same advantages of nature and the use of the same faculties *should* also be equal one amongst another without subordination or subjection . . . The state of nature has a law of nature to govern it, which obliges every one; and reason, which is that law, teaches all mankind who will but consult it that, *being all equal and independent*, no one ought to harm another in his life, health, liberty, or possessions.[35]

Given this equality postulate, the challenge to Locke's assumption – the challenge that any theorist who postulates equal rationality must face – is why rational beings do not all recognize and uphold these "self-evident" rights as their prime political interest.[36]

Although Locke is concerned to argue against the view that there exist "innate ideas" given to us at birth, his argument in the *Essay* does not eliminate the possibility that there exist universal truths and principles *knowable* by human reason or intuition.[37] Circumstances and people themselves nevertheless can facilitate or hinder the development of rational understanding. Locke, for example, claims that,

in fact, all men everywhere are sufficiently prepared by nature to discover God in His works so long as they are not indifferent to the use of these inborn faculties [reason and sense perception] and do not refuse to follow whither nature leads. Thus it is clear that men *can* infer from sense experience that there exists some powerful superior who has right and authority over themselves.[38]

The possibility of a just revolution is an important indication in Locke that people are naturally prone not only to acknowledge the minimal foundations of just rule but to resist the imposition of unreasonable dominance. The right to revolt precedes and is reinforced by the natural ability and inclination to perceive the dictates of political right. Martin Seliger's suggestion that "the right of the majority of all citizens to give effect to their dissent through revolution represents an unqualified concession to political equality" can be extended: This right of all in Locke also represents a *qualified* political concession to the rational potential of every citizen.[39]

The most fundamental political implications of Locke's equality assumptions are those relating to constitutional government and majority rule. Seliger points out that "the procedure of majority decisions recommends itself because it is morally superior to obligate all by virtue of what most approve than by what one or a few approve, not to mention that generally political decisions affect the majority more, and certainly no less than the minority."[40] Taken alone, this deduction ignores the significant constraints on majority rule that the rationality postulate demands. Because people are equal not simply in their right to pursue their passions but in their right to certain definable goods that they all can (at least potentially) recognize, majority rule must be limited to a sphere within the universe of guaranteed individual rights to life, liberty, and property. The precise definition of those rights is crucial to an assessment of their political significance and is also contingent on the meaning of the rationality postulate itself. But it is significant to note here that sovereignty in Locke is constrained at the very time it is popularized by the assumption of human rationality: Participatory rights are equalized among rational beings, but democratic decision making is constrained within the bounds of the principles of political right.[41]

Locke's justification of the particular rights that the liberal state is to protect appears to have both a secular and a religious foundation. His political writings suggest two distinct *sources* for deriving rights and two corresponding *methods* for engaging in the enterprise of justification. The first source is God;[42] the corresponding method is biblical exegesis and God-given human insight. (This method, human insight, converges on the method tied to the second source. But the justificatory power of the two remain distinct.) The second source is human experience; the faculty of human reason coupled with sense perception provides the appropriate tools for such a justification.[43]

Ultimately one must choose between the Christian and secular justifications of Lockean liberalism, as the two sources and methods diverge on issues crucial to liberal egalitarianism. To those interested in developing a stronger liberal argument for egalitarianism than Locke himself provided, Locke's secular method and source are more appropriate, and more compelling to a modern consciousness.[44] Why would atheists not keep mutually advantageous contracts? Surely, human rationality dictates that promises should be kept, as it suggests to Locke that individual liberty be respected. If atheists can be trusted to keep contracts, then a justification of the state must admit that they too will be capable of obedience and obligation. Locke's attitude toward atheists can be dismissed as inessential to his politics so long as we simultaneously question the foundation of obligation to the liberal state in the existence and belief in God and the nature of God's will.[45] The secularization of Lockean liberalism broadens the scope of toleration; every rational being, atheists and Catholics included, can now be assumed capable of keeping contracts. Yet as the foundation of rights and obligations shifts from a belief in God to a capacity to assess one's rational political interest, the appropriate source for defining the nature of individual rights also shifts.

Beginning with the second method and source of justification, Locke arrives at his idea of what constitutes human rights from a conception of human reason: "The freedom . . . of man, and liberty of acting according to his own will, is grounded on his having reason which is able to instruct him in that law he is to govern himself by, and make him know how far he is left to the freedom of his own will."[46] Granting that the rights to life and liberty are plausibly based upon individual reason, what connection does the right to property have to this reason? At an early point in the *Second Treatise,* Locke introduces the notion of "self-ownership": "Though the earth and all inferior creatures be common to all men, yet *every man has a property in his own person;* this nobody has any right to but himself."[47] Self-ownership naturally excludes people from having rights over others unless they consent. The right to order one's life as one wills is thus tied to a view that (absenting God's ownership) people own themselves and not one another. Their rationality is particular to the satisfaction of their own desires and designs for life. Rationality is tied to self-ownership in a moral as well as a factual sense; because people are rational beings they can be assumed to be responsible for their own actions. Thus people *own* their actions in two senses: They have the right to do what they will so long as they do not infringe upon another person's equal right to life, liberty, or possessions; and as mature persons they are presumed responsible for the harm as well as for the benefits accruing from their actions. The right to punish individuals for the harm they have caused flows from this belief that they are responsible for causing that harm and could have decided to do otherwise. Similarly, the idea that a person is entitled to the product of his labor seems to be tied to an argument about individual responsibility and desert: "The labor of his body and the work of his hands, we may say, are properly his. Whatsoever then he removes out of the state that nature has provided and left it in, he has mixed his labor with, and joined to it something that is his own, and thereby makes it his property."[48]

Property rights thereby become a metaphor for human rights.[49] The equal right to life is identified with the claim that all people own themselves and their own actions; the equal right to liberty with the claim that each person should be free to do with his life and possessions that which he chooses; and the equal right to property with the claim that each person should be entitled to whatever "flows" from his own actions. For Locke this meant that people were entitled to whatever they mixed their labor with and thereby added value to. The self-ownership metaphor carries the implication that people are their own possessions. Property – at least in oneself – thereby becomes an essential attribute of personhood.[50] Locke has only to justify the connection of external possession to an individual to render property in the narrower sense an essential individual right as well. But establishing this connection is not easy for several reasons. If my body is simply another piece of property like any other, then to assert that I own myself simply begs the question whether I can own other, nonattached property. If, as is obviously the case, my body is not simply another piece of property, then the metaphor of self-ownership is too weak to establish the right to own other things in a *way* different from self-ownership. But even if we were to ignore these limi-

31

tations to the self-ownership metaphor, we would soon confront the two Lockean provisos that intervene between a person's labor and the possession of the product of that labor: (1) "Enough and as good" must be "left in common for others," and (2) no more may rightly be possessed than that which can be used without waste.[51]

The Lockean metaphor of self-ownership has often been used to prejudge the case for private property and against communal ownership. Its corresponding concept in classical utilitarian theory is that of *self*-interest. Nevertheless, Locke's two provisos may place severe upper limits upon the *amount* of property any individual can rightfully accumulate. Even were land very abundant, as Locke reasonably might have assumed, the waste proviso would limit every person to a fairly modest possession of property[52] – at least until the introduction of money. Then the Lockean argument radically changes, as do its implications for the limitations upon private property. The use of money makes possible a surplus immune from waste. Locke assumes, in addition, that private ownership of the means of production will stimulate the productive use of land, labor, and capital, thereby expanding rather than contracting the resources available for human use and consumption.[53] Private property no longer appears as an absolute right. The provisos have rendered it a limited right, a right based upon a calculation of consequences. Locke can now consistently allow for taxation, if the majority consents.[54]

Nevertheless, given that individuals have equal rights as owners of their own persons and by deduction as owners of their own labor, it is not clear that Locke can so easily sanction great inequalities of property, unrelated to the extent to which individuals have labored. On the basis of the self-ownership assumption such inequalities of propertied and propertyless could be legitimate only if all consented to the system which generated that inequality. This is indeed what Locke claims – that people all consent to the introduction and, he must assume, to the continued use of money.[55] The reason he gives us to believe that people, owners of their own persons as he initially describes them in the state of nature, would consent to a system that admitted such inequalities is that their lives will thereby be improved.[56] (I leave aside for the moment the further question of whether even if they did consent, they would be obliged to accept all forms of inequalities that system generated.) Why else, beginning with a state of society guaranteeing all who worked a modest plot of land and a convenient living, would a man consent to a state in which he might lose not only his small plot but the self-ownership of his labor? Locke cannot simply *assume* consent to the use of money without assuming away the biggest problems that the "enough and as good remaining" proviso creates for a money economy. Only by means of reasoning that the worst-off in the state of nature are better off after the introduction of money is Locke able to sanction a more inegalitarian society than was his state of nature. But why not reason that tacit consent can be assumed only to the arrangement that *maximizes* the position of those worst-off? Without here resolving what the correct distribution would be in a contemporary Lockean society, we can at least begin to see the major theoretical tension that needs to be resolved between Locke's own assumptions concerning individual self-ownership and the inegalitarian results contemporary Lockeans "derive" therefrom.[57]

The concept of human equality in Kant, as in Locke, entails the possession of a rational faculty by each person. The existence of a rational faculty does not ensure its use, because people are often inclined to act against rational precepts.[58] Kant's dualistic view of human nature – of people as both (rational) noumena and (sensual) phenomena – supplies a reason (consistent with postulating a rational faculty as a universal human attribute) why people do not always recognize the dictates of rationality.[59]

Unlike Locke, Kant relies on a secular conception of equal rationality: People are equal insofar as they all are assumed to possess rational faculties capable of autonomous action. The principles of politics derived from that postulate apply consistently to all men qua rational beings. We shall look first at how liberal principles of political right are derived by Kant from an equal-rationality postulate and then ask whether those principles are sufficient and consistent with the full force of the argument from equal rationality.

Every person has the potential for human dignity based upon reason. Human dignity and autonomy are manifested not by the exercise of freedom of choice based upon inclination, constrained only by other people's like freedom, but by a freedom *from* inclination, a freedom constrained by the dictates of reason that stipulate ends valid for all men as rational beings, as ends in themselves. Thus "a free will and a will under moral laws are one and the same."[60] As an end in oneself, one must be treated by others as a person guided by reason and one must act not only *according to* but *from* the moral law.[61]

The manner in which we should be so treated and should so act accords with the principles of, and the obligations to, a liberal state. Principles of political right, correctly constituted, are categorical imperatives. Political principles, as such, substantiate our equal humanity by abstracting from the contingent needs and desires of particular people and formulating rules based solely on people's universal interests as citizens of a liberal state. The "Formula of Limits" expresses this universal noncontingent foundation of political right as an imperative that limits the negative freedom of individual citizens: "Act only on a maxim that recognizes every person as a condition limiting all merely relative and arbitrary ends."[62] Formulating the principle of positive freedom for individuals, the rule is to "act by a maxim that involves its own universal validity for every rational being."[63] Translated into publicly known political principles that are to govern a society through an institutionalized state, Kant's theory provides a firm foundation for a universalistic legal system, an essential characteristic of the liberal state.[64]

Each categorical imperative prescribed by, and addressed to, all individuals can be formulated as a piece of legislation for what Kant calls a "Kingdom of Ends."[65] That kingdom is modeled on the natural world and can be seen as an attempt to create a counterpart to the phenomenal law-governed universe in the noumenal realm of existence.[66] Laws based on the machinery of the categorical imperative can be interpreted as the appropriate lawlike counterparts in our moral world to laws of nature.[67] Whereas the latter are objective, externally given causal principles, the former too are objective but, suitably, given by each person to himself as an autonomous moral being or noumenon. Therefore, the universalistic legislation of the liberal state creates obligatory principles of action insofar as we are to *display* our dignity and worth as moral beings.

The Kantian defense of a minimal liberal state – a defense of equal civil and political liberties, equal opportunity, and equal representation – ultimately rests upon the strong sense of equal rationality and positive freedom underlying the categorical imperative. Kant clearly outlines his defense of liberal constitutionalism in *Theory and Practice* as follows:

The civic state, considered merely as a legal state, is based on the following *a priori* principles:
1. The freedom of each member of society as a *man*.
2. The *equality* of each member with every other as a *subject*.
3. The autonomy of each member of a commonwealth as a *citizen*.[68]

Kant here begins with a simple presupposition in favor of as much negative freedom for each person as is consistent with the same freedom for all in civil society. From the second principle, Kant derives an argument for equal obligation to the law; and from the third an argument for equal civil and political rights.

Our ability to abide by moral law, our *moral* personality, makes us capable of having rights. Having rights in civil society is therefore contingent upon the assumed capacity of our equal subjection to a constitution that guarantees those rights to all (therefore the justification of denying equal rights to certain criminals who show themselves to be incapable of such capacity). Civil rights derived from the first principle are thereby contingent on the equality postulate of the second.

The force of the principle of equal subjecthood in turn depends on the postulate of equal autonomy: "No man can lose the equality [he has in a commonwealth as a subject] except through his own crime . . . For he cannot cease . . . to be master of himself."[69] For Kant, the ability to be master of oneself is entailed by the presupposition of the autonomy of human beings. The third juridical attribute of civil independence "requires that he [a person] owe his existence and support, not to the arbitrary will of another person in the society, but rather to his own rights and powers as a member of the commonwealth (hence his own civil personality may not be represented by another person on matters involving justice and rights)."[70] Because *arbitrary* wills are by definition contingent and idiosyncratic for Kant, civil independence as well as equal subjection requires authorship of laws by people as rational, rather than as passionate, beings. As such, all people are equal citizens.

Because individuals are assumed equal and autonomous moral personalities, principles of right must be universal and grounded upon the full freedom (both positive and negative) of individuals. That is, because people have a capacity both of negative freedom to choose and of positive freedom to choose according to the moral dictates of practical reason, principles of political right must not only be general and universalizable but also capable of being prescribed by all rational beings as legislators in a kingdom of ends.[71]

These three conditions impose important limits on the nature of political principles. The first two are certainly not unique to Kant's philosophy, though the adequacy of his theory as a foundation for a legalistic state is apparent.[72] The "Universal Principle of Right" derived from the three criteria is a strong expression of the liberal foundations of civil rights: "Act externally in such a manner that the free exercise of thy Will may be able to coexist with the Freedom of others, according to a Universal Law."[73] Civil *rights* are thus derived from the *right* to freedom each person has by virtue of his equal rational faculty.

The state for Kant is based on principles of right that, as in the liberal theories of Bentham, Mill, and Locke, command externally.[74] Given that all individuals' rights are not equally enforceable in the state of nature, the state is necessary to supply a neutral authority to publicize and to enforce the universal rights of each person. To act rightfully each person must abide by, though not necessarily be motivated by, the public principles of the state. The laws of the liberal state assume the capacity for obedience but cannot judge the nature of internal acts of will. Therefore, although the liberal state guarantees rightful action, it offers no guarantees or judgments of a lawful person's moral worth: Acting from the moral law cannot be externally distinguished from heteronomous action in accordance with the law. Lawful action is nevertheless sufficient to ensure full citizenship. Kant argues for the state's necessity, and its liberality, based on equality. People, though all potentially guided by right reason, are not saints: Inclinations tempt and incorrect maxims may divert each and every person away from morally worthy actions. Yet even a person's passions may lead him, with the coercive incentives of the state, toward rightful acts.

At least in this respect, the Kantian state, though a means to something higher than lawful action, is not easily distinguishable from the state based upon utilitarian principles. Both command only externally – unlike the state conceived by Rousseau, which attempts to achieve individual moral freedom through political means.[75] A Kantian state enables people to be autonomous by providing safeguards against external interferences with their actions. A utilitarian state may inadvertently facilitate the same ends. But neither attempts, or believes it possible, to force people to act from the moral law.[76]

A minimal liberal form of government provides the best, though not the only possible, expression of the principles of right articulated by Kant. Ultimate sovereignty must rest with the people if justice is to be an expression of the will of each and all: "The sovereign authority resides in the person of the legislator . . . The legislative authority can be attributed only to the United Will of the people."[77] A system of representation must be instituted by which the *acting* sovereign in fact represents the people.[78] Although autocracy, aristocracy, and democracy are legitimate forms provided substantive representation is effected, a limited form of democracy would be the most plausible for effective representation consistent with Kant's rationality assumptions.

Kant's own ambivalence to democracy is generally directed at plebiscitary, rather than representative, forms, just as the logic of his equal-reason postulate demands. Separation of powers is for Kant, as for Locke, a necessary means of ensuring representative government, a government that must preserve individual rights and human dignity regardless of majority sentiment. For the same reason plebiscitary democracy is condemned as a dangerous means, one that would violate the legalistic implications of the dictates of the equal-rationality postulate, were a majority of people to act upon their inclinations rather than upon their reason. Kant is very concerned, as must be any theorist who stipulates universal principles of right based on human reason, that a correct division be maintained between constitutional guarantees and decisions open to majoritarian rule.[79] Consistent therefore with the formulation of the categorical imperative, majority rule must always be constrained by a constitutionalism that guarantees civil rights to all citizens. Though his disdain in *Perpetual Peace* for plebiscitary democracy accords with his liberal constitutionalism, his further reservations concerning democratic rule and the extent of citizenship rights are attributable to his position on private property.[80]

Property for Kant is a *manifestation* of personality: Legal possession allows a person to act, and thereby to display his freedom externally. But no person, Kant tells us, can publicly display his rational, moral will. Acting *from* the moral law must be an assumed potentiality in all who manifest freedom of choice. But Kant claims that only those men (it was only *men* for Kant) with property – those not subject to another person's will to maintain themselves – can publicly manifest freedom of choice (i.e., free *Wilkür*). Like most other liberals of his time, Kant fears that those directly dependent on others for their subsistence will easily succumb to the political wills of their social superiors. Therefore, the landless and the dependent are thought likely to be conservative political forces: They lack a politically free will. Possession of property then becomes the criterion by which Kant judges a person's capacity for full (or active) citizenship, for authorship of (as contrasted to mere subjection to) civil law. Active citizenship is limited to those individuals who possess property sufficient to allow them the external freedom to regulate and order their lives independently of the wills of others:

> Fitness for voting is a prerequisite of being a citizen. To be fit to vote, a person must be independent and not just a part of the commonwealth, but also a member of it, that is, he must will of his own accord, together with others, to be an active part of the commonwealth. This qualification leads to the distinction between an active and a passive citizen . . . [G]enerally anyone who must depend for his support (subsistence and protection), not on his own industry, but on arrangements by others (with the exception of the state) – all such people lack civil personality, and their existence is only in the mode of inherence.[81]

The civil rights that the liberal constitutional state guarantees presuppose in each citizen the juridical attribute of "civil equality – of having among the people no superior over him except another person whom he has just as much of a moral capacity to bind juridically as the other has to bind him."[82] Thus the civil dependency of propertyless artisans, sharecroppers, servants, and women obviates the possibility of complete political equality and independence presumed by the principles of political right.[83] Two categories of citizens emerge: the active ones who are in practice both authors of and subjects to the laws of the state, and the passive ones who are only subjects to the law, as they are subjects also to the private will of other citizens.[84]

One might conclude from this advocacy of unequal citizenship that Kant does not intend the equal-rationality postulate to be as strongly egalitarian as it appears in theory, that he has significantly qualified the postulate upon which the foundations of the metaphysics of morals and of justice were laid. If that were simply the case, Kant's egalitarianism would be severely limited in its importance, as the a priori assumption of human equality would then justify little more than a formally legalistic state, with no need for equal political or social rights.[85] A more consistent and useful case can be made that Kant's position on unequal citizenship was based upon an unjustified acceptance of a given distribution of property. Without such an acceptance, his argument for equality could have significantly stronger egalitarian political and social implications.

It is evident in his further discussion that Kant does not intend the distinction between active and passive citizenship to override all of the political implications of his equal-rationality assumption:

This kind of [civil] dependence on the Will of others and the inequality that it involves are by no means incompatible with the freedom and equality that men possess as human beings, who together make up a people. Rather only by conforming to these conditions can the people become a state and enter into a civil constitution. Under this constitution, however, not everyone is equally qualified to have the right to vote, that is, to be a citizen as well as a fellow subject . . . [I]t follows only that, whatever might be the kind of laws to which the citizens agree, these laws must not be incompatible with the natural laws of freedom and with the equality that accords with this freedom, namely, that everyone be able to work up from his passive status to an active status.[86]

Here, unequal citizenship is not used to imply unequal civil rights, nor does Kant simply accept the distinction between civil dependence and independence as a just basis for a fixed inequality of citizenship. Equal opportunity to become active citizens is necessary to ensure an appropriate discrimination between those able to govern themselves and those capable solely of being governed. Kant, however, does not explore ways of equalizing opportunity. (Presumably, one thing he had in mind was freeing property from its feudal entails.) But why is equalizing opportunity rather than redistributing property the appropriate way to treat free and equal rational beings who just happened to enter the world with unequal possessions? Or, assuming that equal opportunity is the equality that accords best with this freedom, what does that equality demand of the state? Both of these questions indicate an important unresolved issue within a theory of justice that postulates no natural right to property. Because property is a legally constituted rather than a natural right, it is a product of the hypothetical social contract and an instrument of state policy.[87] Now, Kant argues that equal protection of unequal possessions is a plausible condition of the social contract. But one could easily imagine conditions under which equal rational beings would not agree to such grounds for a civil constitution. Kant also tells us that "the mode of having something external as one's own property in a state of nature is physical possession, which carries with it the juridical presumption that, through the union of the Will of everyone in public legislation, the possession will be made into *de jure* possession."[88] But he does not indicate why persons assumed to be free and equal but lacking property would so unite their wills in public legislation that deprived them of active citizenship.[89]

Why provide equal opportunity rather than equal property if all are presumed to have the capacity, while not the external prerequisites, for civil independence? This is a particularly perplexing question for Kant, who abstracts from the externally contingent characteristics of persons to formulate categorical imperatives of political justice. Once taxation is justified, how does one draw the line between taxation (combined with equal opportunity) and property redistribution?[90] Kant's own case for partial citizenship entails an admission that there exist phenomenal prerequisites for civil equality. Yet his arguments concerning property and citizenship fail to live up to the egalitarian potential of his theory's basic equality postulate. Nevertheless, his admission of the relationship between civic equality and property and his recognition of the essential interdependency of members of a commonwealth provide scope for the justification of more egalitarian distributive measures upon Kantian grounds.[91]

Two other basic characteristics of Kant's theory become useful to subsequent liberal egalitarian concerns.[92] His conception of rationality leads directly to a support of principles of right. There is no divergence between what "by nature" is rational for an individual and what is rational for society. In addition, human rationality and freedom are explicitly tied to a concept of human dignity. Kant's conception of human equality as equal dignity is, unlike Locke's, unattached to the metaphor of private property, and it is divorced from the particular nature and intensity of people's passions. The concept of human dignity is apparently absent in classical utilitarianism in its Benthamite form. Every action has its price (to use Kant's terminology) in Bentham's system, the price of the pursuit of happiness.[93] Nothing in the utilitarian characterization of human beings as pleasure and pain machines appears to distinguish humans from other species of animals, as does Kant's attribution of reason. But this contrast ought not to be overdrawn. Reason ultimately enters the utilitarian's portrait of people, even if it is not in their original design; it is a reason, however, that processes rather than masters the demands of the passions. Either extreme view (of the passions as determinative of human rationality or of human reason as totally independent of the passions) dwarfs our commonsensical notion of human nature and hinders the possibilities of a more egalitarian liberal politics.

Perhaps the largest obstacle that the basic framework of Kant's theory presents for liberal egalitarian concerns is the difficulty of giving content to principles of political right beyond the formal criterion of equal treatment of people. This content problem arises because Kant argues that a state may legislate only imperatives that are categorical. [94] For example, a state can supply the means to only those ends essential to the "idea" of a rational being, not to ends contingent upon the particular passions or inclinations of citizens. But because the idea of a rational being is that of a person who acts from the moral law, Kant's formulation of the principles of right appears both circular and formalistic. [95]

Nevertheless, there must be some ends apart from moral worth itself that legislation is designed to facilitate; otherwise, Kantian justice would be an absurd formalism. Freedom of choice, although not the end that gives human beings their unique dignity, nevertheless is recognized by Kant as a universal human end. More broadly still, Kant must assume that all people (necessarily) have ends that they wish to realize. [96] Now, if it could be shown that some goods are necessary means to the satisfaction of every rational person's ends, however diverse those ends may be, or (better still) necessary preconditions for the exercise of human autonomy, then more content could be given to legislation in a Kantian system. Rawls's theory, which is considered in Chapter 5, can be viewed as one such attempt to overcome this content problem in Kant's theory, an attempt that substantially alters Kantian metaphysics and carries with it more egalitarian principles of justice.

THE CONVERGENCE OF THE TWO EQUALITIES

Clearly, no simple one-to-one correspondence exists between postulates of human equality and forms of state, because two substantially different equality postulates both suggest similar, liberal democratic, forms of government. This might be taken as cause for skepticism: Can the liberal state be justified by any, or a multiplicity of divergent, metaphysical premises? I would suggest not, at least not so straightforwardly as by postulates of human equality. This convergence on liberal democracy from a plurality of metaphysical postulates can be explained so as to dispel the suspicion that any assumptions about human nature might serve equally well to justify liberal democracy.

Seliger points out that both post-Lockean utilitarianisn and idealism, though dispensing "more and more with the notion of natural law . . . preserved, with varying emphasis, the belief that political life cannot be ordered without reference to rational standards." [97] This agreement on a general political norm is based on a corresponding convergence on the level of metaphysical premises. What Seliger points out about utilitarianism's need to give weight to dictates of reason applies also to the rationalist's need to give weight to the demands of people's sensual nature in constructing principles of distributive justice:

In utilitarian theories, while man's desires and interests alone constitute the criterion of eventual harmony, they still require the mediation of reason for the attainment of the greatest possible happiness of all. In other words, dictates of reason are reverted to as a means to restrict human arbitrariness, irrespective of whether human motives and ends are predicated on men's personal desires and interests or are subjected to an objective teleological order. In both instances, dictates of reason have the identical function of effecting justice through a rational reconciliation of interests . . . Both utilitarian and idealist political theories agree – though on different grounds – on the necessity of political organization and its major practical purposes; nor do they differ so very much about what they must and must not do to maintain it.[98]

With reference to metaphysical premises, the point is similar. Those who presume equality of passions also appear to assume at some point in their analysis a rational faculty in persons that can be employed to regulate the passions, or at least to order, direct, or postpone gratification so as to attain maximum long-term gratification. This assumption is necessary not only on an individual level, to allow for our long-term happiness, but also on the level of politics, to allow for the possibility of rational decision making.

Locke and Kant, who presume equal rationality, on the other hand, view that equality as a potentiality in all people, or at least assume that potential until it is proven absent. This qualification, which bridges the gap with the equal-passions school from the other side, is most apparent in Locke. Again, people's use of reason is both limited and mediated by their passions, yet the passions do not necessarily lead people to act against what would be the dictates of their reason. Locke argues that

whatever flatterers may talk to amuse people's *understandings*, it hinders not men, from feeling: and when they perceive, that any man, in what station soever is out of the bounds of the civil society . . . and that they have no appeal on earth against any harm they may receive from him, [they will] take care as soon as they can . . . to have that safety and security in civil society for which it was first instituted.[99]

Of course, people's passions do not *always* lead them to act rationally, as they would were everybody always capable of discerning natural law on the basis of the rational faculty. But with respect to the most important political issue – how people are ruled – "ordinary men are clearly believed to be not incapable of passing political judgment according to the standards of natural law" because they "are capable of . . . differentiating between good rulers and successors of another stamp."[100]

Now to say that people are all capable, even equally capable, of knowing or acting upon the most basic dictates of reason in the political realm is not to deny that under certain conditions some people's capacities may be rendered inoperative. The possibility therefore exists that an equal-rationality or equal-passions postulate can lead to advocacy of a nondemocratic state – toward advocacy of rule by an intellectual elite. This might have been the case had Locke, for example, judged people so blinded by their upbringing as to lose sight of their basic political interests in equal rights, and had he had confidence that some distinguishable person or group of persons was not so blinded. That equality postulates need not lead to a political preference for liberal democracy is evidenced by Helvetius's political arguments for rule by an intellectual elite. But his theory does not obviate the general point. Helvetius advocates elite rule only as a temporary means to render ordinary men capable of using their potentially equal rationality.[101] Lacking confidence in the present rational ability of an ascertainable class, unhindered and undiluted by self-interested passions, an equality postulate militates strongly against nondemocratic rule.

Furthermore, Helvetius's advocacy of rule by an intellectual elite contradicts the peculiarly modern view that each human being is uniquely dignified: that every person must be presumed rational until his actions prove otherwise. This presumption of universal rationality is difficult for modern theorists to override. Liberal democratic theorists by no means prove their cases for equal treatment of persons. Rather, they choose not to carry the burden of disproof. The presumption in favor of human equality therefore remains strong for both rationalist and utilitarian schools of liberal thought. Neither believes that a person can be designated as distinctly rational or capable of knowing what is rational for all other people, so as to sanction political rule in the form of traditional monarchy or bureaucratic administration of political life.[102]

The equality postulates of the theorists examined here take them at least as far as the minimal liberal state. How much further their equality assumptions may take *us* constitutes the salient question of the remainder of this essay. I have begun in the belief that the nature of contemporary liberal egalitarianism can be best clarified developmentally, because its roots lie in classical liberal theory. The most critical limits of that egalitarianism also derive from this base.

Before proceeding any further, however, we must answer two important objections to the enterprise of reconstructing foundations and developing a case for liberal egalitarianism. These objections are often voiced against contemporary egalitarian arguments, but they apply equally to classical liberal theory. If valid, they would undermine the entire enterprise. The first criticism is that people are obviously not equal in any significant respect.[103] The second is that, even if they are, one cannot move from empirical claims of equality to normative conclusions concerning distributive justice.[104]

As critics of egalitarianism on the first count object, to claim that people share similar passions, a minimum capacity for rationality, and/or a certain dignity as human beings is a far cry from claiming that they are *equal*. After all, even if we share certain passions (for a commodious living or against violent death), we do not feel those passions with equal intensity. And though all of us may be capable of planning our own lives and of abiding by the laws, surely some of us are more capable of rational planning and of judicious behavior than others. Furthermore, even if all people have a dignity about them or desire self-respect, does not the capacity for self-esteem among individuals vary? Then, the critic asks, what sense does equality retain in the face of all these manifest differences among people?

The most direct reply to the critic is that his contention that people are unequal is simply incorrect, that there exists no clear evidence demonstrating people to be unequal in the ways mentioned above. This reply is not completely implausible if one is careful to speak of equality – especially of equal rationality – as a capacity of all people. The less-than-ideal circumstances of all existing (and previously existing) societies can be invoked as an explanation of the inequalities manifest among existing (and previously existing) persons. This constitutes a weak defense of equality claims for two reasons. Even if people are *potentially* equal, under any presently conceivable circumstances their capacities for rationality and for happiness are very likely to differ. Secondly, although the critic's contentions are not susceptible to hard proof, given the obvious existing discrepancies, the burden of proof would appear to fall on the egalitarian.

However, there exists no good evidence that potentials or capacities differ along racial, religious, or class lines. Here the direct empirical counterargument is much more forceful and constitutes a relevant reply to claims that there are differential genetic capacities for reason among identifiable human groups – between blacks and whites, for example, or between working and middle classes, as Arthur Jensen and Richard Hernstein have recently claimed. Because the evidence and arguments supporting the heritability theories of Jensen and Hernstein have already been quite thoroughly refuted, I refer the reader to those refutations, rather than rehearse them here.[105]

A better direct response to the critic of equality is the following: Granted that inequalities exist among people, nevertheless the political significance of the inequalities you mention is not very great.[106] Those inequalities, like many others you may list, are inessential to politically egalitarian claims. They are not inherently associated with any easily discernible traits, with any class, ethnic, racial, or sexual characteristics of persons. Therefore, you cannot justly design political institutions that favor some groups over others. In addition, the capacities most crucial for a well-functioning polity are those that people – assuming of course just circumstances – can reasonably be expected to share equally: for example, the ability to abide by the law and to choose a reasonable plan of life.[107] Self-respect and human dignity are also capacities that we expect will be equally possessed by citizens of a just society.

Thus an equality claim need not reduce all present differences among people to circumstantial causes in order to retain its meaningfulness. It does mean, at the very least, that a philosopher king would not be the best ruler for a polity – not simply because the possibility of an incorrect choice would make the choice too risky, but rather because everybody is assumed potentially capable of knowing both his own and the public interest better than could any single great mind.

The second major criticism is that no principles of justice can be derived from factual claims, however sound those claims may be: There exists an unbridgeable gap between "is" and "ought" statements. But are postulates of human equality strictly, or simply, factual assertions? To argue in the context of political theorizing that people are equal entails an *evaluation* that their shared characteristics are politically more significant than their differences.[108]

Similarly, the claim that people have equal dignity carries with it the normative proposition that, other things being equal, people *should* be treated with equal respect. That people are of equal dignity or of equal rationality, again, is not simply an empirical claim, for without reconstructing contemporary societies we lack adequate evidence to prove or disprove the claim. Thus we would have to change societies to assess the authenticity of the claim. But the justice of the change is itself contingent upon the validity of the claim.

The argument from human equality to principles of egalitarian justice is therefore circular, but the reasoning is not tautological. Our idea that human beings are equal gains plausibility from our firm belief that certain distributive inequalities are unjust. Our normative intuitions therefore support our descriptive belief in human equality. But the justificatory causation is often reversed. The argument that women are equal to men in their rational capacity is a descriptive claim supporting the argument that they ought to possess equal voting rights. Similarly, in our reply to someone who proposes that dogs, chimpanzees, and children under twelve ought to have the right to vote, we would refer to the relevant dissimilarities of these beings to adult humans.

The skeptic might respond that these references merely serve as rationalizations of our unfounded intuitions that certain beings ought not to share our rights. If the skeptic, with no further argument, charges us with rationalizing unfounded intuitions whenever we cite equality as a reason for equal treatment, then his charge is unrebuttable and philosophically uninteresting. But if there are instances when relevant inequalities can be shown to exist and we still remain committed to equal treatment, then the skeptic can try to convince us by citing the evidence.

If we cannot rebut his evidence or his criterion of relevance and we still refuse to change our normative judgment, then he can rightly charge us with failing to act rationally. But regardless of its outcome, his argument relies on the assumption of a connection between descriptive and prescriptive equality claims. By these standards, liberal egalitarian principles of justice are nontautologically tied to assumptions of human equality.

Relevance criteria mediate between descriptive and prescriptive claims. The view that women are physically weaker than men and therefore ought not to have equal voting rights is best rebutted by denying the relevance, rather than the validity, of the descriptive claim. Therefore, to deny that a descriptive statement in itself *logically contains* or *entails* a normative judgment is only to concede that description alone does not logically yield prescription without a valid (and often implicit) mediating claim that the former is relevant to the latter.

A final response to the charge of having committed the naturalistic fallacy therefore must entail a limited concession to the critic, because relevance criteria cannot be determined on purely empirical or logical grounds, as I shall argue in more detail later.[109] No strictly logical connection can bridge the gap between is and ought statements.[110] Yet having conceded that no political theory is capable of being a purely deductive system, of proceeding from factual claims to normative propositions, we must also recognize that no alternative system is available that begins with objective normative claims and deduces principles of justice from that certain starting point. If we are doomed to moral uncertainty, the claims of human equality are a plausible starting point for political theorizing. The empirical and normative claims attached to classical liberal theory are still susceptible to rational criticism, although at some point common ground between competing theories ceases to exist, because empirical and normative bridges between those theories are lacking or remain to be constructed. This is to concede one significant limit to any political theory even before proceeding to investigate the strongest arguments for liberal egalitarianism. This weakness does not eliminate the need to judge the entire construction, because it remains to be seen whether any alternative theoretical structure can be more solid.

Chapter 2

J. S. Mill and participatory opportunity

THE MILLEAN INTEGRATION

Because it combines the equality postulates of the two schools considered in Chapter 1, John Stuart Mill's revision of utilitarianism results in a more extensive argument for liberal democracy than was made by the classical liberal thinkers previously considered, suggesting that the two equality assumptions taken together can be used to justify certain more egalitarian political principles. Although Mill does endorse some more egalitarian distributive policies (e.g., inheritance taxation), the strength of his own theory from an egalitarian perspective is its strong, principled recommendation of "participatory equality": extending the participatory opportunities available to citizens into many realms of social life. The largest unresolved question within Mill's theory with which I shall be concerned is whether Mill's endorsement of equality of participatory opportunity must necessarily come at the cost of competent (i.e., well-managed) government and of a more redistributive economic policy. These questions arise within Mill's theory in part because he is committed to a view of people as similar both in their capacities for pleasure and in their potential abilities rationally to discriminate among more and less valuable pursuits. The relationship between the distribution of participatory opportunities and of economic goods becomes central to any theory committed to a realization of people's passionate and rational capacities.

As Helvetius's argument indicated, an equal-passions postulate taken singly might sanction elite rule, if one believed that a small, discernible group could – by virtue of superior reason – make the best political decisions in the interests of all. Alternatively, the equal-rationality assumption could be used to sanction unequal political representation or elite rule, assuming that some people derive more satisfaction from politics than others. A division would then be created between *homo civicus* and *homo politicus*,

48

who, though equally rational, are unequal in their political needs, desires, or even abilities.[1]

Mill's synthesis of the two equality postulates is an uneasy one, yet one that allows a stronger defense of liberal democratic forms of government than preceding theories. Great critical weight has been placed on the uneasy synthesis he attempted, without reflection upon the necessary tensions between internal consistency and moral realism of any nineteenth-century philosophy. Critics tend to exaggerate the internal inconsistency of Mill's theory by concentrating on his admittedly time-bound advocacy of a capitalist market economy.[2] Yet at least one critic, C. B. Macpherson, suggests that Mill's conception of human nature is the correct one, but that his deductions from the postulates of human nature to the maxims of distributive justice are misguided (though necessarily so, Macpherson seems to claim, given the historical context of Mill's theory).[3] I take Mill's view of human nature to be the essential core of his theory, and therefore investigate the egalitarian implications of that view given both ideal and nonideal sociopolitical conditions. But I shall not claim that Mill's utilitarian method is *the* correct approach to egalitarian justice. Whether egalitarian justice finds its ideal basis in the postulates of equal passions and equal rationality as combined in Mill's teleological theory remains an open and difficult question, and one to be investigated more fully in subsequent chapters.[4]

Mill's synthesis modifies both equality postulates significantly. As in Bentham's theory, pleasures are not (at least explicitly) morally differentiated. Mill argues for the greatest-happiness principle as a single, maximizing standard by which to calculate and compare different degrees or quantities of aggregate happiness. Yet he also claims that some pleasures are of significantly greater quality than others, and that those pleasures can be discerned as of greater quality by experienced agents.[5] Mill's argument still permits pleasures to be ranked, at least upon an ordinal utility scale; but not everyone is equally qualified to rank all the pleasures. This is not because some people are inherently more rational than others, but because at present, given the inequalities of social inheritance and upbringing, some people have been able to experience the whole range of pleasures, of which others have been deprived. Mill's "choice criterion" of pleasure thus suggests that once each of us is able to experience every significant pleasure, we will more or less agree upon their comparative "happiness ratings."[6] Although one may argue that, in effect, Mill is distinguishing between incommensurable types of pleasure, this is not what his method sanctions or what his reasoning explicitly warrants. According to Mill, Socrates would not be asked to decide whether the pleasures of the mind are morally better than those of the body, but whether in the long run he would experience a far greater pleasure from intellectual than from bodily pursuits (I presume beyond a certain minimum of the latter). Pleasures are still in theory commensurable. If for Mill pushpin is not as good as poetry, then anyone capable of experiencing both would find poetry more satisfying and therefore would give it a more prominent place within his life.

Mill's theory introduces a modified equal-rationality postulate that further complicates, while it sophisticates, the standard utilitarian model.[7] People are potentially equally rational beings as well, who nevertheless cannot be judged equal given contemporary socioeconomic and political conditions. But unlike Locke's and Kant's conceptions, Mill's concept of a rational faculty is one that does not control and morally differentiate between pleasures; rather, it is one that allows people to recognize the higher pleasures and enjoy them more than the lower ones. However, the distinction between a faculty that orders and controls pleasures and one that correctly discerns their quality may have become a moot one. Indeed, that is a reason why Mill's theory can be seen as an integration of the two schools. Rationality becomes the servant of the greatest-happiness principle, while the passions are thought to be naturally ordered, just as social justice would dictate.

POLITICAL CONSEQUENCES OF INTEGRATION: A PRELIMINARY INVESTIGATION

What is the nature and consequence of this integration of equal rationality with an equal-passions postulate? Strikingly, Mill embraces both equality postulates as potentials. People will share the same relative estimate and experience of different pleasures only when all are provided with the opportunity of experiencing both higher and lower pleasures. Similarly, people will know and accept the dictates of justice only when they are raised under conditions that do not necessitate preoccupation with basic needs but encourage self-directed development of intellectual and social capacities – in short, when they are raised under conditions that make possible but do not require an appreciation of the higher pleasures.[8] Mill therefore looks ahead to a time when people will all be progressive beings, not equal in the sense of identity, but similar in appreciating the higher pleasures of intellectual life, of fellow-feeling, and of self-determination.[9] Presumably, people will then integrate the higher and lower pleasures in similar (although not necessarily equal) proportions into their unique, though equally rational, plans of life.[10]

The political consequences of Mill's view of human nature are best understood if the nonideal and ideal cases are separately analyzed. Utilitarianism, even with Mill's revisions, does not provide solutions "in principle": One must assess the consequences of alternative policies within a historically specific situation.

Under ideal conditions, Mill's equality assumptions suggest a one-person, one-vote, representative democracy: "Two very definite ideas are usually confounded under the name of democracy. The pure idea of democracy, according to its definition, is the government of the whole people by the whole people, equally represented . . . [T]here is not equal suffrage where every single individual does not count for as much as any other single individual in the community."[11] Mill forsees that this arrangement will be appropriate in the future when each person's potential as a progressive being is realized. The objects of a person's passions and his rational faculty ideally complement one another. Pleasures will be similarly ranked. But the equality aimed at cannot warrant an egalitarian democracy for Mill as long as the inequalities of both sensibility and rational judgment remain significant and discernible. Yet the equal potential Mill assumes to exist does sanction important, though limited, egalitarian political reforms, even within a context where the higher forms of desire and reason are unequally distributed.

In *The Pursuit of Certainty*, Shirley Letwin emphasizes the elitist tendencies of Mill's political principles. She argues that his concern with "not only . . . reforming the machinery of government but the souls of men as well" led him to concentrate on the distinction between those who "really" know and those who do not, assuming that the latter would, and should, defer to the knowledge of the former.[12] Although this distinction on the basis of knowledge was clearly at the root of Mill's preference for representative government over plebiscitary democracy, Letwin's emphasis on the central political role of an intellectual elite in Mill exaggerates the inegalitarian nature of his politics by obscuring the egalitarian intent and potential of his political philosophy.[13] Two essential aspects of Mill's politics are unexplained and generally ignored by Letwin's analysis. One is that Mill clearly preferred representative democracy to autocracy or to an intellectual aristocracy (at least

51

within developed societies), for no class of people was so superior as to be worthy of the right to rule unconstrained by the political preferences of others. The second of Letwin's oversights is Mill's belief in the *potential* rationality of all persons. His faith in every individual's potential led Mill to value extensive democratic participation as a school for enabling all citizens to become progressive beings, more like their representatives in being and in consciousness than most elitists ever imagine to be possible or desirable.[14] Letwin's oversight is largely due to her failure to distinguish the ideal and nonideal application of Mill's theory, to separate Mill's appraisal of contemporary politics from the potential nonelitist implications of some of his most basic assumptions.

What did nineteenth-century Britain and America warrant in political organization according to Mill's theory? Both Britain and the United States were nonideal societies, judged by the unequal conditions and the character of their people compared to the standard of progressive beings. Although judging the characters of people to be grossly unequal, Mill attributed the cause of human inequality to social, political, and economic factors that failed to encourage the full development of specifiable classes in different ways: Working conditions hindered the participation of the lower classes, commercial culture stunted the middle class's appreciation of nonmaterial values, the lack of more extensive suffrage prevented the disenfranchised from identifying their communal interests and from comprehending political issues in general.[15] Mill's incipient egalitarianism is reflected by the fact that he refused to attribute contemporary human inequalities to the inherent inequality of the human condition. Given the striking inequalities of contemporary Britain and the United States, Mill could argue that a fully participatory democracy would be inappropriate to either nation. Yet he was unwilling to forego all representative democratic forms, even under the grossly unequal conditions he described; and he provided good reasons for that unwillingness.

His reasons are significant both in their own right and in what they tell us about the nature of reasoning from premises of human equality to political forms. Faith in the potential of humans as fully rational beings whose passions will ultimately be directed toward objects of universally recognized value leads Mill to argue more forcefully for a participatory and liberal democratic state. Although his attitude toward Aristotle is otherwise very critical, Mill's idea of the higher pleasure of self-development is closely linked to the Aristotelian notion of perfectionism.[16] Mill therefore views the state in this respect as a polis and all persons as potentially active citizens. Whereas Kant explicitly concentrates on the equal representation of every person's interest as a rational being, Mill focuses upon the *participation* of people as equal citizens of the state.

Of course, Mill also values intelligent representation of people's interests. He advocates the centralization of some important political functions, such as information gathering.[17] More uncertainly, he suggests the desirability of permitting intellectuals to have more influence in government, at least in the short run. But he concedes that he cannot offer an effective and safe institutional means of discerning who is more intelligent.[18]

Participation is not simply of instrumental value in Mill's politics. It may be part of the good life for some citizens and a necessary means to self-development for many more.[19] Because it is more than a means to efficient or just legislation, in the end Mill does not completely sacrifice active citizenship to effective representation of interests.[20] Like Locke and Kant, he safeguards certain spheres of politics from the contingent desires of the majority. The "choice criterion" of pleasure provides the groundwork for an argument guaranteeing civil and political rights of progressive beings. Mill's dual equality assumptions lay claim to a sphere open to the desires of people as passionate and as rational beings. The desires of progressive beings must be elevated to the intellectual challenge and the emotional rewards of the political domain.

A crucial tension in Mill's theory arises from the need to qualify the essential value of participation. Though participation is an end in itself insofar as people realize their potential through politics, it must be qualified by the utilitarian value of rational government, a government that seeks to supply the requisites for a comfortable life and also to provide equal protection of all citizens under the laws.[21] A central conflict for Mill is that between rule by the competent and rule by the people, or what I call participatory government. I shall use the term "rational government" interchangeably with "competent government" to mean that government which enlists the aid of the most capable citizens in public office *and* which correctly interprets and protects the public's interest. Competent government is distinct from the notion of an efficient government, one that implements its goals with minimum cost, whatever those goals might be. "Competence" as I use and assume Mill used the term entails both a formal (means-oriented) and a substantive (end-oriented) rationality.

J. S. Mill and participatory opportunity

RATIONAL AND PARTICIPATORY GOVERNMENT: THE TENSION OBSERVED

Utilitarianism claims to provide a relatively simple method of weighing and balancing important but seemingly incommensurable values, such as participation, efficient government, material welfare, and equal rights. First one determines the social utility of each value, and then one accords each a priority corresponding to its relative utility. Sophisticated utilitarians like Mill often sacrifice the most apparent advantages of utilitarianism as a clear and precise method of political decision making to a moral realization that things frequently *are* as complex as they seem. Not that Mill forsakes utilitarianism entirely in confronting problems of moral conduct. Rather, his discussions in *Representative Government, The Principles of Political Economy,* and his essay on Tocqueville reveal that his solution to the conflict between participatory and rational government is by no means definitive, but contingent on many difficult judgments concerning how to weigh the relative costs and benefits of alternative forms.[22]

Mill's "solution" to the tension between participatory and rational government under nonideal conditions is most consistently as follows: The highest levels of policy making, demanding the most intellectual competence, are to be nationally representative positions. The Hare Plan will insure, within the limits of effective representation in a large nation, that every adult is represented by a single delegate of his choice. Mill is not bothered by the likely prospect that most national representatives will be of upper- and upper-middle class backgrounds, so long as they are, taken together, truly representative of all national interests.[23] Politics and administration are to be clearly differentiated: Again, the more specialized and complex skills that Mill considers essential to administration of political decision are to be placed in the hands of experts.[24] (Mill may overlook the practical problem of experts also gaining control of policy through a monopoly of information. Such a problem, if real, warrants a rethinking of his utilitarian solution.)

Finally, and most significantly from our perspective, Mill sanctions widespread decentralization of lower-level decision making.[25] Though he considers the local levels of government less significant and generally less efficient, he argues strongly for the preservation and creation of local political forums that will allow all those who so desire to take part in political decisions and administration. Local politics, he suggests, should seek to encourage

54

the development of those faculties that make good citizens. Some citizens will thereby become more competent representatives, but all will become more intelligent judges of their interests as citizens and therefore will better control and select their own representatives at all levels of government. Local politics thereby serves as a "school of political capacity and general intelligence."[26] Ultimately, the creation of a society of equal citizens – one in which every person is a progressive being – constitutes Mill's vision and directs his recommendations for nonideal political means.

The problem raised by this reconciliation of competent government and popular participation reveals the major tension between Mill's equality assumptions under nonideal conditions. True, he permits both a participatory sphere within which the political desires of citizens are equally considered and a sphere of competence in which the value of rational decision making predominates. At the same time, his reconciliation is a compromise that satisfies neither the participatory nor the rational government ideal completely. In the end, his theory provides no principled reasons for the political solution he chooses.

For Mill, political participation is both a means to the inclusive end of human self-development and in itself a valuable aspect of progressive human social activity. His model of a progressive being is a composite one, consisting of two ideals: (1) free development of one's personality – *determining* what one's interests are; and (2) rational intellectual development – *discovering* what is in one's interest as a social being, and, of course, how to achieve that interest. Now, taking people as they are, the role Mill grants to political participation appears largely intended for (and appropriate to) the satisfaction of the latter provision – extending people's knowledge of their role as citizens of the state. For Mill explicitly limits the actual decision-making powers of local participatory groups so as to avoid jeopardizing the competence of government.[27] Though he separates politics from administration at higher levels of government, he limits representative groups (even at the national level) to monitoring rather than to initiating policy. Thus the ideal of popular participation – a seemingly essential aspect of egalitarian democracy – is significantly constrained by the ideal of competence that is based upon the potential equality of people as rational beings. Here the *actual* inequality of citizens is given more weight than their *potential* equality and is used by Mill to sanction a significantly limited, although necessarily democratic, politics. The necessity of a democratic politics reflects the bounds imposed by Mill's theory on political elitism.[28]

Nevertheless, the question remains how Mill would draw the line between participatory and rational government under conditions more favorable to equal development. Is this tension between rational and participatory government an inevitable one? He appears to assume that participatory institutions often will not elevate the most competent citizens to office. He therefore attempts to separate spheres of competence from those of participation and to devise methods of election that might give extra weight to the more intelligent.[29] But one might challenge him on his own ground and ask whether this particular tension is a necessary product of inherent human inequality or a result of the unfavorable social and political environment in which many people have been raised. Perhaps well-informed, well-educated, and well-fed citizens would be more likely to choose the most competent as their own representatives. Thus, in a society in which all people live commodiously, participatory institutions would become the best means to the ends of competent government. Participation becomes an essential form of political education.

Yet this does not completely resolve the tension between participatory and rational government even in the ideal case. There remain economic preconditions for commodious living that Mill, in his concern for competent administration, neglects. We shall return to consider how this tension might be resolved in Chapter 7. Taken this far, Mill's own arguments contribute to our awareness of how a liberal's assessment of the relationship between the ideals of rational and participatory politics may often depend upon an assessment of people's capabilities at a given historical moment, rather than upon an appraisal of their natural or potential capacities.

Mill's ideal of rational politics is constrained in practice by the need to educate people to be active and intelligent citizens of the state. He recognizes that the desire to participate does not logically or practically entail a present ability to rule others, or even to determine one's own fate intelligently. Yet participation may ultimately be a means to the end of competent, *democratic* government as Mill understands it. Given that he does not argue for participation on the basis of the *right* to participate, it remains unclear both in theory and in practice precisely how one is to weigh the long- and short-run benefits of democratic versus rational politics. This is a somewhat ironic limit of Mill's theory, because it is precisely this aspect of utilitarianism that is generally said to be its strength. On the level of casuistry, utilitarianism lays claim to an ability to provide a clear rule by which to resolve conflicting human goods. Mill does not provide us with such a clear, practicable rule. Nonetheless, his conception of human nature – which is not peculiarly utilitarian – provides an indication not only of the tensions between strong egalitarian premises but of the potential egalitarian results such premises may permit, if not clearly sanction, given adequate empirical assumptions.

The clearest indication of the egalitarian implications of Mill's assumptions concerning human nature can be found in his essay *The Subjection of Women*. Mill's argument reflects the presumption in favor of equality offered by a genuinely liberal theory in the face of evidence of large existing inequalities among groups or individuals. He begins by criticizing the common practice of taking historical givens as one's normative authority:

If, after trying various other modes of social organisation – the government of women over men, equality between the two, and such mixed . . . modes of government as might be invented – it had been decided, on testimony of experience, that the mode in which women are wholly under the rule of men . . . was the arrangement most conducive to the happiness and well-being of both; its general adoption might then be fairly thought to be some evidence that . . . it was the best; though even then the considerations which recommended it may . . . have subsequently . . . ceased to exist.

He concludes that

the opinion in favour of the present system, which entirely subordinates the weaker sex to the stronger, rests upon theory only; for there never has been trial made of any other; so that experience, in the sense in which it is vulgarly opposed to theory, cannot be pretended to have pronounced any verdict.[30]

After suggesting a simple hypothesis to explain why women originally became the "second sex" – their relative physical disadvantage – Mill puts forward a series of arguments about why women cannot now be expected to manifest or to assert their real equality with men.[31] The revealed or apparent nature of women, he concludes, is "an eminently artificial thing – the result of forced repression in some directions, unnatural stimulation in others."[32] None of his arguments can prove his positive case for granting women equal political and social rights: that women are by nature equal to men. The moral strength of the original equality assumptions nevertheless triumphs in his argument, if only by history's default. Beginning with the presumption that people are equal in their rational and passionate capacities until otherwise demonstrated, Mill concludes that history has not proven the inegalitarian's case: "History . . . teaches another lesson: if only by showing the extraordinary susceptibility of human nature to external influences, and the extreme variableness of those of its manifestations which are supposed to be most universal and uniform."[33]

In the course of reasoning toward the conclusion that women should be accorded full rights of citizenship with men, Mill maintains that a society of equals is both the only means of maximizing social happiness and "the only school of genuine moral sentiment."[34] But his aim in *The Subjection of Women* – to extend existing social and political rights to women – nevertheless leaves open the further question whether a universalization of existing political and social rights will suffice to create a genuine society of equals among as well as between women and men.

THE LAISSEZ-FAIRE PRINCIPLE

Like Locke and Kant, Mill sets forth certain apparently inegalitarian intermediate principles of distributive justice that have subsequently drawn much criticism.[35] He does not answer the question of what an ideal distribution of goods would be, because as a utilitarian, he did not believe that question of ideal theory very meaningful. Instead, the egalitarianism of his distributional theory is left wide open to moral and empirical argument. That openness constitutes a strength of his theory vis-à-vis previous liberal political economics, while it reveals a weakness of his utilitarianism in comparison to subsequent egalitarian theory.[36]

On what grounds does Mill argue for the laissez-faire principle? This question must be answered before we can judge whether that laissez-faire principle is an inevitable and essential outcome of Mill's liberalism, rendering the egalitarian postulates of his philosophy less egalitarian in purpose and effect than first appearances would suggest. Laissez-faire is a second-order principle: one that, given the socioeconomic conditions he observed, Mill feels is a just and useful rule of thumb in applying the greatest-happiness principle, grounded on the interests of progressive beings. This recognition is important in order to understand that, given different empirical conditions or a different interpretation of the conditions that Mill observed, the greatest-happiness principle might sanction more interventionist and more egalitarian secondary principles of distributive justice. As the Fabians' argument was later to indicate, how basic the laissez-faire principle is to Mill's utilitarianism depends in large part on the accuracy of his interpretation of contemporary socioeconomic conditions or on the permanence of the situation he describes. Before claiming Mill's presumption to be a practical principle without a future, one should notice that Mill himself sanctions several exceptions to the laissez-faire rule. In fact, his exceptions significantly limit the appropriateness of the laissez-faire principle even with reference to the situation of nineteenth-century England, and certainly with reference to developments within twentieth-century England and the United States.

Mill's argument for the laissez-faire principle is consistent with one he sets forth in *On Liberty* for individual freedom. There, he establishes a presumption in favor of noninterference in matters that concern only the interests of an individual or that affect others *only* through an impact on their personal moral sensibilities.[37] Clearly, even with a strict interpretation of "interests" (one that does not assimilate interests to desires but views them as universal or basic needs), the realm of private concerns is small compared to that of matters which affect other people's interests, particularly with reference to economic issues. But in the public sphere, interference is not sanctioned a priori. Mill explicitly recognizes this in *On Liberty*, when speaking of questions of free trade:

As the principle of individual liberty is not involved in the doctrine of Free Trade, so neither is it in most of the questions which arise respecting the limits of that doctrine . . . Such questions involve considerations of liberty, only insofar as leaving people to themselves is always better, *caeteris paribus*, than controlling them; *but that they may be legitimately controlled for these ends, is in principle undeniable.*[38]

In the public sphere, therefore, the greatest-happiness principle must be employed to determine the proper balance between liberty and equality of income and wealth, either in each unique or in the general case. Mill tells us that if an action is other-regarding, it may be interfered with if, but only if, the greatest-happiness principle so dicates. Debate must be entertained on the costs of the interference compared to the benefits of redistribution – with one proviso: The subject's own good cannot be argued as the grounds for interference, on the assumption either that he is already a progressive being and therefore most capable of judging his own interests or that he can only become a progressive being if the proper opportunities for *self*-development are made available.

Mill seems to think that in most of those cases in which utilitarian calculations are warranted, the scales will tip in favor of noninterference of government into the public's affairs. His basic reasons for defending laissez-faire are consistent with his primary end of developing humans as progressive beings: "To be prevented from doing what one is inclined to, from acting according to one's own judgment of what is desirable, is not only always irksome, but always tends, *pro tanto*, to starve the development of some portion of the bodily or mental faculties, either sensitive or active."[39] Nevertheless, while he defends the general policy of laissez-faire in the *Principles*, Mill lists and discusses five significant and general exceptions to that policy, each at least potentially of such extensive applicability as to warrant pause before assuming his utilitarianism to be essentially a theory of the free market or a theory sanctioning a grossly inegalitarian distribution of goods and services.

Mill discounts the presumption in favor of the market (1) if the buyer is not the best qualified to judge the commodity;[40] (2) if individuals can only manage their concern by delegated agency;[41] (3) if government interference is necessary to give effect to individual preferences;[42] (4) if "energy and self-dependence are . . . liable to be impaired by the absence of help";[43] *or* (5) if the long-term interests of the society will not be served by private initiative.[44] In each of these cases, if the greatest happiness is served by interference, Mill's utilitarianism sanctions restrictions on the market principle.

Mill himself cites examples in each category which confirm that his basic commitment is to the principle of equal development rather than to a principle of negative freedom (letting people do as they wish). In the first case, Mill cites education as part of a wide class of things "of the worth of which the demand of the market is by no means a test; things of which the utility does not consist in ministering to inclinations . . . and the want of which is least felt where the need is greatest."[45] He points out that long experience may be required before the advantages of such goods are "proven" to the people benefiting from them. The proviso that the subject's own good cannot be invoked as a reason for public interference does not apply in this instance, because children rather than mature adults are the affected parties. Mill looks behind simple freedom of choice here and explicitly argues that in the case of children, "freedom of contract . . . is but another word for freedom of coercion."[46]

Although parents rather than children are the contractees in the case of education, Mill suggests that the principle behind the education example might have more extensive application. There are situations where the interests of the contracting parties, although they are mature persons, must be protected: situations where the effect of the service cannot be clearly discerned by the contractees or where they are not completely free in their choice of goods, services, or employment. "Besides," Mill points out,

a thing of which the public are bad judges, may require to be shown to them and pressed on their attention for a long time, and to prove its advantages by long experience, before they learn to appreciate it, yet they may learn at last; which they might never have done, if the thing had not been thus obtruded upon them in act, but only recommended in theory.[47]

In the second category, Mill includes all those ventures undertaken by what we today recognize as large corporations. His argument, that work done by delegation "may be as well, and sometimes better done . . . by the state,"[48] is quite radical in its present implications, given the growth of shareholding corporations. Once ownership and management are separated, Mill's argument opens the door to government interference. No moral defense of capitalism remains on the grounds that individual owners exercising their entrepreneurial skills and initiative deserve the fruits of their labor. And Mill's argument that things are done best that are done by those most directly affected tells against ceding corporate power to an unresponsive management. Once again we discover that interventionist policies are completely consistent with Mill's utilitarianism.

Mill justifies minimum-wage and similar work regulations in the third category of exceptions. He argues, in a manner congruent with Mancur Olson's subsequent explanation of the logic of collective action, that in many cases "it is the interest of each to do what is good for all, but only if others do likewise."[49]

State provision of public assistance to the destitute but able-bodied is warranted under the fourth class of exceptions, for "it is even more fatal to exertion to have no hope of succeeding by it, than to be assured of succeeding without it." Nor does Mill succumb to the plausible argument that the lazy and destitute will thereby think themselves deserving social parasites. Mill replies to his imagined critic that "the state must act by general rules. It cannot undertake to discriminate between the deserving and the undeserving indigent. It owes no more than subsistence to the first, and can give no less to the last."[50]

Finally, Mill's argument justifies long-range investments by the state – in research and resource development or control – when those investments are not profitable and therefore are unlikely to be undertaken by private individuals.

Rather than being rendered inoperative by changing economic and social conditions, the final point Mill makes in *On Liberty* and in the *Principles* against government interference remains a plausible one to consider: that the growth of a centralized state's power may be dangerous to the potential free development and self-determination of that society's citizenry. Given the aims of his theory, this argument is a cogent one, although it is not clear what practical conclusions are to be drawn from Mill's warning. Certainly, he does not intend the sphere of government interference to be reduced to the point of nonexistence. But because in each general or unique case considered, the increase of state power resulting from an interventionist policy would be incremental, deciding where to draw the line between issues that warrant interference and those that do not is a perplexing problem. Utilitarian considerations of each case will not necessarily suffice for either of two reasons. It is likely to be difficult, if not impossible, to balance the costs against the benefits of government intervention in the specific case under consideration. Or, even if the cost of government interference seems to be outweighed in the particular case, the additional power of the government may be just enough to tip the scales toward what Mill, following Tocqueville, disparagingly calls democratic despotism: an overcentralized political authority that renders citizens of an otherwise democratic society passive instruments in its hands. In any given case, utilitarian considerations of the relative costs and benefits of increasing state power are likely to be indeterminate. Perhaps Mill therefore sanctions state interference only in those previous instances where free individual action seems to be rendered *very* costly without it.

A philosophical system that by secondary argument originally supported a free-enterprise system, thereby indirectly sanctioning unequal distribution, is also capable of sanctioning extensive spheres of government interference, subsidy, and control over the otherwise freely contracting public. Mill is led in many cases to discount people's present preferences when their real interests as progressive beings are apparent and can be rationally discerned by the choice criterion of pleasure. His faith in people as rational beings also leads him to place great weight on the sociopolitical environment as determinative of the present rationality (or irrationality) of citizens. He therefore can consistently advocate policies that will encourage the development of individuals' rational capacities.

Yet Mill's concern for the problem of state power cannot be totally discounted. It is, as we have seen, intimately related to his
assumption of human rationality and the concomitant goal of self-
development. Yet the proper balance between the costs and benefits of state interference suggested by his several valued ends is
never resolved by his utilitarian method. The tension between
providing for the needs of citizens and containing the power of
centralized authority continues unresolved into twentieth-century
liberal thought. It is an issue we leave behind here only to defer it
to subsequent discussions.

THE PARTICIPATORY IDEAL EXPANDED: ECONOMIC LIFE

Mill concentrates his attack on inequalities of power in the more
strictly political sphere. Yet he also makes a cogent and compelling
case for participatory equality in the economic realm.[51] In his
chapter in the *Principles* entitled "On The Probable Futurity of the
Labouring Classes," Mill takes his major stand against the inequalities that contemporary industrial relations fostered. He contrasts two theories of how the working classes should be treated:
"The one may be called the theory of dependence and protection,
the other that of self-dependence."[52] Proponents of the former
theory, he tells us, hold that

the lot of the poor, in all things which affect them collectively, should be
regulation *for* them, not *by* them. They should not be required or encouraged to think for themselves, or give to their own reflection or forecast an
influential voice in the determination of their destiny. It is supposed to be
duty of the higher classes to think for them, and to take the responsibility
of their lot, as the commander and officers of an army take that of the
soldiers composing it.[53]

Clearly this is not the picture of the relations between laboring
and capitalist classes that Mill wishes to endorse. Such an endorsement would legitimize grossly unequal power relations, running directly counter to his ideal of every person as a progressive,
potentially rational, being.

Basing his views on the second model of the desired relations
between classes, Mill supports cooperative industrial enterprises
among workers (rather than proliferation of single proprietorships
or peasant landholders), because, as he tells us,

if public spirit, generous sentiments, or true justice and equality are desired, association, not isolation of interests, is the school in which these

excellences are nurtured. The aim of improvement should be not solely to place human beings in a condition in which they will be able to do without one another, but to enable them to work with or for one another in relations not involving dependence.[54]

With respect to the political means of achieving that egalitarian vision, Mill contends that

no man or woman who either possesses or is able to earn an independent livelihood, requires any other protection than that which the law could and ought to give. This being the case, it argues great ignorance of human nature to continue taking for granted that relations founded on protection must always subsist, and not to see that the assumption of the part of the protector, and of the power which belongs to it, without any of the necessities which justify it, must engender feelings opposite to loyalty.[55]

Two questions arise here in regard to Mill's positive case for equal relations between persons in the economic sphere. First, to what extent is his ideal of industrial relations an egalitarian one? Second, and related as a question of means to the first, what protection to the working class does he think ought to be required of the law?

Mill's ideal appears in theory quite egalitarian, although in the *Principles* he appears to underestimate what the demands upon law and the state in general might be, given his egalitarian goal. It is not clear whether he would sanction more state control over industrial relations were that required to equalize economic power. The problem of balancing goods – in this case equalization of power against self-determination – again arises within the utilitarian method of determining the right. Here is a potential conflict that might be perceived even within Mill's single ideal of self-development. In the short run it may matter greatly whether one supports negative freedom of free choice or positive freedom for future self-development on any given issue: One's interpretation of that composite ideal may decide crucial issues concerning the structure of industrial relations and the consequent relative power of capitalists, workers, and the state in society.

Mill values three major characteristics of cooperative associations in industry: (1) the equal relations entailed between persons, (2) the communal participation fostered, and (3) the "common interest of all workers in the work" maintained.[56] These three values are of course constitutive of his ideal image of progressive beings as self-determining yet communally minded. But Mill also believes that workers will freely combine and that cooperatives will thereby gradually proliferate, combining all the advantages of capitalist-owned enterprises with none of the disadvantages: "Eventually, and in perhaps a less remote future than may be supposed, we may, through the cooperative principle, see our way to a change in society, which would combine the freedom and independence of the individual, with the moral, intellectual and economical advantages of aggregate production."[57] He therefore finds no difficulty in supporting cooperative enterprise within an otherwise freely competitive system, explicitly disagreeing with the socialists on this ground. His "solution" to the problem of inequality within the economic sphere is consistently liberal: He sees that unequal relations *within* industry may deny individuals the opportunity to develop as free and progressive beings, though he sees no reason to stifle competition *among* industries that will encourage production for the greatest good of all citizens.[58]

But Mill's solution here again tends to ignore the complexities arising from the potential conflict among the ends he values: individual liberty, equal development, communal participation, restricted state power, and human industry. His theory provides us with no explicit, well-grounded priorities, as he does not seem to have believed that hard choices would be necessary. "The prospect of the future," he tells us, "depends on the degree in which they [the laboring class] can be made rational beings. There is no reason to believe that prospect other than hopeful. The progress indeed has hitherto been, and still is, slow. But there is a spontaneous education going on in the minds of the multitude, which may be greatly accelerated and improved by artificial aids."[59] To the extent that Mill is skeptical about the future, he relies on education as the means to human development.

As the presumption in favor of laissez-faire suggests, Mill seeks equality in freedom from dependence upon the wills of others. Yet he argues that the means to future freedom of choice will not necessarily be constituted at any given time by a like freedom, if all people are not yet competent judges of their own interests. And even if all were competent judges, some of Mill's exceptions suggest that pure freedom of contract – given the logic of collective action – will often be incapable of implementing the actual preferences of individuals, and incapable of securing the greatest happiness of a nation in the long run.

Then in what sense, if any, is the laissez-faire principle significant in Mill's theory? What is central to Mill's argument for laissez-faire is the need to preserve spheres of individual initiative and collective participation so as to allow people to develop and exercise their higher faculties. Mill allows for "governmental interferences which do not restrain individual free agency" and notices that certain restraints increase effective freedom immediately or in the long run. But with reference to politics he staunchly maintains that "there cannot be a combination of circumstances more dangerous to human welfare, than that in which intelligence and talent are maintained at a high standard within a governing corporation, but starved and discouraged outside the pale. Such a system . . . embodies the idea of despotism."[60]

Mill's rationale is fully consistent with the postulates of human equality attributed to him here: To be human is to be approximately equal to other humans in potential rationality, to have the capacity for the higher pleasures, especially the desire for self-determination. Thus a government that centralizes expertise and control is despotic because it fails to recognize, or even actively stifles, the potential equality of people.[61] Centralization is a dangerous means of governing because the only security against political slavery is the check over governors provided by the diffusion of intelligence and public spirit among the governed.[62] But more essential to Mill's case is his recognition that centralized political authority also entails a negation of the end of equal human dignity: "A democratic constitution, not supported by democratic institutions in detail, but confined to the central government, not only is not political freedom, but often creates a spirit precisely the reverse, carrying down to the lowest grade in society the desire and ambition of political domination."[63] Mill argues for political freedom as the greatest possible diffusion of power, initiative, and skill. Laissez-faire, to the extent that he endorses it, is meant to be a means to that end, rather than an end in itself.

In the posthumously published "Chapters on Socialism," Mill explicitly affirms that the question of laissez-faire or state intervention is an empirical one. It is in these chapters that he demonstrates greatest concern for the effects of distributive inequalities. Mill agrees with the socialists that the present state of economic distribution is an unjust one:

No longer enslaved or made dependent by force of law, the great majority are so by force of property; they are still chained to a place, to an occupation, and to conformity with the will of an employer, and debarred by accident of birth both from the enjoyments and from the mental and moral advantages, which others inherit without exertion and independently of desert.[64]

Acknowledging that (1) the present state is an unjust one, (2) existing private-property rights are not inviolable or deserved by their possessors, and (3) the "working classes are entitled to claim that the whole field of social institutions should be reexamined," Mill goes on to challenge various socialist arguments concerning what institutional *means* will best elevate the working classes to a position of social freedom and will achieve a society in which "every one would be a gainer by every other person's successful exertions."[65] He concedes that existing institutions are inadequate to these ends but contends that the communal institutions preferred by socialists or communists would be only a second-best solution. A society in which industrial partnerships between employer and employee were the rule would be more desirable.

My purpose here is not to assess Mill's contentions but rather to indicate the nature of the debate in which he was engaged. His arguments in the "Chapters" concern almost exclusively what the *effects* of limited competition versus unlimited communal ownership might be, Mill claiming against socialists (such as Fourier, Blanc, and Owen) that a regulated system of competitive industry will have a more salutary effect than would a system of state ownership in (1) lowering prices to consumers, (2) stimulating innovation, (3) discouraging fraud, and (4) raising wages for the working classes.[66] In the end, Mill's disagreements with the socialists are still further qualified by a concession that once higher standards of moral and intellectual education for all citizens were achieved, communism might conceivably gain the advantage over a system of limited private enteprise. Mill's conclusion, that "society is fully entitled to abrogate or alter any particular right of property which on sufficient consideration it judges to stand in the way of the public good," opens the door to twentieth-century critics of capitalism who look back upon his preferred solutions with a historically enlightened skepticism.[67]

Given this openness of Mill's theory regarding economic institutions, and recalling the exceptions to the rule of laissez-faire cited here, Mill's theory seems to be a potentially egalitarian one. At the same time, the basis of its egalitarian strength entails several important weaknesses of Mill's utilitarianism as a theory of distributive justice. The first, as we have seen, is directly related to the flexibility of utilitarian principles and the inclusiveness of its calculations when applied to actual historical situations. Utilitarian cost–benefit calculations appear so flexible as to be largely indeterminate. Once one admits the practical limits of human knowledge, the multiplicity of uncertain empirical factors that must be included in cost-benefit analyses tends to ensure that no clear policy position can result. Will Mill's presumption in favor of laissez-faire then become, by default, the preferred utilitarian policy in every ambiguous case? On the other hand, if the presumption in favor of laissez-faire can easily be overridden in each ambiguous case (i.e., in most cases), what has happened to Mill's case for the preservation of individual liberty and initiative as a means of ensuring the development of individuals as progressive beings? Can we postpone economic liberty for one generation, or for many, if utilitarian calculations warrant, and still preserve the ideal of equal self-development? If not, the original utilitarian calculations should be revised to include more long-range calculations. But then we return to our first problem: When can we expect human knowledge to be so extensive as to permit confidence in complex, long-range estimates of the greatest happiness? Mill's utilitarian method is potentially very egalitarian in its distributive implications so long as one claims that economic liberty – the liberty of the free market – is inessential to human self-development. But the utilitarian proof of the validity of this claim seems to require a species of omniscient calculators. We shall return to Mill's defense of participatory equality in our final extension of liberal egalitarian justice with the purpose of uniting Mill's concerns about participatory equality with the stronger case for distributive equality put forward by Rawls's theory of justice.

Chapter 3

The Fabians and their allies:
the minimal welfare state and beyond

A statesman differs from a professor in a university; the latter has only the general view of society; the former . . . has a number of circumstances to combine with those general ideas and to take into his consideration. Circumstances are infinite, are infinitely combined, are variable and transient: he who does not take them into consideration is not erroneous, but stark mad; . . . he is metaphysically mad.[1]

Burke may have overestimated the "generality" of the professor's view of society, but the distinction he draws between professors and statesmen is relevant to interpreting the Fabians' thought. Any interpretation of the Fabians as egalitarian thinkers must take into account their concurrent role as engaged political actors in late nineteenth- and twentieth-century British politics. Rather than focus upon their political practice, however, I wish to reconstruct Fabian arguments for greater equality in order to assess their extent and limits. This means, of course, that I shall ignore many of the more inconsistent, indeed even incoherent, arguments they made, in the interests of understanding the potential theoretical strengths of their case. Such a reconstruction can serve as a prelude to assessing the consistencies and inconsistencies within Fabian politics. More central to my immediate theoretical concerns, a reconstruction will indicate how liberalism continued to be pushed in more egalitarian directions by reappraisals of existing social circumstances.

Members of the Fabian Society were united by their criticisms of capitalist democracies as inegalitarian societies. From the beginning (1883–4), the Fabians were and remained divided over what form social democracy would take and how best to achieve it. G. D. H. Cole, the most prominent internal critic of the early Fabians (particularly of Sidney and Beatrice Webb), focuses upon the participatory face of democratic socialism that the Webbs and many English neglected. R. H. Tawney's work provides still another democratic socialist point of view from which egalitarian arguments more extensive than those of the Webbs emerged. The

69

perspectives of both Cole and Tawney foreshadow later, more consistent, philosophical arguments for equality. Cole might be considered the first of a number of Anglo-American participation theorists, to whom I return for a more extensive critical analysis in Chapter 7. Tawney relies heavily upon relevant-reason arguments to attack what he calls the established "religion of inequality." In Chapter 6, I return to assess this form of egalitarian argument. Here I shall move on more quickly to consider some problems faced by subsequent Fabians in their attempt (in the 1950s) to revise egalitarian theory to "fit" their political practice.

BENTHAMITE UTILITARIANISM REVISITED

Bentham's staunch support of equal universal suffrage and Mill's early advocacy of equal opportunities for women impressed the Fabians: They were fighting for very similar reforms half a century later. Although the Fabians' egalitarianism was largely consistent with the basic premises of classical utilitarianism, their arguments constituted an explicit internal critique of the principles of distribution Bentham and Mill derived from these premises. The Fabians' major egalitarian claim against classical liberalism was that the distributive inequalities flowing from the unequal ownership of property undermined the realization of human equality, striking at the heart of human dignity. A utilitarian argument that took account of this empirical claim would support a minimal welfare state: a state providing every citizen with goods, services, and opportunities essential to a decent way of life.

The Fabians were united in political fellowship by their criticism of widespread poverty even before they concurred on the need for finding a gradual, democratic path to a socialist society. Despite their early efforts to say *What Socialism Is*,[2] they never concurred on what a socialist society would be. That they initially and lastingly agreed upon a critique of existing inequalities supports the view that egalitarian purposes originate in an intuitive discomfort with the knowledge that "millions of . . . fellow creatures . . . sweat and suffer in hopeless toil and degradation."[3] The Fabians may have become egalitarians out of sympathy for the poor, but they also found reasons to support their sentiments.

In its simplest form, Benthamite utilitarianism provided a philosophical basis for the Fabians' understanding of what appeared an apparent injustice of liberal capitalism. Given that adequate shelter and sustenance are universal prerequisites to happiness, that each person's happiness counts equally, and that the marginal utility of income and wealth progressively diminishes, then the satisfaction of the basic needs of the poor ought to have priority over the satisfaction of the desires of the rich. At the same time, Bentham's defense of secure expectations takes on a new meaning. Shaw agreed that secure expectations are an important source of happiness, but denied that most people in a capitalist society can have expectations – other than those of continued poverty and unemployment – to secure. The capitalist economy worked more like a capricious nature than like Smith's invisible hand.[4] New "facts of life" therefore warranted a new social policy:

Fifty years ago it would have been assumed that absolute freedom in the sense of individual or "manly" independence, plus a criminal code, would spontaneously result in such an arrangement for each particular nation; and the effect was the philosophic apotheosis of *Laissez-Faire*. Today every student is aware that no such optimistic assumption is warranted by the facts of life.[5]

In short, where many lack the primary requisites for a secure and moderately pleasurable existence, the secondary utilitarian principle of securing expectations makes little utilitarian sense.

Bentham himself admitted that, other things being equal, his equality assumption warranted an equal distribution of resources. Other things were not equal according to Bentham. Incentives were necessary to stimulate production – hence the first constraint on the equality principle in the greatest interest of the social whole. But Bentham quickly elevated that constraint into a principle of freedom completely overriding the equality principle against which it originally was to be weighed. Granted the need to induce people to produce, Bentham still gave no argument why complete freedom of enterprise would be the necessary means. Clearly, he thought *absolute* freedom was not required, as he believed taxation another justified, because necessary, means to the greatest happiness. Why, then, was the apparent good of equal distribution completely forsaken? When Sidney Webb challenged Bentham's priority of liberty over equality, he did not challenge directly the value of liberty in utilitarian theory, but rather the conditions under which it can be realized:

The result of [the development of Sociology] is to compel a revision of the relative importance of liberty and equality as principles to be kept in view in social administration. In Bentham's celebrated "ends" to be aimed at in a civil code, liberty stands predominant over equality, on the ground that full equality can be maintained only by the loss of security for the fruits of labor. That exposition remains as true as ever; but the question for decision remains, how much liberty?[6]

The Fabians demonstrated that a cogent Benthamite argument can be made for equal provision of adequate sustenance,[7] arguing that a guaranteed effective opportunity for a decent living will provide greater happiness for the poor than superfluities do for the rich, as it is a prerequisite to all other pleasures and to the very possibility of a dignified existence for the majority of people.[8] Human dignity became the surrogate criterion for happiness. The minimal dignity suitable to human beings was not at the time accessible to the great mass of the population – even the anticipation of a proper burial was unavailable to many Englishmen. "Give me neither riches nor poverty" – the epigraph of Fabian Tract no. 17 – was the demand echoed in the Webbs' fight for a guaranteed national minimum.

THE MINIMAL WELFARE STATE: SOCIALISM VERSUS LIBERALISM?

The Webbs' argument for what they called a "National Minimum" is an important one once the classical liberal view that the free market would secure for all industrious persons a commodious living is found wanting. The Fabians' case for socialism began by setting forth an extensive design for alleviating the problems of what later became known as "primary poverty": unsatisfied individual *needs* for more goods necessary to life, needs that remained unfulfilled even within a developed, free-enterprise system:

"The poor ye have always with you" is merely a statement of the fact of inequality of wealth; and it affords no evidence as to the chronic existence in Judea of any mass of what is now called destitution, still less of its inevitableness. By destitution we mean the condition of being without one or other of the necessaries of life, in such a way that health and strength, and even vitality, is so impaired as to eventually imperil life itself.[9]

One might dispute where the precise line was to be drawn between poverty and destitution, but the Webbs were clearly willing to recognize that hard cases and wavering lines existed. The ground they stood on was fairly firm: Up to the point of full subsistence, people suffer from a condition whose diagnosis is analogous to that of a physical disease.[10]

The medical analogy was extended so as to suggest the proper method of cure. Treating only the symptoms would not rid society of its problems. "To prevent the occurrence of destitution we must, it is clear, first ascertain its causes and then arrest their operation."[11] If a cure for the disease, once rampant, is difficult to discover, one must concentrate on preventive medicine. The Webbs thus looked for both short-term causes and long-term preventions. As the disease they were observing had multiple causes, they recommended simultaneous cures for each significant cause: unemployment, poor medical care, inadequate child-care services, poor education, and insufficient provision for old age. The most significant cures therefore would attack these five "germs" of the problem.

Sidney Webb claimed that state prevention of primary poverty would signal a shift from individualism to collectivism. The individualist premise on which he rested his critique of liberalism was therefore the Spencerian assumption that each man's self-interest is so radically divorced from every other's that a state can at most balance the satisfaction of interests or erect barriers between people to minimize the number of serious collisions.[12] Webb was thus arguing against a liberal whose conception of human nature was more radically individualist than was Locke's, and certainly more so than was J. S. Mill's.

Without noting the target of their attack, one cannot understand the meaning of the Webbs' collectivism. Ultimately they slid into an unprincipled collectivism, which condoned the sacrifice of the individual to society, a sacrifice that all classical liberals and the Fabians themselves were anxious to avoid. But their most consistent "collectivist" argument was a liberal one. The individuals on which their state was to be built required social support and collective effort to satisfy their interests. The interests of society transcended those of individuals only insofar as utilitarian calculations required that some people's interests be sacrificed to those of the greater number, a general problem of utilitarianism to which I shall return in Chapter 5:

To the employer and to the landlord, all this enactment of "common rules," and all this enforcement of a "National Minimum" low as it might be, loomed as a limitation of his personal freedom. It limited the range of his power over the lives of others . . . But the other side of the shield, seen by the wage-earner as the outcome of this same legislation, is an enormous growth in practical freedom of action, a liberty positively enlarged by law, increased leisure, better health, greater amenity of life, further opportunities of advancement for his children, and sometimes even higher money wages.[13]

The Fabian case for collectivism was most fundamentally an argument against laissez-faire, based upon observation of the necessary social preconditions for achieving the greatest happiness or for providing all people with the opportunity for a decent and dignified existence. Certain remedies for the injustices of the free-market system – entailing collective provisions of goods, services, and opportunities – came readily to mind: tax reforms, extension of factory acts, educational reforms, reorganization of poor-law administration, extension of municipal services, and reformation of the machinery of political democracy.[14]

Sidney Webb was impressed by the natural evolution of many of these remedies out of the individualist anarchy of classical liberal society, and by the extent of the existing socialistic reorganizations of capitalism.[15] He did not recognize that these reorganizations might be consistent with the premises of liberalism operating under social and economic conditions unforeseen by classical liberals. With Spencer as his archetypal liberal, Webb simply contrasted capitalism to socialism and individualism to collectivism. Because the policies he supported coincided with those toward which the capitalist state was gradually moving, he concluded that a new socialist era was commencing. William Clarke echoed Webb's pronouncement: The new government regulations of industry, "involving collective checking of individual greed and the paring of slices off the profits of capital in the interests of the working community," were "of a Socialistic character."[16] Clarke, of course, did not think that the early restrictive legislation on industry *was* socialism itself. But what he took to be lacking was more of the same: state control. The democratic state that he, and most other Fabians, envisioned was a state in which "some very large and definite extensions of collective authority" would be made.[17]

"The best government," argued Webb, "is . . . that which can safely and successfully administer most."[18] The ambiguous qualifiers, "safely and successfully," left a great deal about the socialist ideal unspecified. The early Fabian Tracts emphasized the need for more government regulation – of industry, of municipal services, of education – always presupposing that such regulation would operate safely, within a democratic framework, and successfully, for egalitarian ends. But many of the extensions of political authority to which they referred were not primarily redistributive (between classes).

The Fabians rightly claimed that redistributive aims of socialism might be accomplished by further extensions of government authority over economic life, yet Webb and many fellow Fabians sorely neglected another socialist ideal – the redistribution of political power. And, as G. D. H. Cole was to remind the Fabians, an equalization of power was as important a precondition for securing the equal dignity of individuals as was greater material welfare. If socialism was understood as the extension of democratic politics to the "soil" of practical life, material welfare would provide the precondition for democratic participation, and the decentralization of government and democratization of industry the opportunities. Webb's optimistic hopes for the coming of socialism rested upon his one-eyed vision of what socialism was, reflected in his claim that "the difficulty in England is not to secure more political power for the people, but to persuade them to make . . . sensible use of the power they already have."[19]

TWO FACES OF SOCIALISM

An important analytical, and historically relevant, distinction must be made between the two rationales for what is commonly called "socialization of the means of production." Socialism has been viewed as a means of elevating the masses to a minimum standard of living and of human decency and also as a means of equalizing political power among individuals. The Fabians were champions of the first cause, and they provided a case for accepting their cause as the more urgent one.

The idea of equality served a singular critical purpose for most early Fabians – as a critique of a society that denied the effective opportunity for all citizens to live decently. Those who supported the second sort of equality rightly claimed that this use of the equality ideal was inadequate to the socialist cause. By illuminating another side of the democratic socialist ideal, Cole's writings shed light on a deficiency in mainstream Fabian argument.

Cole recognized the grounding of the Fabian case for the welfare state in Benthamite utilitarianism and argued that the logical extension of this Fabian argument would lead to a form of socialism in which a highly centralized state controlled "the entire economic machine."[20] The Fabians supported administrative decentralization only for the sake of greater efficiency, in both the political and economic spheres. They were content to rely upon existing mechanisms of universal suffrage allied with the politicization of economic issues (which followed from nationalization of the means of production) as a means of ensuring collective control for the common good.[21] Cole objected that these mechanisms for controlling state power in the common interest would not suffice, as the state by Webb's own admission would centralize expertise (if not decision-making authority) on important issues. [22]

Following good utilitarian reasoning, the Fabians wanted to entrust to the civil servant the responsibility for the efficient running of governmental services, for the best employment of productive resources, and for the general maximization of happiness. Even democratization of industrial organization for the Fabians meant centralization of professional authority in the interests of efficiency and only retrospective popular control over representatives:

> To balance the professional civil servant we have, in fact, the professional representative . . . The fundamental requisites of government are the same in the democratic state as in the Trade Union. In both cases the problem is how to combine administrative efficiency with popular control. Both alike ultimately depend on a continuance of general assent . . . [But] in the democratic state as in the Trade Union, the eventual judgment of the people is pronounced not upon projects but upon results. [23]

Cole did not doubt the legitimacy of the *aim* of the state machinery the Fabians supported, nor even its *effectiveness* in satisfying the basic needs of citizens. Rather he wondered whether the Fabians' explicit goals would ultimately undermine the liberal ideal of free and equal citizenship:

> There is a feeling that the great State has got out of touch with the people, and that no mere democratic machinery at elections will be able to bring it back again. There is individualism, an assertion that the individual . . . is after all ultimate . . . And there is a claim, on behalf of the individual, for a greater measure of *effective self-government* than can be given by the ballot-box and the local constituency. [24]

Armed with the alternative socialist standard of equalizing political power as well as material satisfaction, Cole challenged the means the Fabians had chosen to achieve their ends. [25] He never denied that material satisfactions are a necessary condition for human dignity, but he contended that justice must be constituted as well by the realization of more equal participatory or power relationships within society.

The standard of equalizing political power is only a partial expression of Cole's socialist ideal and his critique of Fabianism. He saw a more inclusive standard of human equality as a seriously devalued end in Fabian socialism. Modern industrial organization had made the ideal of human *self*-development – control over one's principal life activities – increasingly difficult to achieve: "There is a great difference between the common-sense ideal of high wages, and the other ideal of enabling men somehow to express, in their daily work of their hands, some part of that infinitely subtle and various personality which lives in each one of them."[26] In order both to control bureaucratic power and to provide citizens with more democratic control over their lives, Cole demanded a broadly democratic, federated trade-union movement. The Webbs also supported trade unionism but in a much more qualified and less democratic form.[27] With respect to nationalization, Cole acknowledged the need to unite both egalitarian perspectives – of economic distribution and participatory equality – within an adequate socialist vision: "If it is no use to nationalize industry without obtaining real control over it, it is of equally little use for the workers to control industry without getting more out of it."[28]

Trade-union power – rather than welfare statism – remained Cole's preoccupation, whereas centralized administration of industry, of services, and of education, in the name of a "National Minimum" was the linchpin of Fabian socialism. Although the power of collective bargaining was an important trade-union weapon, its significance to Sidney Webb and most Fabians was clearly as a means to a "more than minimal" egalitarianism; its success would be evidenced by the steady rise in material wages and improvements in working conditions. Decentralization and democratization of industrial organization was for Webb at best a "utopian" ideal, at worst a call for "industrial anarchism."[29] A case might be made for the *priority* of equalizing basic opportunities over equalizing human powers in industry, but not for the total neglect of the latter ideal. Webb supported democratic control over the state and democratic state control over trade unions. Yet he shortsightedly ignored the restriction of human aims and capacities, if not of material interests, that a centralized state coupled with a centralized trade-union movement might ultimately effect.

State regulation of the economy and state provision of free services, the background conditions for equal access to the market, constitute the logical limits of the Webbs' case for socialism. Unlike Cole, most of the Fabians rested largely content with the basic political foundations of the existing liberal order. Their contribution to the critique of laissez-faire capitalism was coupled with a residual complacency with the existing organization of liberal democracy – well captured by Margaret Cole's report of the compari-

77

son Beatrice Webb drew between the Webbs and the guild socialists: "Beatrice said they [the Webbs] were 'B's, benevolent,
bourgeois and bureaucratic,' contrasting themselves with the 'A's,
who were aristocratic, anarchist, and arrogant.'"[30]

The gap between these two egalitarian perspectives had logical
roots in the distinct liberal foundations of equality. The Fabians
largely built upon the strict utilitarian assumption of equal passions and extended it in the light of a new, or at least newly interpreted, historical situation. Cole, on the other hand, reminds us
that the strict utilitarian view of equality is one-eyed. His arguments hark back to Mill's critique of Bentham and tell us of the
possibilities of a reconciliation of the two liberal traditions: a rein-
tegration not, however, realized in his own thought.

Although Cole's critique makes us conscious of the one-sided-
ness of the Fabians' vision, neither he nor the Fabians completed
the integration of the two faces of democratic socialism: democratic control *over* industry and politics constrained so as to effect
a more equal distribution of goods and services; and democratic
control *within* industry reflecting a greater equalization of human
powers and realization of human capacities through political participation. In their more philosophical moments, both Cole and
the Webbs recognized several serious problems that such an integration presented: balancing consumer against worker interests in
the product of labor and determining to what extent democracy
can be considered *self*-control. Yet without a fuller account of distributive justice, the Webbs were unable (and perhaps otherwise
unwilling) to consider the possible integration of Cole's critique.
Like Bentham, they considered social efficiency so great a value
that bureaucratic means to that end were not seriously questioned.

TAWNEY'S PERSPECTIVE: EGALITARIAN FELLOWSHIP

A contemporary of the Fabians, R. H. Tawney shared many of
their egalitarian goals and criticisms of laissez-faire capitalism, although unlike the Webbs, he self-consciously remained faithful to
the liberal democratic tradition in his vision of a fully socialist
society.

For Tawney, the notion of human equality had its most meaningful and explicit foundation in Christian thought: the idea of a
human brotherhood deriving from the equality of all people in the
eyes of God. Yet, conscious as he was of the predominant secular
vision of his age, Tawney accommodated that Christian vision to a

secular society and attempted to make a case for its relevance to
social justice. In its application to secular justice, the implications
of the classical Christian notion of human equality are significantly modified.[31] The convergence of the two images of human
nature – secular and religious – rather than the peculiar legitimacy
of the Christian basis, lends support to the foundations of modern
egalitarianism.

Although Tawney appealed to a Christian ideal, the equal dignity
and worth of human beings of which he repeatedly spoke is not
radically distinct from the secular notion of human beings as equal
moral persons that we later encounter in Williams's "The Idea of
Equality" and in Rawls's *A Theory of Justice*. Stemming from that
notion are a large number of egalitarian arguments about the distribution of both goods and power in liberal capitalist society.
Tawney built upon the classical liberal case for equal political and
civil rights a case for what T. H. Marshall called equal social rights:
a guarantee to all people of those social amenities, such as health
care, housing, and education, necessary for the meaningful exercise of political rights and individual freedom.[32] In addition, Tawney argued for an upper limit on the disparities of wealth a society
may tolerate. The ideas of fellowship and equal human dignity
imply a relatively egalitarian distribution of power within the economic sphere as well. Tawney would agree with at least two of
Rousseau's preconditions for the realization of a general will in
any society: that no man be capable of buying another and that no
one identify himself as a member of a privileged class rather than
as an equal citizen.[33]

Tawney endorsed the Fabians' egalitarian position on the issue
of guaranteeing each citizen a decent living. He therefore supported the extension of social services, universal secondary education, inheritance taxation, and industrial legislation.[34] But his
egalitarianism went beyond, and sometimes stood in tension
with, that of the Fabians. He interpreted the ideal of human equality with which he began as requiring three secular goals to be
attained by a system of distributive justice. That system should be
one that (1) allowed all people to *live* decently (as self-respecting
individuals), (2) enabled them to *appear* dignified, and (3) encouraged them to be *conscious* of their common humanity. By concentrating upon the latter two goals, Tawney's argument went beyond that of the Fabians, and it therefore deserves closer
attention.

The aim of Tawney's egalitarianism was to provide people not only with a decent life but with a decent *communal* life as well. The existing appearance and the consciousness of inequality weighed heavily in his critique of contemporary capitalist democracy. Both were affected by the existence of what he called class privilege.[35] Privilege he observed on many fronts – in the distinct mode of work of the working and capitalist classes, in their differing use of leisure time, in their differing access to goods, in the disparities of their public influence, and, above all, in their distinct cultures.

The Fabians had solved the problem at the lower end of the income scale but contributed confusion concerning the proper distribution over the remaining range. Tawney's approach largely ignored the middle ranges to concentrate on an attack at the upper end of the income and wealth spectrum. There he believed that undeserved *and* unbeneficial inequalities existed: undeserved because no one could contribute that much more than others to the social product or be worth that much more as a person; unbeneficial to society for a reason logically distinct from the Benthamite utilitarian criterion of happiness maximization, the Lockean criterion of just entitlements, or a criterion of proportionate incentives. Large inequalities of wealth have a tendency to corrupt the relations between different classes of citizens in a democratic society by enabling the upper classes to dress lavishly and thereby to have the appearance of a superior subspecies among humankind.[36] The market for fine clothes reflects a reverence for superficiality that capitalist society has condoned, if not encouraged.

Tawney sought an end to those economic inequalities that "spilled over" into other realms of human existence, realms in which it was irrational to distinguish among people on the basis of differentials in their income or wealth:

A society which values equality will attach a low degree of significance to economic and social differences between different groups . . . , [whereas a] society which is in love with inequality will take such differences seriously, and will allow them to overflow from the regions, such as economic life, where they have their origin, and from which it is difficult wholly to expel them, till they become a kind of morbid obsession, coloring the whole world of social relations.[37]

It was not the division of labor between the working and capitalist classes that disturbed Tawney. Rather, it was the sight of a society in which social distinctions were based upon the economic divisions of classes. Such a society necessarily constituted an unsettling vision for anyone who began with a conception of basic human equality and wished that conception to be made socially apparent.

An egalitarian society would therefore not only end the misery to which the Fabians had addressed themselves but also would abolish those social distinctions among people based solely on class (or, more generally, economic) position.

Although economic inequality corrupted social relations,[38] Tawney also observed the reverse causal relation between the subjective consciousness of human equality and objective factors of social equality. Instilling a common egalitarian consciousness presented itself as a critical means to Tawney's egalitarian design. From this perspective one can understand his concerted attack upon what he called the "acquisitive ethos" of liberal capitalist society.[39] The ethos was that of a society in which people sought wealth as an end in itself and as the basis of social rank. Tawney viewed money's role in twentieth-century England much as Marx had described it in his early manuscripts, as exercising a tyranny of power over and between people.[40] That tyranny both caused the acquisitive ethos and was perpetuated by it. Capitalism in England thereby brought with it a culture that not only elevated wealth to the overriding and inclusive goal of social life, but devalued social life to a competitive battle rather than a cooperative venture.[41] Tawney wished to replace that culture of competition with a new culture, one that gave voice to fraternal relations and to the multiplicity of ends a dignified and free human existence might serve.

The overriding value of fellowship tied to a belief in human equality provided grounds for granting citizens the right to a minimum standard of living. The goal of fellowship would place an upper limit on the rewards accruing to a person by virtue of his talent, however great. No job would justifiably carry a remuneration so great that its occupant would feel too elevated to associate with those in less lucrative professions. In a society in which the value of fellowship was institutionalized, communication between people would be possible regardless of their incomes or occupations. And equal political consideration of everyone's interests would be a publicly recognized norm, for only if everyone understood that his wants would be considered as seriously as would any other's in the political process could citizens relate to one another on the basis of mutual respect. Self-respect would thereby become (at least in part) a politically determined category.[42] In addition, because fellowship would require as a background condition universal self-respect, it would be essential that all people pursue ways of life in which they might find self-fulfillment.

By emphasizing fellowship as an end to which society should be oriented, and by insisting that socialism would be morally successful only if the acquisitive ethos of modern capitalism were superseded by a new, more humanistic social purpose, Tawney avoided the dehumanizing social ideal of a meritocracy, a society in which all citizens are rewarded according to their contribution to the common good, that good being defined as maximization of the social product. Tawney recommended instead an economic equality sufficient to prevent some classes from being effectively barred from the higher culture of their fellow citizens:

What is repulsive is not that one man should earn more than others, for where community of environment, and a common education . . . have had a common tradition of respect and consideration, these details of the counting-house are forgotten or ignored. It is that some classes should be excluded from the heritage of civilization which others enjoy, and that the fact of human fellowship, which is ultimate and profound, should be obscured by economic contrasts, which are trivial and superficial.[43]

Tawney explicitly recognized ends other than that of fellowship upon which a socialist society needed to be built. Indeed, any political thinker who sought to reconstruct a just, or even a better, society would have to consider a plurality of values relevant to the moral and practical design of social institutions and to evaluate the possibility that some values require the sacrifice of others within a society in which institutional priorities are not clearly determined. Now, although Tawney wished fellowship to be an end toward which British society would be increasingly oriented, he also argued that "distribution should never fall out of relation to service rendered to the community. Reward follows function."[44]

Aside from its ambiguity, this principle invites a serious criticism of Tawney's theory. Once a society rewards citizens according to some publicly understood standard of social contribution, it invites the creation of a status hierarchy. The possibilities for avoiding this problem will depend upon social psychology: Even guaranteed employment or provision of basic goods and services may not be sufficient to foster self-respect among citizens if, as Tawney's own argument indicated, self-respect is a strictly comparative social category.[45] Tawney failed to consider the possibility his own argument left open: that leveled distinctions in income, tied to equal opportunity *and* a principle of reward according to function, may also make fellowship psychologically untenable, because people may then base their self-respect on their relative ability to contribute to the common good. Inequality

82

in England was undesirable to Tawney in part because it led to the deference of the poor to the rich. But if social justice might also produce deference, would that be preferred? Even if so (as I shall later argue), Tawney's discussion of equality, directed primarily at reducing established class privilege, offers few clues as to why.

The problem of defining the common good also remained. Here was the widest gap in Tawney's argument for a socialist society, though it is a gap not easily bridged by any committed liberal theorist. Tawney clearly wanted the common good to be collectively defined. Its precise content was therefore to be an open question. This attitude toward the common good contrasted sharply with that of the Webbs, for whom the common good was a scientific rather than a moral problem.[46] Tawney was never tempted to conceptualize society as an organism whose interest transcended that of its constituent elements.[47] The interest of democratic citizens could not be defined without taking the real will of the people into account. But far from solving the problem of the common good, Tawney's approach raised new problems. For although he wanted each person to contribute to the definition of his own social welfare, he also argued that people must consciously agree upon some common social end. In short, Tawney faced Rousseau's problem of how people can freely come to agree upon their common interests as citizens.

What a social purpose or the common good meant to Tawney is not clear, although he repeatedly declared the need for a new social ethos to replace that of the acquisitive spirit of capitalism, an ethos that would constitute a collective rationale for social life: a common recognition of a purpose for which society exists, rather than of an end toward which all social actions need be oriented, an "inclusive" end akin to the greatest-happiness principle in Mill's theory.[48] This interpretation coheres best with Tawney's belief in the need for a plurality of goals for which citizens can strive and be socially rewarded. Principles of social justice must take account of the legitimacy of these goals. Once social purpose is understood as an inclusive end, the seemingly straightforward principle of "reward according to function" becomes a very complex distributional principle.

Democratic socialism was to be the product of this new social consciousness of the common good. Yet how was such consciousness to precede the very reforms that Tawney saw as necessary to support a new humanism? If it was inequality to which Tawney attributed the acquisitive spirit, how was that spirit to be transcended before the class structure was reformed? Tawney never supplied a theoretical answer to this question, but his hopes for British society clearly lay in the unusual opportunities afforded by the upheavals of the Great War and the economic crisis of the thirties.

From the British war experience, Tawney inferred the possibility of fellowship and social unity based upon common purpose. The disorientation following the war presented an opportunity to reorganize social institutions and to redefine institutional goals. Tawney thought that in times of economic stress people would realize the value of fellowship and would begin to question the previous rationale of economic institutions.[49] Although he had indicated that the public spirit created by military or economic crises could not suffice to ensure progress toward a common culture, the war experience clearly bolstered his faith in the potential for a common culture, although the realization of a humanist culture would have to await concrete egalitarian reforms in social and economic institutions.[50] Founded on the public spirit produced by wartime mobilization, Tawney's faith was relatively blind. His conception of a common culture was so amorphous as to obscure the severe theoretical limitations of the practical analogy he employed. Though the war had created a social consciousness of cooperation toward a communal goal, the wartime purpose was hardly the democratically chosen good of Tawney's ideal. Nor was it an inclusive end of social life; indeed, it was not even a purpose we would describe as a good, and certainly not one that would be desirable to impose upon a just or nearly just society. Few subsequent egalitarian thinkers were to share Tawney's faith in the democratic development of a desirable social ethos once both wars passed. Yet neither has any subsequent liberal egalitarian theorist been able to avoid the theoretical need to postulate attainment of collective agreement upon social purpose. That consciousness will be characterized by Rawls as an agreement upon principles regulating a just society and by Williams and Walzer as an agreement upon the relevant reasons governing social institutions.

Although Tawney's argument for a common culture raises problems for liberal egalitarian theory, it provides insight into the need for the idea of equal human fellowship to operate not only as a theoretical basis for just distributional principles but as a conscious social ideal within an egalitarian society. Otherwise, no amount of distributional justice will secure a society in which people *appear* to be equals. Without such a consciousness, any inequality may be established as the principle of a new social hierarchy, in which those with more than that unequally distributed good or trait rise to the top.

Tawney contributed to that consciousness of equal humanity as a historian by reinterpreting the past as the history of the rural and urban working classes, not simply as the isolated accomplishments (or culture) of an elite.[51] But in the end, Tawney the social critic does not provide us with sufficient criteria for what might constitute the common culture upon which a future egalitarian society would thrive. The revitalization of Christianity was not only implausible (as Tawney himself recognized) but also inadequate to a secular egalitarian culture. Insofar as the classical case for Christian fellowship had little concern for questions of distributive justice, the philosophical task of detailing the specific contours of distribution within a just secular state remained a task that Tawney only began, and one that has yet to be completed.

One important component of Tawney's egalitarianism remains to be considered: his case for the equalization of power in society. In his concern over this issue, Tawney followed Mill's lead. Although Mill, too, was a critic of the unequal economic relations under capitalism, Tawney placed greater emphasis upon this issue, perhaps because he observed industrialism in fuller force. Nevertheless, Mill's theoretical argument remains essential to Tawney's case.

Rather than setting forth a notion of freedom distinct from that of Mill, Tawney applied Mill's exceptions to the laissez-faire principle to the problems of industrial organization in capitalist society. He claimed that the free action of individuals could not secure individual preferences without some external enforcing agency – hence the need for stricter government regulation of private enterprise in the interests of the vast majority of citizens (consumers and workers). Without such regulation, the existing monopolistic, hierarchical organization of industry would remain unchallenged, or more accurately, ineffectively challenged.[52] Because Tawney did not claim for the state a *right* of ownership divorced from the interests of individuals to live freely and to develop fully, he did not support wholesale state ownership. Public ownership was required only in those cases where the conditions of that freedom – in particular, relative equality of social and political power – would be forsaken or severely impaired:

There are certain great services which cannot safely be resigned to exploitation for private profit, because the public welfare is so intimately dependent upon them, that those who own them become, in effect, the masters of the nation. There are certain others in which the consumer is at the mercy of the monopolist. In all the first, and some of the second, regulation is insufficient. What is required is public ownership.[53]

Tawney's arguments for the necessity of regulation, control, and/or ownership by government were thus couched in terms consistent with the exceptions to laissez-faire policy that Mill recognized.

Tawney attempted in three ways to avoid Mill's dilemma of the concentration of political power that may result from more extensive government controls. First, he did not argue for a uniform policy of state ownership of all industry. Second, when he did sanction state control, it was only with the proviso that there be mechanisms of public, that is, democratic, accountability. Finally, and most significantly, he redescribed the alternatives of private and state controls as choices between second bests. If monopolistic private industries were domains of completely unaccountable power, state-run enterprises might at least be partially, if not wholly, responsible organizations: "The important question is not whether an undertaking is described as private or public; it is whether, if it is private, adequate guarantees can be established that it performs a public function, and whether, if it is public, it performs it effectively."[54]

Though Tawney had not entirely solved the problem with which Mill began, he had roughly outlined the possible consequences of different forms of economic control in terms of equalities of power. By his model, monopolistic private enterprise and nationalization by an unaccountable state would be similarly inegalitarian and detrimental to individual liberty; some combination of workers' and consumers' control would become the most egalitarian. Tawney did not describe what the latter mode of organization might entail, nor was he critically attuned to the more specific problems of *who* should decide *what* economic issues. Though these unanswered questions complicate his case for collective ownership and democratic participation, Tawney consistently added to the case for equalizing power by extending more completely into the economic sphere the Millean argument for an egalitarian politics. The problems that remained were substantial. As they were reconsidered by subsequent participation theorists, we shall return to them in Chapter 7.

FABIANS OF THE FIFTIES: CROSLAND AND CROSSMAN

Members of the Fabian Society continued to argue and fight for democratic socialism at a time when many believed democracy and socialism to be an impossible combination. The events that intervened between the Fabians and their political heirs of the 1950s may help explain the alteration in tone of the new Fabians' moral argument. The "Great Terror," Hitler's Germany, and the political fantasies of 1984 and Brave New World certainly instilled the fear of totalitarianism and mass politics into a new generation of British Labourites. Yet this explanation of the new Fabians' politics is too simple. The Fabians' anti-Marxism and their insistence on a democratic road to socialism antedate these experiences of the new generation. And at least in Anthony Crosland's case, the domestic situation in Britain – in particular the temporary economic boom of the fifties – could also be used to explain his greater acceptance of the status quo.

The new Fabians generally agreed that "the belief in social equality . . . remains the most characteristic feature of socialist thought today."[55] As Richard Crossman put it, "Our Socialism is based on the traditional radical demand for a society of free and equal citizens, reinforced by the empirical postulate that great concentrations of power become a menace to freedom and equality unless they are subjected to public control."[56] Subjecting great concentrations of private economic power to public control was an important goal of the old Fabians. The problem they generally had neglected was how to subject the new economic institutions of a formally democratic state to more effective public control. Here the new Fabian program continued to fall short. Crossman himself confessed: "I wish that in nationalising we had taken more trouble to preserve the best units of self-government and responsibility built up by previous generations of socialists or believers in municipal enterprise."[57]

Crossman's concern for redistributing political power was not matched by every new Fabian, nor has it been realized by their political practice, but it shows that Cole's concern for more participatory equality did not disappear from Fabian thought. Indeed, Crossman added to Cole's argument two important provisos: that workers often had an interest in remaining independent of management and that collective bargaining would work fairly only if all industries within the economy, as well as each party to a particular contract, shared relatively equal bargaining power.[58] Their political experience no doubt assured new Fabians that Cole's vision of one national guild representing all industries – one association of producers united by a common purpose and counterpoised against the state (the "association of users," in Cole's terms)[59] – was neither practicable nor desirable. But many new

Fabians still failed, in theory as well as in practice, to appreciate Cole's argument for redistributing power by politicizing industrial organization. The guild socialists often claimed too much political power for producers, but Crosland totally dismissed the plight of the industrial workers, reflecting his own blindness to the remaining force of the guild socialist's participatory ideal.[60]

While clinging to the aspiration for equality, Crosland contended that "if we want more equality, the case for it must rest on statements largely, if not entirely, unrelated to economic welfare."[61] Previous egalitarian thought was considered inadequate to present social conditions for two reasons: The growth of the welfare state had rendered concern with economic welfare generally obsolete, and socialization of industry would not remove the new threat of managerialism. On what grounds could the case for social equality then rest?

"More equality . . . would yet conduce to a 'better' society. This I believe for three reasons, relating respectively to the diminution of social antagonism, to social justice, and to the avoidance of social waste."[62] By social justice, Crosland meant effective equality of opportunity, but he did not pursue the potentially radical implications of this Fabian standard. Social waste was avoided by full employment, allowing people of all abilities to contribute simultaneously to their own and to the social good. This was a narrower interpretation of the equal-opportunity maxim, with concern for equality deleted. The elimination of social waste would not attack differential rewards based upon functions but would support full employment and an income floor to ensure that no rewards were so small as to render the more poorly endowed useless or unwilling to be of use. The argument for equality that appeared to carry the greatest weight in Crosland's case for socialism was the need to decrease social antagonism. His concentration on the "personal envy argument" indicated the new Fabians' persistent uneasiness with any evidence that might be used in favor of the Marxist case for class conflict and their overriding concern with the psychological reactions to social inequality, rather than with its socioeconomic correlates.

Inequality became a state of mind in Crosland's analysis. If some people are envious of others' higher positions, their feelings, Crosland declared, "are neither unnatural nor deplorable, but based on a simple view of what is just and fair."[63] In order to distinguish justifiable from unjustifiable envy, one would need a conception of justice logically separable from a person's immediate emotional state, or a more precise definition of the background conditions for a society in which envy would reflect, and reflect only, distributive injustice. Rawls subsequently has attempted to specify such a framework, which we shall critically explore in Chapter 5. But in his own argument for the "justness" of envy, Crosland did not present any criteria of what "*is* just and fair" apart from that which people's envy would judge. His theory served as a solution not for *inequality* as socialists had previously understood it, but for *class resentment*. And the need to abolish class resentment (rather than class) was Crosland's major case for socialism. It was a case apparently well suited to the new Fabians' claims against Marxism. Inequality based on economic distribution was no longer the major issue to which socialists need address themselves, for the welfare state had solved the most pressing economic problems of class society. If a class society persisted, it was largely in the minds of citizens who resented the resulting distribution of privilege (class *power* was a thing of the past).[64]

Although valuing social unity above social equality, Crosland might still argue for the latter, given the resentment some inequalities fostered. Insofar as inequalities fostered potential social conflict, already "visible both in politics and industry . . . making society less peaceful and contented than it might be," Crosland professed a revisionist egalitarianism.[65] Both equality and social justice were viewed as a means of avoiding the threat of class politics. Their *independent* value was not very apparent in Crosland's analysis.

The subsequently developed concept of "relative deprivation" is intimately linked and readily applicable to Crosland's social view. Relative-deprivation studies seek to understand under what conditions the less advantaged resent, or accept as just, distributive inequalities present in their society. In the most extensive study of relative deprivation in Britain, W. G. Runciman discovered that distributive inequalities between the upper and lower classes were generally not resented or even perceived by the lower strata of society.[66] To the extent that resentments existed, they were directed at similarly disadvantaged groups closer in the stratification hierarchy to the observed group. Rather than providing fuel for Crosland's egalitarian concerns, Runciman's study would suggest that little or no egalitarian movement is required, given present working-class consciousness. Coupling relative-deprivation studies with Crosland's egalitarian guidelines, we can see how complacency about the status quo is readily warranted, despite recognition of gross disparities in the distribution of advantages among classes. Taken alone, relative-deprivation accounts do not warrant such complacency: Runciman himself supports a potentially more egalitarian political program by coupling his empirical study with an early version of Rawls's conception of justice.[67] But Crosland's normative view – that egalitarian values are primarily justified by social resentment or by class consciousness of inequality – can readily be used to justify existing unequal distribution, given the absence of conscious (or at least of easily communicable) social resentments among the less advantaged in the social hierarchy.

Another critical question arose within Crosland's case for the importance of the subjective dimension of equality: Why was the threat of class politics, of perceived and resented inequalities, still present in the newly managed welfare state? Lacking an objective conception of distributive justice going beyond that of the Fabians, Crosland and many other new Fabians were at a loss for a convincing answer. Their greatest justification of the managerial state was its necessity. Even granted that necessity, the new Fabians never justified the particular distribution the managerial state oversaw. During the full employment period of the fifties, Crosland interpreted the lingering presence of perceived injustice among citizens as a by-product of past class-based ideologies unsuited to a new bureaucratic politics and as therefore inappropriate to the new objective conditions of the welfare state: "The objective (of socialism) has become not only less clear-cut, but also . . . less urgent. But people want something to crusade about."[68]

Another central fact of the new reality upon which the new Fabians commented was the phenomenon of secondary poverty: substandard living patterns attributable to wasteful habits rather than to low earnings. Crosland interprets the social consciousness he observes as an irrational response to an altered social reality. The phenomenon of secondary poverty was understandably difficult for a committed egalitarian to crusade about, for secondary poverty in Crosland's analysis was not "really" poverty at all, as it was due to "ignorant or imprudent spending of earnings."[69] As one consequence, objective indexes of poverty based on income would no longer be adequate measures of distributional justice or injustice.

This argument went even further than Crosland realized, or perhaps desired, in undermining previous socialist thought. For now guaranteeing all citizens a *minimal* share might be irrational if some people would waste their shares, whereas others would use theirs prudently. How could one believe in the liberal justice of "to each according to his basic needs" if many people either did not recognize their own needs or were not oriented to satisfying them? Three replies are possible here: The first two present a challenge implicit within the original Fabians' egalitarianism; the third was a reply explicitly provided by the new Fabians themselves. Each of these replies contains more than a grain of truth, and all – if properly qualified – are mutually compatible.

The first reply suggests that services in kind rather than money be provided, thereby constraining people to make proper use of the welfare state if they are to use it at all. This solution raises the dilemma of state power with which the new Fabians were very concerned: If people cannot be trusted to act in their own interest, the attractiveness of state control in the interests of citizens increases. At the same time, the practical fear of its misuse may arise. The old Fabians were less disturbed about containing state power, perhaps because they had not lived to witness the consequences of fascism and totalitarianism disguised as state socialism. But as Cole pointed out, the Fabians also had separated in theory the role of the state as a service institution from its role as a policing agent, and had focused upon its service role. Within the context of a democratic state, this separation was reasonably well founded. We might add that the expansion of the service sector need not be thought of as creeping paternalism – if paternalism is understood as the curtailment of individual liberty in the interests of the individual whose liberty is curtailed.[70] All citizens have a right to medical care, to housing, and to education, but none of these rights need entail the right to the cash equivalent of those goods (to be used as the recipient wishes). A national health service need not be a paternalistic institution so long as its internal practices are not paternalistic.[71] This reply to the problem of secondary poverty therefore forces us to discriminate between state functions that do and those that do not necessarily threaten or limit individual freedom.

A second reply to the new Fabians' dilemma is the counterargument that people will know and act upon their own interests when the proper social conditions are provided. This reply rejects Crosland's claim that the economic foundations of egalitarian justice had been well laid by the welfare state.[72] If equality of opportunity was still a goal rather than a reality (as Crosland for a time maintained), then the new Fabians could have consistently retained faith in the potential rationality of disadvantaged citizens. This argument is especially forceful when applied to the family for, as Crosland recognized, the most significant instances of secondary poverty occurred within family units where the husband failed to distribute sufficient funds for his wife's use and where mothers were inadequately informed of ways to satisfy their children's medical and other basic needs. At least some of these problems of family structure could plausibly be attributed to the unequal economic and educational opportunities available to women in British society.

The new Fabians themselves concentrated on the role of education. The question of alleviating secondary poverty was one of how to teach people to be both rational individuals and worthy citizens, or how to provide "education as a preparation for life," as Margaret Cole put it.[73] The problem of what would constitute an education adequate to the new welfare and managerial state thereby became one of their central concerns.

For any committed liberal egalitarian, educational goals tend to take over where economic and political policy leave off. As a consequence of their satisfaction with the accomplishments of the welfare state and their retreat from more extensive egalitarian measures suggested by previous democratic socialists, many new Fabians relied heavily on the educational system to fill in the large gaps that, they argued, must remain between an egalitarian economic policy and a fully egalitarian society. The fact of the new Fabians' concentration on the politics of educational reform may be as significant as the substance of their suggestions. Cole began her essay "Education and Social Democracy" by noting the challenge to this concentration voiced by previous democratic socialists: "When the plan for this task was being discussed, a Fabian who had heard something of its prospective contents commented, 'Why a chapter on education rather than on any other of the social services?'"[74] The answer implicit in Cole's essay, as well as in the work of Crosland and Jenkins, was that education must carry the burden of socialist hopes for a future egalitarian society.

Given the enormity of that burden, the new Fabians were anxious to explore in detail the ends that an education should serve and the means by which those ends might plausibly be attained. Cole criticized previous socialist thinkers, including Tawney, for neglect of this issue.[75] Although Cole listed and discussed ten "essential purposes for a democratic socialist education in the modern world,"[76] the primary burden placed upon education in the new Fabians' vision became apparent in her concluding statement that "whether the managerial–technical society which we are now creating turns in this country into a Burnham or Orwell nightmare . . . or a socialist democracy, depends in very large measure on how far education can create social consciousness."[77]

Though their educational goals were multiple and diffuse, two general ends predominated in, and made sense of, the new Fabians' staunch support for comprehensive schools. The first argument for comprehensive schooling was that "the techniques of living together can be fully and satisfactorily developed only by people who do actually live together."[78] But a comprehensive school plan could not by itself bring the different social strata to live together. The rationale behind this argument was that it fulfilled some of the new Fabians' more immediate hopes for lessening class antagonisms or resentments, rather than those for altering objective class distinctions. Having children from diverse classes *learning* together might inculcate liberal democratic loyalties as well as a belief (justified or not!) in the existence of equal opportunity. A more generous interpretation would indicate that all liberal egalitarians must ultimately find a means of establishing consciousness of human equality – or fellowship – among citizens with different ethnic or religious, or simply different family, backgrounds. A system of public education is likely to carry some of this burden. The crucial question is, How much? Those new Fabians who thought that the goal of an equal and classless society could not be attained by more extensive political and economic redistributions clearly placed, and continue to place, too great a burden upon educational reform.[79]

Comprehensive schooling was also viewed as a means of attaining a "democratic quality of leadership," and thereby of avoiding political elitism. The men of Promethean social conscience to whom Crosland had previously referred his hopes for a reformed managerial state would be those same students who were educated to democratic values and who, coming from the masses, recognized their social debt.[80]

Crosland admitted that comprehensive schools were, after all, not unique in the equal opportunity they afforded to citizens.[81] A system of free "separate but equal" secondary schools with nonrestrictive admissions and additional aid to the less advantaged could fulfill, with similar effectiveness, the equal-opportunity principle. But that opportunity was not the only, or perhaps even principal, end of educational reform. The possibility of instilling a democratic social consciousness – "a parity of esteem," as Cole had called it; a perception of human fellowship, in Tawney's terms – made equal educational opportunity even more desirable and necessary (but not sufficient) to a social democracy.

Yet many new Fabians placed too large a burden on education and too little on economic justice. It is of course possible that a reformed educational system would be capable of *reducing* social antagonisms. The gaps between the new Fabians' egalitarian goals and the political program they defended and between the objective and subjective correlates of the social equality they professed were too great to be bridged by a simple faith in comprehensive education. Education will always carry a burden in the liberal case for social equality. But the burden must be shared by a set of more egalitarian principles of distributive justice that can be applied (1) to institutions distributing goods, services, and opportunities to mature citizens to use as they may choose; and (2) to institutions providing opportunities for mature citizens to participate in decisions affecting their lives and the intermediate groups of which they are a part. Otherwise, significant internal contradictions arise between the liberal desire to preserve freedom and the need to implant a consciousness of social equality that might have been mediated by unfettered choice.

The new Fabians showed some realization of the need to spread the burden of egalitarian justice beyond a defense of the existing welfare state and a program for comprehensive educational reform, but their lack of a more egalitarian theory of distributive justice was sorely felt. Crossman criticized the Labour Party for having "lost its way, not only because it lacks a map of the new country it is crossing but because it thinks maps unnecessary for experienced travellers."[82] Neither Crossman nor Crosland abandoned the old Fabians' commitment to the unity of political theory and political practice, but because their map of the new country to be crossed by liberal egalitarians remained (by their own admission) incomplete, it is often difficult to tell whether their theory guided their political practice or whether they had simply forsaken their egalitarian aspirations for "successful" political practice.

The role most compatible with their socialist, egalitarian aspirations was that of persistent critics of British politics. In a speech before the Fabian Society in 1971, Galbraith aptly characterized the advantage of a political organization whose members are not intent on perpetually competing for or maintaining political office: "Even the most plausible of reforms, on first being broached, look dangerously impractical – and seem so to voters. They become commonplace, then banal, then basic human rights, only by discussion. It is the business of those who do not expect to hold office to initiate that discussion."[83] Crossman had previously taken a position very similar to Galbraith's. He had criticized new Fabian revisionists (Crosland, Jenkins, and Douglas Ray in particular) for subordinating old Fabian principles to new election strategies. Crossman's argument was not simply one for retaining the moral purity of Fabian principles. He also contended that the political success of an organized opposition to the British establishment would ultimately depend upon the maintenance of theoretical integrity.[84] Whether another generation of Fabians will have the opportunity to "strike" successfully – as Fabius Cunctator is said to have struck Hannibal after patiently waiting for the right moment – is not an answerable question. But the appeal of Crossman's position from an egalitarian point of view is that if political success comes to new Fabians, it will not come at the cost of equality. Crossman's work, however, shared one general weakness with that of other new Fabians. While taking account of circumstances, they neglected to find general principles of egalitarianism that would take them beyond the minimal welfare state for which the old Fabians had patiently and persistently fought.

Chapter 4

The relevant reasons for liberal egalitarianism

THE RELEVANT-REASONS APPROACH

Corresponding to the weakening of the egalitarian stance of many social democrats of the 1950s, there occurred a period in the practice of political philosophy when widespread doubts were expressed about the very possibility of using moral concepts, and of making moral arguments within a context of rational (opposed by many philosophers to merely political) discourse. The term "rational" had been stripped of any moral content, and political thought was said to carry the sole (and in this view, sorry) burden of being normative and nonrational. Equality as a standard of justice for many new Fabians was judged largely by the subjective satisfactions of citizens, however situated. The use of equality as a moral concept for many analytic philosophers of the fifties and early sixties was considered solely a statement of personal preference in otherwise objective academic discourse.[1] Both political and academic discourse were thereby stripped of critical moral substance. From the fact of equal humanity, one could not deduce the moral imperative of equal human rights or of a more equal distribution.

It was in the context of moral skepticism within the philosophical community that Bernard Williams wrote what has become a seminal article in twentieth-century egalitarianism – an essay entitled "The Idea of Equality" – and it is in this context that the egalitarian arguments he sets forth must be understood.[2] One of the purposes of Williams's article is to suggest a way around moral skepticism by shifting arguments concerning equality from the level of *moral* discourse to a more objective level, a level either of conceptual truth or of ordinary language. The second purpose of Williams's essay is, more substantively, to make an egalitarian argument: to criticize the prevailing distribution of goods within liberal societies.

Both the distinct method and the substance of Williams's argu-

96

ment make "The Idea of Equality" a significant contribution to twentieth-century thought. Williams suggests not only that Anglo-American societies should be more egalitarian but also that a simple and readily discernible "justification" exists for the egalitarianism he recommends. I shall be concerned in this chapter to explore both his method and the substance of his argument, as extended also by Michael Walzer in "In Defense of Equality."[3] I shall suggest that the egalitarian politics for which Williams and Walzer argue will flow from their method only when employed by individuals who share a certain form of social life and moral understanding reflected in theory by classical liberalism. Williams's and Walzer's egalitarian conclusions – if they are to stand at all – must stand upon firmer but also more historically specific ground than their method indicates.[4]

Let me begin by looking at the methodological ground upon which Williams's argument might rest. Williams finds the foundations of egalitarian justice within an established social logic. His mode of argument appears close to the form of moral argument that gained currency among British analytic philosophers following the lead of Wittgenstein's *Philosophical Investigations*. Philosophy was considered an exercise in the "logic of everyday life." Though many moral statements could not be rationally grounded in further argument, standards of rationality were said to exist within the forms of our social life, to be discovered in what we have naturally accepted as legitimate "truth sentences" in our everyday discourse.[5] The basic truth sentence on which Williams and Walzer place the burden of their egalitarian arguments takes the form "*a* is the relevant reason for distributing *x*."

This approach to the question of distributive justice is by no means new. The appeal to ordinary language and to relevant reasons can be derived from Aristotle's argument in the *Politics*:

The good in the sphere of politics is justice; and justice consists in what tends to promote the common interest. General opinion makes it consist in some sort of equality . . . In other words, it holds that justice involves two factors – things, and the persons to whom things are assigned – and it considers that persons who are equal should have assigned to them equal things. But here there arises a question which must not be overlooked. Equals and unequals – yes; but equals and unequals in what? This is a question which raises difficulties, and involves us in philosophical speculation on politics.[6]

The problem Aristotle points to is, How can one determine what is and is not a relevant reason for distributing any particular good?

With respect to politics, Aristotle argues, claims "must be based on the ground of contribution to the elements which constitute the being of the state."[7]

Contemporary analytic philosophers have in this sense followed Aristotle's method of analysis.[8] Many, however, view the ideal of equality as one that *eliminates* distributions based upon *irrelevant* reasons, rather than as one that enables us to stipulate the relevant reasons for distributing a given good. Benn and Peters, for example, argue that "claims to equality are . . . in a sense, always negative, denying the propriety of certain existing inequalities."[9] They therefore do not solve the problem Aristotle posed of how to determine criteria of relevance for purposes of distributive justice: Rather they claim that the relevance or irrelevance of reasons in any given situation is ultimately a matter of choice, though not choice based upon pure whim or fancy.[10] They seem to believe that the problem is philosophically unresolvable. No strictly rational criteria exist to determine the solution.

Williams and Walzer, by contrast, argue that the logic of relevant reasons is not merely formalistic and that it can offer us substantive answers to questions posed in the form: What is the relevant reason for distributing *x?* I shall concentrate upon their essays for this reason, and because the substantive principles that emerge from their use of relevant-reasons logic are significantly egalitarian ones.

NEEDS AND ECONOMIC DISTRIBUTION

Williams presents us with one very obvious statement of the relevant reason for distributing medical care:

Leaving aside preventive medicine, the proper ground of distribution of medical care is ill health: this is a necessary truth . . . When we have the situation in which . . . wealth is a further necessary condition of the receipt of medical treatment, we can once more apply the notions of equality and inequality . . . since we have straightforwardly the situation of those whose needs are the same not receiving the same treatment, though the needs are the ground of the treatment.

For equally sick people to receive unequal medical treatment, Williams argues, "is an irrational state of affairs."[11]

With respect to medical care, Williams's argument is an egalitarian one – and radically so.[12] It suggests that medical services be distributed *strictly* on the basis of medical need. ("For what other relevant criteria might there be in this case?" Williams would ask.) One would therefore have grounds for criticizing a national health service that either demanded payment for essential medical services *or* provided better care for fee than for clinic patients. The argument from relevant reasons points in the direction of a maximum welfare state: one that distributes exclusively on the basis of need those goods and services for which need is *the* relevant distributive reason.

What are those goods and services for which our language provides necessary and sufficient relevant reasons for distribution in Williams's terms? In addition to medical care, one might argue that the relevant reason for distributing housing is the need for shelter, for providing employment the need for work, and for distributing legal services the need for legal aid. If one takes care in interpreting Williams's arguments, these relevant-reason arguments also make sense as distributional principles. It is an irrational state of affairs, Williams would argue, to distribute housing to people on the basis of money when some people are without any decent shelter. Similarly, to provide a skilled person with a *better*-paying job when another person entirely lacks work appears irrational (and ipso facto, according to Williams, unjust). Again, to distribute legal services to the accused who happen to be rich but not to those who are poor is irrational *and* inegalitarian in his terms. In these cases, our conceptions of equal justice have already been built into our language. Our language tells us to provide housing, legal aid, and medical care to those who have the relevant needs. The relevant-reason argument therefore provides additional support for extending the services provided by the welfare state into areas of medical care, housing, employment, and legal aid by pointing to the notions of distribution according to need that are firmly embedded within our social discourse.

It is equally important to note what these relevant-reason arguments do not, and cannot, comprehend. Williams can assert that illness is a necessary and sufficient condition for distribution of medical care. One can rationally make a similar claim about housing and job opportunities *narrowly understood*. A right to decent housing and to gainful employment follows from our understanding of the relevant reasons for shelter and sustenance. But above certain minima, housing and work cease to be simple needs. At the same time our language ceases to provide simple or singular criteria to assert the appropriate grounds for distribution. Thus, Williams's argument sanctions radical redistributions within the social spheres in which needs are fully operative relevant reasons. Beyond those spheres, we are left free to question the proper moral grounds for distribution.

Tied to this observation is the need to define carefully the nature of the good for which the relevant distributive reason is sought. Once that good is precisely defined, Williams's argument is a cogent one. For example, the relevant reason for being supplied with job opportunities is being unemployed, yet that is not the relevant reason for the right to any particular job or for the right to a better-paying job. This limitation on Williams's argument also affects the extent of its egalitarianism.

Williams argues that "in the case of needs . . . it can be presumed for practical purposes that the persons who have the need actually desire the goods in question, and so the question can indeed be regarded as one of distribution in a simple sense, the satisfaction of an existing desire."[13] But even granting this congruence of need and desire in some cases (at least for "practical purposes"), what should be done in those cases in which we can objectively specify basic needs but in which we cannot assume that all people want their needs satisfied in the same, or similar, ways? This may not be a central problem for health care or for legal aid. But what about the cases of housing, where we certainly cannot assume (especially for "practical purposes") that people in need of housing all desire a particular form of public housing. In such cases three alternative policies come to mind.

First, in cases of need, one might reject as irrelevant the standard of satisfying people's preferences concerning *how* their needs should be satisfied. More often than not, welfare-state policies in England and the United States have followed this path. Yet although there is good reason to override people's preferences when they are in conflict with their needs, I can think of no compelling reason to deny people's preferences when they are congruent with their needs, unless one establishes that those preferences entail unreasonably large social costs.

The second alternative solution to this problem would be to provide money instead of goods in kind in those cases where preferences about how to satisfy a given need diverge. Such grants could of course be tied to the satisfaction of the given need. There are several disadvantages to this policy when used within a society that relies heavily upon a private market.[14] Recipients must rely upon that market to supply the goods that will satisfy their preferences. If their cash grant is a fixed amount, the market may not supply the relevant goods at that price, whereas if the grant is of an amount sufficient to meet the market price, private suppliers of the good may take advantage of the elasticity of purchase price to charge the government more than would otherwise be necessary. In addition, there are costs of monitoring the use of such grants, not the least of which are the costs to the recipient in privacy.[15]

The third, and most desirable, alternative means of satisfying needs that entail indeterminate preferences is for the state to allow welfare recipients to determine how their needs might be satisfied. A range of preferred choices might be democratically determined. One major advantage of this alternative is that, in addition to satisfying people's preferences, it also encourages participation by those citizens who otherwise are the least likely to participate in politics.[16] This is one way of resolving an important issue that Williams's argument implicitly raises. Yet the resolution of this issue clearly demands considerations beyond those suggested by relevant reasons.

THE RELATIVISM OF RELEVANT REASONS

To understand its limits, we must look more carefully at the logic of relevant reasons. Williams never poses the simple question, Why *should* we accept relevant reasons as necessary and sufficient conditions for the distribution of the goods or services in question? Even if he is correct in claiming that "whether a certain consideration is *relevant* to a moral issue" is not "an evaluative question," he still cannot simply use relevant reasons to dispose of moral arguments.[17] We need to confront directly the moral dilemma of how primary goods such as medical care, job opportunities, legal services, and political power should be distributed in a relatively affluent society.

Let us go back to Williams's argument for medical care: "The proper ground of distribution . . . is ill health: this is a *necessary* truth." Necessary to what? Williams means either "necessary to make sense of our *use* of the term 'medical care'" (as I have assumed so far) *or* "necessary to make sense of our normal ways of *conceptualizing* medical practice." In neither case does "necessary" carry with it the connotation of *logical* bindingness. Our language does not preclude moral arguments such as those Robert Nozick puts forward in favor of profit-oriented doctoring – "schmoctoring," to use Nozick's neologism.[18] Nor is it a necessary conceptual truth that the proper (and *sufficient*) ground for the distribution of medical care is ill health, unless one takes the prevailing theory of medical practice more seriously than the prevailing practice itself does *and* unless one can convincingly argue against those (like Nozick) who would justify the practice of schmoctoring with arguments that are more compatible with medical practice in the United States than are Williams's arguments for a non–market-oriented practice of doctoring.

The stronger defense of Williams's idea of equality is a conceptually and institutionally based one. Our commitment to equality is *justified* not by brute citation of our moral or practical discourse but by an elucidation of our common *moral* assumptions concerning what constitutes correct medical practice within our institutions. But Williams's argument then cannot proceed so quickly. It would not even be enough for him to cite the fact that doctors *claim* to be practicing the science of curing the sick rather than that of making money, because many, if not most, doctors in the United States and Britain also claim the right to be schmoctors, part-time schmoctors at least. One problem with a purely conceptual or institutional criterion of medical justice is that our principles of medical justice do not rest simply upon institutional claims or professional self-definitions. The internal purposes of institutions and professions are often rightly constrained by broader and more important social purposes. Williams's idea of equality therefore must ultimately be situated within a theory of justice that reconciles these purposes when they conflict. His conceptual argument may not be a necessary one, but it is nonetheless a very powerful one within a society where the claims to independence of an existing medical profession are based upon their professed acceptance and satisfaction of his relevant reasons for distributing medical care. Taken as distributive principles, relevant reasons are therefore relative – they are parasitic upon the existence of particular social practices and institutions, and they are dependent upon the existence of a broader theory of justice that can incorporate them consistently with other distributive principles and practices.

An example of the relativism of Williams's relevant-reason position emerges from extending our view back from modern liberalism to ancient political theory. Historically, needs have not been universally recognized as a sufficient basis of rights to their fulfillment. In the *Republic*, Plato puts forward an argument which suggests that a sick carpenter who, if maintained alive by medicine, could no longer perform his trade would be as good dead. Plato's argument suggests that the carpenter can be *justly* denied medical care.[19] Where justice is modeled on the good life, hierarchically defined by individuals' natural roles, the implications of arguments from relevant reasons may be significantly altered. Or, one could say that in Plato's terms what we now consider "nonrelevant" reasons ought partially to determine who receives medical care. Other factors – in this case capacity to fulfill one's natural role in society – may be rationally considered necessary (but not sufficient) conditions. (Here I assume that sickness is a necessary condition for medical care in any rational conception of distributive justice so long as scarcity is an issue). Alternatively, one may retain the form of Williams's argument, but claim that two reasons for distributing medical care are relevant (each necessary and only together sufficient) to a society modeled on Plato's conception of justice: sickness, and the ability to fulfill one's function in the polis (or, correspondingly, to fulfill the function of one's soul).

Williams does not explicitly deal with this seemingly forceful argument that needs are socially and historically relative in ways that defy definitions of the particular and universal needs of human beings.[20] Nevertheless, his approach can provide us with a way of accepting such criticisms without undermining the case for distribution of many goods according to relevant reasons.

Suppose one argues that people's needs are those conditions that are essential to their chosen life plans.[21] However, one also notices that certain goods such as health care, legal aid, and housing are essential to all people's life plans *within a given society.* Then one may still find that the relevant-reason argument provides a correct standard for just distribution *within that society.* The usefulness of the relevant-reasons argument as an *independent* standard for determining what constitutes a just distribution will therefore depend upon how closely the language of relevant reasons reflects the universal needs of citizens within the society one is addressing.

For example, were one to say that the relevant reason for possessing a flute is being a good flute player, and therefore that flutes should be distributed in our society to good flutists, the relevant-reasons argument would be insufficient (or irrelevant) to determine the *just* standard of distribution of musical instruments in *our* society. Only on the level of needs does the relevant-reason argument seem to attain the level of sufficiency on questions of distributive justice, and even then one must ascertain whether the reasons given for the distribution – for example, of housing or jobs – are needs of all citizens within the society considered. One can determine this by examining the life plans of individuals as they exist within one's society or by exploring what the life plans of the same individuals would be were they living under more favorable conditions. Each method has its attractions and pit-falls.[22] Were one to take existing plans of life as the standard by which to ascertain needs, one would ignore the possibility that the life plans of many individuals would be significantly altered were they able to count upon the use of greater resources and were they to develop certain skills and talents upon being provided with greater social opportunities. If one chooses the latter, more hypothetical criterion of need, one must take care to specify those favorable conditions with sufficient determinacy to avoid the cir-cularity that "as long as people do not show a need for x in their life plans, their conditions of life have not been favorable to realiz-ing their basic needs."[23]

The normative implications of relevant-reason logic – even when applied to services fulfilling what we consider basic human needs – therefore may vary with the form of social life within which one poses the question, What is the relevant criterion for distributing x? The particular implications of the relevant-reason logic Williams suggests are undoubtedly those that strike many people as most sensible. Williams's argument thus possesses the force of sufficiency for distributive justice to those who reject (for example) the form of life represented by Plato's *Republic*, having accepted a view grounded upon belief in the equal worth or dig-nity of individuals. In a world in which a conception of the basic equality of persons has gained currency (at least in our individual moral beliefs and social norms, if not in our social practice), sick-ness will appear as *the* relevant reason for distributing medical care. The ability to practice one's trade will appear irrelevant to one's right to medical care, because occupation is insufficient to the definition or value of a self.

An important, perhaps essential, support to Williams's case therefore is the fact that answers to the specifically moral ques-tions of just distribution have tended to converge in twentieth-century liberal thought with the corresponding relevant reasons. Relevant-reason arguments would have less currency in our moral discourse, and would lack the status of sufficient grounds for dis-tributive justice, without those equality assumptions upon which liberal theory and contemporary liberal societies are based. Had liberal society not been founded upon an assumption of human equality, the relevant reason for distributing medical care might not now appear as a *sufficient* criterion upon which to establish the justice of distribution on an institutional level.

Williams comes close to acknowledging this convergence of lin-guistic or conceptual argument with our particular form of social life when he argues that in cases of need, as distinct from those of merit, one can assume that people in need also *desire* the good in question.[24] His case for medical care thereby rests upon the idea that people have similar passions for certain basic goods – the same idea upon which the Fabians argued for a minimally decent human existence. Williams brings to our attention that the equal-passions assumption upon which classical liberalism was built may demand more than the *minimally* equal distribution for which the Fabians campaigned. At least with reference to the vast majority of medical services, the relevant reason of illness seems to be both a necessary and a sufficient condition for distributing medical care.

Under conditions of scarcity, one would have to place constraints on the distribution of basic goods and services. Yet the constraints imposed by scarcity should not obviate the force of the relevant-reason principle.[25] It would still appear unjust, or irrational in Williams's terms, to distribute medical care on a free-market principle. The urgency of basic needs will outweigh the utility of allocating scarce resources through the market, once human equality is given its due weight. External contingencies are not the primary threat to the egalitarian's use of the relevant-reason standard. What *may* run counter to egalitarian intent is the internal logic of the relevant-reason standard when applied to questions of distributive justice beyond satisfaction of basic human needs.

CONSENT AND POLITICAL POWER

When extended beyond the question of what considerations are relevant to the supply of basic human services, relevant-reason logic may lead to conclusions that stand in tension with liberal egalitarian ideals. To understand its inegalitarian potential, we can look back to how Aristotle used such logic. It was in the very nature of certain goods that they be distributed on certain grounds. Those grounds we might call the "desert bases" for distributive justice. Just as the sick deserved medical care and the destitute deserved shelter by virtue of being human, talented flutists, in Aristotle's terms, deserved flutes by virtue of their distinct ability.[26] Similarly, one might suppose that talented politicians deserve political office and superior intellects higher education.

Walzer's essay supplies a counterargument to this interpretation of the relevant-reason view, an argument most clearly set out with reference to the distribution of political power. Though he suggests a familiar alternative to the Platonic view of the relevant reason for distributing political power, his discussion also reveals the limits of the relevant-reason approach to moral argument when this approach is understood apart from the form of social life of which it is a necessary component.

The relevant reason for distributing political office once was thought to be political wisdom: knowledge of how a polis should be organized and of the ends toward which collective human endeavors ought to be directed. According to Plato, the wisest person ought to rule the polis just as the most skilled navigator ought to pilot a ship.[27] The ship-of-state metaphor suggested the classical relevant reason for allocation of political power – knowledge of how to run the state. Consent followed from expertise and wisdom properly employed, rather than preceding and determining who should rightfully rule.

A distinct relevant reason has obviously gained currency since Plato: democratic determination of political leadership. According to this view, consent to be ruled by X must precede and causally determine X's right to rule. It is this relevant reason for which Walzer argues: "The freely given support of one's fellow citizens is the appropriate criterion for exercising political power and, once again, it is not enough, or it shouldn't be, to be . . . ideologically correct."[28]

With respect to political leadership, not only are there two relevant reasons in our language for allocating political power, but the two reasons will, in important instances, conflict: The popularly chosen leader may not be the wisest (or the most ideologically correct) of citizens. The choice between those two reasons for allocating political power is then a normative one – a choice concerning the correct grounds upon which political leadership *should* be allocated.

Returning briefly to Walzer's remark, we must ask, What are the grounds upon which he can argue that the consent of the governed is *the* relevant reason for distributing political power? Walzer cannot simply *claim* consent to be *the* relevant reason for, as we have noted, other reasons have been and are still put forward as the relevant ones, reasons which conflict with that of popular consent. Walzer's choice is a clear rational decision, or a matter of social logic, only within the context of a liberal society. That is, the relevant reason he selects can be justified only with reference to the liberal foundations of human equality. Once one accepts those assumptions of human equality, assumptions now deeply embedded in liberal democratic societies, the reason Walzer cites for distributing political power will appear to be *both* the relevant and the right ground for choosing political leaders. Walzer's own argument then harks back to the liberal view of people as equally dignified beings. The moral argument implicit in his case is that human dignity would be negated in practice were anyone to be denied a vote equal to all other votes in determining political leadership. Thus, Walzer can assert that "each citizen is entitled to one vote simply because he is a citizen."[29] But if equality were not constitutive of one's conception of humanity, the relevant reason for distributing political power might be wisdom or ideological astuteness. Political leaders might rightly be appointed by a council of elders or by a ruling party, were these procedures more likely to ensure that the competent or the ideologically astute would rule.

Furthermore, even if we agree with Walzer that consent is the relevant reason for exercising political power, we must go on to stipulate those conditions under which consent can be considered a valid indication of free choice. Under many conditions, consent as measured by voting will not constitute the "freely given support of one's fellow citizens." I doubt whether Walzer would deny that one's acceptance of voting as consent must be conditional. But any such proviso placed upon his statement points to the insufficiency of the logic of relevant reasons in establishing the correct grounds for consent. Perhaps the relevant-reasons approach solves this problem indirectly by establishing that housing, medical care, and legal aid be supplied to all citizens on the basis of need, these then being the necessary preconditions for considering consent to be a voluntary act. But a more direct way of pursuing the same problem consistently with the relevant-reasons approach is first to ask what the relevant reason for citizenship is. The liberal egalitarian's answer is, being a free and equal being. One then asks: What are the preconditions for that freedom and equality? The answer is, that which is necessary to a decent life for all citizens – that is, those goods that make possible the satisfaction of every citizen's basic needs for medical care, housing, job opportunities, legal aid . . . (the list might be extended as individual needs expand).

DESERT AND EQUAL OPPORTUNITY

Williams also explicitly discusses the logic of relevant reasons as it applies to cases of merit, as distinct from those of need. In cases of merit, he argues, the nature of the good supplied is generally in question, so that we cannot be sure which distributive reasons are the relevant ones.[30] Williams suggests here that it is inherent in cases of merit that relevant reasons are either multiple or indeterminate. The example he uses is education. Williams is genuinely uncertain of the purpose of education, unlike that of medical care. What is the nature of the educational "good"?[31] Do we desire education to develop each person's mind to its utmost capacity, or to perpetuate a tradition of social leadership, or to socialize citizens of the liberal state? Education clearly is among the more difficult cases for relevant-reason logic and perhaps not simply because the nature of the good itself is in question, but also because education will be a multivalued good in any liberal society. There are a multiplicity of relevant reasons suggested by contemporary egalitarian thinkers for its distribution.

But let us return to some goods that appear once to have been more clearly defined, goods ranging from Aristotle's example of musical instruments to jobs demanding definite expertise. These are examples of goods for which relevant-reason logic at one time supplied fairly straightforward answers to the question, What are the relevant grounds for distributing x? The relevant reason for supplying musical instruments (and training as well) was musical talent. The positions of bureaucrat, physician, and lawyer were to be allocated to the most skilled in those trades. In each of these cases relevant-reason logic suggests that the naturally talented deserve their appropriately, and naturally, defined rewards.

The problem is more apparent here than in the case of needs. For in the case of goods that supply basic needs, though relevant-reason arguments do not directly respond to moral questions, they furnish answers that we can accept as necessary *and* sufficient to establish principles of distributive justice; whereas in the case of goods that people are said to merit, the relevant-reason argument either does not establish the justice of distributing those goods in the "all things considered" sense, or does so only at the cost of ignoring certain reasons that are now reasonably claimed to be relevant ones. In cases of merit, unlike those of needs, there may be reasons of justice that override the relevant ones (as classically understood) for distributing the good in question, reasons in most cases having to do with the conception of man upon which liberal theory is founded, particularly the value of each individual's freely chosen life plan, which has been derived from that liberal conception of equality.

In those cases where Aristotle used the logic of relevant reasons to argue for distribution according to merit, Williams supports instead the principle of equal opportunity as a means of obtaining the goods in question.[32] Institutionalization of the equal-opportunity principle is relied upon to create a distribution of positions according to merit. Merit is now best viewed as a developmental quality – a potential that, under favorable conditions, some of us will realize by our own application. It is not an innate differential trait to be discovered in children and subsequently encouraged and rewarded by society. Only those societies that provide a thoroughgoing equality of opportunity can even hope to assess individual desert fairly in the end.

However, support of the *process* of equal opportunity may begin to undermine faith in our ability to distinguish relative merit from those qualities that relative environmental advantage has produced. Williams alerts us to this problem when he wonders where the institutional process of equalizing opportunity must stop: at the family? genetic endowment? The possibility of judging desert on an institutional scale will depend upon whether we can ever draw a clear and principled line between environmentally caused and freely developed individual talents.[33]

But if one is not skeptical about the ultimate possibility of judging differential human desert, one must determine the conditions under which fair equality of opportunity can be said to exist. Williams suggests that fair equality of opportunity cannot be said to exist in any society in which ascribed group characteristics are correlated with economic position, intellectual achievement, social status, or other important socially valued goods.[34] The same premise underlies both the argument *against* interpreting the distribution of social rewards within society as indicative of relative personal desert or merit and the argument *for* extending the meaning of equal opportunity beyond the formal institutional requirements of nondiscrimination. In order to treat people *fairly* one must abstract away from the environmental determinants of their behavior, even of their character. "This line of thought," Williams tells us,

points to a connection between the idea of equality of opportunity, and the idea of equality of persons, which is stronger than might at first be suspected. . . . [T]here is a necessary pressure to equal up the conditions: to give Smith and Jones equality of opportunity involves regarding their conditions, where curable, as themselves part of what is *done* to Smith and Jones, and not part of Smith and Jones themselves. Their identity, for these purposes, does not include their curable environment, which is itself unequal and a contributor of inequality. This abstraction of persons in themselves from unequal environments is a way, if not of regarding them as equal, at least of moving recognizably in that direction; and is itself involved in equality of opportunity.[35]

In practice, Williams's argument entails treating distinct human attributes as undeserving of social recognition, for these attributes are not believed essentially to constitute a person. Williams recognizes a danger here: that our notion of personal identity might give way entirely to our belief in human equality. In Chapter 6, I shall assess the criticism made by Robert Nozick that such a view of *equal* persons (people stripped of any uniquely identifying features) directly contradicts the notion of *autonomous* persons (people with abilities to choose ends, direct their lives, and develop their characters as they will), a conception of persons upon which liberalism claims to be built.[36]

Williams ends his essay with a different, although related, critique of the equal-opportunity maxim – a critique he directs at the liberal theory of contemporary Anglo-American society: A significant tension may arise within an egalitarian society owing to the conflict between the psychological effects of the equal-opportunity maxim and the ideal of creating equal respect among people. Williams seems to object to the emphasis that he assumes is now placed upon equal opportunity as a process by which the social worth of individuals is determined. There is, today, "the feeling that a thoroughgoing emphasis on equality of opportunity must destroy a certain sense of common humanity which is itself an ideal of equality."[37]

The most vivid portrait of the dehumanizing effects of a society in which opportunity is radically equalized is found in *The Rise of the Meritocracy*, by Michael Young, which summarizes the disillusioning transition from the "Golden Age of Equality," when people had faith in the potential equality of all citizens, to the "Meritocratic Age," when equality of respect is lost to a purportedly fair social determination of personal merit. In the Golden Age:

Subjective and objective status were often poles apart. The worker said to himself: "Here I am, a workman. Why am I a workman? Am I fit for nothing else? Of course not. Had I had a proper chance I would have shown the world . . . I never had the chance. And so I am a worker. But don't think that at bottom I am any worse than anyone else. I'm better."[38]

Young concludes from his futuristic fantasy that "educational injustice enabled people to preserve their illusions, inequality of opportunity fostered the myth of equality. Myth we know it to be;

110

not so our ancestors."[39] From this perspective, we are presented
with a despairing picture of the meritocratic era when "for the first
time in human history the inferior man has no ready buttress for
his self-regard."[40]

Young's portrait of the results of equal opportunity warns us of
the potential tension between the ideals of equal respect and equal
opportunity, both of which are tied to assumptions of human
equality: respect for individuals and respect for their freely chosen
life plans. But Williams does not argue that either ideal *logically*
entails a sacrifice of the other, because "one might hope for a society in which there existed both a fair, rational and appropriate
distribution of these goods, and no contempt, condescension or
lack of human communication between persons who were more
and less successful recipients of the distribution."[41]

We can still reasonably expect, therefore, that increasing equality of opportunity beyond the point presently established will re-
inforce rather than threaten equality of respect. The point at which
equal opportunity will undermine equal respect is too far in the
distance either to serve as a critique of equalizing opportunity or
to permit us sufficient evidence to assess its potential psychological effects on individual self-regard. Williams is no doubt correct:
How much we fear this problem depends upon our view of human nature. We have here a potential problem within liberal egalitarianism, but one for which we will not have an apparent solution so long as we do not have an accurate theory of human
nature. Yet a more critical look at the justice of the equal-opportunity principle as interpreted by meritocratic accounts may deflect
some of our concern away from the psychological effects of the
equal-opportunity principle as a standard of justice per se to a
concern over the possible mistaken interpretations of the principle
itself.

Where do the adverse sociopsychological effects of the equal opportunity principle arise? The most frequently cited source of this
problem is that within a society of equal opportunity, people *know*
that their positions are *merited* in the sense that (1) they had every
social opportunity possible, consistent with that of all other persons within society, and (2) the rewards accruing to their positions
are proportionate to their contribution to the social good. (This is
a society based upon a conception of merit in which merit is defined as contribution to the social product.)[42]

But what if we separate the effects of equal opportunity of the first sort from the practice of rewarding people in proportion to their contributions to the social good? It is the latter practice – that of attaching monetary rewards to positions on the basis of contribution to the social good, however defined – that Walzer most effectively challenges from an egalitarian perspective. Even *if* one wants to defend a meritocracy, one would have to recognize that there exists a plurality of valuable human capacities and talents. Few people have all *or* none of these talents; one person rarely is the most accomplished businessman as well as the best athlete, parent, or lover. Which talent (or group of talents) should be rewarded with a medium exchangeable for so many other goods?[43] A consistent meritocrat cannot claim that the distribution of income in our society accurately reflects the distribution of all socially valuable capacities among individuals. Indeed, it is extremely difficult to imagine how any society could distribute income to people in proportion to all their valuable social contributions. In addition, because money is never valued for its own sake and because few human accomplishments deserve to be rewarded with everything that money can buy, money rarely appears to be the relevant reward for merit. The incommensurability of money and desert therefore seems to follow from money's very nature as a pure exchange value.

Perhaps there will be social utility in rewarding people in accordance with, but not in strict proportion to, their contribution to the social good – as measured either by the market, as the neo-conservatives claim,[44] or by some other socially determined standard, as Young' society depicts.[45] Incentives may be necessary to elicit from some citizens the scarce goods and services that others desire. But Walzer's view challenges a standard deduction from this axiom: that contribution to the social good must be judged in terms of increased production or of marketable services, as the neo-conservatives assume.[46]

We need not consider a just society to be a meritocratic one – meritocratic at least in the sense of being one in which (1) only some people possess most of the talents that are socially valued, and (2) each person's comparative social value can be assessed within a single social hierarchy (of income, power, or any other scarce good). Instead, there should be many distributive hierarchies – of power and intellect, athletic prowess, artistic ability, and the many other human talents – all socially recognized and rewarded in a liberal egalitarian society. If this were so, no simple measurement of personal merit or social value could be taken, and thus there would be a diminished likelihood that self-respect would be based upon social ranking. The meaningfulness of making such judgments would be called into question by the absence of a single, or aggregated, social scale.[47]

Underlying this conclusion is the plausible egalitarian assumption that the distribution of talents among people is quite far ranging and that therefore many more people will be rewarded in a society in which money ceases to tyrannize over talent. As a consequence of defining the social good more broadly, more people will be rewarded and honored as contributors to that good. But what happens to those who, even by Walzer's pluralistic criteria, fail to contribute anything of value to society? Walzer might doubt whether anybody would be so unfortunate. But were we to concede that the self-respect of some people would suffer, our alternative would be to imagine a still more egalitarian and pluralistic society.

A striking practical consequence of Walzer's, like Tawney's, argument for a plurality of distributive principles would be the reduction of real income inequalities among classes:

It would be immediately necessary to have a national health service, national legal assistance, the strictest possible control over campaign contributions. Modest proposals . . . but they represent so many moves toward the realization of that old socialist slogan about the abolition of money . . . [I]t makes a great deal of sense if it is interpreted to mean the abolition of the power of money outside its sphere. What socialists want is a society in which wealth is no longer convertible into social goods with which it has no intrinsic connection.[48]

In this, Walzer also follows Marx's argument in the early manuscript where he criticizes the "all-purpose" role money plays in a capitalist society. Marx tells us that money exerts a tyranny over every sphere of human existence in bourgeois society by enabling the wealthy to buy those human qualities or semblances of human qualities that are socially valued.[49] The logic of relevant reasons tells Walzer that society should instead "pay equal attention to the different qualities,' and to the 'individuality' of every man and woman, that we [may] find ways of sharing our resources that match the variety of their needs, interests, and capacities . . . Our goal" he concludes, "should be an end to tyranny, a society in which no man is master outside his sphere. That is the only society of equals worth having."[50] And so Walzer converts Marx's indictment of the role of money in bourgeois society into an egalitarian statement of purpose.

BEYOND THE LOGIC OF RELEVANT REASONS

There are two questions to be asked of this form of egalitarianism. The first is whether the logic of relevant reasons extends further than is consistent with Walzer's liberal egalitarian intent. The second is how, or to what extent, might Walzer's ideas be realized. Is there an inherent difficulty with a society in which money does not exert power outside its "own" sphere?

Walzer's proposed solution to the tyranny of money in bourgeois society diverges in important ways from Marx's own solution. This is significant because it indicates a problem, or at least an ambiguity, within Walzer's case for egalitarianism similar to the problem within Williams's essay. In the last paragraph of the manuscript on money, Marx extends the relevant-reason logic, the same logic later employed by Williams and Walzer. No longer does he concentrate on an attack of bourgeois society, but here we catch a glimpse of the political theory of a "just" society: a society in which the logic of relevant reasons would come into its own.[51] "Let us assume man to be man," Marx tells us,

and his relation to the world to be a human one. Then love can only be exchanged for love, trust for trust, etc. If you wish to enjoy art you must be an artistically cultivated person; if you wish to influence other people you must be a person who really has a stimulating and encouraging effect upon others. Every one of your relations to man and to nature must be a *specific expression,* corresponding to the object of your will, of your *real individual life.* If you love without evoking love in return, i.e., if you are not able, by the manifestation of yourself as a loving person, to make yourself a beloved person, then your love is impotent and a misfortune.[52]

Walzer suggests that this passage of Marx "is *only* meant to suggest a humane form of social accommodation."[53] Yet the form of social accommodation Marx suggests is a very particular one, one that is much less *humane* (in the ordinary sense of the word) than "to each according to his needs," and one that is at the same time very radical.

Marx, unlike Walzer, seems to be arguing for a society in which people will get what they *merit* and quite precisely what they merit in the sense of what suits their "real individual natures." Under socialism, Marx tells us, if you are not a loving person, you do not deserve to be, indeed you should not be, and perhaps you will not be, loved: "Every one of your relations to man . . . must be a specific expression . . . of your real individual life."[54] Marx applies this relevant-reason view to both nature and human society – realms that for him logically confirm and will historically reveal each person's essence as a social being in a very strict sense. So he says in "Free Human Production" that "our productions would be so many mirrors reflecting our nature."[55] And he argues there and elsewhere in the early manuscripts that a person's work would be so many tasks confirming his natural human talents. Human personalities would be socially confirmed at the very same they were exposed. The social organization of an ideal society not only would *permit* people to develop their capacities and talents (in this Marx and liberal egalitarians agree) but would also lead to the public realization of who individuals "really" are – what their capacities, including their shortcomings, are. In a communist society, as I understand Marx's vision, people really *are* just what other people take them to be.

Walzer, on the other hand, does not extend the logic of relevant reasons from the critique of bourgeois society to advocacy of a society based upon distribution according to social merit. The liberal egalitarian view as developed by Williams and Walzer and the Marxist view agree upon the use of relevant reasons as a critique of the grossly inegalitarian distribution of money and power in capitalist society. But to complete the logic of relevant reasons, Marx suggests that social justice must extend beyond a more egalitarian distribution of money and power to a distribution of work, praise, honor, and perhaps even love congruent with the real – that is, social – merits and talents of citizens: a distribution grounded upon and appropriate to everyone's true social worth. But social worth can become a critical standard in Marx's terms only if one believes (1) that there is a social (and natural) essence to each human being included in which are his unique talents as well as his needs and desires; and (2) that citizens in a correctly organized society will freely distribute goods – income, power, praise, honor, and love – according to each individual's essential qualities.

Liberal egalitarians use nature as a critical standard only insofar as its critique is consistent with the assumptions of human equality already embedded in the foundations of liberal society. To go further, to argue that people will be given (or will receive) just what they merit, is to express a belief that distributive justice can actually reflect the true differential nature or worth of individuals. In Marx's scheme, the social tyranny of money is to be conquered, but so are the limitations of egalitarian politics. Ultimately, all egalitarian patterns are to be transcended in the name of each person's social, and perhaps unique, nature. This I take to be the meaning of a Marxian argument against liberal, even liberal egalitarian, politics. People are social beings not simply in the commonly accepted sense of being created or conditioned by their environment but in the more specific, and deeply controversial, sense of becoming fully known by society.

Liberal criticisms that indict Marx's ideal for its deliberate subordination of individual freedom to societal needs are therefore misleading. The liberal ideals of freedom and equality are criticized by Marxists because they are incomplete. They are inadequate *political* substitutes for a society so constituted as to realize and to recognize each individual's true social nature. It is the value of privacy, not freedom, that Marx's theory denies, privacy understood as retreat from public scrutiny and recognition. My understanding of myself as more or other than what people take me to be is not the self-understanding of a socialist woman. In a socialist society, my nature would be totally "publicized." I would still be a unique personality, but a unique combination of social recognitions. My private self-understandings would then amount to nothing. Now, they can plausibly be interpreted as the frustrations of a socially unrealized being.

I know of no firmer grounds upon which liberal egalitarians can persuasively criticize Marx than by introspection and by rejection of the practical possibility of establishing or of recognizing a society in which everyone's nature is socially realized. But the very standard of introspection may presuppose a liberal understanding of the self as partially concealed from society, an understanding Marxists can consistently claim to be socially relative and capable of being socially transcended. And if, as a result of egalitarian alterations in economic institutions, people do freely distribute goods according to the real nature of individuals, we would have no reason to object to the resulting distribution. Yet liberal egalitarians neither anticipate nor place great value upon such an extended vision. Although Marx's vision cannot be disproved, liberal egalitarians generally doubt the possibility that people will ever be known to be just what they "naturally are."[56] Rawls also implicitly rejects Marx's hopes for a society based upon a principle of social merit because he wants to deny the appropriateness of any notion that people merit the *differential* goods they receive, even from a just society.[57]

Although Walzer explicitly and consistently as a liberal rejects distribution according to social desert, he does not provide any grounds for so doing, grounds that might ultimately distinguish his view from that of the young Marx. This is a weakness of Walzer's argument that he shares with Williams: Both wish to rely upon relevant reasons as the standards of distributive justice without looking forward to a time when the tyranny of money would be replaced by distribution according to differential human capacities and talents. Nature is endorsed by both Williams and Walzer only as a partial standard of justice. Yet neither theorist explores the moral foundations of his chosen standard or of the limits he places on relevant-reason logic.

A final question to be asked of the relevant-reasons position is how determinately egalitarian it is. Walzer's argument certainly suggests a *more* egalitarian distribution of income than presently exists in the United States or Great Britain, more egalitarian so as to prevent individuals from exercising power outside the sphere in which money should operate or from acquiring those human qualities (or the semblances of human qualities) that money should not buy. Yet Walzer never makes clear *how* equal such a distribution need be. Were this strictly a practical dilemma, to be determined on empirical grounds, one need not be so concerned. But once Walzer rejects nature as an ultimate standard for distributive justice, it is hard *in principle* to know how much equality would, or should, suffice to restrict money to "its own sphere."

Walzer himself suggests that money really does not possess its own realm. Once one discounts extraworldly motivations, it is hard to imagine a rational individual pursuing wealth simply for its own sake. (Money making, we might then suppose, would become a harmless, but rather overdemanding and ungratifying, sport.) Yet Walzer argues that money not only can but should buy some things – even in a society operating in accordance with relevant reasons. But what goods should money buy and how much "money power" can individuals rightly possess?

The abolition of money, as Walzer argues, is a socialist slogan suggesting "the abolition of the power of money outside its own sphere."[58] But neither contemporary Marxists nor Walzer have made clear how money can be so contained, without being abolished entirely. Ultimately, this may be a greater problem for Marxists than for liberal egalitarians; for Marx, as we have seen, wanted not only to contain the power of money but, in the process, to realize a society in which people got precisely what their individual natures warranted. The choice then is between a society in which money is abolished in the strict sense and one in which money allows people to seem what they are not (at least to some extent).[59] Walzer, and liberals generally, may opt for the latter alternative, and remain theoretically consistent in doing so. The liberal freedom to be what one chooses admits of the latter possibility: that people need not be socially "exposed" if they do not choose to be. And the equality postulates of liberalism suggest an image of men in which nature's different endowments are less decisive or deserving of social recognition than basic human similarities.

So, Walzer's solution is potentially consistent and also suggests an extension of liberal egalitarianism. But he proposes only a partial conception of egalitarianism, for we are never told, even in principle, how much differential "money power" is consistent with a liberal egalitarian order, an order "in which wealth is no longer convertible into social goods with which it has no intrinsic connection."[60] The argument from relevant reasons clearly sanctions redistribution of basic human services, for which the needs of the poor should become a fully sufficient and operative distributive reason. But with respect to those goods and services for which no relevant reason exists, or for which the relevant reason is an insufficient distributive criterion, Walzer has only a weak and ambiguous prescription for distributive justice: "So long as money is convertible outside its sphere, it must be widely and more or less equally held so as to minimize its distorting effects upon legitimate distributive processes."[61]

Walzer also admits that he is tempted by a radically egalitarian distribution of wealth because "it is so hard to see how a man can *merit* the things money can buy."[62] But because he does not argue for a society in which merit wins out, inequality of wealth cannot be judged unjust simply by virtue of the fact that the goods money can buy are not deserved by their purchasers.[63] Nor can the justice of an equal distribution be deduced from the argument that a meritocracy rewarded by income is unjust.

Williams's and Walzer's arguments provide a strong presumption in favor of a more egalitarian society than now exists, one based upon the assumption of human equality and the absence of relevant reasons for inequalities that have been perpetuated in the name of individual merit. Yet a strong *presumption* is all they provide for an egalitarian redistribution of income beyond the free supply of basic human services and for a redistribution of political power beyond formal political democracy. We remain without a full conception of justice and without an account of those values – such as individual liberty and community – not explicitly considered by the logic of relevant reasons.[64] We therefore are still left to wonder how far beyond the welfare state liberal egalitarianism can *rightly* extend.

Chapter 5

John Rawls and distributive equality

A Theory of Justice is the most remarkable contemporary attempt to situate the concept of equality within a comprehensive theory of egalitarian justice.[1] The importance of Rawls's theory to egalitarian concerns derives from both its substance and its scope. After exploring the strengths of his theory as the newest form of liberal egalitarianism, we shall consider a concern of egalitarian justice that is absent, or at least hidden from our view, in his presentation: a concern for expanding the opportunities for citizens to participate actively in the public life of their society. Although Rawls rightly takes an unrefined classical utilitarianism to task for its aggregative principle of maximizing happiness, we still find in Mill's revisionist utilitarianism an important piece of egalitarian justice missing from Rawls's explicit consideration.

We shall begin by examining the equality postulates of Rawls's theory and from there question how egalitarian *A Theory of Justice* is with respect to the distribution of goods: the primary goods and services that are used to satisfy basic human needs, and the residual goods that are not. This distinction between primary and residual goods will enable us to see how Rawls's theory goes beyond those of previous liberal egalitarians in justifying redistribution beyond what is necessary for basic human welfare. The role of self-respect and the fair value of liberty are investigated in this context as additional constraints on the distributive inequalities Rawls's theory may sanction.

A Theory of Justice is not necessarily—in any strictly logical sense – egalitarian in its distributive implications. But by the most consistent interpretation of Rawls's intent and of his explicit argument, *A Theory of Justice* is very likely to have significant egalitarian implications when applied to twentieth-century Anglo-American societies. This discussion is intended to question how significant some of those implications are. Finally, we shall compare the nature of Rawls's egalitarianism to that of Mill. The similar ways in which their theories assess the interests of individuals will provide us with an important insight into the method by which the egalitarian implications of liberal theory have been expanded.

EQUALITY AND THE ORIGINAL POSITION

Rawls begins by establishing a point of view – the original position – from which principles of justice can be rightly discerned.[2] This is his greatest contribution to liberal egalitarian theory. However, there are many questions to be asked concerning the status of this point of view, the most comprehensive being, Does it provide an Archimedean point of justification or does it simply suggest a framework that organizes the firmest intentions of someone who is already a committed liberal egalitarian?[3] For the moment at least, this problem of justification will be bracketed. Even if only the latter, weak form of justification holds for Rawls's theory, the coherent world view that *A Theory of Justice* presents is significant in itself. And the egalitarian extent of its resultant principles will be important evidence of the potential egalitarian scope of liberal theory.

Men in the original position are characterized as equal moral persons, whom Rawls defines as people who "have a conception of the good and a capacity for a sense of justice."[4] The latter part of this definition harks back to the Kantian conception of humanity.[5] In Rawls, too, every person is assumed capable of obeying and (in a hypothetical sense) of prescribing the moral law. Furthermore, everyone is assumed capable of pursuing a conception of the good, although it is not part of the original position that each person know his conception of the good; and each person's conception provides rational ends toward which just distributive principles can be oriented. Of course – given people as we know them – were every person to know his particular conception of the good, agreement on principles of justice would be impossible, and, even if possible, would effect an unfair and grossly unequal distribution of goods.[6] Now the resultant inequality itself does not constitute an *argument* against an alternative original position that would include substantive knowledge of one's own particular conception of the good. Rawls, however, provides three independent reasons for eliminating such particular information from the original position: Information concerning one's own conception of the good (1) permits "self and group-interest to distort the parties' deliberations," (2) "refers to contingencies and accidents that should not influence the choice of moral principles" and (3) "represents the very moral conceptions (or aspects thereof) that we seek to understand in the light of other and more basic notions."[7]

Once people in the original position understand that each has a conception of the good but that none can fairly choose distributive principles based upon knowledge of his *particular* conception, the original position becomes a radically egalitarian choice situation.[8] For now "original men" rather than actual people are being asked to stipulate what their interests are; they are forced to choose distributive principles based upon those goods that *all* can reasonably be expected to desire in order to fulfill their particular life plans once the veil of ignorance is lifted.

While abstracting from the contingent desires of real men, Rawls's theory provides a solution to the content problem in Kant.[9] This solution assumes that rational people do share certain common ends or desire certain common goods – liberty, self-respect, income, and wealth being prime examples.[10] These goods provide content for the distributive principles chosen in the original position. Rawls avoids considering all natural attributes of people as contingent, or "morally arbitrary," in his words, by separating Kant's phenomenal world into two additional realms.[11] One criterion for this separation is the postulate of equality among persons. The original position that builds upon this assumption is not therefore morally neutral.[12] Certain natural desires, technically part of Kant's phenomenal world, are not considered as merely contingent desires because they are constitutive of moral personality insofar as they form a part of every person's conception of the good.[13] Hence certain passions are constitutive of the characterization of people as equal moral beings: those passions that permit individuals who otherwise have distinct conceptions of the good to agree upon substantive distributive principles regulating a system of mutual cooperation. Rawls claims that a starting point which thereby incorporates human equalities – whether those equalities be of the noumenal or the phenomenal realm – is a fair (not a neutral) starting point for theorizing about justice.[14]

The nature of human equality has not diverged from the Kantian conception of individuals as equally dignified beings, but the idea that a dignified being must both act and be treated as an end in himself now has a distinct implication. Acting from inclination (or being treated in accordance with one's desires, as opposed to one's reason) may be a means of publicly demonstrating one's dignity (or having one's dignity publicly demonstrated) so long as

these desires are universally shared and consistent with social justice. Rawls's theory separates two characteristics of the passions
that Kant's conflated: that our passions are not self-controlled and
that they are idiosyncratic.[15] Rawls seems to be revising Kant on
both counts, first by implying that Kant was wrong in suggesting
that all human passions are uncontrollable (or that, even if he was
correct, the exercise of our rationality may not be distinct from the
exercise of our inclinations on this ground, and Rawls does not
want to dispose of rationality as grounds for justice for this reason). Second, Rawls suggests that Kant was incorrect in thinking
that the *objects* of our passions are all idiosyncratic; some are universal and essential to our understanding of human nature.[16] This
latter claim of Rawls's forms one basis of the criticism that his
theory is ahistorical in assuming the possibility of stipulating
some relatively timeless notion of individual interest apart from
the particular time and society in which individuals live.[17]

Rawls's theory is not ahistorical in that it quite explicitly recognizes two distinct sets of principles, a general and a special conception of justice, applicable to less and more economically developed societies respectively.[18] In addition, Rawls argues that in the
legislative stage of decision making, "it is permissible . . . to take
into account the interests and needs of the persons in [a] particular
society. This does not violate the idea of an Archimedean point,
nor does it reverse the proper relation between harmony and justice . . . because the principles of justice are already on hand, and
these set limits on what a just harmony can be."[19] However, I
think there is considerable force remaining to this criticism insofar
as it questions whether any set of primary goods, however general, can be considered to apply to all individuals within all societies at all times. A more modest claim for Rawls's theory is that
primary goods can be considered essential to the life plans of all
rational individuals who are members of liberal advanced industrial societies. But even in so weakening the universal claims of
Rawls's theory, one goes still further in overcoming the content
problem in Kant's theory while constraining the applicability of
the particular principles thereby generated.

THE TWO PRINCIPLES REVISED

Rawls tells us that people in the original position will agree upon
two principles of distributive justice. The first, with priority over
the second, guarantees such liberty to each as is consistent with a

like liberty for all. The second principle establishes that "social and economic inequalities are to be arranged so that they are both (a) to the greatest benefit of the least advantaged . . . and (b) attached to offices and positions open to all under conditions of fair equality of opportunity."[20]

Rawls describes the equal and basic liberties to be guaranteed by the first principle as, "roughly speaking, political liberty (the right to vote and to be eligible for public office) together with freedom of speech and assembly; liberty of conscience and freedom of thought; freedom of the person along with the right to hold (personal) property; and freedom from arbitrary arrest and seizure as defined by the concept of the rule of law."[21] The equal rights to these freedoms are the most deeply embedded equalities of the liberal tradition. Priority of the first principle ensures that basic liberal freedoms are not sacrificed for greater socioeconomic advantages under broadly specified conditions: (1) a just or nearly just society with (2) a fairly advanced level of socioeconomic development. These two provisos are significant in situating Rawls's theory historically in the liberal tradition as a response to the question of justice within an advanced industrial civilization, and philosophically as a theory of ideal justice. The two principles of Rawlsian justice might be significantly altered either under economically underdeveloped or nonideal political situations.

Although less developed and therefore less conclusive with reference to conditions other than those of advanced industrial societies, Rawls's theory does suggest that to equalize all liberties prior to primary-good distribution in a society in which most (or perhaps even some) people do not have a minimum standard of living would be to misconstrue the intent of the liberal commitment to equal freedom.[22] Although Rawls is unfortunately ambiguous as to precisely what priority principles apply to an affluent society in which pockets of poverty unjustly persist, his argument for the fair value of liberty suggests that a minimal level of primary-good distribution must be achieved before the equal-liberty principle is recognized as a prior concern of rational individuals. In addition, in advanced industrial societies, the original position sanctions the equalization of "fair value of liberty" as far as is consistent with equal formal rights and the interests of the least advantaged.[23]

The point to be emphasized by those interested in extending the egalitarian implications of Rawls's theory is that he incorporates the classical liberal position on equalizing formal (or negative) liberties with a potentially radically egalitarian stance on maximizing the worth (or positive side) of liberty to the worst-off within any given society:

Liberty is represented by the complete system of the liberties of equal citizenship, while the worth of liberty to persons and groups is proportional to their capacity to advance their ends within the framework the system defines . . . Taking the two principles together, the basic structure is to be arranged to maximize the worth to the least advantaged of the complete scheme of equal liberty shared by all. This defines the end of social justice.[24]

Rawls also extends the meaning of the classical liberal ideal of equal opportunity. In theory at least, he can avoid both the criticism that equal opportunity legitimizes a society of inherited inequalities and the problem of "egalitarian collapse" – that equal opportunity taken to its logical extreme may entail a radical identity of persons. The first criticism is met because the two principles of justice ensure *fair* equality of opportunity, requiring extensive public subsidy and control of what classical liberals took to be the private realm, including of course economic enterprise.[25]

Because individuals in the original position want above all to preserve their self-respect, the rewards accruing to any position may be restricted still further in that cause.[26] Inequalities attached to equal opportunities will be limited not only by the increased supply of talent one might expect to result from the proposed governmental implementation of equal opportunity, but also by the broader implications of the conception of equal moral persons with which Rawls's theory begins. Rational individuals in the original position will ensure that the unequal rewards attached to equal opportunities are only those necessary as incentives to labor and those consistent with the public characterization of themselves as equal moral persons.

Now it is an empirical question (to be explored further on) how egalitarian the results of these provisos on the equal-opportunity principle will be in a contemporary context. Nonetheless, the original position does suggest a *theoretical* limit on the egalitarianism of equal opportunity that avoids the problem of "egalitarian collapse." Because all individuals in the original position are known to possess and value their own conceptions of the good (although ignorant of the unique content of these conceptions) and to view themselves as protective of a line of descendants, the futuristic fantasy of genetic manipulation will be considered an irrational one, one destructive of that conception of self with which each person in the original position begins.[27] Even the less radical version of egalitarian collapse entailed in abolition of the nuclear family is viewed by Rawls as unnecessary once the two principles of justice guarantee to the least advantaged both equality of self-respect and a greater share of primary goods than they now possess.[28] One might also argue that an attempt to equalize opportunity by abolishing the family would fail so long as any natural ties between parents and their children are permitted to exist. Of course, because each individual in the original position considers himself representative of a line of descendants, the destruction of the nuclear family is precluded by the very nature of the original position.

In building the conception of equal moral persons and of natural family loyalty into the original position, Rawls is clearly building upon a belief in the sacredness of personality and in the "naturalness" of family that is deeply embedded in the liberal tradition, but that is by no means a universal one. The limits of justified modifications of individual personality and intrusions on the family have, of course, also been modified over the centuries of liberal thought. It is significant that Rawls builds the most minimal of these limits on egalitarian collapse into the original position. Because the logic of radically equalizing opportunity might entail that all ties between parents and children be severed and that all socially consequential and distinctive natural attributes of persons be eliminated, liberal egalitarians intuitively draw the line of equalizing opportunity at preserving the family and preserving the inherited natural attributes of persons. Rawls's original position does not provide an argument supporting this intuition; it simply characterizes it. All other equalizing measures – including the abolition of inheritance of wealth – remain consistent with the potential province of legitimate egalitarian reform.

After the guarantee of equal opportunity as far as is consistent with equal liberty, the final part of the second principle of justice goes into effect. The "difference principle" establishes equality as the base line of primary good distribution. An unequal distribution is justified if and only if it will maximize benefits to the least-advantaged group within that society.[29] Assuming (only for the moment) that the incentives necessary for encouraging competent people to fulfill more difficult or demanding jobs and for stimulating desirable social investment are nil, the difference principle suggests that absolute equality in the distribution of income and wealth would be the equitable policy.

But once one unties the bundle of goods for which income and wealth are the surrogates of exchange, the justice of an equal-distribution base line may be questioned in Rawls's own terms. The reasoning in support of the difference principle suggests that individuals in the original position would be extremely averse to risks in choosing distributive principles that are to determine their basic life chances and, by extension, the life chances of their progeny. Now, in addition to formal rights and liberties, certain basic human goods and services are prerequisites to the free and enjoyable use not only of all other goods but of basic liberties as well. These goods are essential to one's very ability to pursue a life plan: education and job training, housing and employment, medical care and legal services. The first two pairs are recognized by Rawls as essential and included in the fair equality-of-opportunity principle. This principle also suggests that medical care and legal services be distributed according to need rather than according to the difference principle.

If people in the original position agree to the distribution of all income and wealth in liquid form according to the difference principle, they risk being unable to meet a sudden demand. By their nature, both legal and medical care rather frequently require large amounts of money at unpredictable times during most people's lifetimes – often so large as to place enormous strain on their resources. Therefore, granting that people within the original position are for good reason risk-averse agents, a strong case can be made either for distributing services in kind or for providing payments tied to the satisfaction of medical and legal needs. The distribution of medical and legal services according to need would be a more rational decision from the perspective of the original position.[30]

The egalitarian addition to the first principle just suggested requires an equal treatment of objectively determined needs in addition to the guarantee of equal civil and political liberties, so as to equalize self-respect among citizens and to guarantee a basic minimum value of individual liberty.[31] "Welfare rights" are thereby elevated to a level of priority with the first principle of equal liberty in order to secure what I shall call "basic effective liberty" to all people. One might consider basic effective liberty a multiplicative function of formal liberties and basic welfare rights, whereas effective liberty might be considered a function of formal liberties and the total store of primary goods.[32] Revising Rawls's first principle so as to grant priority to basic effective liberty accords with what I take to be a compelling judgment from several critics of Rawls concerning the necessary preconditions for the employment of political and civil liberties.[33] Of course, this revision of the first principle does not eliminate the need to place additional limits upon absolute levels of income inequality in accordance with the difference principle and other values to be discussed later.

Residual goods then remain to be distributed as equally as is consistent with maximizing benefits to the least advantaged: They may be used freely by individuals in pursuit of their chosen life plans. The first form of equal distribution of economic goods and services underwrites the maximum welfare state within a Rawlsian system. The second form, explicitly supported by the difference principle, expands justice beyond the welfare state to a potentially more egalitarian system of distribution than that supported by previous liberal theorists. Distributive justice by Rawls's theory is thereby divided into two egalitarian spheres: (1) a distribution of basic human services in which some version of *equal treatment of needs* operates, and (2) a distribution of residual goods (presumably in the form of money) in which a principle of *equal shares to individuals* (modified in the interests of the poorest sector) operates. Given the relative urgency of the needs met by basic welfare rights, the first egalitarian principle will be prior to the second, within broad limits.

The revised egalitarian first principle clearly requires additional specification. The precise nature of the function constituting basic effective liberty must be further specified. Plausible limiting conditions are also necessary to avoid the problem of resource drainage that extreme cases now present, but these conditions can only be determined once the contours of need and income distribution are known in any given society. We leave open here what the process or nature of that specification might be.[34] Barring extreme cases, it remains rational for individuals in the original position to accept the risk of moderately lower income prospects in exchange for the certainty that their health will be protected and maintained at all but outrageous cost to society.[35]

The skeptic here should note that even within our present system, medical needs as severe and costly to satisfy as perpetual dependence on kidney machines are often met at the expense of the state. Of course, the problem of resource drainage would be heightened within a society that satisfied such needs as universal rights. Yet, as recent certificate-of-need programs in the United States were intended to indicate, our present system needlessly duplicates many major medical services to a degree that presumably would not obtain in a system that allocated essential medical services as far as possible according to need, rather than according to income or geographical proximity to an affluent community.[36] So, though the principle of ensuring basic welfare rights certainly requires more precise definition of the needs and the magnitude of needs that individuals have the right to satisfy at the expense of the state, those questions can remain open without destroying the central argument for basic welfare-state services.

We should note here two important consequences of revising Rawls's argument by elevating basic welfare rights to a priority over difference-principle considerations. As Rawls's theory now stands, no specified distribution is guaranteed by the difference principle. Were welfare to be simply contingent upon difference-principle considerations, the incentive structure of any given economy would have a potentially enormous impact upon the welfare expectations of all individuals, particularly upon the expectations of the least advantaged. The revised first principle guaranteeing basic effective liberty is preferable to Rawls's first principle for reasons similar to those Rawls gives for preferring the difference principle to that of utility maximization.[37] The difference principle explicitly specifies a concern for how goods are allocated among people and a clearly related concern for the least advantaged that utilitarian principles tend to obscure, or at best indirectly reflect. Similarly, stipulating the basic effective liberty of each citizen as a right makes that priority clear *in principle*, although it is a priority that might well be effected in most situations by the application of the difference principle or the principle of maximizing average utility.

The second advantage of this revision is that welfare now has the status of a right for all citizens. Were we to derive a theory of obligation from this revised liberal egalitarianism, we would be likely to endorse the right to civil disobedience and perhaps even to revolution for those citizens who are denied their basic effective liberty by a denial of basic welfare rights. I say "likely" because I shall not attempt here to derive a theory of obligation from this revised form of liberal egalitarianism. Nevertheless, the more principled this guarantee of basic welfare.is, the wider the door opens to legitimate claims of disobedience on the part of those whose basic welfare rights are not guaranteed by the present system.

Of course, we might find ourselves in a society so poor that not enough exists to satisfy the basic welfare needs of all citizens. If that were the case, the basic-effective-liberty principle would collapse into Rawls's general conception of justice. In advanced industrial societies, there is no reason to anticipate such a collapse. Once applied, the basic-effective-liberty principle will publicize an egalitarian commitment to certain welfare rights and separate this commitment from that of maximizing the income and wealth of the least advantaged. Because the former commitment is stronger (in many senses) than the latter, our argument has the advantage of allowing us to judge the validity of the difference principle separately from that of the aim of guaranteeing people basic welfare rights. We turn now to an assessment of the practical implications of the remaining difference principle.

THE DIFFERENCE PRINCIPLE AND EQUALITY

Many critics have suggested that the difference principle will be less egalitarian in practice than its theoretical appearance might seem to suggest, that it is another inegalitarian principle after all.[38] If the difference principle does not work in the direction of equalizing shares, it is unlikely that anything short of a principle of strict equality will.[39] But of course this is not to say that the difference principle will work. Nor can we with great intellectual assurance determine how it will work; that this is a matter of some speculation must be admitted from the start. Any attempt to resolve this dispute between Rawls and his critics ultimately must rely upon empirical evidence and extrapolations from that evidence. And, to complicate the matter further, evidence from our own decidedly nonideal society generally supplies very unreliable data for the purposes of extrapolating predictions of the behavior of individuals in a society to be run according to principles quite distinct from our own. Nevertheless, we shall rely upon empirical evidence as best we can to achieve a tentative resolution of this dispute concerning the difference principle, although we have grounds upon which to criticize Rawls's own use of empirical findings in support of his case.

Our selective use of empirical evidence relies upon three simple but I believe generally valid rules. First, we cannot legitimately expect to change the basic principles upon which a society is run without changing the knowledge that people within that society have of how their society is run. Therefore, we cannot validly extrapolate from present data by relying upon the assumption that people in a just society will know only what they now know about the workings of their society. This rule calls into question Rawls's reliance upon relative-deprivation studies, as indicated later.

Our second working rule of thumb is that extrapolations from studies of contemporary societies are valid if, taking people as they are now, one discovers that more (or less) egalitarian policies can operate in our own society without significant harmful effects upon other desired ends. Extrapolations from such studies are valid insofar as they can tell us what it is possible to achieve without changing "human nature" as we now know it. (It is possible of course to suggest that people may change for the worse in an ideal society. However, few of Rawls's critics entertain that argument; the dispute is over whether people will change for the better – better, that is, with regard to egalitarian possibilities – or whether they will remain the same.)

Our final rule is the following: Studies whose findings are based upon an acceptance of people's present motivation (to work, to obey the law, etc.) cannot be used to *disprove* the possibility of a society run according to distinct principles of justice. This follows from the postulate that people's motivation may reasonably be expected to change within a new social order. (The more difficult issue this raises is *how much* change can reasonably be expected. We shall explore this question in Chapter 6, but an answer to it is unnecessary to establish our third, more general, rule.)

Now these rules concerning the use of empirical evidence taken together appear to be, and indeed are, "biased" toward the argument that a just egalitarian society is a possibility (although they have nothing to say about its desirability, if it is possible). Empirical studies of contemporary societies are more likely to help prove than to disprove the very possibility of a more egalitarian society. But this is not an unfair bias to establish. The rules are fair on grounds independent of their resulting bias, and the bias itself is probably a fortunate one. Given that the status quo has the practical advantage of having proved its possibility, it is not unreasonable to counter that practical advantage by placing the intellectual burden of disproof upon those who claim that other well-ordered societies are impossible. This burden of disproof is an inducement to those who wish to defend the status quo to defend it upon moral rather than upon practical grounds. This would be an indirect and salutary effect of our burden-of-proof argument. (But clearly, the latter argument cannot alone establish the reasonableness of such burden-of-proof standards.) Having established reasonable rules for empirically based arguments, let us first move back a step to investigate the potential egalitarian force and attraction of the difference principle *in theory* and then ask what its effect is likely to be *in practice*.

The difference principle and equality

A principle more egalitarian than the difference principle would be inefficient from the point of view of the least advantaged: An increase in their level of primary goods would still be possible and desirable.[40] Nevertheless, the efficiency claim of the difference principle has already been qualified in the name of equality: Efficiency is a value in Rawlsian terms only insofar as it *maximizes* benefits in the form of primary goods *to the least advantaged*.[41]

Unlike Walzer's argument for more equality, the difference principle provides a rule in the form of the maximin criterion for determining *how much* inequality is permitted to fulfill the demands of social justice: that which maximizes benefits to the least advantaged consistently with the equal freedoms of all. Now though this criterion is determinate, it is not necessarily simple. There are several dimensions of advantage to be considered: income and wealth, powers and prerogatives of authority, and self-respect. If, as Rawls indicates, these primary goods are generally and closely covariant, the maximin criterion will be both simple and determinate.[42] If covariance does not exist, some indexing of primary-good advantages will be necessary.

Powers and self-respect will present the more complex and more nearly unique problems for the difference principle, if indexing is necessary. We shall assess the nature of those problems and suggest some solutions consistent with the egalitarian spirit of Rawls's theory later in this chapter and in the next. But if we initially consider only the nature of a just distribution of income and wealth (assuming for the moment that self-respect and powers are covariant), we still might want to know how much equality is likely to result from the application of the difference principle to contemporary Anglo-American societies.

Let us begin with one possible challenge to the egalitarianism of the maximin rule against which Rawls explicitly defends himself. Lester Thurow has argued that a society governed by the difference principle might provide inordinately large rewards to high-income groups in exchange for small "trickle-down" effects to the least advantaged.[43] Rawls provides a rebuttal to a very similar hypothetical challenge in *A Theory of Justice*. He contends that although there is no theoretical guarantee against great inequalities, the context of just institutions governed by fair equality of opportunity in which the difference principle operates will militate against such possibilities: "The disparities likely to result will be much less than the differences that men have often tolerated in the past."[44] But a significant misunderstanding underlies Thurow's

131

criticism. Thurow appears to assume that *any* resulting benefits to the least advantaged can justify allowing the rich to have more. Rather, the difference principle as consistently stated can justify activities with marginal trickle-down effects only if they provide greater benefits to the least advantaged than *any possible* alternate arrangements. Set within the context of more egalitarian background institutions, it is hard to imagine the results of the difference principle as other than egalitarian relative to income and wealth disparities within contemporary societies. One commentator seems to recognize this in conceding in an otherwise critical essay that "of course, Marxists do suppose that a permanently stable society would have to be one which, at least roughly speaking, realizes the difference principle."[45]

As an example, let us take a significant contemporary case of the grossly unequal income distribution between doctors and nurses (lawyers and their legal secretaries would serve as well). In a Rawlsian society, with fair equality of opportunity and governmental subsidies for vocational training, doctors would not be able to ensure their scarce supply, and access to medical schools would be less limited as long as medical care was a high social priority. This assumes, of course, that the supply of medical services is artificially rather than naturally limited today by the high cost of medical training, by the scarce supply of places within medical schools, and by the skewed allocation of doctors across communities – fairly plausible and easily documented claims. In a just society, doctors might still earn larger incomes than nurses (for example, to compensate for the more difficult work or the longer training periods required), *if* income incentives were necessary to call forth the desirable supply of competent physicians. But there is little reason to believe that this income differential, if any (nonmonetary incentives might suffice), would be as great as presently exists, and good reason to believe it would be radically lower.[46] As the oligopolistic position of doctors diminished, so would the inequalities in their income presently caused by economic rent. Furthermore, in a society organized for mutual and maximin benefit to the least advantaged, the structure of the medical profession might be more graded, so as to eliminate many of the enormous gaps in training, skill, and professional responsibility between the present-day ranks of doctors and nurses.

Rawls assumes that advantage in such cases is measured to the exclusion of the effects of envy. But in any case we need not expect that extending the gradations of employment in medicine would produce another hierarchical structure of authority more demeaning to those on the bottom than the one that presently exists. Rather, the plurality of skills necessary to different medical practices (surgical expertise, bedside manner, general diagnostic skills, etc.) would be distributed among, rather than ordinally ranked by, a large variety of job slots. Therefore, we would not expect a serious conflict to exist within the goal of maximizing benefits to the least advantaged, whether the least advantaged were identified as those most in need of good medical services, those generally worst situated in the population, or those presently denied dignity by their extreme subordination to physicians within the hospital. Nor would it be surprising to learn that these groups overlap substantially in the present population.

Some persuasive evidence exists in support of the greater egalitarian potential of the difference principle coupled with fair equality of opportunity, both in equalizing job opportunities among social groups and in equalizing income and wealth through taxation. Thurow, for example, argues that job (and corresponding income) discrimination against many minority or disadvantaged groups is "statistical" rather than ad hominem in nature.[47] Employers may now be acting rationally in choosing their workers exclusively from more-advantaged groups in the population even though there may be well- or better-qualified individuals within discriminated-against groups. By playing the lower odds in choosing among their potential employee pools, employers minimize their chances of hiring someone who is less competent or more expensive to train.

Guidelines that require employers to consider each person among the discriminated groups on his *individual* merit are one way to overcome this statistical discrimination in contemporary society.[48] This may be an irrational use of time from the point of view of the individual employer but necessary from the perspective of social justice. In a just society, modeled on Rawlsian principles, affirmative-action programs would be unnecessary even if the motivation of employers remained unchanged. Employer rationality would coincide with social justice because, given fair equality of opportunity, there would be no reason for employers seeking to maximize the quality of their employee pool to discriminate prejudicially against members of any specified social group. The policies recommended by a fair equality-of-opportunity principle would militate against statistical discrimination and eliminate the need for government-imposed affirmative-action guidelines. A "natural lottery" would result where no group would be statistically discriminated against because of the "handicaps of race, sex, age or adverse macro-economic policies." Thurow estimates that with no other equalization policies, "income dispersions would be reduced forty percent if the national economic lottery [in the U.S.] yielded a structure of prizes as equal as that now generated for fully employed adult white males" (those currently exempt from statistical discrimination).[49] Of course, this does not tell us how we can or should get from a society in which individuals are presently disadvantaged owing to past discriminations against their race or sex to a society in which fair equality of opportunity flourishes. But it does tell us where we might want to go and what sorts of problems can be avoided once we get there.

Does the difference principle open the door to a justification of gross inequalities under the rationale that incentives are necessary for the middle class to do highly skilled, productive work and for the rich to contribute by means of investment to the welfare of the poor? Several empirical studies have indicated that increased taxation of income (within broad limits) has minimal effects on work incentives and productivity among the middle class; people may work just as hard if not harder in order to maintain their previous incomes or to achieve their desired income level.[50] Nor is it clear that unemployment will rise significantly among working classes with the institution of guaranteed income floors.[51] The most reasonable conclusion from available studies may be that no firm evidence exists to determine whether income floors will decrease benefits to the least advantaged by diminishing the total social product.[52] Rawls's difference principle nonetheless shifts the burden of redistributive argument from the need to demonstrate that income supplements will not decrease total social productivity to a demonstration that supplements will not diminish the welfare of the least advantaged in the long run – by weakening the economy and thereby offsetting the income gains to the least advantaged – or lower another group below the formerly least advantaged.

With reference to the effects of progressive taxation on investment incentives, the evidence is similarly ambiguous and the policy implications of existing evidence are even less clear, because investment need not be undertaken by individuals. Savings could instead be made by the state.[53] But assuming that one wanted to rely upon private decision making as much as possible, the present low effective tax rates on inheritance and capital gains would still not be justified. The amount of investment currently undertaken by individuals is not well correlated with the degree of risk involved or with the expected rate of return. Rather, business economists report that there exist substantial random factors in the individuals' investment decisions, as well as in their actual returns.[54] In addition, the political structure of contemporary capitalist societies may thwart more efficient capital-investment decisions by offering an important noneconomic incentive for wealthy individuals to translate their personal economic accumulation into personal and, more seriously, into political power.[55] This alone might be sufficient reason to equalize wealth accumulations under a Rawlsian system.

Policies that would simultaneously remedy the inefficiencies of the real capital market and effect a more egalitarian distribution of wealth include raising inheritance taxation and closing existing loopholes, raising the tax rate on capital gains, and treating corporations for tax purposes simply as aggregates of individual stockholders.[56] Profits to corporations could be treated as accretions to individual (rather than corporate) wealth, just as profits and savings accruing to salaried employees are now treated. No corporate body would be permitted to absorb and transfer profits into internal savings, and no individuals would be allowed to avoid taxes through the accumulation of unrealized capital gains. If Thurow's analysis is correct, this extension of an equal-treatment maxim into revised tax policy would also go far in equilibrating a presently skewed real capital gains market. Of course, these are just several possible, and debatable, examples of governmental policies consistent with the difference principle that are potentially productive both of greater efficiency and of a more equal distribution of income and wealth in society. It is up to political economists concerned with equality to suggest more particular policies, as well as to analyze how alternative economic systems differentially accommodate egalitarian values.[57]

SELF-RESPECT AND THE FAIR VALUE OF LIBERTY

But surely there must be some equalization policies that might reasonably be expected to conflict with increased productivity in the interests of the least advantaged. What if there are situations in which the best policy in accordance with the difference principle generates a wide gap between the incomes of the most and of the least advantaged? It is important to ask how such challenges to an effective egalitarianism would be resolved in a Rawlsian society. In order to do this, we must examine the distributive implications of two additional factors included by Rawls within his argument that have been excluded from consideration until now. One is the "sense of one's own worth," or self-respect, included among those primary goods whose distribution must be governed by rules of justice. The second is the need to preserve the "fair value of liberty" within a just system.

Rawls consistently lists self-respect as the most important primary good. The meaning he ascribes to self-respect makes apparent its priority among the primary goods remaining after rights and liberties have been equally allocated by the first principle:

We may define self-respect (or self-esteem) as having two aspects. First of all . . . it includes a person's sense of his own value, his secure conviction that his conception of his good, his plan of life, is worth carrying out. And second, self-respect implies a confidence in one's ability, so far as it is within one's power, to fulfill one's intentions. When we feel that our plans are of little value, we cannot pursue them with pleasure or take delight in their execution. Nor plagued by failure and self-doubt can we continue in our endeavors. It is clear then why self-respect is a primary good. *Without it nothing may seem worth doing, or if some things have value for us, we lack the will to strive for them.* All desire and activity becomes empty and vain, and we sink into apathy and cynicism. Therefore the parties in the original position would wish to avoid *at almost any cost* the social conditions that undermine self-respect.[58]

Given Rawls's definition, a strong argument can be made from the perspective of individuals in the original position for the necessity of distributing self-respect equally. If without self-respect "nothing may seem worth doing," accepting a less-than-equal distribution will directly undermine the rationale behind the difference principle's maximization of the interest of the least advantaged. Supplying the poorest with more primary goods will be insufficient if their sense of self-worth or their very desire to pursue their conceptions of the good is undercut by self-doubt.

If a person's sense of his own worth is considered a national good, one dependent on his position relative to others in society, then the attempt to equalize self-respect may have further radical distributive implications, depending upon the causal connections thought to exist between distributive justice and individual psychology. Rawls often appears to view self-respect as a relational good, but in a more limited sense: Self-respect is causally related to the distribution of basic rights and liberties, rather than to the distribution of income or wealth within a society. This is probably true only within certain significant limits, for example, only given a guarantee of basic welfare rights such that all persons could effectively pursue a wide range of life plans. The ability to choose more expensive life plans might still be unevenly distributed (again, within limits) without undermining the equal distribution of self-respect.

Is there a causal relation between self-respect and unequal distribution under the difference principle? This is not a question that can be clearly answered without prior agreement on what constitutes self-respect and what its manifestations are. If we accept the two principles of justice, we are likely to dismiss as unjustifiable envy negative psychological reactions to those inequalities otherwise sanctioned by the difference principle. Nevertheless, we can go some distance here in understanding the potential egalitarianism of Rawls's theory by postulating clearly discernible psychological effects of distributive inequalities other than those Rawls appears to believe will ensue from the institution of basic liberties and fair equality of opportunity. If the self-respect of the least advantaged were shattered or seriously injured by economic disparities that otherwise could be justified by the difference principle, the priority of self-respect as a primary good would warrant a more equal economic distribution, regardless of its resulting inefficiencies. The moral urgency of such a policy is another important indication of the subordinate role of economic efficiency in an egalitarian theory of justice. The problem now of course is that we are ill equipped both theoretically and practically to determine what connections exist between self-respect, as distinguished from envy, and distributive principles.

If Rawls's psychological assumptions are correct, and distributive inequalities otherwise in accordance with the difference principle would not injure the self-respect of the least advantaged, no further adjustments in the name of self-respect would be necessary. Those inequalities would remain rational from the perspective of individuals in the original position, beneficial from the point of view of the least advantaged and legitimate in the eyes of all those citizens with the requisite sense of justice. The potential range of income inequality sanctioned by the difference principle constrained by equal self-respect would vary, therefore, depending upon the precise workings of the economy and upon the nature of psychological reactions to the inequalities remaining within a just society. Rawls's theory can accommodate this variation by sacrificing some simplicity in priority rules in order to retain a theoretical consistency and determinacy. Self-respect would take priority over economic efficiency. What Rawls's theory unfortunately does not do is provide us with a reasoned defense of a particular view of self-respect. Nor does his theory provide us with a determinate answer to the partly empirical question how self-respect is to be equalized within a just society. The first task would be part of a moral psychology; the second, of a political sociology. As yet, Rawls's theory lacks these intellectual structures necessary to support one of its major egalitarian themes.

Although lacking a well-developed political sociology, Rawls attempts to employ the conclusions of relative-deprivation studies to suggest that small income inequalities would not undermine self-respect. As I indicated previously, however, the conclusions he draws from these studies are suspect. In *Relative Deprivation and Social Justice*, Runciman demonstrates that most workers do not compare themselves with people in radically higher income or wealth brackets, a finding which suggests that self-respect does not depend upon the total structure of income and wealth within a society, but only upon narrow reference-group structures.[59] But in a just society with increased opportunities, mobility, and widespread belief in the equal moral worth of persons, there is little reason to expect (or hope) that individuals would cluster within noncomparing income strata. Now this is not to say that comparing groups would produce that sort of envy ("excusable envy") destructive of self-respect.[60] But it is to say that relative-deprivation studies conducted within nonideal societies are extremely shaky evidence upon which to base estimates of the psychological reactions to income inequalities within a much more egalitarian and just society.

Even were the difference principle to accommodate self-respect, as Rawls believes likely, a just society in his terms must not only guarantee people equal rights but must also maintain the fair value of liberty, so as to uphold the vision of equal moral persons with which his theory begins. Reasoning from the original position, if the parties to the social contract give priority to equal liberty among primary goods, they presumably would want to ensure for themselves the possibility of equal effective use of that liberty, political as well as civil. As Rawls himself argues:

The liberties protected by the principle of participation lose much of their value whenever those who have greater private means are permitted to use their advantages to control the course of public debate. For eventually these inequalities will enable those better situated to exercise a larger influence over the development of legislation. In due time they are likely to acquire a preponderant weight in settling social questions, at least in regard to those matters upon which they normally agree, which is to say in regard to those things that support their favored circumstances.

He concludes that "compensating steps must . . . be taken to pre-serve the fair value for all of the equal political liberties."[61]

It appears therefore that Rawls gives the *worth* of liberty a more central position in his supporting arguments than he does in his explicit principles of justice. Given the priority of equal liberty in Rawlsian justice, we might reasonably expect the fair value of liberty to take priority over the difference principle, because, as Rawls argues,

historically one of the main defects of constitutional government has been the failure to insure the fair value of political liberty. The necessary cor-rective steps have not been taken, indeed, they never seem to have been seriously entertained. Disparities in the distribution of property and wealth that far exceed what is compatible with political equality have generally been tolerated by the legal system . . . Moreover, the effects of injustices in the political system are much more grave and long lasting than market imperfections.[62]

Or if, as some political sociologists have claimed, inequalities of income or wealth of any sort will translate into a seriously dis-torted distribution of political power, the two principles of justice must sanction a more radically egalitarian distribution of income and wealth than is indicated by the difference principle taken alone.[63] If it is also established that private ownership of the means of production lies at the root of the problem of ineffective equal liberties, Rawlsian criteria would have us seek alternative modes of ownership to preserve the fair value of liberty.[64]

It is important to recognize here what reasoning from the two principles of justice does not warrant. The two principles do not guarantee a system in which all persons will participate equally in the political system, or will possess equal authority or equal wealth.[65] The distribution of wealth needs to be radically equal-ized *only* under the assumption that the inequalities sanctioned by the difference principle in a just society will continue to skew the *opportunities* for individuals to take advantage of political lib-erties. Here, Rawls's argument for the fair value of liberty does not provide a clear criterion by which to determine where to draw the line between fair and unfair inequalities of political power and participation. He appears to think it reasonable to assume that under most conditions the difference principle coupled with fair equality of opportunity will come close to ensuring the fair value of liberty for all. But his assumption of equal moral personality tied to the argument for the fair value of liberty would still provide for the further equalization of income and wealth, and even for the alteration of basic ownership structures, if it were recognized that certain classes of individuals discernible by their wealth, income, or relation to the mode of production had much greater access to political power – to the media, to influencing political leaders, and to gaining political office – than other economic groups.

The presumption in a theory that begins with an equality premise as strong as Rawls's must be that income and wealth disparities, rather than race, ethnicity, religion, or sex (when the two sets of characteristics are covariant), are productive of the observed inequalities in the effective use of civil and political liberties, so long as a plausible causal connection can be posited. Of course, at some point the income inequalities sanctioned by the difference principle may be so small that any resulting disparities in political power or participation among groups of individuals will not be thought to impair justice.

Let us go back for a moment to Rawls's argument for ensuring the fair value of liberty and ask what is the value for Rawls of the "fair value of liberty" with reference to political liberties – those liberties to which he devotes most of his attention on this matter. From within the original position, each person deliberates over principles of justice based upon his individual interest. This interest need not be an egoistical interest *in* the self, but it must be an interest *of* the self rather than a moral interest in how society should be organized or a purely altruistic interest in aiding others despite costs to the self. Rawls's reasoning appears to be that people want to secure the fair value of political liberty as a means of ensuring that their basic interests are not overridden by more advantaged persons who can use their political liberties more effectively and thereby exercise undue influence or control over the political process.

This defense of the fair value of political liberty is remarkably akin to James Mill's argument for equal political rights: It is an instrumentalist and defensive account of the need for equal effective political rights.[66] Of course, James Mill did not support equal *effective* rights; but the reasoning underlying his defense of extending the formal right to vote was very similar. In fact, Rawls's defensive rationale appears to operate on two levels. The first is that any individual's political rights may be rendered ineffective without some protection of the fair value of those rights within society.[67] The second is that any constitutional government is likely to be rendered unstable without some assurance to its citizens of the fair value of political liberty.[68]

Both of these rationales for the fair value of liberty are to an extent valid ones, although the validity of each relies heavily upon the view that the economically powerful, if powerful enough, will exercise their political liberty in their own interests to distort or to destroy constitutional government. But this motivational view is not necessarily entailed by Rawls's theory: The motivation of self-interest is necessarily operative only within the original position. Once out of this thought experiment, we discover that people are communally minded rather than self-interested beings. This discovery ought to suggest an alternative defense within the liberal tradition of the need to ensure the fair value of liberty, a defense that does not rely so heavily upon the assumption of self-interested political behavior among citizens, or at least goes beyond that negative rationale for equalizing effective political liberty. That defense of course is John Stuart Mill's. Mill's defense presupposes a number of things that Rawls's rational-choice theory generally neglects, the most significant being the educative value of political participation and the possible centrality of political participation within an individual's conception of the good life. Neither of these defenses of the fair value of political liberty is precluded by Rawls's theory. Indeed, Rawls's concluding discussion of a well-ordered society as a "social union of social unions" wherein "human beings have in fact shared final ends and . . . value their common institutions and activities as good in themselves" might lead us back to the Millean defense of participation.[69] But in his reasoning from the original position, Rawls is not explicitly concerned with the value of participation other than as a form of defense against subversion of the constitutional rights of individuals and of constitutional government as a whole. Mill's emphasis upon the value of participation suggests the need for an integration of his participatory concerns with the explicit redistributive concerns of Rawls's theory.

RAWLS AND UTILITARIANISM

With Rawls's theory we have an egalitarianism, though significantly distinct in its emphasis, comparable in scope to Mill's. Before exploring major attacks upon Rawls's enterprise, let us consider briefly what it is about this liberal theory that leads to more egalitarian conclusions than we have encountered in previous liberal thought.

If liberal theory is provisionally defined by its method of basing principles of justice upon individual interests, there are two ways in which the particular method of Rawls's theory enables him to stretch the egalitarian boundaries of liberal theory. One is that, unlike classical utilitarianism, his theory does not aggregate individual interests into one homogeneous system to be maximized by social justice.[70] Because maximization neither of interests nor of desires is supported by his method, the manner in which the satisfaction of interests or desires is distributed to individuals will count. Because people are assumed to be equally moral, the presumption of distributive justice will be equal shares. It is important to realize that this is only a presumption and that the distinction between this aspect of Rawls's theory and utilitarianism, especially Mill's utilitarianism, may be more apparent than real.

In Rawls's own terms, an equal distribution of rights may be overridden in certain situations for reasons very close to those that Mill stipulated for limiting equal liberty.[71] In addition, an unequal distribution of other primary goods can be justified by Rawls in the interests of the least advantaged. As we have seen, the most persuasive forms of utilitarianism – from the classical Benthamite to the Millean varieties — establish presumptions in favor of equal distribution of rights and other primary goods by virtue of the equality assumptions they attach to their method: that individuals have equal capacities for happiness, that the sources of their happiness are similar, that the marginal utility of a good decreases as the quantity possessed increases, and (in Mill's case) that equality of rights is the only way to ensure maximization of the total quantity of happiness throughout society.[72] Perhaps the more significant difference between the two theories is that in Rawls's terms an individual's rational interest in primary goods is the base line for measuring justice, whereas in utilitarian terms individual happiness or preference is the basic valued good. Even this sharp distinction begins to fade when Mill's utilitarianism is compared to Rawls's theory, because true happiness for Mill is ultimately judged by a standard that assimilates happiness to a rational system of desires, a system where rational preference and pleasure coincide.[73]

In addition, the method by which both theorists determine rational interests assumes that those interests – at least for purposes of distributive justice – are significantly similar. Rawls does this directly by means of the original position and the veil of ignorance, reducing people's interests to one equivalent set of interests in primary goods. Mill's theory does this somewhat less straightforwardly by introducing the choice criterion of pleasure, which says, in effect, that all people would prefer the higher over the lower pleasures were they rationally situated. So the egalitarian potential of both theories is made possible by their basic assumptions concerning the similarity of individual interests or sources of happiness and by the method by which those interests or preferences are to be aggregated.

The difference principle will often support a more equal distribution of goods than will the principle of maximizing average utility.[74] Nevertheless, if one packs into utilitarianism some very strong assumptions concerning interpersonal comparisons of utility, its distributive implications may come very close to those of Rawls's difference principle.[75] One might claim here that utilitarian theories possess no real techniques for measuring utility. The assumptions packed into this form of utilitarianism are likely to have been derived from some independent notion that egalitarian patterns of distribution are *desirable*, rather than from a true understanding of how to measure or compare utilities among persons.

Whichever theory one accepts, the egalitarian potential of liberal theory has been extended by methods that sanction looking beyond or beneath the revealed preferences and the particular interests of people – which are apparently very diverse – to interests both more universal and more hypothetical. The principles of liberal egalitarianism are still based upon an assessment of individual interests. Neither Mill nor Rawls derives individual interests from a logically prior conception of a just society or of an ideal social order. The individual interests upon which both Rawls and Mill base their theories of justice are clearly interests of socially conditioned individuals. Despite first appearances, the only people who can or must enter into the original position are those who already have certain firm convictions about equality and liberty. It is not a coincidence that these people (many of us) have shared a form of social life that professes to honor individual liberty and to respect human dignity. Because we cannot expect individuals' interests to extend beyond all social and historical boundaries, Rawls must claim that one significant – perhaps the ultimate – test of his theory is whether people already situated in a just society will agree to "reenter" the original position and, once there, to choose the two principles of justice. Mill's choice criterion suggests a similar, socially specific and circular, test. Our judgment of the desirability of social end states has thereby become an important – and in Rawls an explicit – justificatory consideration.

Mill and Rawls may remain liberal theorists, but they are theorists who push liberalism to an extremely attenuated form of individualism and to two extreme substantive positions regarding participatory and redistributive equality respectively. In Chapter 7, we shall push liberal theory one step further in an egalitarian direction by attempting to integrate these two central egalitarian concerns. But first we shall consider several of the more powerful criticisms directed against liberal egalitarianism from the left and the right.

Chapter 6

Contemporary critics of liberal egalitarianism: left and right

Some of the most controversial aspects of liberal egalitarianism have been taken for granted by its proponents. Our discussion has accepted as given certain Humean constraints, namely, a situation in which scarcity exists and in which human desires conflict.[1] We have also tacitly assumed that the liberal state can rightly distribute goods as if – to paraphrase Robert Nozick's critique – those goods came into the world as manna came to the Israelites in the desert, from heaven.[2] These assumptions can no longer remain tacit. Liberal egalitarianism confronts incisive critiques on two fronts: from the left, challenging acceptance of the Humean conditions of justice, and from the right, challenging the liberal state's right to redistribute goods according to any preconceived pattern.

The purpose of this chapter is to assess these challenges, as well as to take the opportunity to make more explicit the basic empirical and normative presuppositions of liberal egalitarianism. Any intellectually respectable theory must admit its limitations as well as its potentialities. The challenge from the left forces liberal egalitarianism to acknowledge certain significant limitations to its aspirations. The challenge from the right enables liberal egalitarianism to demonstrate that its principles are more consistent with the classical liberal assumptions of human equality than are the principles endorsed by its libertarian critics. We shall begin with the theorist I take to be the strongest critic of liberalism from the left, C. B. Macpherson,[3] and end by considering libertarian criticisms of liberal egalitarianism, focusing especially on Robert Nozick's critique.[4]

C. B. Macpherson views Rawls as the most recent in line of revisionist liberals who extend the implications of liberal theory to justify a "liberal-democratic capitalist welfare state."[5] Now this characterization does not obviously conflict with my own reading

145

of Rawls, nor is it necessarily a criticism. But Macpherson does intend to criticize the capitalist aspect of Rawls's endeavor:

His [Rawls's] explicit assumption is that institutionalized inequalities which affect men's whole life-prospects are "inevitable in any society"; and he is referring to inequalities between *classes* by income or wealth . . . Principles of justice designed to show when class inequalities are just do not go very deep. Of course, on his inevitability assumption, that is as deep as they can go. But the assumption is not self-evidently valid. A classless society, in his sense of class, that is, a society without classes which determine what the life prospects of their members are, is not unthinkable and not in principle impossible.[6]

Macpherson's attack on Rawls is characteristic of the dominant left criticism of revisionist liberalism, a criticism which is significant in that it implies a seriously inegalitarian, though perhaps often hidden, dimension of liberal egalitarianism. That inegalitarian dimension is captured by Macpherson's contention that liberalism, even of the Rawlsian form, assumes that institutionalized inequalities *between classes* are inevitable.[7] Macpherson and Marxist critics such as Richard Miller admit that inequalities would exist within a socialist society, but those inequalities that are not between economic classes would be significantly less disturbing.[8] This distinction between inequalities under capitalism and under socialism is relevant to Macpherson and other critics because it reflects a qualitative distinction between the way people relate to one another within the two societies. Inequalities between classes create unequal power relationships among individuals of those different classes; inequalities within a classless society will not entail unequal power relationships, assuming of course that those inequalities are limited by something like the difference principle.

Left critics therefore apply a standard of "equal power" to liberal egalitarian (or what Macpherson calls liberal democratic) theories of distributive justice. The concept of power subsumes a multiplicity of values and consequently may be more clearly understood when translated into a variety of other notions. Yet it has rarely, if ever, been clearly defined or dissected by liberal egalitarians or by critics of liberalism.[9] Macpherson begins to separate the bundle of meanings, concentrating on the ideal of self-development or maximization of human powers, but he provides few arguments for the connection between a severely restricted capitalism and unequal human development. We cannot investigate every meaning of power as commonly understood (nor would every meaning be of relevance to our discussion), but we shall examine two meanings that have appeared most significant to left critics of liberalism and then assess the justice of equalizing those forms of power from the perspective of Rawls's revisionist liberalism.[10]

Macpherson's discussion suggests that one disturbing form of power is that in which one person exerts direct power over another. It is of course very difficult to establish clear criteria that consistently accord with our commonsense judgments of when one person has power over another,[11] but suppose that we argue along with Marx that, by virtue of their relation to the means of production, members of the capitalist class exert power over members of the working class. This specific sort of unequal power relationship seems to be what Macpherson has in mind when he speaks of the exploitative nature of capitalist–worker relationships as the transfer of labor power from employee to employer.[12] Marxists would argue that this power relation is not primarily or interestingly personal, that it must be understood as more than the discrete contractual acts binding individual capitalists and workers. Personal capitalist–worker relations over time and taken together create institutionalized power relations, reflecting the power of one class of individuals over another. The aggregate effects of individual capitalist acts limit the quantity, type, and rewards of employment available at any given historical moment to members of the working class, whereas no single capitalist act considered in isolation would so limit working-class options.[13] A more subtle and indirect effect that has been considered in the same category of power is the injury to the self-respect of those subordinated in the productive process.[14]

Liberal egalitarianism cannot consistently permit institutionalized inequalities of this form of domination (assuming, of course, that we accept this description of capitalist–worker relations). The difference principle takes away from capitalists the collective power to determine wage rates. The fair equality-of-opportunity principle ensures ample training and employment for all. The equal-effective-rights principle is likely to necessitate a highly progressive rate of taxation upon owners of capital. And the argument that autocratically defined worker conditions have deprived workers of their self-respect opens the door to industrial democracy or, at the very least, to legislation of more attractive job possibilities (with or without grass-roots demand). Workers' acquiescence to the existing structure of employment may plausibly be explained as a consequence of the unattractive work opportunities available to them. Capitalism in the strict sense of private ownership may still remain after these policies have been instituted, but the state's regulative powers are intended to reduce significantly the structured inequalities of power between capitalists and workers that Marxists seek to overcome.

Instituting such broad and fairly comprehensive regulations on the power of capital could leave little incentive for private investment in capitalist enterprise, but we need not take this prospect to constitute an argument against regulation of free enterprise by government. The economic failure of regulated capitalism would be a reason to consider public investment in and ownership of industry suitably controlled at various levels by democratic decision-making processes. For if the capitalist structure of industry is exploitative and/or destructive of the self-respect of the least advantaged, public investment can justly replace private investment and at the same time avoid the sacrifice of equal power and self-respect, values prior to efficiency in all advanced industrial societies. (We must leave open the question whether an exception to this priority need be made for the least-developed countries.)

Rawls illustrates his principles by reference to a capitalist economy. But that structure of property ownership cannot consistently be taken as an essential assumption of Rawls's, or of any liberal egalitarian, theory. Rawls himself defends private ownership as more protective of individual liberty than a state socialist system is likely to be, much as Mill argued that an *ideal* system of private ownership would be superior to state socialism in protecting and encouraging individual freedom and self-development.[15] Yet if Macpherson's claim is correct that "substantial equality in liberty and personal rights . . . is inconsistent in a capitalist market society,"[16] – even a capitalist society of the extremely restricted sort permitted by Rawlsian principles – then liberal egalitarianism must look for a more equitable, socialist system that will adequately preserve individual rights and liberties and fair equality of opportunity.

Rawls's explicit priorities are very close to Mill's on this issue. Mill acknowledged in the *Principles* that a socialist system would be a far superior alternative to his present-day capitalist society. But he also maintained that socialism would be second best to a well-ordered free-enterprise system.[17] Although Rawls's conception of a well-ordered alternative to socialism certainly differs from Mill's, the values underlying their preferences for free enterprise over state ownership (the pursuit of one's own conception of the good, self-development, and the preservation of the fair value of liberty) are very similar. Both diverge from Macpherson's belief that private enterprise in any form will inevitably (but unnecessarily) distort the equal effective rights and liberties of the many, in the interests of the few. Yet Rawls and Mill agree that the question which system – restricted capitalism or socialism – is better is an empirical one. In theory, neither disagrees with Macpherson's contention: The system that maximizes individual liberty and the opportunities for self-development must be considered the more just one.[18]

As I have suggested, even if in theory Rawls can meet a Marxist critique, in practice the implementation of the difference principle coupled with fair equality of opportunity may be incompatible with the preservation of a private-enterprise system of any sort. Liberal egalitarianism would then converge with a Marxist theory on this point, advocating a democratic socialist form of property ownership. Yet one important distinction between the two theories remains. Like Mill's theory, Rawls's conception of justice – and, I take it, any revised form of liberal egalitarianism – will establish a presumption in favor of maintaining individual rights, liberties, and self-development. The burden of proof in liberal theory will always fall upon those who would maintain that private enterprise is necessarily incompatible with establishing a fair value of liberty or equal self-respect for the least advantaged. Critics will be hard pressed to demonstrate that an alternative system of property ownership would better fulfill the principles of justice. They will be forced by liberal egalitarians, for example, to face the problems of decentralizing political power in state-controlled industries so as to avoid the concentration of political power in the hands of a bureaucratic, though publicly legitimated, elite. They will also be pressed to explain why entrepreneurs can still be said to exploit workers in a situation in which all workers have reasonably attractive job opportunities and in which the activities of all entrepreneurs are closely regulated by the state.

Marxists, on the other hand, place the burden of proof upon the liberal theorist who assumes that a restricted private-ownership system can be made compatible with the standard of equal power among persons. They point in disbelief of revisionist liberals to the wide-scale distributive injustices of present-day capitalist societies and to the translation of economic into political influence, if not power. Revisionist liberals often cite the record of existing socialist countries that systematically undermine the most basic of civil and political liberties. But direct evidence from existing societies can neither prove nor disprove either ideal case. That is one reason why the initial burden of proof is a significant distinguishing feature of the revisionist liberal and Marxist positions with regard to the institutional means necessary to equalize power relations among classes of people. Otherwise, Marxists and liberal egalitarians agree in theory on the need for equalizing this form of power, so as to avoid institutionalized class domination.

A second form of power is more simply the power to act: A's ability to do x, or become x, where x is something that A desires to do or become. This form of power is closely identified with the ideal of self-development or self-realization, a value on which Mill and the young Marx both placed great emphasis. The equalization of this power is a standard central to Macpherson's case against classical liberalism and, by extension, a standard against which he critically measures Rawls's liberal theory.

Macpherson defines this form of power as *developmental* – "a man's ability to use and develop his capacities" – and contrasts it to the *extractive* form of power, which he claims that classical liberalism sanctioned: "The latter ability is power over others, the ability to extract benefits from others."[19] The previous chapter dealt with a specific manifestation of developmental coupled with extractive power – the ability of people with greater income and wealth to participate more effectively in the political process. As long as this imbalance exists, liberal egalitarianism must insist upon a greater dispersion of income and wealth. But in considering people's ability to develop themselves either as they will or to the utmost of their abilities, Macpherson expands the goal of equalizing power to realms outside the narrowly political, concluding that

any adequate twentieth-century democratic theory, since it must treat democracy as a kind of society and must treat the individual members as at least potentially doers rather than mere consumers, must assert *an equal effective right of the members to use and develop their human capacities:* each must be enabled to do so, whether or not each actually does so.[20]

It is not easy to understand what equalizing power in this sense might mean in actual social life other than (1) abolishing the unequal power that some men now have to *extract* benefits from others *forcibly* and (2) providing people with equal opportunity to pursue their preferred conceptions of the good life. In any fuller sense of an effective right to self-realization, liberal egalitarianism would not grant *equal* power to all citizens (although, again, it is not clear what such an effective right would mean in practice).

If it would mean radically equalizing income or wealth,

Macpherson's goal would contradict one purpose of the difference principle: that of allowing inequalities of income or wealth when these benefit the less advantaged (in this case, those with less effective ability to develop themselves). The difference principle sanctions unequal power as long as that inequality indirectly serves to increase the effective opportunities of the least advantaged (who are likely to be the least powerful in this second sense). Again, there are serious and specific limits to the inequalities the difference principle will permit in the name of equalizing life prospects. Nevertheless, the alternative of radically equalizing developmental power is irrational from the point of view of nonenvious individuals in the original position, so long as it means trading a higher level of power (measured absolutely) for a lower though equal level of power (measured in comparison to others). Of course, if scarcity conditions do not apply, as Macpherson sometimes assumes, no conflict need exist between the two criteria. It would then be in the interests of the least advantaged and in the spirit of equal moral persons to equalize developmental power.[21] Under such conditions, "from each according to his (freely employed) ability, to each according to his developmental powers," would be a painlessly simple and morally attractive distributive principle. I suppose that in this situation we would be spared the problem of distinguishing developmental powers from mere wants or frivolous and possibly ever-expanding desires.

Here we encounter a crucial difference between liberal egalitarians and their radical critics: Liberal theorists accept the Humean circumstances of justice as fair background constraints on moral and political theorizing. Macpherson – like Marx and Marcuse – rejects the idea that the Humean conditions of justice can fairly restrict a theorist's vision of a just society. He does so for two reasons consistent with those of many other contemporary radical critics. He believes that advanced industrial societies will soon enter (if they have not already entered) into a period of surplus production, where surplus is defined as production beyond that required to satisfy people's objectively determined needs. And he also assumes that human nature is so constituted that a rational organization of social institutions will create a new structure of consciousness. Citizens will desire fewer material goods and only those goods essential to satisfying their "developmental powers."[22] Mill's vision of a stationary state comes as close to this radical vision of plenty as does that of any liberal theorist. Yet Mill's theory of distributive justice does not depend upon transcending conditions of scarcity and conflict, as do the theories of radical critics of liberalism from Marx to Marcuse and Macpherson.[23]

If one assumes the Humean conditions of justice, the radical vision of a society that attempts to maximize every individual's ability to be or to do x, where x is anything a person "really" desires to be or to do, will appear to be at best a utopian vision or at worst a vision of perpetual warfare, akin to Hobbes's state of nature.[24] Macpherson rightly avoids this interpretation of the equal-power ideal by distinguishing "essentially human" capacities from other capacities, the former being those talents whose exercise would be harmonious with or beneficial to the development of all other individuals' powers or capacities.[25] He then distinguishes a man's *power* from his *capacities:*

The amount of a man's capacities – physical, mental, and psychic – is neither the same as, nor necessarily correlated with, the amount of his ability to use them. The latter depends on present external impediments; the former on innate endowment and past external impediments . . . It therefore seems best to keep "power" for the actual ability to exercise one's capacities, and to use "capacities" for what is there to be exercised.[26]

So it is the equalization of power as distinct from capacities that Macpherson endorses. Given this distinction, it is less clear what equalizing power will entail, aside from ensuring fair equality of opportunity and the fair value of liberty.

These two qualifications on equalizing individual developmental power bring Macpherson very close to endorsing the difference principle constrained by fair equality of opportunity. Rawls of course emphasizes the justice of the *process* entailed in equalizing power: No one should be *forced* to develop those capacities that are "essentially human" or beneficial to other members of society.[27] But Macpherson also seems to concur on this point in his recent work.[28] He does not wish to accept a nonliberal vision of a society in which the state must force people to develop those capacities that are harmonious with those of other citizens.

So long as a realm of free individual choice is protected, the remaining difference between Macpherson's view and Rawls's consists in Macpherson's faith that under the proper circumstances people will freely and equally choose to develop those capacities that are harmonious with and beneficial to the self-development of others: "The case for a democratic *society* fails without the assumption of potential substantial harmony."[29] Indeed, Macpherson claims that democratic liberals have also accepted such a vision of potential social harmony: "That view has always been at the root of the democratic vision . . . Men's very visible contentiousness might be attributed to intellectual error or to scarcity: both conditions were assumed to be removable."[30] Macpherson's final case against Rawls's form of liberal egalitarianism therefore rests upon the possibility of transcending social conflict, thereby eliminating the need for external constraints on individual behavior in protection of rights and liberties, or constraints on the resource demands of individual conceptions of the good. In eliminating one of the largest sources of potential conflict among persons (once capitalist relations of production are abolished, scarcity is overcome and "inherited intellectual error" consequently fades away), Macpherson has effectively eliminated the major problem giving rise to the modern liberal view of social justice. Liberals have always assumed the existence of at least some conflict among individual interests, desires, and self-fulfillments, given the constraints of scarcity and the possibility if not likelihood of intellectual error.[31]

The alternative, radical formulation of the conditions for a fully egalitarian theory rejects the very limits within which liberal egalitarian theory operates: the assumption of scarcity and potential conflict among individuals' freely chosen life plans.[32] This rejection most often is tied to an argument for socializing the means of production so as to eliminate the major remaining source of competitive egoistic (or possessive individualistic) behavior among citizens,[33] an argument implicit in Marx's early writings and in Marcuse's work (although how to effect a socialization of the means of production remains very problematic in Marcuse's writings).

Another way of interpreting Macpherson's argument would suggest that his critique is not peculiarly radical in this sense but rather is one that disputes the prevailing empirical assumption of classical liberalism: that a private property system can be rendered consistent with the principle of equal effective liberty. On this interpretation, Macpherson and Rawls agree that the power of citizens to pursue their freely chosen life plans must be regulated by a democratic state endorsing and enforcing similar principles of justice, but disagree on what economic structure is compatible with the principle of maximizing effective liberty (of the least advantaged).

The underlying disagreement is whether economic relationships between workers and owners of capital are necessarily exploitative. Macpherson's definition of exploitation – transferring to oneself for one's own benefit some of the powers of others – requires clarification, because Macpherson does not appear to have a strict Marxist theory of surplus value in mind. Let us assume that exploitation on a common understanding of the term entails a one-sided rather than mutual transferral of powers, one that is not in the best interests of the exploited in its *results* and is involuntary (again on the part of the exploited) in its *process*.[34] Macpherson's case against a liberal egalitarian society based upon limited private ownership could very plausibly be that any private employment relationship (1) involves a disadvantageous transferral of powers from production in the worker's own interests to production for the capitalist's interests, and (2) rests upon the involuntary choice of employment by a worker, where both (1) and (2) would not occur under a more just, socialist economic system.

In a full-employment economy, where the state taxes profits at a high rate and ensures equal opportunity to all its citizens, would conditions (1) and (2) still obtain? If the choice of work processes offered to employees continued to be very limited under even a broadly regulated form of private ownership, then the involuntariness criterion still would hold.[35] We might also find that the liberal egalitarian state could not succeed in taxing profits at the optimal rate (for the least advantaged) owing to the collective power of capitalists to withhold information, to collude informally, to restrict entry into their businesses (or professions), to influence political representatives, or to use any of a large number of other means businessmen have used in the past to exert undue power over the political process and (indirectly at least) over workers and other consumers. Macpherson is therefore correct in calling for a theory of the state to resolve the controversy between liberal democrats and their radical critics.[36] What is needed most crucially is a theory addressing the question how autonomous a fully democratic and egalitarian state can be vis-à-vis private enterprise.[37] Liberal egalitarians certainly ought to concur with Macpherson on this point.[38]

There are of course radical grounds of dispute distinct from those upon which Macpherson concentrates his critique of liberal egalitarianism. In an article entitled "Rawls and Marxism," Richard Miller examines several alternative Marxist grounds, the most significant being a psychological critique of the very possibility of Rawls's derivation of justice from the original position and a sociological critique of the possibility of realizing an egalitarian society.[39] Rather than directly denying the justice of Rawls's principles, Miller denies the very possibility of conceiving of justice in a

Rawlsian manner, or of imagining its practical import. Miller contends that people, blinded by their class perspective, cannot possibly imagine themselves in an original position from which just principles, ones impartial by class, can be derived.[40] He then claims that even were such a derivation possible, it would be practically impossible to realize a just society, given the bourgeoisie's inevitable resistance to a major redistribution of primary goods by the state.[41]

At first sight, it is difficult to respond to Miller directly other than on empirical grounds, because he radically rejects the very enterprise of liberal theory.[42] To Miller's first critique, one might cite the counter evidence of the bourgeois origins of many twentieth-century egalitarian and radical social theorists. However, the radical or egalitarian theorists who arise in contemporary liberal societies are admittedly few, and their existence cannot establish that individuals in contemporary societies have a general or extensive capacity to project themselves in thought into something resembling the original position. The more forceful reply to Miller's first criticism is that neither Rawls nor any liberal egalitarian theorist need assume that most people are capable *or* willing to imagine themselves in an original position from which just principles can be derived. If correct, Miller's point demonstrates at most that liberal egalitarian theories will not be persuasive to people in a bourgeois society, not that liberal egalitarian theory is unjustified. The former, in any case, is an odd claim for a Marxist critic of liberalism to make.[43]

A reply to Miller's second claim can also be made on empirical grounds. Members of the bourgeoisie have in the past acquiesced under great pressure to social policies that favor the working class. Marx suggested that such acquiescence was possible even before the event of imminent proletarian revolution.[44] Clearly, this is not to say that the bourgeoisie as a class will advocate and support such policies prior to their institutionalization. But one can plausibly claim that violent revolution is not the only possible means (even in Marxist theory) to meaningful egalitarian reform. Marx himself implied that universal manhood suffrage might be an important and effective step in the immediate interests of the proletariat, and against the long-term interests of the bourgeoisie.[45] The psychological view Miller supports would exclude both the possibility of the bourgeois origins of radical theory and that of bourgeois concessions to egalitarian reform. Historical affirmations of both possibilities could lend credence to the more optimistic psychological postulates of Rawls's liberal egalitarianism.

Although a more extensive argument on historical grounds lies beyond the scope of this essay, another, again more forceful, response to Miller's second claim is possible on theoretical grounds: that liberal egalitarianism no more than Marxism depends for its validity upon the easy or gradual transition to its preferred end state. Liberals too can justify, and have justified, revolutions, especially in situations where recourse to peaceful means of transition have failed.

THE LIBERTARIAN CRITIQUE

Whereas the left has attacked liberal egalitarianism for subordinating equal human development to unequal economic power, the libertarian right has taken the egalitarian component of revisionist liberalism as its prime target of criticism.[46] We have just argued that the left critique, to the extent that it remains a radical one, consists largely of a disagreement concerning the possibility of realizing a society in which the constraints of distributive justice are superfluous. Liberal egalitarianism rejects, at least implicitly, this anti-Humean component of radical thought. Principles like the difference principle, and their minimal but nevertheless inegalitarian possibilities, are assumed necessary because individuals are believed to be (at least to some extent) separate albeit equal systems of desires. Critics on the right, on the other hand, propose to take more seriously than do liberal egalitarians the fact of individual separateness. Because they also generally honor the liberal belief in individual equality (at least insofar as they support equal civil rights), we must ask how and why the balance between equality and liberty is differentially determined by libertarian and egalitarian liberals, and which balance is the correct one.

Nozick, for example, straightforwardly tells us at the outset of *Anarchy, State and Utopia* that "individuals have rights, and that there are things no person or group may do to them (without violating their rights)."[47] In a direct attack upon liberal egalitarian conceptions of justice, Nozick wants to demonstrate that when one begins an investigation of social justice with an assertion of individual rights, one must end with a minimal collective power – a power stripped of all redistributive functions – one just barely large enough to be recognized as a state: the monopolizer of the legitimate use of physical force in a given territory.[48] Given that liberal egalitarians do not want to forsake either the foundations of classical liberalism or the language of individual rights, we must ask whether the libertarian challenge is correct: that the equality assumptions of classical liberalism cannot legitimately yield egalitarian conclusions.

The equality libertarian theorists claim to honor is that equality among people which gives us all equal rights to life, liberty, and property. Some libertarian theorists, of whom John Hospers is an example, explicitly consider these rights a trilogy.[49] Others, like Nozick, view every individual's claim to liberty as the primary right that necessarily entails a right to life and to property.[50] But all libertarian thinkers agree that the right to (almost completely) unfettered private property is one without which the rights to life and to liberty are rendered meaningless or at best completely ineffective.[51] So we are then led to wonder why it is that the right to unfettered private property is so closely bound up in libertarian thought with the basic rights to life and to liberty of all persons considered as equal moral beings.[52]

Our wonderment begins to be abated as we are reintroduced to the Lockean notion of self-ownership. At the root of "the political philosophy that is called libertarianism (from the Latin *libertas*, liberty) is the doctrine that every person is the owner of his own life, and that no one is the owner of anyone else's life." *I am mine*, and therefore I have the "right to act in accordance with [my] own choices unless those actions infringe on the equal liberty of other human beings to act in accordance with *their* choices."[53] Contemporary libertarians thus begin with a view like Locke's, that people "own themselves," that they therefore have a right to their natural assets, and that such a right necessarily entails both a right to use their assets freely and a right to whatever flows from that use, provided they do not infringe upon other people's natural rights or entitlements. All assume that the right to private property, income, and wealth directly flows from this free use of human assets.[54] One might begin by asking, Upon what grounds does a man's right to his own natural assets also entail an entitlement to whatever flows from the use of those assets (given, of course, nonviolation of other people's rights)? A fair Lockean interpretation of the libertarian argument would be that (1) because no one else deserves the fruits of a person's labor, and (2) because it is *that* person's own actions which produced those fruits, (3) it is only he who is entitled to such *self*-generated holdings. The Lockean libertarian maxim might then become "to each according to the fruits of his (successful or unsuccessful) efforts."

But how far along the libertarian path does this reasoning get us? The market, even the *free* market, is obviously not anyone's self-generated system. The market's smooth functioning is only guaranteed by every individual's compliance with its rules, and even the particular rewards accruing to any individual transaction are determined only by the aggregate pattern of supply and demand resulting from each person's participation or nonparticipation. And what of joint products of labor, which are progressively more common under advanced industrial conditions? How is an individual acting "freely" to lay claim to his share of the joint product? And given a "free" market, who is to ensure that private contracts are honored, that transgressions of the market process are prevented, or transgressors punished? A publicly funded state? Then again, market rewards will not be the sole consequence of a particular individual's talents, skills, or services. It is therefore clear that an individual's efforts or actions alone (no matter how responsible in the Lockean sense) do not generate the monetary rewards the market brings. Nor are a person's rewards generated by the actions of those who buy his goods or services.[55] Following libertarian reasoning, should not the rewards that accrue to each individual be divided according to some rule of proportionate contribution among all those who have made that system's smooth functioning and particular distribution possible?

If it is more than just my own action, my effort, my luck, or my fortunate social position that generates my market price, why then am I solely entitled to whatever "flows" in this extremely mediated manner from my actions? Lacking an answer to this challenge, the libertarian's attack on taxation – the most apparent means of welfare-state provision for basic needs – is seriously weakened. Consequently, Nozick's analogy of taxation to forced labor and Hosper's analogy of taxation to legalized plunder both fail.[56] The analogies are convincing only on the assumption that people's *holdings* (accruing from the workings of a free market), are, as Nozick claims, on "a par with" their *actions*.[57] But individuals cannot be considered the sole generators and therefore the absolute proprietors of their productions even if they can or should be considered fully responsible for their actions, as the strong sense of Lockean self-ownership would have us accept. Nozick's claim that "things come into the world already attached to people having entitlements over them" may be true, but it is not obvious which people have the entitlements.[58] So despite what contemporary libertarians claim, it is not clear that Locke's theory commits us to considering taxation on a par with forced labor. If our argument is correct, Locke need not have been contradicting his postulate of equal self-ownership in sanctioning taxation (with majority consent).[59]

Even if one begins with a view of human rights as property rights in oneself – a view that Macpherson, despite his earlier critique of Locke, has recently recommended[60] – one must consider what the conditions for the free exercise of those property rights are.[61] By any broad view of property rights, those preconditions must include public provision of basic individual welfare, because the Lockean condition of bountiful unclaimed property ("enough and as good left for others") no longer obtains in any contemporary society.[62] The remaining problem in Locke's theory is why even a majority need consent. But at least the potential limitation upon the exercise of private property rights that Locke's theory admits is more consistent with his initial equality assumptions than is the principle of absolute (or near absolute) private dominion supported by contemporary libertarians.

Contemporary libertarians want to embrace the free-market principle even though the justifying reasons Locke gave can no longer hold today. The Lockean labor theory of acquisition is just only if after each person has acquired property on the basis of his own labor, enough and as good remains for all other persons to acquire.[63] A neo-Lockean cannot in good faith embrace the same free-market principle under circumstances that do not permit freedom in the form of equality of basic economic opportunity. So libertarians, in the professed spirit of Locke, put themselves in the untenable position of rallying around a procedural principle that no longer has any basis in Lockean reasoning. Similarly, the simpler principle of acquisition explicitly put forth by some libertarians – that of "first come, first served" – cannot be justified unless the first served do not in effect deprive the last of the opportunity to help themselves.[64] One critic of Nozick very aptly sketched a scenario of the landing of the Mayflower: One enterprising Pilgrim immediately runs onto shore and lays claim to an enormous tract of land, while his fellow Pilgrims remain on board long enough to agree upon a political constitution. On libertarian grounds, so much the worse for the communally minded Pilgrims.[65]

Some libertarians concede that after so many generations of property usurpations and contractual frauds, it may now be necessary to redistribute property more equally in order to begin fairly the free-market process. But this limited concession will not suffice, because it still leaves libertarians without any acceptable means of justifying the very limited and unequal life chances that inheritance is likely to create for future generations.[66] If no substantive welfare principles are built into a conception of distributive justice, there will be a perpetual need for a rectification principle so as to get the market process going fairly for each new generation, on these quasi-Lockean grounds. Egalitarian principles of justice are no more disruptive of people's life plans and expectations than a libertarian rectification principle.

DISTRIBUTION ACCORDING TO DESERT REJECTED

If the right to the full product of one's labor does not sanction an unrestricted market and if each individual's right to liberty does not preclude taxation for purposes of individual welfare, the libertarian argument can still fall back upon the intuitive maxim of distribution according to individual desert or merit, where desert is measured by an individual's talent, effort, or voluntary contribution to the public good.

The particular examples libertarians cite often suggest that people's holdings are the result of hard work, applied skill, unusual talent, great contribution to the welfare of others, or a combination of all four factors. It is significant that most of the examples libertarians offer to counter egalitarian claims to a more equal distribution of goods imply that some people *merit* or *deserve* more than liberal egalitarians are willing to let individuals in society give them. For example, Nozick appeals to our intuitive notion that there are cases in which liberal justice should, but cannot, recognize and reward talent, hard work, and contribution to public welfare or happiness, whereas libertarianism can. The Wilt Chamberlain example is by now the best known. Let us say that each of one million fans is willing to pay 25 cents of the total admission price directly to Wilt to see him play basketball. Nozick wants us to ask, Is not Chamberlain *entitled* to keep his $250,000?[67] But are we really wondering instead, on being asked this question, Does not Wilt Chamberlain *deserve* his $250,000? Can libertarians possibly divorce their view of just entitlement to goods from a theory of differential deserts, without sacrificing the major intuitive appeal of their case for the free market?[68] On the basis of the failure of their argument from individual freedom alone, I would reply no. Yet I shall argue shortly that the libertarian argument from desert also fails.

Nozick gives other examples that might be thought to appeal to our sense of just deserts: among them, a philosophy professor who lectures overtime in a socialist society in order to earn enough for his own private library.[69] Yet is there any reason to believe that a libertarian state will better reward talent and hard work than would an egalitarian one? Perhaps the Wilt Chamberlains of our society will be well taken care of in Nozick's utopia, but will the Fouriers and Einsteins and those public-spirited or private, law-abiding citizens whose talents are not so marketable?[70]

Herbert Spencer explicitly set out a libertarian argument based on desert conceived of as achievement in the capitalist marketplace (not as effort). As David Miller has recently pointed out, Spencer assumed that the laissez-faire principle of freedom was equivalent to the desert principle as a statement of justice.[71] Contemporary libertarians avoid the explicit use of desert arguments because they realize that any end-state principle of the form "from each according to his ———, to each according to his ———," might in theory justify placing restrictions upon the pure procedural justice of the free market.[72] In particular, they may recognize that a market — even a perfectly competitive market – will often fail to identify and reward social desert as commonly considered.

So contemporary libertarians have avoided an internal contradiction by explicitly denying that a laissez-faire economic principle must rest upon a principle of social desert or merit. But they have at the same time forsaken the moral underpinnings of their conception of individual freedom. Unlike Spencer, Nozick leaves us completely unenlightened as to *why* we ought to accept his particular understanding of individual freedom as entitlement to possess, to buy, and to sell property within a laissez-faire market system. Furthermore, unless one believes that libertarian principles are based at least in part upon an argument about individual merit or desert, it is hard to understand what underlies efforts such as Nozick's to argue against liberal egalitarianism on the grounds that it does not admit the idea that an individual can merit or deserve certain goods.[73]

A desert argument based upon Lockean assumptions can be made to justify the market process of generating entitlements. One must assume, as Spencer seemed to, that people's contributions to social value are measured by the price they receive for their goods or services on the free market, and that people deserve that price by virtue of their own efforts. A more qualified desert argument might be that people deserve to be rewarded for their contributions (regardless of effort) to the sum of valued goods in society and that a free market measures this form of desert (contributions of social value) better than could any alternative system. A qualified desert argument of this kind at least provides a logically sound answer to the question why the process of the market fully legitimates the individual holdings *it* (at least in large part) generates.

But this theoretical defense raises the crucial question whether the free market in practice comes closer to measuring social worth than any alternative system could. Only if we discount the pervasiveness of externalities unmeasured by the market mechanism and the failure of a free market to provide for collective goods can we simply answer yes.[74] And even were we to answer yes, we would still not have addressed the question whether this form of social desert is an appropriate standard for distributive justice.

Liberal egalitarians reject the libertarian solution to distributive justice because it sanctions the distribution of primary goods, particularly economic rewards, according to factors that are morally arbitrary. Rawls tells us that the greater income that might accrue to some people in accordance with the difference principle, no less than the rewards of an absolutely free market, will be undeserved even though people are *entitled* to the former for other reasons. Then why not substitute distribution according to effort for market success? Rawls argues that "once again . . . it seems clear that the effort a person is willing to make is influenced by his natural abilities and skills and the alternatives open to him. The better endowed are more likely, other things equal, to strive conscientiously, and there seems to be no way to discount for their greater good fortune."[75] Nozick launches a serious attack upon Rawls's argument here. He claims that the line of argument underlying selection of the two principles rather than the libertarian system of natural liberty denigrates a person's autonomy

by attributing *everything* noteworthy about the person completely to . . . external factors. So denigrating a person's autonomy and prime responsibility for his actions is a risky line to take for a theory that otherwise wishes to buttress the dignity and self-respect of autonomous beings; especially for a theory that founds so much (including a theory of the good) upon persons' choices. One doubts that the unexalted picture of human beings Rawls' theory presupposes and rests upon can be made to fit together with the view of human dignity it is designed to lead to and embody.[76]

Is there any sense in which liberal egalitarianism recognizes individual merit, and if not, is this omission a morally problematic one? Now, Rawls, Nozick, and I take it that all liberal theorists agree (1) that people do not *deserve* their natural assets or their initial starting place in society, (2) that the foundations of desert need not be deserved all the way down (otherwise it would never make sense to say that a person deserves anything), and (3) that people have a *right* to their natural assets. But why is it that Rawls says that people do not *deserve* the extra fruits their talents bring them?

Rawls does of course point out that some people are simply lucky in being better endowed than others with natural talents that attract a high price on the open market. But suppose you work very hard to develop your talents (while your neighbor, equally endowed, does not). Nozick argues that Rawls's conception of justice diminishes the importance of *your* efforts to develop those talents by claiming that the efforts people contribute to developing their capacities are causally dependent upon their positions in society, which themselves are undeserved (not *self*-determined). Nozick might then add: Suppose you believed that there is a "you" down there who works very hard to develop your talents; would you then deserve the extra benefits your talents could bring? What might a liberal egalitarian reply?

If egalitarians claim that individuals never can be said to *deserve* what they receive for their labors, then they indeed appear to be denying the possibility of any correct use of the word desert. This would, I think, constitute a serious indictment of liberal egalitarianism.[77] So we must ask: Given Rawls's professed uncertainty of the extent to which people are responsible for their achievements,[78] what would it mean to say a person is morally deserving in the strict sense of having responsibly earned the benefits that accrue to his actions? Nozick's criticism suggests that the notion of desert is indeed meaningless given Rawls's argument, insofar as Rawls denies that people are *ever* responsible for developing their own talents or expending their own effort in the public interest.[79]

Nozick's criticism is wrong, however. Liberal egalitarians can consistently argue that the notion of desert is meaningful but that, for both moral and practical reasons, it is applicable only to micro-situations rather than to distributive principles that are regulative of the basic structure of a society.[80] Rawls does make a practical argument about why institutions of distributive justice could not be based on the principle of rewarding people for their efforts: that effort is extraordinarily difficult to measure on an extensive, comparative scale.[81] There are also a number of significant moral arguments about why distribution according to desert would be an undesirable distributive maxim.

The more intimately we know a person, the more likely are our statements about his personal desert to be well founded. But, given our limited knowledge of how social and economic factors coupled with chance differentially affect people's conscientious (or successful) efforts to be productive and to satisfy other people's wants, a social institution that claimed to reward people in proportion to such desert would be suspect. Liberal egalitarianism then can be plausibly interpreted as making the following claims:

1. No one deserves his natural assets.
2. Some persons are more responsible than other, similarly advantaged persons for cultivating those assets.
3. It has generally been easier for the initially more advantaged to make responsible efforts to cultivate their talents.
4. Therefore, some people can be legitimately said to deserve more than others, but one cannot legitimately judge comparative desert on the broad institutional scale necessary to distributive justice.[82]

Thus liberal egalitarian theory can admit with complete consistency the existence of free choice – that people are even to a large extent free to develop their potentialities – while at the same time maintaining that social institutions cannot judge desert in practice.

I have argued so far only that liberal egalitarian theory does not purport to make a case against the idea that people may deserve certain honors, rewards, and praise. But I also want to explore the reasons liberal egalitarians can give for justifying a society in which social goods will not be distributed according to differential desert.[83] The reasons can perhaps be best illustrated with reference to Rawls's difference principle, because the libertarian challenge to egalitarianism does not arise as directly or consistently when the distribution of civil and political liberties is considered.

Although the members of the most advantaged group in a Rawlsian society will be *entitled* to greater holdings only if they benefit the least advantaged, there is no underlying assumption that they will therefore be more *deserving* of their greater shares. To make such a judgment, society would have to be based upon a full theory of the good which stipulated that contribution to the social store of primary goods was a basic measure of a person's social worth. Neither the difference principle nor any liberal egalitarian distributive principle can be grounded upon such a social ethic. It is certainly plausible to believe that some people will be more talented than others in providing those goods. But so long as one is faithful to the view of equal moral persons with which classical liberalism began, one will deny the validity of any attempt to stipulate a theory of individual worth that considers maximization of social welfare a morally necessary constituent of every individual's life plan.

One of the attractions of Rawls's difference principle is that it upholds a conception of human equality without forcing upon individuals a uniform conception of the good life. In addition, a commitment to this conception of individuals as equal moral persons provides a compelling rationale for rejecting distributive principles based directly upon individual merit and those based upon Nozick's libertarian maxim, from each as he chooses, to each as he is chosen.[84] By eliminating knowledge of our natural assets from the original position, Rawls precludes any possibility of our choosing either a distribution based directly on differential desert or an entitlement principle such as Nozick's, based on "natural liberty."[85] But a hypothetical social-contract view can provide a more persuasive rationale for the elimination of this knowledge than is conveyed by Rawls's assertion that our natural assets are "arbitrary from a moral point of view."

Although there is no more moral reason why people should be born rational than why they should be born talented,[86] a plausible reason still can be given why Rawls includes rationality as a criterion for individual choice yet excludes knowledge of other human attributes from the original position. The original position creates an egalitarian perspective by including only knowledge of those individual attributes that characterize people as equal moral beings: "The purpose of these conditions is to represent equality between human beings as moral persons, as creatures having a conception of their good and capable of a sense of justice."[87] It is on the basis of those traits that characterize us as equal rational and moral beings – capable of giving our lives meaning and of recognizing political and moral duties and obligations – that we are differentiated from other animals, and that political societies are therefore capable of distinguishing between those beings who are to be accorded equal rights and those who (or which) are not. It is not that talents and other characteristics that differentiate among individuals are arbitrary from all moral points of view but that these characteristics are not necessary to, and may distort, the process by which people who share certain essential equalities are to consider themselves partners to a political and social contract.

Were a just society created, we would not need simply to assume that all people were equal by virtue of their minimum human capacities and therefore entitled to equal welfare rights. Having been granted these rights, we would all demonstrate ourselves worthy of this assumption (and worthy of at least *some* of those rights) by abiding by the rules of a just society.[88] The plausibility of this characterization of people is of course also significantly enhanced by its provision of a firm and credible basis (at present lacking in libertarian theory) for the mutually accepted judgment by libertarians and liberal egalitarians alike that all individuals should be accorded equal rights to life and to civil liberties.[89]

Essential to Rawls's and to any liberal egalitarian conception of justice is the assumption that we have a fundamental interest in ensuring our self-respect in any society that we enter. The institutions of a just society must therefore affirm the equal moral worth of all citizens. This requirement places significant constraints upon the operation of a distributive principle, namely: (1) the distributive principle should minimize the degree to which the effective liberty of individuals to pursue their life plans is reduced by those attributes and contingencies that are not essential to their characterization as free and equal moral persons; (2) the distributive principle should help all individuals pursue their own conceptions of the good (for it is in large part by virtue of their freedom to pursue their life plans that men and women affirm their moral being) and therefore should not, if possible, favor certain conceptions of the good over others; and (3) the distributive criterion in its role as a publicly known principle should reaffirm *belief* in the moral equality of all citizens.[90]

Now each of these constraining criteria militates against choosing either the libertarian conception of justice or a distributive principle based directly on desert: the first because our deserts and market prices are intimately linked to our natural talents and to other factors beyond our control, whereas our effective liberty to pursue freely chosen life plans is dependent on the resources to which we are entitled; the second because a distributive principle based on desert or on market price is likely to attach so great a reward to those of us whose conceptions of the good contribute to the store of goods other people desire as to make it difficult for others to pursue their conceptions of the good successfully; and the third because both desert principles and libertarian entitlement conceptions are unpatterned principles of justice that will, in theory at least, permit a wide and ever-widening gap between the welfare of the most- and least-advantaged groups in society, and, in the case of desert maxims, that gap may be further widened by public belief that the most advantaged are also the most worthy.

There is one common sense of the concept desert according to which it is fitting to say that egalitarianism distributes social goods in line with (although not in proportion to) desert.[91] The basis for this kind of desert is not any specific action a person performs but simply the minimum conditions of being human (manifesting reason and desire) and being a law-abiding member of a well-ordered society. To say that someone deserves a minimum standard of living is much like saying that he has a right to that treatment. This congruence of usage is interesting insofar as it may suggest some situations in which our notions of what people naturally *deserve* and what they are (or should be) *entitled* to in a well-ordered society are the same. With reference to what we consider essential social goods, to say that people deserve those goods and that they have a right to them may be two sides of the same moral argument: In both cases we are referring to our basic moral intuition that people deserve certain goods (consistent of course with other people's deserts) in virtue of being moral and rational beings. Given my previous analysis of the liberal egalitarian commitment to viewing people as free and equal moral beings, it is not surprising that this is the only sense of desert that may plausibly be said to underlie liberal egalitarian principles of distributive justice.

EQUALITY AND THE NATURE OF JUSTIFICATION

A critical question concerning the relationship between human equality and distribution remains to be raised from a libertarian perspective. Are these minimal capacities for rational and moral personality sufficient to justify the advantages conferred on individuals by egalitarian distributive principles? Libertarians believe that the present welfare states in the United States and Great Britain supply too much to citizens who simply abide by the rules of a just society, but who contribute nothing of market value to other members of their society. An acceptance of even the more-qualified libertarian views of Hayek or of Friedman seems to commit one to such a critique of egalitarianism. Hayek, for example, argues that "there is no obvious reason why the joint efforts of the members of any group to ensure the maintenance of law and order and to organize the provision of certain services should give the members a claim to a particular share in the wealth of this group."[92] At this point, the only response available to liberal egalitarians may be that there *is* an obvious reason for them: that people as equal moral beings are entitled to a share of the social wealth at least as large as is necessary to provide for their basic welfare (assuming of course that enough remains for others' welfare as well). Also, although less obviously, each person is entitled to as extensive an *effective* liberty to shape his life as is compatible with the life and liberty of others.[93]

When the debate between libertarians and liberal egalitarians reaches this point, we are forced to consider whether any conception of distributive justice can be justified on strictly rational grounds, apart from a reliance upon our (perhaps conflicting) moral intuitions or social habits. And if not, what does the absence of rational *proof* say about the status of liberal egalitarian thought?

Though Rawls's original position does provide one defense of liberal egalitarian principles, we must of course first be led to accept the egalitarian perspective of that situation.[94] Indeed, Rawls does not claim that the original position is the only, or sufficient, defense of egalitarian justice:

There is . . . another side to justifying a particular description of the original position. This is to see if the principles which would be chosen match our considered convictions of justice or extend them in an acceptable way. We can note whether applying these principles would lead us to make the same judgments about the basic structure of society which we now make intuitively *and in which we have the greatest confidence;* or whether, in cases where our present judgments are in doubt and given with hesitation, these principles offer a resolution which we can affirm on reflection. There are questions which we feel sure must be answered in a certain way.[95]

We are therefore unlikely to accept Rawls's definition of the original position unless our firmest considered judgments on substantial moral issues accord with the egalitarian policies suggested by the resulting principles of justice.[96]

No doubt some will refuse to enter the original position on the grounds that individuals are not equal moral persons, that in fairness we cannot abstract away from specific conceptions of the good life, or that the resulting, nonmeritocratic principles are clearly (to their minds) wrong. The claims to justification end where these nonegalitarian intuitions begin, and are firmly rooted. But because this justificatory weakness applies equally to nonegalitarian theories, only the skeptic who is willing to do without any theory of justice can dismiss liberal egalitarianism solely on this epistemological ground. Recognition of this limit to justification makes our contextualist interpretation of Rawls's theory more plausible and leads, I think, to a serious qualification of the applicability of *A Theory of Justice* to past and contemporary societies in which our dominant liberal paradigm (if I may be for-given for using this term once) does not prevail. Our conception of the justice of ancient Sparta or of the Trobriand Islands may be guided by Rawls's general conception of justice, but why we would want to criticize the justice of those societies from this per-spective eludes me. If we speak of *A Theory of Justice* as bringing coherence to our considered judgments and in the process leading us to forsake some of our inconsistent moral judgments about *our* society – assuming it is a society in which many of us hold similar intuitions and share certain considered judgments – then the meaning and purpose of theorizing becomes clearer. We can thereby criticize our society by building upon some fairly firm and enduring moral consensus among our fellow citizens. To the extent that such agreement is possible, it is probably a social prod-uct of a shared liberal political and philosophical tradition. But that realization need not diminish the force – only the applicabil-ity – of our resulting judgments.

The justificatory grounds of Rawls's theory are therefore neither the classical Cartesian nor naturalist ones. No universal, self-evi-dent truths can be provided from which certain moral principles follow with clear deductive logic. Nor, Rawls admits, does his the-ory of justice begin with moral concepts that can be defined "in terms of presumptively non-moral ones" and proceed to "show by accepted procedures of common sense and the sciences that the statements thus paired with the asserted moral judgments are true." The very possibility of finding necessary moral truths in the strict sense is rejected:

I do not hold that the conception of the original position is itself without moral force, or that the family of concepts it draws upon is ethically neu-tral . . . I have not proceeded . . . as if first principles, or conditions thereon, or definitions either, have special features that permit them a peculiar place in justifying a moral doctrine. They are central elements and devices of theory, *but justification rests upon the entire conception and how it fits in with and organizes our considered judgments in reflective equilib-rium.* [97]

Justification, in short, "is a matter of the mutual support of many considerations, of everything fitting together in one coherent view."[98] Everything, for Rawls, includes the substantive charac-terization of the original position as a rational point of reflection, the image of equal moral persons which that position reflects and gives rise to in the resultant distributive principles, and the rein-forcement of our firmest convictions that those principles effect.

Included, finally, is a liberal belief that agreement on principles of justice *can* result from an exercise in rational choice by suitably situated (or characterized) individuals. The coherence of internal elements lends credence – and theoretical beauty – to Rawls's theory, but our familiarity with, and acceptance of, the various parts that cohere is essential to justification: "A proof simply displays logical relations between propositions. But proofs become justification once the starting points are mutually recognized, or the conclusions so comprehensive and compelling as to persuade us of the soundness of the conception expressed by their premises."[99]

From this perspective of the necessary and potential comprehensiveness of egalitarian theory, we have criticized the incomplete egalitarian arguments of Williams and Walzer, and we have expanded Rawls's theory to account for our considered judgments in favor of welfare rights. Of course, such an account also follows plausibly (though by no means certainly) from the characterization of persons in the original position and the proposed method of proof, joining the original position with the principles of justice. Both libertarian and liberal egalitarian theories share the lack of a certain or "self-evident" starting point (or a "brute" fact). We have argued only that egalitarian principles of justice follow more plausibly from the equality assumption of classical liberalism than do libertarian free-market principles.

In addition to the justificatory criteria Rawls mentions, the steady development of a liberal egalitarian tradition is itself an indication of the firmness of egalitarian foundations within Western culture. And the agreement among several diverse strands of liberalism – classical rights theory, utilitarianism, Christian and democratic socialism – that people are potentially free and equal moral beings provides additional foundational support for egalitarian distributive principles. Of course, any past consensus would not in itself be a valid basis for moral construction were its content not philosophically compelling and intuitively plausible. But this image is for many of us a deeply engrained conviction and has been an enduring, even if not undisputed, philosophical assumption.

This assumption of human equality has also been taken to indicate a serious, perhaps even a fatal, internal flaw in the project of liberal egalitarianism until now. The challenge, recently raised by international egalitarians (and suggested all along by Marxist critics of liberalism), is the following: How can liberal egalitarians legitimately draw a line between justice *within* and justice *among* states? And if they cannot draw a principled line, must not liberal egalitarians cease speaking of distributive justice within particular states and extend their distributive principles to include all people, because they assume that all rational human beings, whatever their nationality, are equal moral persons?

This is a troubling issue, on which I offer only some inconclusive thoughts. It is very difficult, particularly in a world of mutual dependence among nations, to find clear principled reasons for differentiating distributive justice *in* and *between* states. At the same time, simple extensions of egalitarian justice to a global scale encounter difficult problems in theory and lack in contemporary political reality even the most basic foundations necessary to their adequate institutionalization. The sort of question raised here is not simply whether (for example) the United States is obligated to supply the Indian population with basic sustenance without any obligation on India's part to limit population growth. For there is an analogous problem among individuals within nations that can be answered within the Rawlsian model.[100] The problem of a world egalitarian order is much greater in scope than this question reveals. If the United States is obligated to feed the Indians, then the United States has a similar obligation to the entire underdeveloped world. Within what sort of *political* order could this obligation be expected to hold? This question has an answer, but it is one that reveals the difficulty of presently criticizing the goal of domestic egalitarianism from the viewpoint of an international egalitariansim based on the Rawlsian difference principle.

The domestic situation of justice is one in which citizens already have a sense of mutual obligations, often a shared political heritage, always a degree of control through the institutionalized mechanisms of political democracy, and a large degree of daily interaction through voluntary associations, the media, the market, and even ritual national observances – much larger than that which exists between citizens of different nations, however economically interdependent their societies might be. If we are to advocate radical egalitarian distributive measures among nations, we must be sure also that we investigate what the nature of a just political (i.e., participatory) order among those same nations might be.

A world egalitarian order is not in theory undesirable. Quite the contrary: It is an exceedingly attractive and harmonious vision. But it is at present also a vision that stretches the limits of our (or at least of *my*) theoretical imagination much further than the vision of a just egalitarian order within established, and *relatively* more harmonious, advanced industrial societies. It is particularly the political dimension of the framework of a just egalitarian world order that eludes us. All the worry about how a world society modeled on Rawlsian principles would function *economically* obscures the problem of how a society among nations might operate *politically* so that people would retain (or gain) the liberties of political participation and so that they would not live in basic fear that the resources they produced were being distributed to people within nations that were as likely as not to make war against them, or at least to have consistently hostile intentions toward them. Should we be willing, if necessary, to sacrifice the political liberties of a small number of developed nations to the greater economic welfare of all? (And would – in the absence of secure democratic institutions among nations – greater economic welfare ensue?) Perhaps the ultimate questions raised here are ones of political psychology: What are the limits of felt obligations and of basic security beyond those of the traditional nation-state? By analogy to the argument made in the following chapter, an advanced industrial world order without democratic institutions could not be considered fully legitimate. Without equal civil and political liberties, the rationale for welfare rights would remain incomplete. Therefore, although liberal egalitarian theory is indeed potentially open to the challenge of an internationalist egalitarian perspective, the prerequisites for establishing such a perspective and the nature of that challenge cannot be understood without a further understanding of the prerequisites and nature of a just egalitarian order *within* nations.

One might also wonder how we would now begin to build a more egalitarian world order that would respect the integrity of existing nations. Several redistributive policies have been suggested, among them tariff preferences, transfers of capital and technology, commodity price stabilization, loan guarantees, and special drawing rights for poor countries. But were these redistributive policies now instituted, we would no doubt discover that the poorest citizens in the richest countries bore the major burdens of subsidization. (Increased inflation and unemployment are the likely domestic effects of several of the proposed measures.) So long as we are concerned about welfare and justice for *individuals,* we must look for more egalitarian justice within existing rich societies in order that the costs of international egalitarianism may be borne fairly.[101] In this sense at least, the realization of an egalitarian world order depends upon the realization of just equality within existing societies.

Chapter 7

Participatory and distributive equality reintegrated

TWO FACES OF LIBERAL EGALITARIANISM, OR ONE?

Rousseau painted a picture of an ideal democratic society in which the conflict between democracy and substantive justice would never arise: "Each man, in giving his vote, states his opinion on that point; and the general will is found by counting votes. When therefore the opinion contrary to my own prevails, this proves neither more nor less than that I was mistaken."[1] Now this happy concurrence of majority decision and justice was not a natural phenomenon for Rousseau. He suggested background conditions without which one could not say that the general will emerges from majority rule.[2] Nevertheless, Rousseau envisaged a situation in which voting becomes, or at least comes very close to, a pure procedure for determining justice.

Nozick's critique of democratic theory – although invalid as a general critique – can rightly be applied against Rousseau's vision.[3] Rousseau, in effect, attempted to free individuals from slavery to their own passions in order to make them slaves to the will (and one might read "passions" here) of the majority, a will not necessarily congruent with principles of a just society. Such a critique of Rousseau's democratic theory raises the question when, if ever, we can rightly say that the majority will defines what is just, and hence defines what individuals (especially, of course, those in the minority) should be obligated to do.[4]

The question how to reconcile our commitment to democratic rule with our belief in principles of distributive justice comes up in different forms within Rawls's theory and within Mill's defense of participation, as well as within many contemporary theories of participatory democracy. If one does not think that an ideal participatory democracy can serve as a form of pure procedural justice or that a philosopher king can legitimately rule an ideal society, then how does one combine distributive and participatory values within a just society?

The question we are asking here must be distinguished from

that of how we can legitimately *achieve* a just society: by democratic or by nondemocratic means? The two questions are to a significant extent independent, although if we envisaged a completely nondemocratic ideal society, we surely would have fewer problems justifying a nondemocratic transition to that society.[5] The question we ask here is what place democratic participation can have within (rather than on the way to) a just society, given that justice depends upon the implementation of correct egalitarian principles of distribution of primary goods such as health care, housing, job opportunities, income, wealth, and self-respect (in a certain sense at least), regardless of the desires of the majority of citizens.[6]

This leads to the following question: Were we to develop a picture of an egalitarian society built upon Rawlsian distributive principles, suitably expanded and revised, could that society conspicuously lack a political life? It certainly would be strange and disturbing if individuals as participants in political life had no secure and valued place within an egalitarian society. We have argued that the qualities which enable a person to interpret the moral law or to take other people's interests into consideration in pressing for new laws are an essential part of both Kant's and Mill's visions of a community of equal moral persons. A state whose constitution was based upon the two principles of justice, whose courts consistently upheld civil liberties, and whose legislatures faithfully translated those principles into just distributive laws might still be a state of passive citizenry. Yet as long as the legislatures, serviced by efficient and accountable bureaucracies and reviewed by a competent judiciary, were faithful to the spirit and letter of egalitarian justice, need we look further, to the participatory ideal, for the source of our discomfort with this vision of social justice?

Rawls's characterization of a just society leaves the participatory ideal implicit while concentrating upon an outline of those distributive principles that are to regulate the most inclusive "social union of social unions."[7] Those, like Mill, who have explicitly argued for the participatory ideal, on the other hand, have rarely faced the question whether a belief in just principles of economic distribution conflicts with a commitment to participatory democracy or communal self-determination. If democratic participation is simply interpreted as in general the best means available to desired social goals, then in cases where one could determine what those goals are and who would faithfully effect them, democratic means might legitimately be dispensed with. Alternatively, if all one values is the freedom of each to participate equally in decisions made by all, regressive taxation or a highly uneven income distribution could be sanctioned on the same grounds as more egalitarian distributive policies. Both may be products of democratic decision making.

Rawls himself says remarkably little about the participation of citizens in the political affairs of a just society. Yet the first principle of Rawlsian justice stipulates the priority of liberty, included in which is the priority of political liberty. Rawls clearly has in mind the freedom to vote and the less frequently used freedoms to run for office, to campaign for competing candidates and parties, to petition one's representatives, and, I assume, to demonstrate peacefully against one's representatives or even against one's government.[8] But a defense of these political freedoms still may leave us far from defending the establishment of those widespread participatory institutions for which Mill, Cole, and many modern participatory theorists have argued.

Rawls emphasizes the value of participation as a protective means, most specifically as a means of safeguarding individuals from the tyranny of government and of other groups within society.[9] Participation as an opportunity for citizens who so desire to share in the decision making and management of their society, to educate themselves in political life, and to develop their faculties of communal feeling and political competence does not have a central place within Rawls's explicit argument for participatory institutions, nor does participation as a chosen part of the good life of men and women. Any of these goals may warrant a more extensive system of participatory institutions than that now present in the United States and England and than that suggested by Rawls's first principle. Nonetheless, expanding participation to the level suggested by Cole and modern participatory democrats may threaten some of the principles of distributive justice Rawls's theory intends to secure.

If we do value participation as more than a defense against government, the question we must ask is whether a liberal egalitarian theory like Rawls's must remain a partial egalitarian vision or whether it can consistently integrate those values of participation presented by Mill, Cole, and other democratic theorists. Similarly, one might ask of participation theorists whether they can accommodate the values of distributive justice Rawls's theory supports. Whichever way one tackles the problem, one might wonder whether there is, not one liberal egalitarian tradition, but two: one guaranteeing a just distribution of primary goods (excluding extensive participation from this category of goods) and one maximizing participatory opportunities (regardless of the effect on the distribution of other primary goods within society). How can we consistently integrate these egalitarian ideals into one liberal egalitarian vision?

If we accept that the two forms of liberal egalitarianism are irreconcilable, then we must resign ourselves to one of two "ideal" worlds in which there will still exist inherent moral conflict, because one cannot reasonably deny the value of either the distributive or the participatory ideal. I am willing to assume that our present society creates many "surplus" moral conflicts by its unnecessary injustices, but I am not willing to assume that we must embrace the same irreconcilable conflicts of values within our vision of a just society. At least, my vision eliminates a substantial number of those conflicts, while no doubt leaving several others to be resolved in the future.

The tension between the participatory and the distributive ideals[10] of egalitarian justice has been reduced to the following "paradox" by several philosophers of democratic theory:

1. We believe it a matter of justice that x ought to be the outcome of decision n.
2. We also believe that p is the correct process by which n ought to be decided.
3. However, the process p leads to the outcome not-x.

The question we are left with is how to deal with the conflict between our first two beliefs as reflected in outcome (3).[11]

One reasonable way to deal with this tension is to argue that p is the best procedure available to determine n, admitting that it is an imperfect procedure. The outcomes of this procedure will not always be just, and therefore they need not always be accepted by the dissenting minority. We accept this path most often in thinking about how to get to a more just society from where we are now. We often argue that democratic rule is the *safest* even if not the most efficient way to achieve a better society, although we cannot reasonably expect majorities always to discover what is just, nor can we always reasonably bind minorities to majority will, especially on issues in which disputed rights are at stake.[12]

We can offer a second reasonable resolution to this democratic dilemma (so far, at least, no paradox has surfaced) by precluding the use of simple democratic procedures when we clearly know that x ought to be the resulting policy and x is to be greatly preferred on grounds of justice to any of its leading competitors. The most obvious policies in which we employ this "nondemocratic" alternative are those involving people's basic rights. In such cases, we rightly do not allow n to be determined by an imperfect democratic procedure once we know that the institution and perpetuation of x can be all but guaranteed by other means. Civil and political rights in liberal societies fall under this category of solution, or rather avoidance, of the democratic paradox. I shall argue shortly that once a just society is instituted, welfare rights should also fall under this category of cases. If any procedure is permitted to alter just rights policies it would be akin to the amendment procedure in the United States Constitution, a procedure that protects rights against all but the *most* determined and widespread public disapproval. This amendment process might be justified on two grounds. It might guard against persistent judicial misinterpretation by allowing citizens to revise the wording of particular constitutional rights. It also would allow for genuine substantive changes in the nature of rights as changes in social conditions might demand.

The existence of a democratic paradox is also called into question once one recognizes that there are many issues in which we cannot or at least do not know what ought to be decided, except that the decision should be that of a democratic majority. These are cases in which individual rights or people's basic life chances are not at stake. I suspect that in a just society there will be many issues that fall into this category: Citizens will feel strongly and be divided over the political outcome of a decision, although none of the proposed outcomes would violate anybody's rights. And though each of the participants may think that his preference is the best one, no one can rightly claim that the majority's preference is unjust. In these cases, the democratic process will be the valid, and probably the only valid, method of determining the outcome. Here we consider democratic politics a form of pure procedural justice. Aspects of educational policy and of industrial and bureaucratic organization will fall into this category, as we shall argue later.

We shall now examine more carefully several realms in which the conflict between distribution and participation has arisen in contemporary society, in an attempt to foresee ways in which those specific potential conflicts can be avoided or resolved by a just liberal society. The three issue areas we shall focus upon are community control of schools, industrial democracy, and participation within and control over bureaucracies. The case of community control of schools is important because education has been the main area of community participation in this country as well as the main focus of egalitarian hopes for equalizing opportunities for all potential citizens.[13] The debate over industrial democracy raises the question whether what liberal theorists have traditionally considered a private sphere should become a political sphere, controllable (at least in part) by its now subordinate constituents.[14] The question of participation within bureaucracies challenges the main locus of nonparticipatory decision making in the United States and Britain, the locus that many have claimed is the actual center of decision-making power in contemporary societies.[15]

The debates concerning participation within educational, industrial, and bureaucratic institutions in recent years have been complicated by the fact that the problems addressed by participants to these debates are problems of decidedly nonideal societies. Our task here is to assess the role of participation in these institutions within a *just* liberal egalitarian society. This enterprise is at least in part a prior one: We would want to know the ideal mix of democratically determined and constitutionally defined principles of justice before judging the correct balance of power and principle within a nonideal social order. We shall not resolve the additional problem of how to achieve such a just structure.

THE VALUES OF EQUAL PARTICIPATION

Four significant arguments for equalizing participatory opportunities have recurred within liberal theory. Perhaps the most deeply embedded within liberalism is the "self-protection" view: that the right of equal participation is a means of protection against the tyranny of others, specifically of protection against tyranny by the state. This value of participation was, as we have seen, already evident in the works of Bentham and James Mill, and more recently it has had a place in Rawls's defense of equal political rights. The defense of what has become known as social pluralism and its corresponding qualified support of political participation has been based largely on fear of state power. Madison's argument in the *Federalist Papers* provides an excellent example of a pluralist argument for limited democratic participation as a means of safeguarding constitutionalist government.[16] The consistent pluralist's support of participatory rights always remains contingent upon the effectiveness of those rights as weapons against state power. Were equal political rights unnecessary to guaranteeing constitutional order, or inefficient in doing so, the pluralist might support an unequal distribution of rights, so long as relatively equal countervailing powers among groups prevailed. But

178

the liberal egalitarian must continue to defend equal participatory rights, even in situations where they are proven inefficient – that defense reflecting at minimum a commitment to supporting the equal dignity of all citizens.

A second "consumer-sovereignty" view is that equal participation is more likely to result in better policy than would decision making by a few. This is the classic "shoe-pinching" argument that Mill, following his father and Bentham, repeats in the *Principles* with reference to decision-making areas in which people (1) have access to the relevant information and (2) are directly affected by the decisions.[17] This defense of participation is by no means new to modern liberal theory. It goes at least as far back as Aristotle's *Politics* but is still a major basis for the defense of participation by twentieth-century democratic theorists.[18] As we argued in Chapter 2, Mill himself recognized the limits of the consumer-sovereignty rationale in those spheres in which consumers have inadequate product information. Nevertheless, his argument holds for those areas in which citizens can be said both to know their own interests and to be those most affected by the relevant activity: The structure of the workplace is an important example of an appropriate sphere for "worker sovereignty." Mill's defense of participation goes beyond this rationale, and there are good reasons for contemporary liberal egalitarians to follow his lead.

A third rationale for participation emphasized by Mill is the "self-development" view: participation as a "school of political capacity and general intelligence."[19] Although Mill does not stipulate the goals of intelligent decision making, he argues that participation in communal affairs will help individuals develop the mental skills necessary to arriving at adequate personal and public ends.[20] And the extension of participatory rights to new public realms will distribute those skills more equally, ultimately creating a citizenry of progressive individuals capable and therefore desirous of taking account of their interests as part of a larger public interest. Participation so understood is a means of both personal and, by extension, group identity. Individuals learn and give voice to allegiances within the democratic community. They thereby discover and create loyalties within the larger union, and they gain the ability to protect their individual interests through these larger affiliations.[21] Liberal egalitarians can accept this non-individualistic value of participation so long as justification in terms of individual interests is prior to, or at least covariant with, the development of communal identity and political loyalty.

This argument makes the liberal case more adequate: Equal participation creates loyalty because it is a means of simultaneously educating citizens to their communal interests and fulfilling their individual natures as progressive beings. The eventual "natural" compatibility of self- and communal interest is essential to Mill's case for participation and the key to distinguishing his liberal argument for participation from Rousseau's. There is no need to force men or women to be free if they can be educated through freely chosen (although politically facilitated) opportunities for communal decision making. Loyalty to the state can be expected to follow naturally from increased participation, because participatory opportunities enable a citizen to fulfill his own nature by making decisions in which some larger public interest is identified with and *as* his own. Although liberalism may always require an uneasy balance to be freely struck between self- and communal interest, the more optimistic moral psychology of Millean liberalism avoids the necessity of posing the question of participation as a hard choice between the absolute independence of Rousseau's natural man,,and the enforced selflessness and social dependency of the Spartan citizen.[22]

Mill's self-development argument is applied most often in favor of expanding the political arena at the local level, a level at which most citizens can easily identify their own interests and engage in well-informed decision-making processes. This argument forms the other side of the Millean rationale for participation discussed in Chapter 2. Participation in this sense is intended as a means of developing every citizen's moral autonomy by encouraging each to discover where his real interests lie: in some measure, at least, with the broader democratic and egalitarian community of which he is an equal part.

Fourth and last is the "equal-dignity" rationale: The equal right to participate is an end in itself, or a constitutive value, insofar as it is *indicative* (as well as supportive) of equal dignity and mutual respect among citizens.[23] Now this rationale is historically relative in the following sense: Without the expectation of equal treatment among members of a society in other distributive realms, it is possible that the dignity of nonparticipants would not suffer and mutual respect would still exist between citizens with full and those with partial participatory rights.[24] However, once equality is publicly recognized in any realm of political or social life, participatory opportunities cannot be unequally limited without simultaneously challenging the dignity of partial citizens and destroying the potential bonds of fraternity among all citizens.[25] Thus, in the Anglo-American context, only a state providing effective and extensive opportunities for all citizens to participate in politics can be said to respect its citizens equally. This is a rationale of participation on which the theories of Mill and Rawls converge. The argument for equal participatory opportunities must be consistently recognized by both strands of liberal egalitarian thought.

This rationale for participation is by far the most crucial one from a contemporary liberal egalitarian perspective: By opening up opportunities for free and equal participation in political life (broadly understood), an egalitarian society gives credence to the ideal of equal moral persons upon which it is theoretically based. Only by allowing and encouraging equal opportunities for all citizens to participate in a variety of spheres that affect their lives will citizens see themselves and be seen as possessing equal dignity. And only upon serious consideration of the equal-dignity rationale is the participatory ideal fully established as an essential primary good: To deny *effective* equal participatory rights or *fair* equality of participatory opportunities is to deny the equal dignity of individual citizens. The equal-dignity rationale explains the urgency of equal participation as an egalitarian ideal and explains why rule utilitarianism is an unnecessary rationalization of the need for equal voting or other equal participatory rights.[26] The other rationales aid us in locating the most significant and useful spheres for participation.

The liberal egalitarian case for participation can now be distinguished from an alternative extraliberal tradition of participatory theory most commonly associated with Rousseau. That tradition is potentially more egalitarian by virtue of its rejection of the liberal conception of negative freedom.[27] Whereas liberal egalitarians can insist upon expanding and equalizing participatory opportunities, participatory theorists following Rousseau can go still further in forcing men to be free through equalizing participation itself.[28]

Rousseau's case rests upon two important arguments. One is that equal participatory rights are instrumental in achieving a stable polity to which citizens will pledge their primary allegiance. The second is that political participation is a central part of the good life. No person can be considered a citizen free and equal to others or a fully moral individual unless he participates equally with others in political life. Participation, by this view, is at the same time a necessary means to positive freedom as a loyal citizen of the state and an essential part of the good life. Forced equality can be justified by virtue of the benefits thereby conferred through the state upon every individual.

Participatory and distributive equality reintegrated

The creation of loyal subjects is perhaps the least satisfactory liberal rationale for participation, nor is it empirically clear that more participatory rights do in fact create a more integrated or loyal citizenry.[29] In any case, without independent criteria defining the justice of the state, an argument for participation as a means to stability will have indeterminate value. The loyal-citizen rationale therefore fails as a liberal argument for participation: There must be proof of the state's justice in fulfilling individuals' interests before social integration becomes a legitimate end. Participation cannot be consistently valued by a liberal theorist as a means to socialization or loyalty without further justification of the *value to the individual* of social integration. This argument of Rousseau's for equal democratic participation is unavailable to the liberal egalitarian.[30] Neither loyalty nor fraternity can be an end in itself, apart from the justice of the polity to which citizens are attached.[31]

The second part of Rousseau's defense of participation is much more compelling than the first and worthy of more extensive discussion than we can engage in here. The idea of participation as a necessary part of the good life has a distinguished history before Rousseau. Rousseau, however, linked the Greek view of public man as moral man (and private man as idiot) to a more egalitarian perspective, wherein all male individuals were assumed capable of attaining the status of equal moral persons. (I have of course taken the liberty of including women within Rousseau's universe of equal persons, thereby completing his participatory egalitarianism.)

Several important claims are linked to this view of participation as a necessary part of the good life. One is that we cannot become moral without engaging in politics: Our concerns will otherwise remain selfish, even were we to participate equally in partial associations, such as the family or the workplace. Only political participation can teach us the proper habits and principles of communal life: those habits and principles that constitute the essence of what it means to be a moral individual. The good man and the good citizen in a democratic society governed by the general will are one and the same, and the former is created by the habits engendered by the latter.[32]

Another claim often linked to this ideal of equal participation is that politics is a higher form of activity than any other; and therefore, in being forced to be free through extensive political participation, we are also being forced to be better people. Now, Aristotle attached one proviso to this claim: that pure intellectual activity may be superior to political activity,[33] although his political theory, unlike Plato's, does not dwell upon structuring the polity around recognition of the exceptional person who engages in this activity. Rousseau clearly makes no exception for philosophy (or philosophers), because reason itself is a corrupting influence upon the moral virtue of individuals, engendering antisocial egoistical behavior.[34]

It is fairly easy to see how both these claims are related to the claims that citizens will not be loyal to the state if they do not participate within it. One need only attach the claim that selfish behavior is undermining of the just state's legitimacy and authority, a claim certainly entailed in Rousseau's argument for the necessity of participation as a part of the good life of all citizens.

There is a good deal of force behind these two claims for participation as a required activity for the good man and woman and the good citizen. Yet that force diminishes significantly if one rejects (as does Mill, for example) Rousseau's view of human nature: that "natural" man was asocial and that he "naturally" becomes competitive and egoistical once he enters into a civil society. What remains in support of enforced equal participation is another, more qualified claim: that political activity is a necessary part of the good life for all individuals because each citizen of a just society *should be morally obligated* to contribute to the maintenance and perpetuation of his society. This claim cannot be dissolved by a rejection of Rousseau's pessimistic view of human nature, nor is it clearly a claim that liberal egalitarian theorists must reject as beyond the legitimate scope of a liberal state.

THE ARGUMENT FOR COMPULSORY EQUAL PARTICIPATION REEXAMINED

The remaining claim for compulsory participation has two possible supporting bases: one found in Aristotle and another in modern collective-goods theory. Aristotle argued that the contribution of each citizen to the collective good of the state was in a sense cumulative: "Just as a feast to which many contribute is better than one provided by a single person, so . . . the masses can come to a better decision, in many matters, than any one individual."[35] For Aristotle, the deliberation of all is preferable to the deliberation of the few because the outcome of the former is likely to be a better one. From this perspective, one could require all citizens to participate so as to maximize the wisdom of social policy and to ensure that each person contributes his share to the collective good.

This argument for compulsory participation encounters serious difficulties on both an empirical and a normative level. Empirically, even were one to accept Aristotle's claim that many are collectively wiser than a few, the marginal contribution of an average individual to the collective good must diminish significantly beyond a certain number of participants. Beyond that number, an individual's contribution to the collective good might even be negative, if there are any additional organizational costs attached to larger numbers in collective participation. It becomes hard to justify forcing or even morally obligating all citizens to participate if the contributions of some citizens will be at best marginal, and probably much smaller than the costs to them of participating.

Yet a collective-goods argument for participation can come very close to Aristotle's while avoiding the problem of forcing individuals to contribute without demonstrating corresponding benefits to them or to the common good. Given that a just liberal state is based upon the notion that its citizens have a right to equal treatment and correspondingly have certain equal obligations to support the state when no one can expect to gain disproportionately or to be excluded from the benefits of that support, then there may exist certain activities that all citizens must be obligated to perform if fairness is to be upheld.[36] This argument has limited application but is nonetheless forceful with reference to at least one sphere of participation – voting.[37]

The results of voting are a collective good: No one can be excluded from the benefits of election results or from the more general benefits of continuing the democratic system itself. But voting is irrational from the point of view of the cost–benefit calculation of an individual.[38] Because no individual voter can expect to have more than a miniscule effect upon the outcome of a national election, even the smallest costs of voting are likely to outweigh the benefits to the individual voter. Yet voting and competitive politics are viewed as crucial activities from the point of view of the welfare of all individuals, not only from that of the democratic system itself. Those individuals who are solely cost–benefit calculators would become free riders on the system, benefiting from their neighbors' choices to vote out of moral obligation, that being the only truly rational motivation for voting.[39] Voting therefore must be considered a duty of each individual citizen if its effects are indeed to be considered a necessary collective good from the point of view of all citizens (unless, of course, some citizens are considered unfit to participate, but liberal egalitarians will certainly deny this contention, and for good reasons).

Of course, not all moral duties should be legally enforced. Alan Wertheimer recognizes this, although he goes on to argue that the moral duty to vote should be legally obligatory.[40] Though we shall part company with Wertheimer here, we first should recognize how far liberalism has traveled from Locke toward a view that participation is a morally obligatory part of a good citizen's and a good person's life.

Whether the moral obligation to vote should be legally enforced depends on several factors. One is simply whether legal enforcement would be necessary in a just society. Even if no other policies were altered in the United States today, were registration made as easy as it is in many European countries and election days declared national holidays, voter turnout would no doubt significantly increase.[41] Were economic policies also to become more egalitarian, the differential turnout among groups of voters might well disappear. Were all ballots to offer the choice of abstention and write-ins, still more citizens might be moved to vote their preferences. In short, it is not implausible to hypothesize that voting in a just egalitarian society would become a universal political activity and that legal sanctions would be unnecessary to enforce this publicly recognized moral obligation.

On the other hand, one might still think it just to penalize the few who did not vote. The relevant question here is a utilitarian one: Would the costs of a legal sanction outweigh the benefits? The benefits are likely to be very small. No one is noticeably injured by a few people abstaining. The costs of legal enforcement on the other hand may be quite large: Some people will undoubtedly have legitimate personal excuses that will have to be brought before some civil court. Moreover, it is possible that legal enforcement would reduce the moral feelings of obligation to vote that people otherwise would develop quite freely.[42] Those of us who hold a more Millean conception of human nature may reject arguments for a legal compulsion to vote as the only acceptable alternative to socially induced "psychic compulsion," relying upon our assumption that individuals will freely develop a moral sense of obligation within a just democratic society[43] and will consider fulfilling their moral obligations as a part of what it means to be a rational person. Those holding a Rousseauean conception of human nature can and perhaps must opt for legal enforcement. Of course, in an unjust democratic society, compulsory voting may be the best alternative available to overcoming the problems created by free riders and by the otherwise disproportionate representation of the most advantaged citizens within the electorate.

PARTICIPATION BEYOND THE STRICTLY POLITICAL

The preceding discussion of whether there would exist a moral or legal obligation for all citizens to vote in a liberal egalitarian society falls far short of addressing a major concern of contemporary participation theorists for broadening the realm of politics. Before addressing this concern within the context of liberal theory, we might consider the obstacles nonliberal theories have placed in the path of broader participatory goals. Both Aristotle's and Rousseau's arguments suggest that participation within partial associations – associations not inclusive of all citizens – will not serve to educate men and women to civic virtue.[44] Indeed, according to Rousseau, membership in partial associations may undermine the desire of those participants to support the general will, and perhaps even impair their very ability to perceive it.[45] Rousseau's general suspicion of secondary associations might therefore lead one to the view that extending participation to workers within a factory would create still another organized social faction inimical to the general good. Ironically, given his reputation as a participation theorist, Rousseau's view of human nature advises us against broadening participation beyond those realms in which *all* citizens can represent themselves. On Rousseau's grounds, only the smallest, agrarian societies can be broadly and justly participatory.[46]

Aristotle's argument, although not based upon such a pessimistic assessment of human nature, can also be taken as a warning against the expectation that all participatory institutions will educate their members to civic virtue. Those institutions whose membership is less than the entire polis will not necessarily be schools of civic virtue. If accepted, this argument casts doubt upon the idea that workers' control will be a means to a more virtuous citizenry; nonetheless, other values of participation in partial associations may remain.

Rousseau's and Aristotle's ideals of participation raise another problem for the participatory democrat that must be resolved before moving onward. Do those who accept the ideal of universal participation in many political institutions and the concomitant Rousseauean ideal of a small agrarian society (or at least a society in which the division of labor is not highly developed) also implicitly assume that a class of partial (or non-) citizens will exist to tend to the less exalted and menial chores of daily life? Certainly both Aristotle and Rousseau assumed this to be the case; either slaves or women would tend to such activities.[47] A contemporary egalitarian must therefore beware of either a pure Aristotelian or Rousseauean "solution"; even Rousseau's proposed utopia is far from utopian from an egalitarian point of view. And if we cannot assume in good faith that there will exist a class of gardeners, housekeepers, and child rearers, neither can we practically afford to propose an ideal society in which all of us spend most of our time attending political meetings.[48] I can see no solution to this problem short of the dissolution of the nuclear family, and even then one must wonder whether professional child rearers would become our new under- or overclass.

I argued earlier that participation is an essential end of liberal egalitarian justice because, among other reasons, equal participatory rights are necessary to ensure the equal dignity of citizens. On the simplest level, unequal voting rights would be unjust because to deny any persons equal votes would be to deny the assumption of their potentially equal rationality. Both Rawls and Mill appear to have taken too lightly the significance of formal political equality. Rawls cites what he takes to be the strongest of Mill's rationales for plural voting: *If* the least advantaged benefit, then their less-than-equal voting rights may be justified.[49] But given our understanding of the significance of participatory rights, it is hard to imagine that any group of citizens in an advanced industrial society would benefit from such an inequality – an inequality likely to be interpreted by the least advantaged as a denial of the equal dignity of their persons, and rightly so.[50]

With respect to suffrage rights (unlike economic distribution), only strict equality will preserve self-respect. Although a high minimum standard of living may provide the material foundation for equal dignity (despite variations among people above that minimum), universal but unequal suffrage (one vote for some and more than one vote for select others) will undermine the self-respect of the less advantaged, or at least be interpreted as an attempt by the state at such undermining.[51] Political inequality on this basic level will be taken to suggest the unequal worth of citizens. Because voting rights are granted exclusively by the state, no random or self-imposed effects can plausibly account for that inequality. Reasons must exist, and what better reason than to assume the unequal merit of citizens? Again, given the egalitarian's belief in equal desires and equal potential rationality of citizens, unequal voting rights are hard to justify, as Mill himself discovered.[52] The strongest defense of participatory equality, as we have argued, is not a pragmatic or protective one, but one that recognizes the foundations of liberal egalitarianism in the equal dignity of human beings.

But equal voting rights establish only the most minimal participatory sphere. The Millean arguments for participation suggest that without more opportunities to participate in communal decision making, the right to vote in infrequent national elections will be a rather shallow concession to the participatory ideal. Equal dignity does not require that everybody participate equally in all political activities, but it does assume that equal opportunities are provided for all people to join in exercising their political and intellectual capacities in communal self-government. Dignity of persons is therefore further attached to the end of human *self*-development, an end that is dependent to varying degrees on the ideal of intelligent and collective self-determination. Moreover, Mill is joined by many contemporary political scientists in telling us that we cannot expect voting rights to be intelligently exercised without effective participatory opportunities in more immediate spheres of communal life.[53] In addition to local political forums, the workplace is often cited as a crucial participatory sphere in both these respects.[54] The opportunity to participate in decisions affecting citizens' work lives is expected to provide a school of intelligence and political capacity for the working classes and to provide an affirmation of their equal dignity, in contrast to the denigrating effect of their present subordination to externally imposed structures of the workplace.[55]

From the equal-participation ideal are derived arguments for equal voting rights, communal participation on a local level, and some form of industrial democracy. These participatory forms serve as *possible means* to self-development, as *necessary means* to the assertion of equal dignity, and as *affirmations in themselves* of the equal moral worth of citizens in an egalitarian state. The substantive content of those decisions that participatory rights allow or encourage remains undetermined as yet, and for good reason. Participatory government must operate within the context of just government. The former *allows* every person an equal right to employ and refine his passions; the latter *ensures* that the interests of all citizens as potentially rational beings are equally protected by egalitarian distributive principles.[56] Participation is thereby constrained rather than threatened by the principles of distributive justice: for only if citizens are first properly situated can the results of participation be understood as fair from a procedural point of view. Nor is participation a threat to the equal distributional principles of Rawlsian justice: for participatory decision making can operate within the structural context and constraints of those principles. The basis for my argument is that, from the standpoint of an ideal theory of liberal justice, the ideal of an egalitarian distribution of goods is to a significant extent a precondition for equalizing participatory opportunity.

In order for formal participatory rights to become meaningful and effective rights, both a minimum absolute level and a relative equality of primary-good distribution must be guaranteed to all citizens. Mill recognized the presence of distributive inequalities as one plausible explanation for the unequal development of people as progressive individuals within his society.[57] Recent studies of participation clearly indicate a wide "participation gap" between citizens of low and high socioeconomic status, a gap that cannot be plausibly explained by the differential characteristics intrinsic to the two (or more) groups.[58] As the absolute level of education, and of socioeconomic status in general, increases across the population, so too does the absolute level of participation of low-status groups; and for certain (particularly more demanding) forms of participation, the gap between high- and low-status groups decreases significantly.[59] What these studies cannot yet definitively tell us is whether *any* differentials in education or socioeconomic status will produce similar discrepancies in the participation rates among groups. Given the lack of any adequately egalitarian society as a basis for control, extrapolations from present survey data are risky. Nevertheless, it seems plausible to hypothesize that beyond a certain threshold of education and within a certain (relatively small) span of income inequality, participation gaps between groups will narrow considerably and perhaps become so insignificant as to reflect the different personal preferences for political participation within and among groups. But contemporary societies such as the United States and Great Britain violate both standards – of guaranteeing an adequate welfare floor and of establishing a maximum level of income inequality – and thereby render even existing participatory rights effectively unequal.

We can also establish the priority of a just constitution over democratic participation as a more general case of the priority of substantive over procedural principles. This argument emphasizes that any *fair* democratic procedure will stipulate certain necessary substantive preconditions. Of course, some games may not

189

stipulate such preconditions – anyone willing to enter may be considered to have a fair chance of winning. But democracy is not much like a game. The stakes are too high (although even within some games – bowling, for example – handicaps are given to the least advantaged). All plausible consent theories stipulate social conditions from which one can assume that the choices of individuals are free and rational ones.[60] The conflict between classical liberals like Hobbes and Locke and theorists like Rousseau is not over whether consent can be considered a sufficient condition for legitimating a state but over what sorts of preconditions for legitimation are adequate. Here I follow Rousseau: In a society in which a rich person can "buy" a poor person, consent by the poor to a social contract cannot be considered free and rational consent, and the contract therefore cannot be considered just on these grounds.[61]

The argument for liberal egalitarianism is that in a society lacking the foundations established by distributive principles – universal welfare rights and a relatively equal distribution of income and wealth – the results of the actual consent of the majority of political participants must be morally questionable. People who do not have a standard of living sufficient to secure basic welfare for themselves simply cannot be expected to participate in politics as extensively and with as much political information as the more advantaged.[62] One might even say that they are rational (given their situation) in ignoring politics, although on an aggregate level the lesser involvement of the poor may significantly harm their interests. *Relative* equality among all citizens is as necessary a precondition for establishing fair participatory procedures as is a welfare floor under each citizen's estate. Even were all citizens to participate extensively, were some *much* richer than others, it is quite likely that no fair procedure could be devised that would prevent the very rich from having an undue political advantage over all others.

One further argument for the priority of distributive over participatory equalities must be mentioned here. Any participatory procedure, with the possible exception of unanimous consent, will exclude the preferences of some citizens from the resulting policy. Now this observation does not constitute an argument against majority rule or other forms of participatory decision making even if one rejects Rousseau's view of voting as a pure procedure of justice. However, such participatory procedures would be unjust were the basic welfare (needs or objective interests) of those citizens in the minority violated by the resulting democratic policy. Thus substantive welfare rights take precedence over democratic participation even in instances where the preconditions for a fair participatory procedure exist. Democratic majorities have no right to rescind the welfare rights of minorities. In addition, of course, the preconditions for future participation on an egalitarian basis would be destroyed were democratic procedures permitted to take priority over basic welfare principles. In this sense, one might want to say that equality of participatory opportunities has priority over equal distributional principles, because the distributional principles that take precedence are those instrumental to providing fair background conditions for effectively equalizing participatory opportunities.

All liberal theorists have recognized that a system of civil and political liberty is a necessary precondition for considering consent an indication of rational preference. My argument suggests that the system of preconditions must be extended to include the fulfillment of basic welfare rights and a just equalization of income and wealth. Particular desires of participant citizens thus should have an important legislative role in a democratic polity. But only after the basic rights of all citizens are guaranteed and after distributive inequalities, if any, are justified can the results of democratic procedures rightly be taken to be the legitimate outcome of the deliberations of free and rational beings.

COMMUNITY CONTROL OF SCHOOLS

We have tried to establish the necessary (although limited) priority of equalizing distribution over extending and equalizing participatory opportunities by arguing that the ideal of equal distribution is entailed by that of equal participation, albeit in a less apparent form than that in which the ideal of equal political liberty is presupposed by the participatory ideal. Our case rests in part upon some persuasive empirical evidence, which suggests that only given equal civil liberties and a relatively equal and comfortable standard of living will political participation become an extensively and freely valued part of the good life of democratic citizens.[63] The results of the movement for community control of schools in the United States in the late 1960s and early 1970s provide additional support for this argument, as well as a vivid illustration of how the various rationales for participation can be applied in advocacy of a specific form of participatory democracy.

The most recent movement for community control of schools came after an almost reverse movement for centralization during the first two-thirds of this century. Proponents of the earlier movement wanted to separate public education from the political control of neighborhood and ward leaders of the big-city machine and from the mayor himself. Typically, this separation of urban education and politics was achieved by the creation of an appointed centralized board of education for the entire city, to which superintendents and other administrators were responsible and which in most cases was given a significant degree of professional autonomy.[64] (In the last wave of reorganization, the mayor's power to appoint board members was significantly curbed, often by professional nominating or review boards.)

Widespread dissatisfaction with these reforms did not appear until the 1960s and then for some very specific reasons, only indirectly related to the centralized and professional structure of urban school administration. The movement in the North for ending de facto school segregation was rightly perceived to be lagging if not failing.[65] The continuing influx of minorities into the central city, the white flight to the suburbs,[66] and the resistance of urban school administrators (and urban communities) to demands to desegregate "with all deliberate speed" all contributed to the slowdown. What followed in many cities – New York and Detroit are two important and representative examples – was a movement among minority groups, predominantly among blacks, for reversing the processes of centralization of administration, of depoliticization, and of professionalization of city school systems by instituting community control of schools.

The most common demands for community control were (briefly) that a community control board be elected, consisting of a cross section of community residents, and that this organization have total control over the operation of local schools, including hiring and firing of teachers and administrators and control over curriculum, over the expenditure of money, and over the building of new schools (and the hiring of labor), if necessary.[67]

The aims of the community-control movement were as varied as those for participation in general. In fact, each of the rationales for participation that we have discussed had its counterpart in arguments put forward for community control in the sixties. Proponents argued (1) that community control would protect the educational interests of predominantly black and other disadvantaged minority communities against the more dominant white interests existing outside the community and presently administering education to the community's children (the self-protection rationale);[68] (2) that black parents were capable of knowing the educational interests of their children better than were white teachers or administrators or a wider democratic majority (the shoe-pinching rationale);[69] (3) that through community control, black parents would gain skills of both educational superintendence and democratic politics and by extension would become more capable individuals and more effective citizens (the self-development rationale);[70] and (4) that only through increased local participation would blacks and other disadvantaged minorities become self-respecting and ultimately mutually respected citizens of the broader democratic party (the equal-dignity rationale).[71]

A final, extraliberal, rationale voiced by more qualified supporters of community control was that it would help integrate potentially dissenting minorities into the broader democratic system. As Daniel Bell and Virginia Held observe, participation is "a deeply conservatizing institution, for, like property, it gives people a stake in the decision which becomes binding on all."[72] Or as Irving Kristol and Paul Weaver note, "Stability and effectiveness are thereby promoted, and the individual comes to enjoy a just self-regard and the other satisfactions of decent citizenship."[73] This rationale is close to what Bachrach and Baratz call a "cooptive" rationale for participation, the first four rationales being "interest oriented."[74] A significant variation of this rationale was voiced by the most radical proponents of community control: that it would create a new communal identity among its participants inimical to identification with white, middle-class, liberal America – a separatist black identity from which a radical political movement might emerge.[75]

The results of the institution of community control in New York and Detroit fell far short of the hopes and aspirations of all community-control advocates, with the possible exception of those few who hoped only temporarily to placate black and dissident white communities. There is little evidence of the success of community control in improving the educational quality of ghetto schools and some evidence of its failure.[76] Although one of the experimental school districts in New York City during the late sixties suspended the standardized reading exam, the goal of equalizing the educational attainment of disadvantaged students was not suspended; and after several years of community control in New York, Kenneth Clark, an original proponent of community control, denounced it as a disastrous diversionary experiment and argued for developing an educational system that would concentrate just upon teaching "these children to read and do arithmetic."[77]

The shoe-pinching argument, which finds support not only among community-control advocates but among proponents of educational voucher systems, also failed to live up to its promise.[78] Community-control advocates mistakenly assumed that low-income parents had adequate time and resources available to judge and control the educational quality of their children's schools. One survey by an early advocate of community control in New York City indicated that a very small proportion of parents were acquainted even with the major educational programs of their children's schools.[79] This is not to say, however, that parents could not retrospectively discern significant improvements in their children's educational progress; but such improvements were not forthcoming through community control, and the judgment of the means needed to effect such improvements was not within their sphere of competence.

The self-development argument ran into similar difficulties, because it, like the others, depended upon the assumption that political participation would be a priority of the poor. Experience of low turnouts in school-board elections[80] – even where the stakes were quite high – suggested that political participation was indeed treated as a luxury by the vast majority of poor families, unless, as in strikes by welfare mothers, economic gains were expected to be immediately forthcoming.[81] In many important school-board elections in New York and Detroit, candidates running on segregationist platforms have been elected: Turnout among more-advantaged whites tends to be much larger than turnout among less-advantaged blacks, although the latter represent a greater proportion of the population of many local school districts.[82] Similarly, supporters of the United Federation of Teachers have had little trouble taking control of many local school districts in New York City, given the "participation gap" between their constituencies and those of candidates representing a poorer, less-educated population.[83]

Universalizing the community-control principle seems to have led to more rather than less resistance to desegregation in the northern cities. Detroit is the most vivid case in point, but many other cities have had similar histories. After the original hope that community control would be a means for improving the quality of education in segregated schools was reasonably abandoned, the goal of desegregation was further stymied by the legitimization of many predominantly white communities' control over their neighborhood schools. A. L. Zwerdling, the liberal president of

Detroit's board of education until 1970, is reported to have commented that "no one who has come to our public meetings on decentralization is interested in integration. Everyone wants segregation so they will be assured a little piece of control."[84]

Many critics of community control of schools took the moral of these stories to be that community control was a worthless ideal. Rather, it was and perhaps still is an ideal whose time has not yet come in New York, in Detroit, and in most other cities in which existing schools in minority neighborhoods are segregated and of very poor quality, and in which residents in those neighborhoods are very poor and largely uneducated. Those who argued that equal dignity would be accorded to blacks and other disadvantaged minorities by granting them greater participatory power over their children's education ignored the preconditions both for achieving equal dignity and for achieving meaningful opportunities to participate in politics. It is much less costly for a society to offer votes and positions on community school boards to the disadvantaged than to offer them welfare rights, equality of education, and equal effective opportunities for decent employment. One cannot reasonably hope to establish an egalitarian society by concentrating on the former means to the exclusion of the latter.[85]

Yet I do not pretend to have offered an alternative way to achieve the egalitarian reforms that we have argued are preconditions of participatory equality in a liberal egalitarian society. Nor does Kenneth Clark's exhortation to teach disadvantaged children to read supply an answer to the difficult question: How? Nobody has yet found a fully satisfactory answer to the question raised by Clark's statement.

In the particular case of desegregation, the procedures we should support are those that are likely to achieve just results so long as those procedures do not violate anyone's rights. It was Detroit's central board of education that approved a plan providing for nearly total integration of local school districts. A majority of Detroit voters defeated the plan, and many largely segregated community-control districts were instituted.[86] Although four of the eight subsequently created community-control districts were predominantly black, blacks won a voting majority on only two of the eight regional boards, and "in the three regions where opposition to integration was most intense, not a single black was elected."[87] Though Detroit's experience is by no means unique, we cannot generalize more from it than this: Participatory means are not necessarily pure or perfect procedures of justice, and when they are not, we may be more interested in using the procedure (subject to the constraints mentioned) most likely to achieve a just outcome than in creating a new participatory realm.

In order for effective equality of participatory opportunities and more equality of educational results to be achieved, welfare rights must be established for all citizens and economic resources redistributed between the rich and the poor. No procedural principle will guarantee these results. If the best procedure is that which is most likely to bring about these results without violating anyone's rights, then there are two reasons for remaining skeptical about community control of schools as either a pure or a perfect procedure of justice. The ideal of achieving equality of educational results presupposes at least some universal standards of educational attainment; these standards are not likely to be set by majority rule within every small community.[88] And the participatory ideal behind community control itself presupposes the egalitarian end-state principles – effective welfare rights and relative equality of income and educational opportunity – that it seeks to establish. Without these equalities, community control may lead to greater participatory inequalities and perhaps even to more substantive inequalities between advantaged and disadvantaged groups within society, and within local communities themselves.[89]

I have assumed that local communities do not have a *right* to "self-determination," particularly in this case, where that "right" would extend to control over the destinies of their children. And if they do not have such a right, then the priority of substantive over procedural principles suggests that we must search for the procedure most likely to bring about equal educational opportunity before championing the cause of community control of schools. It is possible that a significant degree of centralized control over educational decision making and a reliance upon judicial enforcement of equal educational opportunity is necessary in the nonideal situation under consideration.

But answers to this question – how to achieve a just society – will no doubt vary with the particular society and the particular end-states under consideration. We certainly cannot generalize from this particular educational issue to education in general nor from education to a more general argument against democratic means of achieving a more just society. Much of the pressure for equalizing educational opportunities and for extending welfare rights to the poor comes from the existence of democratic political institutions through which the voices of less-advantaged groups can be heard. In addition, there is historical evidence that more equal participatory rights have led to greater welfare rights (Great Britain being the model case), whereas the evidence now available indicates that welfare rights often do not lead to participatory rights (the Soviet Union being the pivotal case). Democratic institutions are no doubt among the most important instruments in the fight for a just liberal society. And it is a plausible historical hypothesis that people must *fight* for distributive justice in order for it to serve as an effective basis for egalitarian liberal democracy. To the extent that our argument can be extended to questions of non-ideal theory, it might suggest that black militants fighting for community control of schools in the 1960s should have been fighting for redistribution of educational resources and desegregation instead. But this does not constitute an argument against the value or legitimacy of their participation. Perhaps they thereby learned that educational results are more important than educational governance (given the existing meager material resources available to black communities), in which case one might argue that participation in the community-control movement had important educative effects, even if it failed in its direct aims. I am not sure how else they, or we, could have more effectively learned this lesson.

My aim here has not been to discover the best procedure for achieving a just society. Rather, I hope that this brief excursion into the politics of community control has indicated the desirability from a liberal egalitarian point of view of ultimately grounding participation upon the foundations of certain substantive principles. Participatory opportunities will be fairly distributed only once citizens have an *effective* opportunity to participate and once they can meet each other on a relatively equal footing when they do enter participatory forums. To grant to a democratic majority within a particular community the right to determine the entire nature of children's education within their community would be to allow individuals to take away the foundations of fair equality of opportunity for others, perhaps even for a whole generation of others.[90]

REALMS OF PARTICIPATION AND REALMS OF CONSTITUTIONAL PRINCIPLE

One can defend the priority of a just distribution of primary goods while affirming the value of expanding participation. Participation in a just society will be encouraged as far as is consistent with a just distribution and conducive to equal dignity among citizens.

Participatory and distributive equality reintegrated

I have now to specify more completely what sort of decision-making power participating citizens can legitimately assert and be granted in an egalitarian society.

Recalling the discussion in Chapter 2, we can see that the constraints Mill placed upon participatory democracy in the name of rational government were so strong as to challenge his very rationale of participation: equal moral self-development. Our internal criticism of Mill extended further, to claiming that where participatory opportunities are limited to symbolic acts or insignificant decisions, citizens are treated as subjects, rather than as equal moral persons. They cannot be expected to participate vigorously in acts of minimal centrality to their lives, to develop the mental faculties requisite to intelligent participation (for little intelligence is demanded by their political role), or to perceive themselves as individuals with equal dignity in a state in which they are effectively barred from exercising important decision-making capacities.

Now, Mill himself did not consistently hold this position, for he realized that a highly centralized government, no matter how just its decrees, denies the equal dignity of citizens. He argued that the representatives of such a government would treat citizens as if they were a different and lower species of being. A highly centralized government creates a spirit of unfreedom among the population, "carrying down to the lowest grade in society the desire and ambition of domination."[91] But Mill's own brand of utilitarianism was inadequate to the task of integrating the demands of competent and just government with those of equal moral development and equal dignity among citizens. In their extreme forms the two egalitarian ideals conflict both in theory and in practice. Therefore only after assessing the relative priorities of egalitarian distributional and participatory principles are we in a position to explore the potential compatibility of the two refined ideals.

A reasonable defense of the ideal of democratic participation constrained by the principles of a just distribution (of goods other than political power) proceeds as follows. Principles of equal liberty, welfare rights, and the difference principle take precedence over actual democratic procedures because *fair* democratic procedures presuppose these rights and principles. Democracy cannot work the way its advocates claim it ought to without a substantive foundation: an egalitarian distribution of basic civil liberties and of primary goods. These constitutional provisions will therefore take precedence over democratic participation.

One modest proviso may be appropriate here: The precise form of the Rawlsian difference principle may not be essential to ensuring a just democratic process; a somewhat more or less egalitarian distributional principle might do, so long as it too is consistent with ensuring basic welfare rights and with preventing inequalities of income or wealth so large as to undermine the equal effective political liberty of all citizens. Although a just distributional principle of residual goods should ultimately take precedence over actual democratic procedures, one might allow a variety of modifications of or variations upon the difference principle to be chosen by democratic procedures in a society in which the requisite background conditions (equal liberties, fair equality of opportunity, welfare rights, and a significantly more equal distribution of income and wealth than presently exists) ensure equal effective freedom of democratic participation for all.

Only after principles establishing equal basic civil and political liberties, welfare rights, and the distribution of residual primary goods are instituted – representing the stage of constitution making – will democratic participation operate upon a basis of fairness. Fair democratic procedures can then be said to exist in many realms of political decision making. Such procedures are to be established on the most extensive grounds possible, as far as is compatible with the principles presupposed by the ideal of democratic participation itself. A fully egalitarian society thereby will allow for the representation of both the particular desires of all persons in some realms of decision making and the universal interests of rational beings in others.

To outline a general constitutional framework for a liberal egalitarian society, we begin with the creation of a democratic constitution that establishes egalitarian principles of justice as the foundations of a liberal society. Included in the constitution will be:

1. A full bill of rights, corresponding to the spirit of the Rawlsian first principle and emphasizing a belief in the equal dignity of all citizens, included in which will be a guarantee of welfare rights to all;
2. A section guaranteeing fair equality of opportunity to all citizens;
3. Another section including a clear statement of the difference principle; and
4. A final statement delegating remaining authority to representative legislatures, as defined further on.

The constitution will be intended both as a public profession of the most cherished ideals of a liberal egalitarian society and as a document defining the limits that can rightly be placed upon individual freedom of action and majoritarian rule. Provision will be made for the amendment of all additional sections but those containing the most fundamental guarantees of liberties, welfare rights, and fair equality of opportunity. These latter principles, constituting the essential rights of individuals and the foundations of a liberal egalitarian society, will be amendable only by the nearly unanimous consent of all citizens; their safeguard will be entrusted to a judiciary through, among other means, judicial review. The near unanimity requirement for all basic rights reflects the firmest belief of liberal egalitarianism that these equalities are essential preconditions for the fair operation of democracy. The proviso for amendment of the difference principle and additional sections of the constitution (by considerably less than unanimity) corresponds to the belief that any theory of justice must ultimately be subject to *fair* test by citizens who have experienced the full application of that theory.[92]

With the constitution very briefly outlined, issues concerning the nature of political participation can be discussed more easily. On a national level, representatives will be democratically elected according to the principle of one person, one vote. The choice among candidates should be considered by citizens a choice based upon the criterion of "judicial competence": Each citizen should ask who will most justly interpret the spirit and letter of the constitution in particular cases. Nevertheless, democratic choice by citizens must be unconstrained: Elections are to be viewed both as cases of imperfect procedural justice and as statements of faith in the potential judicial attributes of all citizens. On the other hand, national representatives are not to see themselves simply as mandated delegates of their constituencies. They are to be interpreters of the constitution and representatives of the public good first and of the particular interests of their constituencies second, as far as is consistent with the interests of society as an egalitarian whole.[93] Thus there is a place for Burke's idea of representation, suitably and significantly constrained by frequent democratic accountability.[94] Representatives may be seen as "educators" in the judicial virtues of their constituencies, but the ultimate seat of power to elect or reject is meant to make clear that the "educated" are sovereign and therefore must be treated as mature adults capable of discerning their moral interests as citizens.[95]

But national representation will be only a part of the democratic government of an egalitarian society. The broad contours of welfare rights and an incomes policy will be determined by the national legislature and its advisory bodies to help ensure that medical resources and incomes are equitably distributed throughout the nation. Because welfare is a right, the courts can legitimately review the legislature's decisions. But to ensure equal treatment of needs, local communities will contain democratic political forums to deliberate directly upon the particular needs of their citizens. Those communities will in turn send representatives to the more centralized units of government until information reaches the appropriate level: the level at which decisions will be made on the just distribution of resources across communities, given full information about the particular (as well as universal) needs of each community on the demand side and about the aggregate of societal resources available on the supply side of the social-welfare equation.

It might be argued that unlike free-speech rights, welfare rights ought not to be and indeed cannot be constitutionally determined or defended, because the latter rights of recipience are dependent upon a socially relative standard of living, whereas the former rights of noninterference are not socially relative. Certainly the precise level of welfare rights owed to citizens is dependent upon society's established standard of living. Free-speech rights are not relative in the same sense. All that follows from this distinction is that courts cannot rightly apply an absolute or timeless standard in judging the justice of legislatively determined welfare rights. But we must not overdraw the distinction between welfare and speech rights. After all, the specific content of free-speech rights is also determined by certain socially relative considerations, for example, by reasonable time, place, and manner constraints and by socially determined standards of slander and libel. Courts must make some time-bound determinations in both cases – of what constitutes an adequate social standard of welfare in one case and of what constitutes a reasonable understanding of free-speech activity in the other. Undoubtedly, constitutional review of welfare rights will be more controversial than the review of free-speech rights in a society that has long treated free speech as a right but has recently treated welfare as a privilege. However, because welfare rights exist on the same level of principle as do free-speech rights, neither may be left solely to legislative policy determination.

Judicial review may constrain but does not obviate the value of or need for legislative decision making. We must also consider the range of democratic decision-making processes available at local levels. Using the example of education, local communities may democratically decide what optional curriculum to provide for their children. Education in basic mathematical, verbal, linguistic, and logical skills and basic political knowledge – for example, knowledge of constitutional principles – necessary for full citizenship and equal opportunity will have been universally sanctioned. Communities must provide forums in which citizens will be free to decide whether to add to the standard curriculum such matters as local histories or native languages or any of a variety of locally determined options. These forums thereby will be free to work within the constraints set by the overriding goal of education for personal autonomy and equal citizenship.[96]

Heated debates might take place over such choices, especially in very heterogeneous communities,[97] but this does not obviate the rationale or the need for local political participation. Citizens of an egalitarian society will already be integrated by a shared belief in the basic justice of their society. (If they are not, then liberal egalitarians will have failed a significant test of confidence in the basic social nature of human beings.) Disputes on the level of more particular interests *or* differing interpretations of universal interests will be necessary and healthy indications of the freedom of all citizens to express and find support for, or legitimate opposition to, their particular interests or interpretations of the public good.

None of these participatory forums must in theory or practice include every affected citizen of the community in question. But because there will be many issues open to local democratic decision making in every community, many participatory channels will be available for each citizen to choose among, depending on his particular knowledge and interests. Other local democratic institutions may function to delegate authority on certain issues to those with more expertise (a situation to be explored in greater detail later); in these cases democratic accountability should help guarantee that experts remain the servants rather than become the moral masters of their communities.

Clearly, this is a grossly simplified and incomplete sketch of the core governmental framework required by any democratic and egalitarian society. Little or no mention, for example, has been made of what form and substance of foreign policy or of judicial institutions would be consistent with the egalitarian perspective developed. This – along with a more complete specification of the structure of legislative, executive, and local participatory institutions – is a task for (at least) another complete work, one blueprinting the specific institutional design of a liberal egalitarian society. What I have hoped to indicate here is that the task of integrating democratic participation and equal distribution is one that is both possible and necessary to the spirit of a liberal egalitarian theory of justice – a theory that views society not only as a "social union of social unions," as does Rawlsian justice, but also as a "political union of political unions," as the participatory ideal demands.

I have yet to explore two other significant issues regarding the integration of participatory and other distributive concerns: (1) the extent of the need to expand the political realm into the economic life of an egalitarian society – a need previously suggested by Mill's advocacy of participatory democracy and by G. D. H. Cole's critique of the Fabians; and (2) the question whether bureaucratic institutions can and should be open to democratic participation. The major question to be considered in the next sections is how the broader participatory ideal can be accommodated within these two specific realms of an egalitarian social order consistently with other egalitarian distributive principles and the ideal of rational government.

INDUSTRIAL DEMOCRACY

The call for democratizing economic relations has most often been considered the by-product of Marxist theory,[98] an argument based upon a belief in the causal primacy of economic relations of productions. But I want to emphasize here the necessary place of industrial democracy within a liberal egalitarian society viewed as a political union of political unions.

In accord with the constitutionally sanctioned Rawlsian difference principle, the level of rewards attached to particular jobs within the national economy will be regulated by legislatively determined taxes and transfer payments. The outcome of collective bargaining relations between employers and employees thus will be significantly modified. We might expect the focus of collective bargaining to be altered in a society in which income differentials are significantly narrowed by taxation. One frequent criticism of capitalist-worker relations – that unions under capitalism concentrate upon wage bargaining rather than upon bargaining over job-content demands[99] – would be defused by the further removal of income determination from the private economic realm.

But there exists a second side of the leftist critique of capitalist economic relations, which concerns the subordination of worker to capitalist within the work situation.[100] Relative equality of wages is one face of egalitarian justice; relative equality of power over the structure of one's daily life, another. Now even were our radical critic to acknowledge that power cannot be strictly equalized within a free society, he would still have a legitimate case against the Rawlsian model of a just society, on grounds that can be shared by liberal egalitarians. Contemporary Marxists often echo Mill, perhaps even more closely than Marx, in claiming that subordinate work relations destroy public initiative, thwart intelligence, and in general militate against equal self-respect among workers.

Among contemporary participation theorists, Carole Pateman has best expanded the Millean case for participatory industrial democracy, although her account shares several weaknesses of previous arguments for workers' control. Pateman conflates Rousseau's and Mill's cases for participation.[101] She argues that for Rousseau, to force citizens to be free meant little more than to allow them the opportunities of equal participation in decisions affecting their lives.[102] In so arguing, she implies that there is no cost attached to Rousseau's value of strictly equal participation in a direct democracy. Mill avoids imposing this cost by emphasizing the need to expand *opportunities* to participate rather than to force strict equality of political participation per se.

Equal power within society was the only fair alternative for Rousseau to the equal and absolute independence men experienced in the state of nature. Indeed, given his image of natural man, equal surrender to and power over individuals would be the only acceptable terms of the social contract.[103] For in Rousseau's eyes, the source of each person's self-respect in the natural state was his pure independence (in which case self-love could not be challenged or perhaps even realized). After the social contract, the re-creation of self-respect would be dependent on equal submission to, and hence equal power over, others. Mill, with a more optimistic moral psychology, could view the participatory ideal as a means of expanding the possibility of equal dignity without absolutely equalizing the power of each individual over every other, and as a means of realizing man's nature as a progressive being without necessitating the mutilation of a more natural being.

Pateman's case for industrial democracy shares another, more specific, weakness with G. D. H. Cole's argument. Pateman's view of the role of industrial democracy borrows largely from Cole's belief that the substantive principles governing a just industrial society will derive from participatory work organizations. "For Cole," Pateman remarks approvingly, "it is industry that holds the key that will unlock the door to a truly democratic polity."[104] Cole and Pateman thus go beyond Rousseau (or at least clarify an ambiguity in Rousseau's account of participation) in supporting participatory association not only as a school for a newly learned freedom of the social passions but also as the source of just precepts of government:

Society as he [Cole] defined it is a "complex of associations held together by the wills of their members." If the individual is to be self-governing then he not only has to be able to participate in decision making in *all* the associations of which he is a member but the associations themselves have to be free to control their own affairs . . . , and if they were to be self-governing in this sense then they have to be roughly equal in political power.[105]

Cole's full account of the source of social justice is based upon the formal principle of function constrained by the principle of equal political power. A just society (in Cole's own rough terms) would be one in which each person is free to participate or to be freely represented in every function of his social life, given the structural precondition that participatory associations with similar or competing functions be equal in power.[106]

Cole has presented us with the most complete blueprint for, and Pateman with the most complete theoretical defense of, a radical participatory democracy, a society that stresses the *necessity* of "constant participation of the ordinary man in the conduct of those parts of the structure of Society with which he is directly concerned, and which he has therefore the best chance of understanding."[107] Demands by society on every citizen's time and energy are to be very extensive and to constitute *the* essense of individual freedom and self-development. Participatory democracy must be extended "not only or mainly to some special sphere of social action known as 'politics,' but to any and every form of social action, and, in especial, to industrial and economic fully as much as to political affairs."[108]

Though the argument underlying a broad extension of participatory institutions is a cogent one, the emphasis on the necessity of equal and constant participation based upon function is an unfortunate by-product of the second weakness in Pateman and Cole's participatory theory: No principles of equal distribution stand independently of the contingent desires of democratic citizens. Having dispensed with the will of the lawgiver in Rousseau, Cole has replaced it with the united will of the people: the actual balance of power, passion, and rationality between each citizen and every other.[109] Cole's theory is thus a variation on a traditional pluralist argument. The advantage of his pluralism over Madison's (for example) is its emphasis on the need for inclusion

205

of all citizens within political associations and for relative equality among bargaining groups. On the other hand, Cole's theory neglects the means necessary to maintain relative equality among groups: the imposition of constitutional constraints upon pluralist decision making. Cole expects relative equality of wages to result from an ongoing participatory society, but given the mutually constraining nature of participatory institutions within the guild system, he can only hope that equal power among guilds will effect equitable wage scales.[110] Cole thus leaves his theory open to the criticism that any distribution resulting from democratic decision making must be sanctioned as equitable, regardless of how inegalitarian. Justice is defined as the *actual will* of the citizens, and democratic decisions must be considered just, so long as they result from a legitimate structure of participatory associations. End-state principles are out of place in Cole's radically socialist theory, just as they are in Nozick's radically individualist one.

Nevertheless, the core contribution of Cole and Pateman's theory – their emphasis on the value of industrial democracy for self-dignity and development – can be realized without sacrificing the distributive ideal and without invoking an invisible-hand explanation of the necessary egalitarian results of participatory institutions. Exactly how can the participatory ideal be consistently integrated into our previous framework?

Workers' control in a fully egalitarian society will be limited to issues unrelated to wage- and profit-scale negotiations, for these issues must be equitably resolved on an industry-wide or national scale, to account for the affected interests of workers, consumers, and citizens. Yet full decision-making power will be granted to workers on many nonwage, nonprofit issues – particularly issues relating to job structure. These are issues on which I can imagine no just policy apart from that resulting from the democratic will of workers themselves, those whose lives are directly affected by the decision of how work is structured. Fair resolution of such issues therefore falls within the third category we outlined at the beginning of this chapter: A democratic process involving those directly affected by the decision will constitute a form of pure procedural justice (or fairness) so long as the process occurs within the context of otherwise just institutions.

When backed by an equitable national taxation and welfare policy, industrial democracy – although restricted to job-related issues – would serve to alleviate problems tied to the dehumanizing effects of the authoritarian organization of modern industry. In particular instances, where the job-structure preferences of workers are completely unacceptable to owners because of potential profit losses, a neutral government board, or the judiciary, might arbitrate the case, deciding whether unfair profit margins are expected by owners or unrealistic job benefits demanded by workers. More routinely, one would expect workers to have ample leeway in determining their working conditions once an equitable welfare and incomes policy was nationally established.

This form of workers' control corresponds to what Pateman calls full participation at the lower level of management: Workers have complete autonomy to decide issues related to job structure and shop-floor activity.[111] Pateman herself appears to advocate full participation at the higher level of management – democratic control of decisions on investment and marketing – as the ideal of industrial democracy.[112] Taking industrial democracy to represent the complete ideal of social justice in a socialist society, one can understand Pateman's argument for full workers' participation at all levels of management: Without such autonomy, workers would probably be subject to unreasonable structural constraints resulting from high profit margins and investment goals set by owners and managers.

But accepting a prior and more complete framework of egalitarian justice, the necessity of full participation by workers at the higher level disappears. The problem of capitalist power over workers will already have been significantly reduced by limits on profit set by the government. Therefore, neither owners nor managers will have the right to full power at the higher level. Note, however, that this necessary framework for the egalitarian justice of industrial relations – full participation at the lower level for workers, partial power for owners at the higher level – does not preclude the possibility of industries owned and controlled at both levels by workers. Indeed, one might argue that given the constraints placed by the state upon owners and managers, more worker-owned and -controlled industries would arise. Arguably, once wealth was redistributed and industries permitted only profits in line with the incentives required to elicit investment, initiative, and expertise, the competitive position of workers interested in high-level decision making would be likely to improve significantly, compared to the current situation. The crucial factor here is the limited power of ownership. Because the highest-level managers – whether they were sole owners, large stockholders, or rank-and-file workers – would have very limited power over the highest-level issues, and as a consequence very limited power over people within their enterprises, the question of who makes the top-level decisions would no longer be a highly charged moral issue.

A schema of integrating distributional and participatory policies appears, then, to meet often-cited objections to both laissez-faire and industrial democracy. The priority of distributional principles ensures that the universal interests of all citizens as rational beings are upheld by the highest institutions of government, whereas the presence of participatory institutions ensures that the particular desires of citizens can have real effect within those distributional constraints.

This schema also answers several of the major problems left unresolved by Dahl's discussion in *After the Revolution?* of whether and how to democratize industrial organization. At the same time, this resolution satisfies Dahl's basic principles of democratic authority.[113] Dahl rightly suggests that interest-group management (although satisfying the principle of control by affected interests) leaves industrial organization disturbingly hierarchical in its authority structure.[114] At the same time, he is troubled by the idea of ceding complete control of industry to any interest group; he – again rightly – perceives the need for external controls upon all forms of industrial management.[115]

Following Dahl's suggestion that property must be recognized as a bundle of rights, we have unwrapped the bundle. We have argued that democratic control over issues of job structure can, and should, be ceded to workers within industries without granting workers exclusive rights to control other issues of industrial management. Similarly, one must not cede to the owners or managers of industry full control over issues concerning wages, prices, or investment decisions. The external controls on management – aside from the forces of the market – should include imposition by a central government of the egalitarian distributive principles outlined in a just constitution.[116]

The more we unwrap property rights that we are now accustomed to buying and selling in one bundle, the more freedom for personal choice workers can attain, and the more protection those who are affected by a broad range of now private economic decisions can receive without necessarily sacrificing competent industrial management. Of course, this argument for industrial democracy presupposes the failure of Nozick's defense of the right of private owners to the whole bundle of property rights. Our case for industrial democracy rests on the argument made earlier that an owner of capital does not have an a priori (or natural) right to the free-market profits of his enterprise, just as a worker does not have a right to the free-market fruits of his labor. But so does the entire case for liberal egalitarianism rest upon a rejection of these libertarian claims.

BUREAUCRACY, PROFESSIONALISM, AND PARTICIPATION

Are bureaucracies likely to present significantly greater problems for a liberal egalitarian society than they now do for less egalitarian industrial societies? We do not – nor need we – contend that bureaucratic problems will disappear in a liberal egalitarian society.[117] Our principal argument concerns three major obstacles bureaucratic organizations have been thought to place in the way of a more egalitarian or democratic socialist ideal: Those obstacles are not likely to be greater, and in many cases they may be significantly less troublesome, for a liberal egalitarian society than for existing forms of advanced industrial societies.[118]

The three major obstacles are the following:

1. Bureaucracies have been known to subvert democratically established political ends by illegitimately usurping decision-making authority for their own or other special interest groups' aggrandizement.[119]
2. Bureaucracies are often legally ceded power that critics claim should rightly be granted to democratic majorities, rather than to a small group of professional bureaucrats.[120]
3. Within organizations, bureaucracies are hierarchical rather than participatory structures and offer jobs that are stultifying to the personalities of their occupants.[121] Marx's analysis of alienation can be extended here to criticize work within bureaucracies.

Each of these obstacles clearly applies quite broadly to advanced industrial societies; many theorists of modern bureaucracy have accordingly been led to assimilate the major ailments of democratic societies to those of authoritarian societies.[122] Yet some theorists still warn that increasing the role of the state will aggravate the bureaucratic malaise of democratic societies.[123] In creating new bureaucracies (in order to provide new social services or to redistribute income), a welfare state not only increases the opportunities for bureaucracies to usurp unsanctioned authority, subverting the ends of the welfare state, but also increases the dependency of citizens upon bureaucratic rather than upon democratic (participatory) institutions.[124] Finally, critics contend that in direct proportion to bureaucratic expansion, employment opportunities within liberal society become less attractive and more alienating. If these bureaucratic ills are present, they will extend quite deeply into the body of a more egalitarian society, subverting its egalitarian ends, eliminating vast realms of democratic governance, and creating a more alienated and more passive citizenry.

Yet those who directly extend the bureaucratic critique from contemporary to egalitarian societies ignore the fact that the lack of public accountability is often motivated by more than intentional recalcitrance or the desire for self-aggrandizement among bureaucrats. In free-enterprise systems, large, organized economic interests often exert grossly unequal pressures upon public bureaucracies, pressures unbalanced by other groups representing broader public interests.[125] In state socialist countries, the pressures to conform to the party's will are undoubtedly stronger than pressures capable of being peacefully exerted from below. This argument, if correct, has three important implications. First, bureaucracies are unlikely to act more consistently in the public interest in a liberal free-enterprise system than they are in a liberal egalitarian one.[126] Second, a democratic socialist system can be favorably distinguished from contemporary authoritarian state socialist systems. Third, the tendency of bureaucracies to subvert the public interest therefore need not be viewed as a tendency intrinsic to all bureaucratic organizations or to all advanced industrial societies.

The problem of the authoritarian nature of bureaucratic decision making still remains, however. One means of mitigating the undesirable effects of bureaucratic authority is decentralization of administration; a still more participatory solution would be to decentralize and to extend local democratic control over bureaucratic decision making.[127]

Decentralization of bureaucratic administration may produce greater responsiveness to popular needs and desires if local populations are not unevenly divided into rich and organized, poor and disorganized, groups. The grossly disproportionate influence of organized groups that Selznick observed while studying the Tennessee Valley Authority is much more likely to occur within an inegalitarian than within an egalitarian society.[128] We can rationally expect decentralized bureaucracies to be more responsive to the needs and desires of citizens within an egalitarian society, because accountability – the solution to the first criticism of bureaucracy – is more likely to prevail in a society whose citizens are universally well educated and well-off than in a society in which relatively few organized private-interest groups vie with each other for influence, to the exclusion of the poor, uneducated, and unorganized.

However, decentralized administration goes only a small way toward answering the second criticism, which is in many ways a more troubling one: that even when a bureaucracy does perform its egalitarian mission faithfully, it will be usurping from citizens what should be within the province of a democratic participatory institution. This critique challenges the very legitimacy of the role of bureaucracies and of expertise, whether professional or otherwise, in the administration – even the decentralized administration – of a just society. One suggested answer to this challenge has been to create representative bureaucracies, whose members represent a cross section of the citizenry and directly represent by mandate their respective interests.[129] Besides establishing a criterion for representation that is unlikely to fulfill its function,[130] this solution misunderstands the nature and role of bureaucracies in a just society.

Bureaucracies cannot exist as substitutes for political forums; where the public interest remains uncertain, institutions of participatory democracy rather than bureaucracies must be established to determine public ends legitimately. A role for competent execution of the public interest exists within an egalitarian society only after the public interest has been legitimately determined.[131] The distribution of police protection, health care, and basic educational skills and the redistribution of income are examples of ends that are likely to necessitate a significant degree of bureaucratic execution, if they are to be equitably effected throughout society. We do not want a local community to have the right to force the Internal Revenue Service to tax some residents at preferential rates. Nor do we want a police force to treat preferentially the most politically active citizens in its community, although we might well want a police force and a health service to be more decentralized than an IRS, because there is good reason to believe that local communities will have more diverse needs for police protection and for health care than for income redistribution.[132] Accountability may be facilitated and minority interests protected by decentralization in some organizations and by centralization in others.[133]

Beyond decentralization and administration, participatory theorists also suggest the need for local democratic control over decentralized bureaucracies in order to fulfill the educative function of participation.[134] Here they echo Mill's fear that bureaucracies will foster a passive, unenlightened citizenry, although Mill himself took a very ambivalent position regarding the benefits of participation compared to those of competent administration.[135]

Participatory and distributive equality reintegrated

The crucial choice in a society in which income and basic services are much more equally distributed than in contemporary societies often will not be between competent and participatory administration but between decisions that are properly subject to local democratic determination and those properly subject to national democratic or constitutional determination.[136] Here I am assuming that well-educated local majorities will often be able to discern competence in competing candidates and to control local service organizations competently if they so desire, but that they will not always be *entitled* to determine the ends that those candidates or those organizations should pursue. When they are so competent and so entitled, decentralized participatory administration should take priority over centralized or decentralized nonparticipatory administration.[137] But when such entitlement is lacking, participatory control on a local level is inappropriate.[138] Control over the fiscal probity of local police departments and over the ends served by conservation programs are two issues that theorists sympathetic to community control have suggested to be properly national rather than local, in recognition of our being ideally "more than a group of potentially autonomous neighborhoods."[139]

Recognition of the needs extending across local communities for specialized health care, basic educational services, competent police protection, and effective conservation services suggests that there is room for professionalism in a just society, just as there is room for democratic organizations to ensure that professional officeholders remain accountable to the public interest.[140] We need bureaucracies and professionals (among other reasons) in order to help ensure that universal norms, once legislated, are *applied* evenhandedly across communities.[141]

With respect to the role of competence, unless one believes (as Lenin once did)[142] that administration in an ideal society will require no greater skills than those necessary to run a post office (and Lenin probably underestimated the requisite level of those skills), qualifications of technical expertise for bureaucratic and professional offices will remain necessary and desirable. But other characteristics of an egalitarian society will mitigate the troubling consequences of the selective standards of professionalism in our society. Educational opportunities will be equalized throughout society, allowing greater access to professions. And the qualifications for professional and other bureaucratic positions will be appropriate to the work required; this standard of relevance is implicit within the principle of equal effective opportunity. These characteristics of a just egalitarian society combined would help ensure not only that professional and bureaucratic offices are filled by those most qualified to carry out the public interest, but that those offices are effectively open to the broadest range of citizens.

But jobs within bureaucracies, centralized or decentralized, might yet remain so alienating as to militate against attracting the most qualified people or having attracted them, might render them quasi-mindless "cogs" within the bureaucratic machine. If we want bureaucrats who do not discriminate among the different faces of their clients, can we avoid creating a class of people who lack discriminating minds?

That bureaucrats must be rule governed in dealing with their clientele does not preclude their collective participation in defining the organization of work internal to the bureaucracy.[143] Weber's model of a bureaucracy in which all tasks are highly specialized, hierarchically organized, and defined from above is not the only rationally conceivable or workable model of bureaucracy.[144] To reconsider Lenin's example, work within a post office need not be organized so that it is maximally specialized; public employees may have participatory control over the structure of their work so long as that control does not extend to the determination of the basic external ends which the organization must fulfill. One publicly recognized end of an egalitarian society is equal effective liberty; that end can be pursued by expanding participation within sectors of public as well as private employment.[145]

There is, however, another side to the problem of job alienation. Democratic theorists have criticized the excessive degree of self-determination over work possessed by professionals.[146] These criticisms, if consistent, must be directed at the lack of professional accountability to the public interest rather than at the nature of professional work itself. The latter is one positive characteristic of professional occupations.[147] Professionals true to their calling will derive personal satisfaction from work while they consciously satisfy other people's needs. Maintaining a realm for professional expertise is compatible with maintaining institutions to ensure professional accountability to the public: Citizen-review boards may be a necessary measure. But were professions not internally governed by norms regarding the public interest, who would not doubt that political institutions could effectively control their activity? Public accountability, however, is not the same thing as participatory rights over professional work; such rights would only serve to create more alienated work out of a form that might serve as a model for unalienated labor. Public accountability is far from a reality in American and British societies today. Not only are there few institutional attempts to hold the professions accountable but there are structural barriers to such accountability: a scarce labor supply and inappropriate monetary rewards for service to the most advantaged citizens. The United States supports a scarce labor market in medicine, for example, by inadequately funding medical education and offers not only American but British doctors incentives to gain much more by serving rich than poor U.S. citizens. The case of the United States "draining away" British doctors also indicates still another problem – that of establishing even a very limited form of democratic socialism in only one country.

PARTICIPATION AND POPULAR SOVEREIGNTY

One of the major arguments for extending the political sphere within a liberal democracy is to create a greater dispersion of political power than now exists both within the political sphere, narrowly understood, and within a newly politicized economic sphere. This goal of a broad diffusion of political power underlies the claim made by advocates of participation that by democratizing relations within a state, one can minimize inequality of power among persons and, as a partial consequence, maximize equality of self-respect among citizens.

The participatory ideal goes a long way toward answering Anthony Crosland's doubts about the political consequences of an egalitarian ideal of economic redistribution. Crosland was in part correct in pointing to the political dangers of the egalitarian goal as put forward by his intellectual progenitors: Were a highly centralized state to be granted exclusive economic as well as political power, we might rationally fear political tyranny. But like that of the original Fabians, Crosland's vision focused on only one side of the egalitarian ideal: the satisfaction of economic needs. And even on this side, his was a distorted vision of the necessary means toward a more egalitarian distribution. An irony existed within this view (as within those of many other, less egalitarian theorists): Though fearing above all the monolithic potential of state power, he was too quick in assuming that the state, even a democratic one, could only act effectively as a quasi-monolithic, bureaucratic entity. And once the state is perceived as an enormously powerful, democratically unaccountable, bureaucratic machine, only an equally concentrated, bureaucraticized, and politically independent economic sector can be expected to serve as an effective countervailing power to the political Leviathan.

From this critical perspective, the major steps we have taken toward reconstituting a liberal egalitarian vision have been to establish (1) a priority within the egalitarian distributive ideal of guaranteeing equal civil and political liberties and ensuring the fair value of those liberties, and (2) an emphasis upon opening up, within the economic and administrative spheres, forums of democratic participation and control consistent with the principles of equitable economic distribution and the public's own need for expertise beyond that which is available through democratic participation.

We have reinterpreted the egalitarian ideals to ensure maximum civil and political liberty and minimum concentration of political power, again employing the standard of effective liberty and recognizing that political power can be exercised tyrannically by private as well as public organizations. This reinterpretation is perfectly compatible with a liberal state. Redistribution need not be effected by state ownership of all industry but can be carried out by constitutionally sanctioned legislative controls upon investments, profits, wages, and salaries, and perhaps even upon the size and structure of industry. If such controls proved to be ineffective, state ownership would be legitimately sanctioned. But even were we to suppose this less favorable outcome, the second face of our egalitarian ideal would guard against the most fearful aspects of state ownership. In the preferred case of private ownership, implementation of the participatory ideal would protect against a preponderance of power on the side of individual owners or capitalists as a group. In the case of state ownership, partial participatory rights would extend to higher levels of management, militating against the tyrannical tendencies of unbalanced state (or bureaucratic) control over the economy. But in neither case would participatory institutions be the sole hedges on state or capitalist power. Constitutional guarantees of equal liberties and of an egalitarian distribution of primary goods would exist in both cases: in one case limiting the power of private owners of capital, and in the other limiting the prerogatives of the state.

In addition to these practical constraints upon political power, participatory institutions may provide the psychological barriers that many of the new Fabians sought in order to avoid unaccountable or unrestrained political power. Unlike the right to vote in infrequent national elections, the right to participate in ongoing decisions closely affecting one's life places responsibility for self and communal welfare directly on the shoulders of each citizen. The argument against mass political participation – that most citizens, particularly the working classes, are ill prepared for political participation and incapable of political responsibility, given the authoritarian nature of their predominant daily social relationships[148] – will no longer hold in a participatory society in which work relationships are largely democratized. A more fully participatory society is likely to militate against the "authoritarian personality" while it affirms the equal dignity of citizens. This is a more specific meaning than Mill attributed to participation as a school of the passions, yet it is a connection between democratic participation and democratic personality whose potential has been suggested by empirical studies of the relationships between personality and democratic (as opposed to authoritarian) political cultures and between the sense of political or personal efficacy and participatory (as opposed to autocratic) work structures.[149]

Finally, a participatory society whose major institutions are constrained by egalitarian distributive principles will serve as a school in a more direct sense. Although participatory institutions will encourage democratic decision making, the constraints placed upon those decisions will teach citizens what the justice of their society is. From the highest representative officials, whose first public task is to design just legislation and whose second task is to represent the particular desires of their constituencies, to representatives on local workers' councils who must design job structures within the possibilities of difference-principle guidelines, each participating citizen will be made aware of the meaning of distributive justice in his society. Nonetheless, as Rawls has indicated, each citizen may not ultimately accept all aspects of the two principles of distributive justice. Representation and, in this schema, participation will be circumscribed by a just constitution; "but in due course a firm majority of the electorate is able to achieve its aims, by constitutional amendment if necessary."[150] All but the most basic liberties, equal opportunity and welfare rights – the bedrock of any democratic and egalitarian society – may be justly amended by majoritarian means. Citizens are educated by the principles of justice: Basic constitutional rights are amendable only by overwhelming democratic approval. But the ultimate test of the *viability* of those principles, even the most basic liberties and rights, must rest upon their compatibility with the moral sensibilities of citizens.

Participation and popular sovereignty

The participatory ideal of an egalitarian society is, then, both an internally powerful and an externally demanding one. It is powerful because ultimate sovereignty must lie with the citizens of a just society. And it is demanding in requiring our faith in the potential dignity and uncoerced, but socialized, sense of justice of democratic citizens.

Conclusion: the limits of liberal egalitarian politics

At the center of the debate concerning equality in recent years has been the contrast between the so-called "new" and "old" egalitarianism. The new egalitarianism takes as the primary aim of distributive justice equality of results, whereas the old took as its primary aim equality of opportunity. The old egalitarianism is believed to be a direct application of classical liberal principles to contemporary society, and the new egalitarianism – associated most frequently with Rawls's theory – is said to be extraliberal in character, denying the individuality, particularly the moral individuality, of persons.[1]

In tracing the foundations of contemporary egalitarianism back to classical liberalism, I have called into question this interpretation of the new egalitarianism. I have attempted to demonstrate that Rawls's theory is a form of *liberal* egalitarianism in its attempt to derive principles of justice from an understanding of individual interests. The arguments for welfare rights and for economic redistribution derived from the difference principle can be understood as outgrowths of a relatively new liberal awareness of the material prerequisites for equalizing opportunity among individuals that appears within contemporary advanced industrial societies.[2]

I have also extended the view of liberal egalitarianism beyond that of redistributing economic goods to include a further expansion and equalization of opportunities to participate in political life, now broadly understood. There then arises the need to integrate these two primary egalitarian concerns of redistributing material goods and equalizing participatory opportunities, and I suggested how a revised Rawlsian framework of justice could consistently accommodate both ideals.[3]

Although I have claimed that Rawls's theory is not a new egalitarianism in the sense of a theory that rejects the classical liberal method or the classical liberal principle of equal opportunity, I want to suggest in conclusion that there exists another egalitarian model that lies outside liberal egalitarianism and that serves as a critical alternative to it. I call this alternative model of justice radical or communal egalitarianism.

Communal egalitarianism is not new. Though often employed or alluded to by radical critics of Rawls, it finds its modern foundations in Rousseau.[4] Whereas liberal egalitarianism is characterized by arguments for a more equal distribution of primary goods based upon the interests of individual citizens (characterized as equal), communal egalitarianism views equality as a good for society taken as a whole, independently (at least to a significant extent) of how equalizing distribution will satisfy the interests of individual citizens.[5] Put differently, the radical egalitarian argument is that an understanding of what constitutes an individual's interest cannot precede an understanding of what constitutes a desirable political community.[6] Equality is considered a primary value insofar as it is constitutive of a fraternal social order, regardless of whether fraternity is in the interest of all individual citizens.[7]

The Rousseauean roots of this perspective are not hard to find, although another interpretation of Rousseau might place his argument within the individualist framework of liberal egalitarianism.[8] A radical egalitarian interpretation of Rousseau emphasizes the desirability of establishing a community within which people are equally dependent, economically and politically, upon the state, rather than upon particular private individuals. For Rousseau, equal dependency can create freedom: not only freedom from dependence upon the particular wills of others but a new, moral freedom.[9] In order for all people to be equally dependent on the state, they must rule equally and possess relatively equal amounts of primary goods.[10] Even were it in the interest of the least advantaged to have more distributive inequality, political and economic equality will be considered a preferable state of affairs. We can find two reasons in Rousseau for reaching this counter-intuitive conclusion: (1) given the invidious effects of competition and comparisons among people generally, only approximate economic equality and strict limits upon economic competition will establish a fraternal society;[11] and (2) without strict equality of political participation, some people will become slaves to the political wills of others, again preventing the establishment of a fraternal society, assuming (as did Rousseau) that fraternity depends upon the equal political autonomy of persons.[12]

219

Now, Rousseau placed much more emphasis on the need for the latter, participatory mode of equality than upon the former, economic mode. With regard to economic equality, he merely specified that no one be so rich or poor as to permit one person to buy another. Yet he also set as a precondition for democracy that absolute levels of wealth be so low that there be "little or no luxury."[13]

Contemporary radical egalitarians may place more emphasis upon economic equality than did Rousseau once they concede the impossibility of a return to small-scale communal life, and hence the impossibility of all citizens' equally and directly participating in law making.[14] A stricter equality in the economic realm (including of course equal treatment of needs, rather than the same treatment for all regardless of need) may be viewed as a necessary and desirable, even if an incomplete, substitute for equalizing political participation. Once each person cannot be directly involved in every legislative decision, economic equality becomes a major means of preventing some individuals from exercising more political power than others by virtue of their economic position. But more significantly, economic equality serves publicly to characterize a society of equal individuals wherein no one wants more, or less, than is available for anyone else. The interests of individuals are transcended in a radically egalitarian society by the moral order of the community. Each individual's interest in social equality is an irreducible moral interest realized only by living and participating in the political life of that society.[15]

Here is the major criticism addressed by radical to liberal egalitarians: that the moral interest of individuals in equality cannot be reduced to individual interest, but must be directly derived from a vision of an egalitarian moral community. This underlying assumption accounts for the numerous attacks upon liberalism, and upon Rawls's liberal egalitarianism, as individualistic and ahistorical.[16] Liberal egalitarianism is considered individualistic in that its starting point is the self rather than the moral interest of rational individuals,[17] and ahistorical in that it assumes the possibility of stipulating some relatively timeless notion of individual interest apart from the particular time and society in which individuals live.[18] Closely related criticism often charges liberal egalitarianism with systematically underestimating the harmonious social nature of individuals, a nature that will be evident when (but only when) a good social order is created.[19]

Liberal egalitarianism is obviously individualistic in the sense that priority is given to individual rights and liberties,[20] and in a deeper sense in that it begins with a notion of individual interest and attempts to justify only those principles that can be derived from the needs or desires of individuals. Rawls's original position, taken as a characterization of individuals in a state of equality, is in addition an abstraction from any existing social condition, and people within the original position are indeed characterized as rational, mutually disinterested beings. There is, however, a certain irony in this radical critique of the original position, because the original position is not meant to characterize people either as they are or as they should be (i.e., as rational maximizers of their self-interest). Rather, it is only because "people" within the original position are really all the very same person – and hence have no distinctive interests, wants, or desires – that the original position provides a starting point from which principles of justice can be derived. In this sense, the original position is a very *non*individualistic starting point.[21] There is another, even more fundamental, sense in which Rawls's framework for deriving principles of justice is nonindividualistic: One has to conceive of one's interests as lying to a considerable degree outside one's self to agree to enter the original position in the first place. That is to say, in accepting a Rawlsian framework, we are committing ourselves to viewing our interest in social justice as identical to the interest of every other member of the community of which we will become a part.[22]

Therefore, what remains of the radical critique is that liberal egalitarianism is too individualistic because it reduces the value of equality to individual interest. Equality is a value for a community taken as a whole, rather than a means of satisfying the interests of individuals within that community taken separately. A less radical translation of this criticism, however, might be the following: Because people must be nonindividualistic if they are to enter into the original position, the reasoning from self-interest within the original position can be more accurately viewed as reasoning from a *moral* interest in community that each of us as real, particular individuals has outside the original position. The advantage of this latter translation of our interest in egalitarian social justice is that it not only makes clear its status as a moral interest but it avoids the problem of ahistoricity leveled against Rawls's formulation.

There is considerable force to the criticism of ahistoricity insofar as it questions whether any set of principles, however general, can be applicable to all societies at all times.[23] Our rational capacities are stretched beyond their limits by Rawls's attempt to stipulate a just savings principle as if we were individuals whose rationality was unbounded by time, not knowing in which of thirty centuries we might be living or to which of thousands of societies we might

221

belong, but being capable of agreeing upon a principle to govern our society's investment for the future.[24] But once we set the problem of the just savings principle aside and concentrate upon the set of principles that are intended to apply to contemporary, advanced industrial societies, more modest claims can be made for liberal egalitarianism, claims that go a significant way toward meeting the charge of ahistoricity.

My more modest proposal has been the following: that the two principles of justice, suitably revised, are those principles that would be chosen by individuals within advanced industrial societies who already accept a basic assumption of Rawlsian and liberal egalitarianism – that people are equal moral individuals and should be treated as such by the institutions of a well-ordered society. By this formulation, liberal egalitarianism makes no claim to being a timeless conception of justice or even a conception that is capable of capturing the minds of those who do not share its basic tenet of human equality. On the other hand, this claim of liberal egalitarianism, however limited, is still a powerful one. I have earlier provided liberal theorists' arguments for establishing this assumption and for considering it a meaningful one upon which to base principles of justice.

Another advantage to this historically specific formulation of liberal egalitarianism is that it can give more determinate content to the notion of primary goods, and particularly to the notion of self-respect that most contemporary egalitarians regard as the most basic of primary goods. Michael Teitelman objects to Rawls's use of self-respect as a primary good because it is, he claims, an almost vacuous concept, an indictment reminiscent of Tocqueville's warning concerning the abstract terms that abound in democratic societies.[25] But abstract terms gain more explicit meaning when tied to a particular historical and social context. Perhaps self-respect has not been a primary good in all sociohistorical contexts.[26] Or even if it always has been a universal good for human life, the economic and political prerequisites for achieving equal self-respect among persons are very likely to have varied over time and among societies at different levels of development.[27]

Teitelman's charge against Rawls is well taken if he means to suggest that the meaning of self-respect as a primary good must be attached to a particular sociohistorical setting.[28] However, once we consider the requirements for equalizing self-respect in the contemporary United States, for example, the abstract concept gains a good deal of concreteness, at least with reference to some necessary preconditions for its attainment. For example, it is difficult to imagine people achieving equal self-respect in contemporary America without universal suffrage, or without basic welfare rights.[29] There will remain, of course, room for political disagreement, even in a liberal egalitarian society, concerning the prerequisites for achieving self-respect, but that does not diminish the force of the standard as a constraint upon distribution. To argue, as does Charles Frankel, that more attention needs to be given to the possibility that "an aristocracy, which assigns every man a place in the social procession, is better for self-respect than an egalitarian society that generates loneliness, anxiety, and identity crises" is wrongly to assume that the preconditions for creating self-respect are infinitely malleable within a given social and historical context.[30] Not surprisingly, Frankel goes on to admit that "I would not myself wish to defend very hard any of the arguments for inequality I have given here."[31] Why, then, present these arguments as viable alternatives to Rawls's egalitarianism? The answer is, I think, that Frankel reads Rawls as presenting an argument that has the same egalitarian implications for all times and places. As the radical critique of Rawls should remind us, in abstracting away from a specific historical setting, we render the principles of egalitarian justice both more ambiguous or formalistic in their implications and more problematic in their justification.

On another level, radical critics of liberal egalitarianism appear to view these ties to historical context as dispensable chains rather than as welcome anchors to contemporary reality. This radical argument, taken more straightforwardly from Marx than from Rousseau, suggests that human beings will come into their true, socially harmonious nature with the passing of certain competitive and exploitative economic institutions. (The Rousseauean argument is more complicated, because it is not clear that there exists a human nature to be realized in Rousseau, although Rousseau does leave open the possibility of social harmony by viewing human nature as extremely malleable by social institutions.) The liberal argument for egalitarian distributive principles assumes that the Humean constraints of scarcity and a conflict of individual interests apply even for considerations of ideal theory.[32] Thus there always remains within liberal egalitarian theory a balancing of individual interests, rather than a vision of their ultimate harmonization. We might view this simply as a limitation of the project of liberal egalitarianism, with radical egalitarian thought lying beyond liberalism, both in its historical perspective and in its ultimate vision of what constitutes an ideal society. Surely no liberal egalitarian could object to the radical vision of a socially harmonious society as a positive step beyond a more strife-ridden one![33]

But this reconciliation of liberal and radical egalitarianism, however hopeful, is too simple, because liberal egalitarianism may not be the best means of arriving at a radically egalitarian society. In his critique of Rawls, Brian Barry suggests that a distributive principle offering more to those whose productions benefit the least advantaged may be counterproductive to the achievement of a society based upon altruistic human relationships, wherein no one expects to gain from his contributions to the welfare of others.[34] Though I cannot find any direct, definitive empirical evidence for this claim, the possibility of altruism is philosophically defended by Thomas Nagel, and its sociological practicability is explored by Richard Titmuss in his comparative study of blood-donor systems in Great Britain and the United States.[35] Titmuss's argument suggests that distributive institutions that even partially reward self-interested motivation will stifle altruistic behavior that would otherwise be freely forthcoming from citizens of a society like the United States. However, the empirical grounding for Titmuss's conclusions is not secure. Other differences – for example, the smaller and more socially homogeneous nature of the British population – may account for the greater proportion of altruistic donors in that country. But even granting that this explanation of the differential rate of blood donations is accurate, we might still question whether we can therefore expect altruism to be an effective motivation when sacrifices (in the work involved and the potential income forsaken) are much higher than those involved in donating blood, as sacrifices would be in a society in which distributive institutions relied much more heavily upon the altruistic behavior of citizens to stimulate production for the needs of others.[36]

There is still another possible end of radical egalitarianism that is necessarily neglected by the liberal vision of a just society. A liberal egalitarian society cannot guarantee equality of self-esteem among its citizens.[37] Self-esteem – a favorable appreciation or opinion of oneself – is a quality that people possess in varying degrees, depending in part upon the distribution of praise and honor within their society.[38] Self-respect – proper regard for the dignity of one's person – is of an "all or nothing" quality. It is plausible to think that self-respect can be equalized in a liberal egalitarian society through a more equal distribution of primary goods, coupled with the full range of equal civil and political liberties.[39] But because self-esteem accrues to people by virtue of their relative success within their chosen pursuits, as a consequence of the relative level of public appreciation of their specific accomplishments, and perhaps also because of nonrational elements within their psyches not amenable to public manipulation, its distribution probably cannot be equalized without sacrificing either the liberty of all individuals to choose their own life plans (consistent with the like liberty of others) or the freedom of all citizens to distribute praise and honor to their peers as they judge fit. In this sense, also, liberal egalitarianism can be said to be based upon an individualistic notion of equality, which stipulates that a just society can be achieved by suitably equalizing the external conditions of people's existences, rather than by equalizing the psychological interactions of individuals more directly. Were the strictly interpersonal zero-sum forms of inequality most crucial to a person's sense of self-respect (as distinguished from honor or self-esteem), then one would be required either to step outside the bounds of liberalism in seeking an egalitarian society or to sacrifice the equality ideal to that of individual freedom. Here again, a liberal vision of equality depends upon a non-Rousseauean belief in the present external sources of unequal self-respect among citizens and the potential internal bases for a cooperative egalitarian order, one that admits multibased inequalities of self-esteem without threatening mutual self-respect and a cooperative spirit among citizens.[40]

As to the practical limits internal to the liberal ideals of equal distribution and equal participation, we can only rely upon extrapolations from past and contemporary empirical studies of income distribution and participation within unjust or nearly just societies. Though I have explored the possible implications of several of these studies, I have argued that the implications drawn from any contemporary empirical study are likely to vary significantly, depending upon one's underlying optimism or pessimism concerning the potentialities of human nature. Therefore, I claim only to have mustered *plausible* support here for the possibility of a well-ordered liberal egalitarian society characterizing an equal humanity.

Yet this vision does not depend upon an unfounded or unlimited optimism. With respect to the practical possibilities of a more equal income distribution, I have cited relevant contemporary studies that have examined the effects of progressive taxation and income floors upon work incentives.[41] These studies point to the practical possibilities of a significantly greater equality by challenging the conservative's empirical claim that a more progressive taxation or a more generous support of the less-advantaged classes will be counterproductive.[42] Of course, that challenge must await proof through actual social practice, as must the conservative's own claims. No doubt disincentive effects will at some point arise – but that point is at present so distant as to evade calculation and perhaps also warrant less critical concern.

Given differential desires for political activity among individuals in a just society, the participatory activities of individuals are unlikely to be radically equalized. But the liberal democratic ideal does not demand absolute equalization of participation among individuals or perhaps even among all groups. We can reasonably expect that participation rates among income categories would be equalized, as there is little evidence to suggest that small differences in income would produce large differences in preferences for political participation. Present extreme differentials in income and in the availability of leisure time among classes help account for the great participatory gaps between classes, especially in those political activities (campaigning, for example) that demand a great deal of time and effort. Not only income but enforced leisure differentials among groups would diminish significantly in a just society. Freely chosen differentials in use of leisure among individuals may then limit equality of participation, but those remaining inequalities would not be class based, but based more acceptably upon individual preference, influenced perhaps by group subcultures.

I have implicitly dealt with both the internal psychological limits and the external psychological boundaries of the liberal egalitarian ideal. Internal to liberalism is the view that people are at least partially independent centers of emotion and rationality. Liberals therefore concede at the outset the likelihood of perpetual conflict among individuals in an unregulated society, as well as the potential for stable cooperation once a just state is instituted. The liberal egalitarian state therefore seeks to establish the fairest terms of agreement so as to avoid the potential conflicts between individual desires. The view that individual interest will always contain a significant component of "self" – allowing either for egocentric interests or for unique, though possibly altruistic, conceptions of the good life – leads liberal egalitarians to a social design permitting individuals both a degree of self-control over their life chances and a degree of unequal capacity (though not power over other persons) in carrying out their life plans. Were people not to some degree inherently separate and conflicting systems of desires, a more radically egalitarian society might result. But that radical vision rests upon what liberals take to be a highly counter-intuitive conception of moral psychology: that individual consciousness can become freely merged with that of the collectivity.

Clearly, there are more pessimistic views of human psychology than that which underlies a liberal egalitarian vision, views that, when accepted, undermine liberal designs for a stable egalitarian order. At the extreme, the belief that envy is the necessary and sufficient source of *all* quests for equality would reduce the difference principle to a mere rationalization of resentment, significantly undermining its independent moral status. This is one interpretation of Nietzsche's critique of the morality of the liberal state.[43] At the same time, were one to postulate universal envy of all inequalities, one might be forced to choose between advocating absolute equality in order to achieve a stable society (despite one's cynicism concerning the source of the passion for equality) or advocating a very authoritarian regime in order to maintain social stability amidst inequality. Both alternatives are opposed by liberal egalitarianism in the name of freedom for citizens to pursue their own unique plans of life.

Alternatively, a radical pessimist might adopt a Nietzschean solution: abandoning the goal of equality entirely and establishing a society in which the strong will win out, morally if not physically. What this new nonslave morality would look like Nietzsche never tells us. He implies, though, that its superior human source will justify its moral content insofar as the overman will naturally deserve the right to determine the rules of the game: For who else could possibly lack any reason to envy? Only the overman will possess the dignity, in Nietzsche's terms, the independence from the motive of envy, for true moral reason. But Nietzsche's argument at the same time suggests that were people in fact potentially equal and did they therefore not desire equality solely for envy's sake, the basis of morality would rightly be that equality which constitutes the source of human dignity. As I have argued, it is this potential equality of moral persons that lies at the foundations of liberal egalitarian justice.

Liberal egalitarians claim that as equal moral persons people are entitled to equal liberties and welfare rights. The institutions of distribution do not base differential entitlements upon judgments of personal desert, for the liberal state lacks both the right and the capacity to do so. Thus liberal justice does not even approach divine justice in its operation. As the absence of an overman prevents a justified political and moral tyranny, so also does the absence of a divine overseer to guide the state eliminate the goal of divine judgment; the differential worth of persons must remain unknown to the secular state. People therefore remain the sole overseers of their inner lives, judging the worth of others at their own intellectual risk. Our opacity is the source both of our protection against tyranny and our ineluctable (partial) separation from our fellow men and women.

Distribution based upon desert, then, is a goal liberal egalitarians cannot consistently pursue, and for good reason. However, there remain two essential, largely unexplored, ways in which my study falls short of the goals a liberal egalitarian theory of justice might ideally, and plausibly, attain. The first is the application of an ideal theory of liberal egalitarian justice to situations of non-ideal justice. The worth of ideal theory does not depend upon its direct application to contemporary situations of political conflict. Yet an ideal theory of equality may be able to guide us in seeking just solutions to some problems encountered within unjust societies such as our own. Given the added problems created by established expectations amid accumulated past injustices, the precise nature of that application of ideal to nonideal justice – to questions how one can rightly move from a less to a more just society – must remain unanswered here. Quite plausibly there may be no just solution, as Sidgwick's paradox of conservative justice suggests.[44] And though Joel Feinberg's claims for the ineluctability of moral conflict are too sweeping, on the level of nonideal theory his case may be well taken.[45]

The second conspicuous omission from my consideration has been a discussion of the relevance of egalitarian ideals to distributive justice *among* states. I have challenged the view that this omission necessarily indicates an apparently fatal flaw within liberal egalitarianism. Nevertheless, the importance of an internationalist perspective on equality remains. We must only recognize that an egalitarian theory of justice within nations cannot be directly extended to a world egalitarian order without serious consideration of the problems of political liberty mentioned in Chapter 5. The egalitarian structure I have erected remains compatible, within the constraints I have discussed, with the original ideals of human equality. Yet even assuming the meaningfulness of established nationhood and of a national egalitarianism, my theory lacks a principled specification of an egalitarian nation's obligations to less-advantaged nations, obligations that I expect would be extensive even in a world order in which the more-advantaged states had rectified their past injustices to the less advantaged.

What I have done here is to lay the groundwork for, explore, and further develop the outlines of an egalitarian theory of justice applicable to contemporary postindustrial societies, and consistent with the classical liberal tradition. That theory, like classical liberalism, takes people as they are and attempts to build political societies that will be most consistent with their interests as passionate and rational beings. But a liberal egalitarian state, unlike Hobbes's, will not leave people as it finds them. True to the liberal belief in human equality, a just political order would cultivate the potential for cooperation among people while protecting their individuality from unjustified social intrusions. Thus moral transformation is expected to follow from the institutionalization of a just political order – for only with that creation can people securely contribute to a mutual cooperative enterprise without risk of sacrificing their individual dignity or public recognition of their individual needs in the process.

But liberal theory does not presuppose a *radical* moral transformation of individuals from their present condition: Neither a complete altruism nor an identity between individual and collective wills is required.[46] Rather, liberal egalitarianism looks forward to a further development of the cooperative nature of individuals already revealed in the development of the liberal welfare state. Even the liberal's most radical expectation – that the most advantaged will willingly and in a fraternal spirit contribute to the interests of the least advantaged – does not require a complete remaking of moral consciousness. For the perceived entitlements of the rich today have been in large part conditioned by the rules of the present economic system, as their much greater past expectations of entitlement reveal. And even given our less than fully egalitarian rules of the game, we often find the rich justifying their larger shares by a rationale approaching that of the difference principle: claiming that their greater shares are justified insofar as they have contributed to the greatest welfare of the poor. A fully egalitarian society would ensure that such claims to cooperative spirit on the part of the most advantaged were made in good faith. And, perhaps as significantly, with the institutionalization of an egalitarian society, those with more would lack the need to rationalize their greater shares: A just rationale for inequalities would have become a publicly acknowledged and operative standard.

Some have argued that new and devastating perceptions of inequality will arise to take the place of the old in a society where everyone has reached heights of well-being, participation, and education attainable today only by a few citizens: "Self-esteem is based on *differentiating characteristics:* that's why it's *self*-esteem."[47] We have willingly granted that self-esteem may still be unequal in a liberal egalitarian society – even in a society of Aristotles, Marxes, and Goethes. But so long as every citizen is respected and self-respecting, a liberal egalitarian society would be a significant, indeed an enormous, improvement over our own. If this projection of the effects of distributive and participatory equalities turns out to be wrong, someone ought to argue for a better society. No doubt any account of a just society must be bounded by our imperfect empirical knowledge, as well as by our limited theoretical vision. Still, we can make a good case for liberal equality now.

Notes

PREFACE

1. See Alexis de Tocqueville, *Democracy in America*, ed. Phillips Bradley (New York, 1945), vol. II, bk. II, chap. 1, pp. 100–3. Even critics of contemporary theories of equality acknowledge the significance of questions raised by the "new egalitarians." For example, Daniel Bell argues that

   > What is at stake today is the redefinition of equality . . . [T]he principle of equality of opportunity, is now seen as leading to a new hierarchy, and the current demand is that the "just precedence" of society . . . requires the reduction of all inequality, or the creation of equality of result – in income, status, and power – for all men in society. This is the central value problem of post-industrial society.

   "On Meritocracy and Equality," *Public Interest*, no. 29 (Fall 1972), p. 40.
2. John Kenneth Galbraith, *The Affluent Society* (New York, 1958), p. 76.
3. For some of the most helpful literature concerning the concept of equality and its many meanings, see the essays by Hugo A. Bedau, Richard E. Flathman, Stanley I. Benn, John Plamenatz, and George E. G. Catlin in J. Roland Pennock and John W. Chapman, eds., *Nomos IX: Equality* (New York, 1967), pp. 3–27, 38–111. See also John Rees, *Equality* (London, 1971); and S. I. Benn and R. S. Peters, *The Principles of Political Thought: Social Foundations of the Democratic State* (New York, 1965), pp. 124–47.
4. See, e.g., Gabriel Kolko, *Wealth and Power in America: An Analysis of Social Class and Income Distribution* (New York, 1962); and Letitia Upton, *Basic Facts: Distribution of Personal Income and Wealth in the U.S.* (Cambridge, Mass., 1972). See also Hayward R. Alker, Jr., and Bruce M. Russett, "Indices for Comparing Inequality," in Richard Merritt, ed., *Comparing Nations* (New Haven, 1966), pp. 349–72; G. Garvey, "Inequality of Income: Causes and Measurement," in National Bureau of Economic Research, *Studies in Income and Wealth* (New York, 1952), XV, 25–47; and Yaakov Kandor, "Value Judgements Implied by the Use of Various Measures of Income Inequality," *Review of Income and Wealth*, 21 (1975): 309–21; and for a comparative analysis of the degree and causes of the increased economic equality among industrial societies, see Harold L. Wilensky, *The Welfare State and Equality: Structural and Ideological Roots of Public Expenditures* (Berkeley, 1974).
5. Tocqueville, *Democracy in America*, vol. II, pt. II, bk. I chap. 16, p. 74.

6. There are several discussions of equality within the context of a tradition or a theory of justice that I do not specifically cite in the text but to which I am generally indebted: Christopher Ake, "Justice as Equality," *Philosophy and Public Affairs* 5 (Fall 1975): 69–89; W. T. Blackstone, "On the Meaning and Justification of the Equality Principle," *Ethics* 77 (July 1967):239–53; Norman E. Bowie, *Towards a New Theory of Distributive Justice* (Amherst, Mass., 1971), pp. 50–76; E. F. Carritt, "Liberty and Equality," *Law Quarterly Review* 56 (1940):61–74 (reprinted in Anthony Quinton, ed., *Political Philosophy* [New York, 1967], pp. 127–40); Alan Gewirth, "The Justification of Egalitarian Justice," *American Philosophical Quarterly* 8 (October 1971):331–41 (reprinted in Richard E. Flathman, ed., *Concepts in Social and Political Philosophy* [New York, 1973], pp. 352–65); Richard J. Lampman, "Recent Thought on Egalitarianism," *Quarterly Journal of Sociology* 71 (May 1957):234–66; Steven Lukes, "Socialism and Equality," in Leszek Kolakowski and Stuart Hampshire, eds., *The Socialist Idea: A Reappraisal* (New York, 1974), pp. 74–95; J. Roland Pennock, *Liberal Democracy: Its Merits and Prospects* (New York, 1950), pp. 80–96; and John Wilson, *Equality* (New York, 1966). For a useful survey of the place of equality within the history of political theory, see Sanford A. Lakoff, *Equality in Political Philosophy* (Cambridge, Mass., 1964).

7. A note on terminology: Throughout, whenever I use the masculine pronouns or the word "men," I intend the generic sense unless otherwise specified.

INTRODUCTION

1. See Felix E. Oppenheim: "Egalitarianism as a Descriptive Concept," *American Philosophical Quarterly* 7 (April 1970):143–52. For an important qualification of the descriptive status of egalitarianism as Oppenheim understands it, see Virginia Held, "Egalitarianism and Relevance," *Ethics* 81 (April 1971):259.

2. I shall be discussing throughout the justice of a state rather than its legitimacy in obligating particular individuals. Although the two are closely related, I do not enter into a discussion of consent, which may be fundamental to the latter problem of obligation. Interestingly, the liberal *method* of political legitimation appears similar to that of justification, in that all citizens are said to have delegated their original sovereignty "to be exercised on their own behalf." (Quentin Skinner, *The Foundations of Modern Political Thought* [Cambridge, 1978], vol. II, 182). For a detailed understanding of the origins of this view of the modern state, see ibid., esp. vol. II, pt. II.

3. See Robert C. Tucker, *The Marxian Revolutionary Idea* (London, 1970), pp. 85–91, for a discussion of Marx's rejection of the state.

4. Even Durkheim can be interpreted as a methodological individualist by reading back into his notion of individual interest the prerequisites of social solidarity. Durkheim himself, however, did not proceed in this manner. There are other good reasons for resisting an interpretation that completely assimilates his functionalism to methodological individualism. See Ernest Wallwork, *Durkheim: Morality*

and Milieu (Cambridge, Mass, 1972), esp. pp. 103–19, 166–81. In Durkheim's work, see esp. *Moral Education*, trans. Everett K. Wilson and Herman Schnurer (Glencoe, Ill., 1961), and "The Determination of Moral Facts," in *Sociology and Philosophy*, trans. D. F. Pocock (London, 1953), p. 37. See also Steven Lukes, "Alienation and Anomie," in Peter Laslett and W. G. Runciman, eds. *Philosophy, Politics and Society*, 3d ser. (Oxford, 1967), esp. pp. 141–2, 154–5.

For Durkheim's argument concerning the appropriateness of liberal principles of justice to societies that are characterized by an extensive division of labor, see his *The Division of Labor in Society*, trans. George Simpson (New York, 1933), bk. 3; and especially his "Individualism and the Intellectuals," in *On Morality and Society*, ed. Robert N. Bellah (Chicago, 1973), pp. 43–57.

5. See, e.g., Isaiah Berlin, "Two Concepts of Liberty," in *Four Essays on Liberty* (New York, 1969), pp. 121–31, 164–6; and L. T. Hobhouse, *Liberalism* (New York, 1964), pp. 16–29. Moreover, both Berlin and Hobhouse go on to support a particular interpretation of liberty that accords best with the Anglo-American liberal tradition. See also Hobhouse's discussion of the proper function of the liberal state: ibid., pp. 83–7, 91–2.

6. See F. A. Hayek, "The Principles of a Liberal Social Order," in *Studies in Philosophy, Politics and Economics* (New York, 1969), pp. 160–77. Liberalism as a conception of limited government corresponds to Hayek's first kind of liberalism. He claims that limited government is that form of liberalism which best supports individual freedom.

7. Compare Berlin, "Two Concepts of Liberty," pp. 145–54.

8. Ibid., p. 125.

9. Ibid., p. 126.

10. John Locke, *The Second Treatise of Government*, in *Two Treatises of Government*, ed. Peter Laslett (Cambridge, 1963), chap. 6, para. 57.

11. Berlin, "Two Concepts of Liberty," p. 125.

12. For a more thorough examination of this triadic concept of freedom, upon which my argument rests, see Gerald C. MacCallum, Jr., "Negative and Positive Freedom," *Philosophical Review* 76 (1967):312–34 (reprinted in Richard E. Flathman, ed., *Concepts in Social and Political Philosophy* [New York, 1973], pp. 294–308).

13. See Berlin's discussion, "Two Concepts of Liberty," pp. 131 ff.

14. See John Stuart Mill, *Utilitarianism*, in *Collected Works*, ed. J. M. Robson (Toronto, 1969), vol. X, chap. 1, par. 5, pp. 207–8.

15. See John Stuart Mill, *Principles of Political Economy*, in *Collected Works* (1965), III, 947–70.

16. John Stuart Mill, *On Liberty*, in *Collected Works*, (1977), vol. XVIII, chap. 5, par. 4, p. 293.

17. Robert Nozick, *Anarchy, State and Utopia* (New York, 1974).

18. Here and throughout this essay, I shall use "redistributionalist," "redistributive," and "distributive" in contradistinction to "participatory" principles and concerns, the former referring to the allocation (or reallocation) of material goods (income, wealth, and services), and the latter referring to specified rights of engagement in democratic deliberations.

CHAPTER 1. THE CLASSICAL LIBERAL FOUNDATIONS

1. See, e.g., George H. Sabine and Thomas L. Thorson, *A History of Political Theory* (Hinsdale, Ill., 1973), p. 439; Elie Halévy, *The Growth of Philosophical Radicalism*, trans. M. Morris (London, 1934), p. 504; and Berlin "Two Concepts of Liberty," pp. 127–8. See also Louis Dumont's discussion of modern vs. traditional societies, in *Homo Hierarchicus: The Caste System and Its Implications*, trans. Mark Sainsbury (Chicago, 1970), pp. 8–11.

2. Arthur O. Lovejoy, *The Great Chain of Being* (Cambridge, Mass., 1964), p. 6. See also Max Weber, *The Protestant Ethic and the Spirit of Capitalism*, trans. Talcott Parsons (New York, 1958), p. 222, n. 22.

3. Steven Lukes, *Individualism* (New York, 1973), chap. 18, p. 137. See also Dumont, *Homo Hierarchicus*, pp. 4, 9. For the historical roots of the modern liberal doctrine of individualism, see Skinner, *Foundations of Modern Political Thought*, esp. pt II, chap. 9.

4. See Claude-Henri Saint-Simon, *The Doctrine of Saint-Simon: An Exposition, First Year, 1828–9*, trans. G. Iggers (Boston, 1958), pp. 178–82; Edmund Burke, "An Appeal from the New to the Old Whigs," in *Works* (Boston, 1877), IV, 57; Edmund Burke, "Speech on the Plan for Economical Reform," in *Works*, II, 265; and Edmund Burke, *Reflections on the Revolution in France, and on the Proceedings in Certain Societies in London Relative to That Event* (London, 1790), pp. 143–5 and passim.

5. The metaphor of exposed nerves is borrowed from Sheldon S. Wolin's *Politics and Vision* (Boston, 1960), p. 326.

6. See Thomas Hobbes, *Leviathan*, in *The English Works of Thomas Hobbes of Malmesbury*, ed. Sir William Molesworth (London, 1839–45), vol. III, pt. I, chap. 6, p. 41; and Jeremy Bentham, *Introduction to Principles of Morals and Legislation*, in *The Works of Jeremy Bentham*, ed. John Bowring (Edinburgh, 1843), vol. I, chap. 1, pp. 1–4.

7. See Locke, *Second Treatise of Government*, sec. 6, p. 311; and Immanuel Kant, *Groundwork of the Metaphysics of Morals* (hereafter cited as *Groundwork*), 403–5 (Prussian ed.), trans. H. J. Paton (New York, 1964), pp. 71–3.

8. See the section entitled "The convergence of the two equalities," later in this chapter.

9. For a recognition of the centrality of this universal fear in Hobbes's justification of the state, see Richard S. Peters, *Hobbes* (Baltimore, 1956), pp. 154, 161–2, 191, 194.

10. Bentham, *Introduction to Principles of Morals and Legislation*, chap. 10, p. 48.

11. Hobbes, *Leviathan*, pt. I, chap. 8, pp. 161–2.

12. Jeremy Bentham, *The Book of Fallacies*, in *Works*, vol. II, pt. IV, chap. 10, sec. 5, p. 466.

13. James Mill, *Essay on Government* (Indianapolis, 1955), pp. 62–3.

14. Thomas Hobbes, *De Cive; or The Citizen*, ed. Sterling Lamprecht (New York, 1949), chap. 1, sec. 7, p. 26. Emphasis added.

15. Thomas Hobbes, *Elements of Law, Natural and Politic*, ed. F. Tönnies, (Cambridge, 1928), pt. I, chap. 14, sec. 6, pp. 54–5. Emphasis added.

16. See Hobbes, *Leviathan*, pt. I, chap. 13, p. 116.
17. Mill, *Essay on Government*, p. 54.
18. Ibid., p. 61.
19. But is democracy not a more desirable means of governance, as, according to Hobbes, people not only should but *do* desire security above all else (hence Hobbes's utilitarian justification for the state)? Two answers are possible. First, there still exists in Hobbes a gap (based in large part on his mechanistic psychology) between the act of human choice and the inferred fact of human preference, such that the Leviathan cannot securely rely on ongoing, democratic consent. Secondly, if security is taken to be the only universal and invaluable good, why would people want to withhold their consent from any sovereign who would so protect their overriding interest? Democracy then would be logically as well as practically redundant. However, even were one to accept Hobbes's ranking of human interests, one might question whether a Hobbesian sovereign could be best relied upon to protect this one overriding human interest.
20. For a thorough discussion of this idea of representation see Hannah Fenichel Pitkin, *The Concept of Representation* (Berkeley, 1972), chaps. 2, 9, pp. 14–37, 190–208.
21. Mill, *Essay on Government*, p. 67.
22. Ibid., p. 67.
23. Cf. John Stuart Mill, *The Subjection of Women* (London, 1869), passim.
24. Mill, *Essay on Government*, pp. 85–6. Note also Mill's assumption about man's educability.
25. Of course, the validity of this claim rests on the assumption that politics is never valued *exclusively* or *merely* as a pleasurable activity in itself.
26. Cf. Jean-Jacques Rousseau, *The Social Contract*, in *The Social Contract and Discourses*, trans. G. D. H. Cole (New York, 1950), bk. IV, chap. 2, p. 106.
27. See Mill, *Essay on Government*, pp. 89–91.
28. Ibid., p. 86.
29. Ibid., p. 86.
30. Ibid., esp. secs. 3, 10, pp. 51–4, 84–91. L. T. Hobhouse aptly summarizes Mill's case for democratic government and its limits in *Liberalism*, pp. 39–42.
31. See Bentham's *Constitutional Code*, in *Works*, vol. IX, book I, chap. 15, p. 107: "The happiness of the most helpless pauper constitutes as large a portion of the universal happiness as that of the most opulent members of the community. Therefore the happiness of the most helpless and indigent has as much title to regard at the hands of the legislator, as that of the most powerful and opulent."
32. This is a more complicated determination than first appearances might suggest, once one considers the question whether each individual case must be considered separately, on its own merits, or whether some general rule should be employed that on the whole would yield the best results – i.e., the greatest social utility. On the question of act versus rule utiliarianism, see J. J. C. Smart and Bernard Williams, *Utilitarianism: For and Against* (London 1973), pp.

9–12; and H. J. McCloskey, "An Examination of Restricted Utilitarinism" in Thomas K. Hearn, Jr., ed., *Studies in Utilitarianism* (New York, 1971), pp. 231–49.

33. See Bentham, *Constitutional Code*, bk. I, chap. 3, sec. 5, pp. 14–18.

34. Note, however, that it is not the subsequently developed notion of Pareto optimality which Benthamite principles warrant, but rather a maximization of total (or possibly average) social utility. This leaves the redistributive potential of the state far more open than does the rule of Pareto optimality: The rich can legitimately be made worse off if the poor consequently benefit more. For a further critical discussion of Bentham's preferred distributive principles and of the status of the equality assumption in Bentham's utilitarianism, see Bhikhu Parekh, "Bentham's Theory of Equality," *Political Studies* 18 (December 1970):478–95.

35. Locke, *Second Treatise of Government*, chap. 2, par. 4, p. 309. Emphasis added. Here and in subsequent quotations from Locke, I have taken the liberty of omitting some capitalizations and changing some punctuation for better conformity to modern usage.

36. For one answer directly addressed to this question in Locke, see Voltaire's "Letter to Crown Prince Frederick," October 1737, in *Voltaire's Correspondence*, ed. Theodore Besterman (Geneva, 1954), VI, 230–1. For another answer to a similar question, see Mill, *Utilitarianism*, chap. 2, par. 7, pp. 212–13. Martin Seliger's interpretation of Locke attempts to avoid this problem altogether. Seliger interprets the *should* in Locke's description of natural equality (cited in the text at no. 35) as indicating a moral imperative rather than a statement of the fact of natural human equality. Yet judging from its construction, that passage appears more plausibly to indicate a political imperative concerning the implication of the moral *fact* of equality. Locke appears to be arguing that men who *are* born with equal rational faculties *should also be treated* as equal politically, "one amongst another without subordination or subjection." Nevertheless, the conclusions Seliger draws from Locke's notion of equality are sound even if one embraces the moral fact of natural equality. See M. Seliger, *The Liberal Politics of John Locke* (London, 1968), p. 80.

37. See John Locke, *Essay concerning Human Understanding*, in *Works*, ed. J. A. St. John (London, 1889). vol. II, bk. IV, chap. 2, sec. 1, p. 134.

38. John Locke, *Essays on the Law of Nature*, trans. and ed. W. von Leyden (Oxford, 1954), chap. 4: "Can Reason Attain to the Knowledge of Natural Law through Sense-Experience? Yes," pp. 155–7.

39. Seliger, *Liberal Politics of John Locke*, p. 172.

40. Ibid., p. 80.

41. This is an important Lockean limitation upon majority rule that is often overlooked or denied by critics of Locke. See, e.g., Willmoore Kendall, *John Locke and the Doctrine of Majority Rule* (Urbana, Ill., 1959), esp. pp. 90–123. Cf. Richard I. Aaron, *John Locke*, 2d ed. (Oxford, 1955), pp. 280–6.

42. See Locke, *Second Treatise of Government*, chap. 2, par. 6, p. 311.

43. See ibid., chap. 6, par. 63, p. 352; and Locke, *Essay concerning Human Understanding*, bk. IV.

44. By contrast, recent historiographical accounts emphasize the religious roots of Locke's political thought. As an excellent example of this scholarship, see John Dunn, *The Political Thought of John Locke* (London, 1969), passim.
45. The argument from God does allow Locke to give content to the notion of political and civil rights: God gave man the earth to use for his benefit, and rights to private property are thereby justified (given, of course, the validity of Locke's contention that communal-property rights would effect significantly less production than private-property rights). Yet, at the same time, the liberal state which is to protect that property is less liberal than it might be if a secular justification of the same rights were possible. As significantly, the reasoning from God to human rights is by no means obvious. In the example of property rights, accepting Locke's definition of God's will with respect to man's use of property, one might plausibly argue that men could collectively cultivate property in a productive manner, providing for a commodious living as God dictates. Property rights may not be as apparently derivative from God's ownership and will regarding mankind as Locke believed.
46. Locke, *Second Treatise of Government*, chap. 6, par. 63, p. 352.
47. Ibid., chap. 5, par. 27, p. 328. Emphasis added.
48. Ibid., p. 329.
49. Cf. C. B. Macpherson's argument in favor of this metaphor, "Human Rights as Property Rights, *Dissent*, Winter 1977, pp. 72–7.
50. See, for a compatible, historically grounded argument concerning the status of property rights in Locke, Karl Olivecrona, "Locke's Theory of Appropriation," *Philosophical Quarterly* 24 (September 1974):220–34.
51. See Locke, *Second Treatise of Government*, chap. 5, pars. 27, 31, pp. 328–9. 332.
52. Robert Nozick points out that were property *ever* to become scarce, the Lockean claims to land made by the first person would be invalid. If this argument is correct, the Lockean proviso would certainly place a serious limit upon private-property rights! I will return to assess Nozick's use of Locke in Chapter 6. See *Anarchy, State and Utopia*, pp. 174–8.
53. Cf. Leo Strauss, *Natural Right and History* (Chicago, 1953), pp. 202–51; and C. B. Macpherson, *The Political Theory of Possessive Individualism* (Oxford, 1962), pp. 211–14.
54. Locke, *Second Treatise of Government*, chap. 11, par. 140, p. 408.
55. Ibid., chap. 5, par. 37, pp. 335–6.
56. See ibid., chap. 5, pars. 37–50, pp. 335–44. Cf. Macpherson's discussion in *Political Theory of Possessive Individualism*, pp. 199–220.
57. Strauss's analysis, unlike Macpherson's and my own, assumes that there is no tension between Locke's assumptions governing human nature and a justification of a laissez-faire market economy. See Strauss, *Natural Right and History*, pp. 240–51.
58. Kant, *Groundwork*, 413, p. 81.
59. Ibid., 405, pp. 72–3.
60. Ibid., 447, p. 114.
61. Ibid., 431–3, pp. 98–100.
62. Ibid., 436, p. 104.

63. Ibid., 437, p. 105.
64. For an interpretation of Kant's legalism, see Philip Kretschmann, "An Exposition of Kant's Philosophy of Law," in George Tapley Whitney, ed., *The Heritage of Kant* (Princeton, 1939), pp. 245–76.
65. Kant, *Groundwork*, 433–5, pp. 100–2.
66. Cf. Onora Nell, *Acting on Principle: An Essay on Kantian Ethics* (New York, 1975), pp. 64–5.
67. For a lucid formulation of the "machinery" of the categorical imperative, see ibid., chap. 5.
68. Immanuel Kant, *On the Old Saw: That May Be Right in Theory but It Won't Work in Practice*, 290 (Prussian ed.), trans. E. B. Ashton (Philadelphia, 1974), p. 58 (quoted from Immanuel Kant, *The Philosophy of Kant*, ed. Carl J. Friedrich [New York, 1949], p. 416).
69. Kant, *On the Old Saw*, 293, p. 61 (quoted from *The Philosophy of Kant*, p. 419).
70. Immanuel Kant, *The Metaphysical Elements of Justice* (hereafter cited as *Justice*), 314 (Prussian ed.), trans. John Ladd (Indianapolis, 1965), sec. 46, pp. 78–9.
71. Act "such that the will can regard itself as at the same time making universal law by means of its maxim." (*Groundwork*, 434, p. 101). "Act on a maxim which at the same time contains in itself its own universal validity for every rational being" (ibid., 438, p. 105).
72. See n. 64 to this chapter.
73. Kant, *Justice*, 231, p. 35.
74. See Kant's Introduction to *Justice*, 219, p. 19.
75. See, e.g., Rousseau's discussion of the need for a civil religion in *The Social Contract*, bk. IV, chap. 8, pp. 129–41.
76. Cf. ibid., passim.
77. Kant, *Justice*, 313, sec. 45, p. 78.
78. Ibid., 341, sec. 52, p. 113.
79. Ibid., 341, sec. 52, pp. 112–13.
80. See Immanuel Kant, *Perpetual Peace*, in *On History*, ed. L. W. Beck (Indianapolis, 1963), 352, p. 96.
81. Kant, *Justice*, 315, sec. 46, p. 79.
82. Ibid., 314, sec. 46, pp. 78–9.
83. Ibid., 314, sec. 46, p. 79.
84. Ibid., 315, sec. 46, p. 80.
85. See Marcuse's critique of Kant's legalism in *Studies in Critical Philosophy* (Boston, 1973), pp. 93–4. See also Hegel's critique in *The Philosophy of Right*, trans. T. M. Knox (Oxford, 1942), pars. 29, 135, pp. 33, 89–90.
86. Kant, *Justice*, 315, sec. 46, pp. 79–80.
87. The contrast to Locke must not be overdrawn, however, because even Locke contends that in the state of nature an individual's property rights are constrained by the provisos.
88. Kant, *Justice*, 257, sec. 9, pp. 66–7.
89. A similar question was asked of Locke's idea of free and universal (tacit) consent to money. I have assumed that Locke must also be speaking of hypothetical contracts and consent. For the view that the Lockean argument makes sense only as a hypothetical social-contract theory, see Hannah Fenichel Pitkin, "Obligation and Consent: I and II," *American Political Science Review* 59 (December

1965):990–9, 60 (March 1966):39–52. This interpretation of Locke puts him close to Kant on a methodological level as well.

90. Kant, *Justice*, 326, sec. 49, p. 93.
91. Cf. Robert Nozick's basic denial of this essential interdependency, or the redistributive implications that might be drawn therefrom, in *Anarchy, State and Utopia*, passim.
92. Cf. Alasdair MacIntyre, *A Short History of Ethics* (New York, 1966), pp. 190–8.
93. See Kant, *Groundwork*, 435, p. 102.
94. Of course, not all categorical imperatives may be legally enforced. See Nell, *Acting on Principle*, chap. 4.
95. For an extended criticism of this view, see ibid., passim.
96. See ibid., p. 87, for a similar point.
97. Seliger, *Liberal Politics of John Locke*, p. 47.
98. Ibid., p. 48. See also Hobhouse, *Liberalism*, pp. 42–3: "Though their starting-point was different, the Benthamites arrived at practical results not notably divergent from those of the doctrine of natural liberty."
99. Locke, *Second Treatise of Government*, chap. 7, par. 94, p. 372.
100. Seliger, *Liberal Politics of John Locke*, p. 56.
101. See Helvetius, *De l'Esprit*, in *Oeuvres* (Paris, 1975), vols. I, II. William Godwin provides the most explicit rejection of Helvetius's use of the basic equality postulate. First, Godwin argues that there will exist no adequate criterion for identifying a superior being among men. Second, and as a partial explanation of the first point, he argues that all share in the essential faculty of reason. Third, political tyranny will be most effectively excluded by shared governance. Finally, democracy most nearly approaches self-control in fostering the uncontrolled exercise of private judgment. Here we find Godwin's ultimate rationale for political democracy: its characterization of men as equally dignified persons. Godwin himself goes on to argue that only anarchy might ultimately protect man's dignity. See his *Thoughts on Man* (New York, 1969), and *Enquiry concerning Political Justice*, ed. G. G. Robinson and J. Robinson, 3d ed., corr. (London, 1798).
102. Rousseau, of course, directly confronts this problem in *The Social Contract*. He admits there that a legislator adequate to a just society would of necessity be super- (or non-) human: "A superior intelligence beholding all the passions of man without experiencing any of them . . . This intelligence would have to be wholly unrelated to our nature." Not giving us reason to believe such an intelligence could exist, Rousseau's undemocratic founding remains utopian. See *The Social Contract*, chap. 7, p. 37.
103. For a classic statement of this position, see James Fitzjames Stephen, *Liberty, Equality, Fraternity*, ed. R. J. White (Cambridge, 1967), p. 220. See also J. R. Lucas, "Against Equality," *Philosophy* 40 (October 1965): 296–307 (reprinted in Hugo A. Bedau, ed., *Justice and Equality* [Englewood Cliffs, N.J., 1971], pp. 138–51 [esp. pp. 139–40]); Richard S. Peters, *Ethics and Education* (London, 1966), pp. 118–20; and John H. Schaar, "Some Ways of Thinking about Equality," *Journal of Politics*, 26 (1964): esp. 867–8, 875–82. Cf. David Thomson, *Equality* (Cambridge, 1949), chap. 1, pp. 1–24; B.

A. O. Williams, "The Idea of Equality," in Peter Laslett and W. G. Runciman, eds. *Philosophy, Politics and Society*, 2d ser. (Oxford, 1962), esp. pp. 110–14 (reprinted in Bedau, *Justice and Equality*, esp. pp. 116–20); Herbert Spiegelberg, "A Defense of Human Equality," *Philosophical Review* 53 (March 1944):104–6 and passim; and L. T. Hobhouse, *The Elements of Social Justice* (London, 1922), pp. 94–95.

104.   See, e.g., Peters, *Ethics and Education*, pp. 94–100, 119–20; and H. J. McCloskey, "A Right to Equality? Re-Examining the Case for a Right to Equality," *Canadian Journal of Philosophy* 6 (December 1976):633. The same sort of "nonnaturalist" argument has been leveled numerous times against Mill's derivation of the greatest-happiness principle. See G. E. Moore, *Principia Ethica* (Cambridge, 1903), pp. 64–81. Cf. Norman Kretzmann, "Desire as Proof of Desirability," *Philosophical Quarterly* 8 (1958):246–58; and Everett W. Hall, "The 'Proof' of Utility in Bentham and Mill," *Ethics* 60 (October 1949):1–18.

105.   The relevant works by Arthur Jensen are "How Much Can We Boost IQ and Scholastic Achievement? *Harvard Educational Review* 39 (Winter 1969):1–23, and *Educability and Group Differences* (New York, 1973). Richard Hernstein's major work is *I.Q. in the Meritocracy* (Boston, 1974). See also his original article, "I.Q.," *Atlantic Monthly* 228 (September 1971):43–64. For forceful and cogent rebuttals of both the methodology and the empirical findings upon which Hernstein's and Jensen's work is based, see N. J. Block and Gerald Dworkin, "IQ: Heritability and Inequality, Pts. I and II," *Philosophy and Public Affairs 3*, no. 4 (Summer 1974):331–409, and 4, no. 1 (Fall 1974):40–99; Leon Kamin, *The Science and Politics of IQ* (New York, 1974); and esp. Philip Green, "Race and IQ: Fallacy of Heritability," *Dissent*, Spring 1976, pp. 181–96; Philip Green, "The Pseudoscience of Arthur Jensen," *Dissent*, Summer 1976, esp. pp. 294–6; and Philip Green, "IQ and the Future of Equality," *Dissent*, Fall 1976, pp. 398–414. See also David Hawkins, *The Science and Ethics of Equality* (New York, 1977), passim.

106.   John H. Schaar makes a similar point about the intention of the "great liberal and constitutional theorists of the modern era (Locke, Kant, Madison, Bentham)" in "Some Ways of Thinking about Equality," p. 884. He goes on to criticize the consequences of the political egalitarianism of classical liberalism: see pp. 884–92. My argument suggests that attempts to resolve the tensions Schaar notes between political equality and private inequality constitute a central dynamic in the development of liberal egalitarianism.

107.   Schaar argues that "the most important consequence of this [liberal egalitarian] way of thinking about politics is that men come to regard the public arena as a place where ordinary men will appear as naturally and act as capably as extraordinary men. The public realm is not seen as the place where great men most naturally gather and where great actions most naturally take place" (ibid., p. 889). Yet it need not be the case that by equalizing the rights and opportunities for political participation one reduces the value of politics or degrades the status of political participants to "second-rate men [who] gather to pursue their second-rate ends" (ibid.). Additional as-

sumptions concerning human nature and the value of politics must be admitted into an argument before one can arrive at such conclusions, of which Schaar is rightly critical.

108. See Hugo A. Bedau, "Egalitarianism and the Idea of Equality," in J. Roland Pennock and John W. Chapman, eds., *Nomos IX: Equality* (New York 1967), pp. 4–13. Cf. Oppenheim, "Egalitarianism as a Descriptive Concept," p. 143.
109. See Chapter 4.
110. Cf. Alan Gewirth, "The 'Is-Ought' Problem Resolved," *Proceedings and Addresses of the American Philosophical Association* 47 (1974):34–61.

CHAPTER 2. J. S. MILL AND PARTICIPATORY OPPORTUNITY

1. Compare Kant, *Justice*, 314–15, sec. 46, pp. 78–80. For a contemporary exposition of a division of this sort, see Robert Dahl, *Who Governs?* (New Haven, 1961), pp. 223–38.
2. See, e.g., Graeme Duncan, *Marx and Mill* (Cambridge, 1973), p. 259 and passim; C. B. Macpherson, *Democratic Theory: Essays in Retrieval* (Oxford, 1973), pp. 39–76; 97–100; and Gertrude Himmelfarb, *On Liberty and Liberalism: The Case of John Stuart Mill* (New York, 1974), pp. 135–9.
3. Macpherson, *Democratic Theory*, pp. 97–100, 174–5.
4. I use the word "teleological" to refer to the fact that both equality postulates are integrated into a theory of justice with the unitary end of maximizing the good of human happiness.
5. Mill, *Utilitarianism*, chap. 2, par. 6, p. 211.
6. See, ibid., par. 7, p. 212.
7. Cf. Noel Annan's claim that Mill's revisions of classical utilitarianism complicate the theory without solving any of its (many) original problems ("John Stuart Mill," in Hugh Sykes Davies and George Watson, eds., *The English Mind* [Cambridge, 1964], p. 222).
8. Mill, *Utilitarianism*, chap. 3, par. 10, p. 231.
9. Mill discusses these three constituent elements of the higher pleasures in ibid., chap. 2, par. 13, p. 215. Cf. Mill, *On Liberty*, chap. 3, p. 260.
10. Mill, *Utilitarianism*, chap. 2, par. 14, p. 216.
11. John Stuart Mill, *Considerations on Representative Government*, in *Collected Works*, ed. J. M. Robson (Toronto, 1977), XIX, 448–9.
12. Shirley Robin Letwin, *The Pursuit of Certainty* (Cambridge, 1965), p. 240.
13. Cf. Dennis F. Thompson, *John Stuart Mill and Representative Government* (Princeton, 1976), passim; and Alan Ryan, "Two Concepts of Politics and Democracy: James and John Stuart Mill," in Martin Fleisher, ed., *Machiavelli and the Nature of Political Thought* (New York, 1972), esp. p. 111.
14. Letwin's analysis also leaves entirely unexplained the fact that Mill argued against philosophers, such as Comte, who did advocate rule by a scientific, intellectual elite. See Auguste Comte, *Cours de philosophie positive* (Paris, 1877). Cf. John Stuart Mill, "Auguste Comte and Positivism" in *Collected Works* (1969), X, 347–51.

15. See John Stuart Mill, "M. de Tocqueville on Democracy in America," in *Collected Works* (1977), XVIII, 191–204.
16. See Mill, *Utilitarianism*, chap. 2, pars. 4–8, pp. 210–13; and Mill, *Principles of Political Economy*, pp. 942–3. For Mill's criticisms of Aristotle, see John Stuart Mill, "Grote's Aristotle," in *Dissertations and Discussions* (New York, 1875), V. 169–215. Also, cf. John Rawls on perfectionism in *A Theory of Justice* (Cambridge, Mass., 1971), pp. 426 ff., 426 n.
17. Mill, *Representative Government*, chap. 4, pp. 543–5.
18. Ibid., p. 476.
19. See Ryan, "Two Concepts of Politics and Democracy," pp. 103–11; and Thompson, *John Stuart Mill and Representative Government*, chap. 1.
20. See Mill, *Principles of Political Economy*, pp. 943–4.
21. See Mill, *Representative Government*, pp. 542–3.
22. See ibid., p. 545, for Mill's recognition of the precarious balance between participation and competence. See also Thompson, *John Stuart Mill and Representative Government*, passim, for a more thorough discussion of Mill's resolution of this tension. My much briefer account accords with Thompson's; however, I am more interested here in investigating the further conflict between principles of participation and those of economic distribution in Mill's theory.
23. The idea of representation in Mill corresponds only roughly to that which Hannah Pitkin calls "representing people who have interests." Pitkin's discussion points to the difficulties utilitarians may encounter in defining what it means to represent truly a person's interests. But her discussion is of limited relevance to J. S. Mill insofar as she largely assimilates his conception of representation to Bentham's. See Pitkin, *The Concept of Representation*, pp. 198–207.
24. Mill, *Representative Government*, chap. 5, pp. 424–8.
25. Ibid., chap. 15, pp. 534–45.
26. Ibid., p. 539.
27. Ibid., p. 536.
28. Cf. Letwin, *The Pursuit of Certainty*, p. 306; and Bruce Mazlish, *James and John Stuart Mill* (New York, 1975), p. 401. Gertrude Himmelfarb, *On Liberty and Liberalism*, neglects even to consider Mill's arguments for democracy and participation; *Representative Government* is largely ignored.
29. See Mill's discussion, including his qualifications on the feasibility of a plural voting scheme, in *Representative Government*, chap. 8, pp. 467–81. Cf. his *Autobiography*, ed. Jack Stillinger (Boston, 1969), chap. 7, pp. 153–4. Here Mill appears to present a challenge to his previous advocacy of plural voting similar to the one I suggest below. See also Thompson, *John Stuart Mill and Representative Government*, pp. 98–101.
30. Mill, *The Subjection of Women*, pp. 7–8.
31. Many of Mill's arguments can be found in some more recent feminist writings concerning the origins and maintenance of the system of sexual inequality. See esp. *The Subjection of Women*, pp. 24–52, 148–52; and cf. Simone de Beauvoir, *The Second Sex* (New York, 1953); and Juliet Mitchell, *Woman's Estate* (London, 1971).

32. Mill, *The Subjection of Women,* pp. 38–9.
33. Ibid., pp. 40–1.
34. Ibid., p. 79. See also ibid., p. 177.
35. This combination in Mill of inegalitarian distributive principles and assumptions of human equality has been explained as one of the inevitable paradoxes of liberal thought. Roberto Unger regards inegalitarian principles of distribution as simple associative correlaries of any liberal theory that values individual liberty based upon the particular passions of individuals. But Unger fails to support his argument with reference to any liberal theory in particular, dismissing too quickly the equality assumptions of liberalism as ineffectual or at best paradoxical. His line of argument is particularly perplexing with respect to Mill's theory because Mill does not seem to ground the laissez-faire principle in the a priori natural right of all persons to negative liberty. The critique of liberalism from the standpoint of its inevitable inegalitarianism – its priority of negative liberty over equality of distribution – is not applicable to Mill. Mill does not argue for the "absolute" priority of free enterprise over a more equal distribution of goods. Many empirical assertions intervene between the utilitarian first principle and the secondary principle of laissez-faire. These assertions are the appropriate initial targets for Unger's criticism; but were he to challenge Mill on these grounds, his critique of liberalism would appear to be an immanent, rather than an undermining, one. See Roberto Mangabeira Unger, *Knowledge and Politics* (New York, 1975), pp. 180–7. Cf. Ronald Dworkin's illuminating discussion of Mill's position on liberty in *Taking Rights Seriously* (Cambridge, Mass., 1977), pp. 259–65. Dworkin rightly suggests that liberty (understood as independence) and economic equality need not conflict in Mill's own terms because Mill did not contend that economic liberty (understood in the "negative" sense) was a basic right people need be granted by a just state.
36. The question will be investigated in more detail in Chapter 5.
37. See Mill, *On Liberty,* chap. 4, pars. 3, 6, 8, pp. 276–80; and Mill, *Principles of Political Economy,* p. 937.
38. Mill, *On Liberty,* chap. 5, par. 4, p. 293. Emphasis added.
39. Mill, *Principles of Political Economy,* p. 938.
40. Ibid., p. 947.
41. Ibid., p. 954
42. Ibid., p. 956.
43. Ibid., p. 961.
44. Ibid., p. 970.
45. Ibid., p. 947.
46. Ibid., p. 952.
47. Ibid., p. 948.
48. Ibid., p. 954.
49. Ibid., p. 959. See Mancur Olson, Jr., *The Logic of Collective Action* (Cambridge, Mass., 1965).
50. Mill, *Principles of Political Economy,* p. 962.
51. Two contemporary works that focus upon Mill's case for participation in the economic sphere are Pedro Schwartz, *The New Political Economy of John Stuart Mill* (London, 1968), pp. 221–6; and Carole

Pateman, *Participation and Democratic Theory* (Cambridge, 1970), pp. 33–5.

52. Mill, *Principles of Political Economy*, p. 759.
53. Ibid.
54. Ibid., p. 768.
55. Ibid., p. 761.
56. Ibid., pp. 775, 792.
57. Ibid., p. 793.
58. Ibid., pp. 794–6.
59. Ibid., p. 763.
60. Ibid., p. 943. Again, it is remarkable that Letwin completely overlooks this aspect of Mill's theory.
61. Ibid.
62. This, of course, is the major basis of James Mill's case for democratic representation in *Essays on Government.*
63. Mill, *Principles of Political Economy*, p. 944.
64. John Stuart Mill, "Chapters on Socialism" in *Collected Works* (1967), V, 710.
65. Ibid., pp. 711, 716. Cf. Rawls's second principle of distributive justice, *A Theory of Justice*, pp. 60–75.
66. Mill, "Chapters on Socialism," pp. 737–49.
67. Ibid., p. 753.

CHAPTER 3. THE FABIANS AND THEIR ALLIES

1. Edmund Burke, "Speech on the Petition of the Unitarians," in *Works* (London, 1900–1), VI, 113–14.
2. See Fabian Tract no. 4 (London, 1886).
3. George Bernard Shaw, "The Transition to Social Democracy" (1889) in Shaw, ed., *Fabian Essays in Socialism* (Gloucester, Mass., 1967), p. 200.
4. See George Bernard Shaw, "Redistribution of Income" (1914), in *The Road to Equality: Ten Unpublished Letters and Essays*, ed. Louis Crompton (Boston 1971), pp. 206–7.
5. Sidney Webb, "The Historic Basis of Socialism," in Shaw, *Fabian Essays*, p. 78.
6. Ibid., p. 81.
7. The principle of securing expectations was not adequate even to Bentham's own case. He strongly desired to break the yoke of custom and customary habit over the lives as well as the politics of Englishmen – hence his reputation as a radical. Yet the principle of securing expectations alone was certainly inadequate to this task: Tradition in the form of customary expectations might as easily be consecrated in this manner. Bentham tacitly accepted as just those expectations fostered by the emerging free-market system, because he wholeheartedly took that system to be the most beneficial to society in encouraging productivity. But by his own admission, and consistently with his utilitarian calculus, the greatest happiness might otherwise be served by the equal provision of goods and services to all. Without offering an adequate argument why equality should be entirely sacrificed to the free market, Bentham failed to

ground the principle of secure expectations on a plausible notion of what constitues *just* expectations. See Bentham, *Constitutional Code*, bk. I, chap. 3, sec. 5, pp. 14–18.

8. See Fabian Tract no. 17, *The Reform of the Poor Law* (London, 1890) p. 15; and Sidney Webb and Beatrice Webb, *The Prevention of Destitution* (London, 1911), pp. 1–6.
9. Webb and Webb, *The Prevention of Destitution*, p. 1.
10. Ibid., p. 3.
11. Ibid., p. 6.
12. Webb, "The Historic Basis of Socialism," p. 73. See Herbert Spencer, *The Man versus the State* (New York, 1884), for Webb's model of liberal philosophy and explicit target of attack.
13. Webb and Webb, *The Prevention of Destitution*, p. 321.
14. Ibid., pp. 74–8.
15. Webb, "The Historic Basis of Socialism," pp. 68–9.
16. William Clarke, "The Industrial Basis of Socialism," in Shaw, *Fabian Essays*, p. 127.
17. Ibid., p. 128.
18. Sidney Webb, Fabian Tract no. 69, *The Difficulties of Individualism* (London, 1896), p. 6.
19. Ibid., p. 5.
20. See G. D. H. Cole, *Some Relations between Political and Economic Theory* (London, 1934), p. 46. Cf. Clarke, "The Industrial Basis of Socialism," pp. 128–9.
21. See Sidney Webb and Beatrice Webb, *Industrial Democracy* (London, 1902), chap. 2.
22. Cf. Mill, *Principles of Political Economy*, bk. V, chap. 11, sec. 1–6, pp. 936–44.
23. Webb and Webb, *Industrial Democracy*, p. 60.
24. G. D. H. Cole, *The World of Labour* (London, 1913), pp. 4–5. Emphasis added.
25. Ibid., p. 4.
26. Ibid., p. 9.
27. See Sidney Webb, *The Basis and Policy of Socialism* (London, 1908); and Sidney Webb and Beatrice Webb, *The Consumer Co-operative Movement* (London, 1921), esp. chap. 6.
28. Cole, *The World of Labour*, p. 73.
29. Webb, *The Basis and Policy of Socialism*, pp. 60, 69.
30. Margaret Cole, *The Story of Fabian Socialism* (Stanford, 1961), p. 148.
31. For a discussion of the classical Christian notion of human equality and its social implications, see Ernst Troeltsch, *The Social Teaching of the Christian Churches*, trans. Olive Wyon (London, 1931), I, 120–38.
32. See T. H. Marshall, *Citizenship and Social Class and Other Essays* (Cambridge, 1950), esp. pp. 43—56.
33. Rousseau, *The Social Contract*, bk. II, chap. 3, pp. 27–8; Jean-Jacques Rousseau, *On the Origin of Inequality*, in *The Social Contract and Discourses*, trans. G. D. H. Cole (New York, 1950), pp. 267–8; Jean-Jacques Rousseau, *A Discourse on Political Economy*, in ibid., esp. pp.
34. R. H. Tawney, *Equality*, 4th rev. ed. (London, 1952), pp. 52, 119, 147, 150.
35. Ibid., p. 90.

36. Cf. Burke, *Reflections on the Revolution in France,* p. 114.
37. Tawney, *Equality,* p. 58.
38. Ibid., p. 87.
39. See both Tawney's *Equality* and his *The Acquisitive Society* (New York, 1921).
40. Tawney, *Equality,* p. 58.
41. Ibid., p. 100.
42. Compare Rawls's discussion of the preconditions for self-respect in *A Theory of Justice,* pp. 544–6.
43. See Tawney, *Equality,* p. 113.
44. Ibid., p. 112.
45. Ibid., p. 106. The comment of Michael Young's observer of the meritocracy is relevant here: "Educational injustice enabled people to preserve their illusions, inequality of opportunity fostered the myth of human equality. Myth we know it to be; not so our ancestors" (ibid.).
46. Shirley Letwin's description of the Webbs' vision of socialism provides an illuminating contrast to Tawney's ideal society: "Under scientific socialism, personalities and personal judgments, with all their uncertainty, were dispensed with. The rule of science eliminated matters of opinion. Everything could be reduced to a question of social health, and settled rationally, efficiently, and impersonally." Letwin is mistaken concerning the comprehensiveness of the Webbs' scientific socialism, but her point about the impersonality of questions of social justice, as far as they went in the Webbs' vision, is well taken. See Letwin, *The Pursuit of Certainty,* p. 378.
47. Tawney, *Equality,* p. 164.
48. See John Stuart Mill, *A System of Logic,* in *Collected Works,* ed. J. M. Robson (Toronto, 1974), vol. VIII, bk. VI, chap. 12, sec. 7, p. 952
49. Tawney, *Equality,* pp. 189–93. See Ross Terrill's discussion of the place of the Great War in Tawney's hope for a socialist fellowship (*R. H. Tawney and His Times* [Cambridge, Mass., 1973], pp. 169–72). Terrill's account is helpful in situating Tawney's politics in the British socialist tradition.
50. Tawney, *Equality,* p. 192.
51. See esp. Tawney's essay "Social History and Literature," in *The Radical Tradition* (London, 1966), pp. 191–219, for an appreciation of the popular roots of Elizabethan culture: "It voices the outlook on life, not of an elegant elite, but of the world of common men" (p. 208). Tawney apparently looked forward to a revival of this sort of cultural populism, although one tied to a more egalitarian distribution of other economic and social goods. As an example of his concern for the role of the lower classes in social history, see *The Agrarian Problem in the Sixteenth Century* (New York, 1967).
52. Tawney, *Equality,* pp. 169–73.
53. Ibid., p. 182.
54. Ibid., p. 183.
55. C. A. R. Crosland, *The Future of Socialism* (London, 1956), p. 113.
56. Richard H. S. Crossman, *Planning for Freedom,* (London, 1965), p. 64.
57. Richard H. S. Crossman, Fabian Tract no. 286, *Socialist Values in a Changing Civilization* (London, 1950), p. 6.

58. Crossman, *Planning for Freedom*, p. 62.
59. See G. D. H. Cole, *Self-Government in Industry* (1917; reprint ed., London, 1972), p. 10.
60. See Crosland, *The Future of Socialism*, rev. ed. (New York, 1963), pp. 52–9.
61. Crosland, *The Future of Socialism* (1956), p. 113.
62. Ibid., p. 192.
63. Ibid., p. 193.
64. See ibid., pp. 119–39.
65. Ibid., p. 116.
66. W. G. Runciman, *Relative Deprivation and Social Justice* (London, 1972), pp. 227–45.
67. See ibid., chaps. 11, 13. Runciman himself reaches an ambiguous position on the desirability of reform, given social consciousness as it exists. But he recognizes the need to separate a theory of just distribution from issues of the justice or prudence of political action. (On the precise distinction between the two, he remains vague.)
68. Crosland, *The Future of Socialism* (1956), p. 99. See also p. 100.
69. Ibid., p. 46.
70. An important essay on paternalism that employs this definition is Gerald Dworkin, "Paternalism," in Richard A. Wasserstrom, ed., *Morality and the Law* (Belmont, Calif., 1971), pp. 107–26.
71. For other reasons why providing goods in kind may not be paternalistic, see Albert Weale, "Paternalism and Social Policy," *Journal of Society and Politics* 7, no. 2 (April 1978):157–72.
72. See Crosland, *The Future of Socialism* (1956), p. 104.
73. Margaret Cole, "Education and Social Democracy," in Richard H. S. Crossman, ed., *New Fabian Essays* (London, 1970), p. 92.
74. Ibid., p. 91.
75. Ibid., pp. 93–4.
76. Ibid., pp. 102–5.
77. Ibid., p. 105.
78. Ibid., p. 110.
79. Dennis Marsden makes this criticism in a subsequent Fabian Tract, no. 411, entitled *Politicians, Equality and Comprehensives* (London, 1971), p. 1: "Comprehensive schools were allowed to appear as machines to engineer equality without the redistribution of resources in the educational system or the rest of society."
80. Crosland, *The Future of Socialism* (1956), pp. 267–70.
81. Ibid., p. 270.
82. Crossman, *Planning for Freedom*, p. 36.
83. John Kenneth Galbraith, Fabian Tract no. 405, *The American Left and Some British Comparisons* (London, 1971), p. 36.
84. Crossman, *Planning for Freedom*, pp. 118–19.

CHAPTER 4. RELEVANT REASONS FOR LIBERAL
EGALITARIANISM

1. For an extended statement of this interpretation of the proper role of philosophical and political argument, see T. D. Weldon's *The Vocabulary of Politics* (London, 1953). See also Margaret Macdonald, "Nat-

ural Rights," in Peter Laslett, ed., *Philosophy, Politics and Society*, 1st ser. (Oxford, 1956), pp. 35–55.

2. Williams, "The Idea of Equality," pp. 116–37.

3. Michael Walzer, "In Defense of Equality," *Dissent*, Fall, 1973, pp. 399–408.

4. Stephen W. White makes a similar argument against A. I. Melden's linguistic justification of equal rights. White argues that "normative commitments transcending language are involved." See White, "The Equality Principle: Is It Linguistically Justifiable?" *Personalist* 55 (1974):57. Cf. A. I. Melden, "The Concept of Universal Human Rights," *Proceedings of the American Philosophical Association: Eastern Division* 1 (1952):167–88.

5. The linguistic method has been employed on another level to determine what truths are presupposed by our very use of moral discourse. See H. L. A. Hart, "Are There Any Natural Rights?" *Philosophical Review* 64 (1955):175–91 (reprinted in F. A. Olafson, ed., *Society, Law and Morality* [Englewood Cliffs, N.J., 1961], pp. 173–86). The use of relevant reasons has also been "justified" linguistically by employing Hart's method. See, e.g., Peters, *Ethics and Education*, pp. 121–5.

6. Aristotle, *The Politics of Aristotle*, trans. Ernest Barker (Oxford, 1958), 1282b, p. 129. Compare Aristotle, *Politics*, trans. H. Rackham (Cambridge, Mass., 1972), p. 231.

7. *The Politics of Aristotle*, trans. Barker, 1283a, p. 131. Compare *Politics*, trans. Rackham, p. 235: "Claim to office must necessarily be based on superiority in those things which go to the making of the state."

8. See, for example, Monroe Beardsley's Equality Injunction: "All persons are to be treated alike unless good reason can be given for treating them differently" ("Equality and Obedience to Law," in Sidney Hook, ed., *Law and Philosophy* [New York, 1964], p. 36). Beardsley's claim is that the Equality Injunction is a metamoral rule presupposed by all moral discourse and therefore requires no justification. There are three problems with this justification. One, well stated by Stephen W. White, is that "it offers counterfeit support for a genuinely ultimate first order *moral* principle. Assuming for the moment . . . that the principle of equality and the principle of utility are logically incompatible in certain contexts, couldn't the utilitarian, e.g., turn the same argument on Beardsley to justify the utility injunction?" ("The Equality Principle," p. 55.) The second problem is that if there is more than one injunction of this nature, the linguistic argument fails to provide any priority rule(s) for choosing between metamoral rules when they conflict. The third is that even if the first two problems were solved, we would still not know which reasons for treating people unequally are relevant and which irrelevant. In other words, the Equality Injunction, if valid, still remains a formal principle until it is connected to an argument establishing standards of relevance or irrelevance.

9. Benn and Peters, *Principles of Political Thought*, p. 132. Cf. W. von Leyden, "On Justifying Inequality," *Political Studies* 11 (February 1963):60.

10. Benn and Peters, *Principles of Political Thought*, p. 131, and Leyden,

"On Justifying Inequality," pp. 69–70, both consider possible standards of relevance, without addressing the question whether there exist rational criteria for determining which standards should be applied in any given situation. See also Peters, *Ethics and Education*, pp. 120–6. Peters here considers the very demand for reasons to be a sufficient claim against the arbitrariness of the resulting principles. Cf. J. R. Lucas, *The Principles of Politics* (Oxford, 1966), p. 245.

11. Williams, "The Idea of Equality," p. 127. The qualification Williams makes with respect to preventive medicine need not weaken his argument. One would expect equal distribution of preventive care (assuming equal susceptibility to illness), based upon a presumed equal need among individuals for prevention of disease and illness, to be the logical distributive principle.

12. I take egalitarianism here, as elsewhere, to consist in treating people equally rather than in distributing goods to them in equal quantities. Cf. Isaiah Berlin, "Equality," *Proceedings of the Aristotelian Society* 56 (1955–6):314.

13. Williams, "The Idea of Equality," p. 127.

14. Compare Milton Friedman's defense of maximizing use of free markets to supply goods, even those subsidized by the state, in *Capitalism and Freedom* (Chicago, 1962), pp. 193–4.

15. Of course, because such grants would be based upon rights rather than privileges, unannounced searches – such as those that the U.S. Supreme Court has sanctioned with respect to welfare recipients – would be unjust. But I assume that some just method of monitoring the use of funds would still be necessary. Cf. the U.S. Supreme Court's decision in *Wyman* v. *James*, 91 St. Ct. 381 (1971).

16. For the value of encouraging such participation, see Pateman, *Participation and Democratic Theory*, pp. 22–44; and Dennis F. Thompson, *The Democratic Citizen: Social Science and Democratic Theory in the Twentieth Century* (Cambridge, 1970), pp. 67–72.

17. Williams, "The Idea of Equality," p. 129, Cf. William K. Frankena, "The Concept of Social Justice," in Richard B. Brandt, ed., *Social Justice* (Englewood Cliffs, N.J., 1962), pp. 9–11. Frankena suggests that even if relevant reasons are given by our language, we cannot simply assume that those reasons are "just-making," i.e., sufficient to constitute principles of justice.

18. See Nozick, *Anarchy, State and Utopia*, pp. 234–5.

19. Plato, *The Republic of Plato*, trans. Allan Bloom (New York, 1968), bk. II, 406c–7a, p. 85. For a contemporary Platonic argument, see Roger D. Masters, "Is Contract an Adequate Basis for Medical Ethics?" *Hastings Center Report* 5 (December 1975): "Instead of basing medical ethics on presumed 'rights' of isolated individuals, the classics insist that there be a balance between the interests and obligations of human beings as they relate to the entire community" (p. 27).

20. See Benn and Peters, *Principles of Political Thought*, pp. 166–8; and M. Halbwachs, *L'Evolution des besoins dans les classes ouvrières* (Paris, 1933).

21. Here, I follow David Miller's argument in *Social Justice* (Oxford, 1976), p. 134. Cf. Morris Ginsberg, *On Justice in Society* (London, 1965), p. 73.

22. By neither method, however, could one simply contend that "where poor sight is common and spectacles rare, there would be no basic need for spectacles" (Benn and Peters, *Principles of Political Thought,* p. 168). We should not eliminate from our conceptions of society the commonly encountered situation where social resources are inadequate to fulfill people's needs. See also Miller's criticism of this point in *Social Justice,* p. 138. The implications of Miller's account and my own might differ in the following case: The least advantaged within a society have no opportunity to acquire glasses and therefore lack consciousness of their (objectively determinable) *need* for glasses. My account would also diverge from Miller's in a situation where more expensive goods were unavailable to one isolated segment of a society but readily available to another.

23. Marcuse's analysis of needs sometimes seems to border upon this sort of circularity. See *One-Dimensional Man* (Boston, 1964), pp. 241–6. One need not, however, conclude from Marcuse's failure to stipulate those conditions under which people's life plans will reflect their true needs that any such enterprise is doomed to circularity. Cf. Miller, *Social Justice,*. pp. 129–31. Mill's discussion of a choice criterion of pleasure can be viewed as a noncircular attempt to discriminate between true and false needs. See *Utilitarianism,* chap. 2, par. 6.

24. Williams, "The Idea of Equality," p. 127.

25. These constraints, however, do make decisions concerning medical care that fall within the bounds of relevant-reasons logic much more difficult than were scarcity not at issue (or were scarcity only the result of a maldistribution of income within a society). Whom to save and whether to save one person from sure death rather than five people from serious illness will not be easy decisions even in a society where ability to pay is not an issue. Yet such dilemmas often arise within medical practice. For an exploration of this issue in a broader context, see Guido Calabresi and Philip Bobbitt, *Tragic Choices* (New York, 1978), pp. 186–91 and passim. For more specific treatment of medical ethics, see J. Katz and A. M. Capron, *Catastrophic Diseases: Who Decides What?* (New York, 1975). Note that in an egalitarian society, socioeconomic considerations would not contaminate medical selection criteria. Compare ibid., pp. 191–5.

26. Aristotle, *Politics,* trans. Rackham, 1282b, p. 233.

27. Plato, *The Republic of Plato,* bk. VI, 488a–9b, pp. 162–9. Compare Aristotle's recognition of the existence of multiple standards for political rule depending upon the nature of the society in which leadership is exercised. Aristotle's argument appears to support the notion that standards of justice are relative to forms of social life. See Hannah Fenichel Pitkin, *Wittgenstein and Justice* (Berkeley, 1972), chap. 6 and pp. 326–7; and Aristotle, *Politics,* trans. Rackham, 1279a–84b, pp. 205–47.

28. Walzer, "In Defense of Equality," p. 404.

29. Ibid., p. 404. Compare Alan Gewirth's more general argument for egalitarian justice: "The description under which or the sufficient reason for which any agent rationally must claim that he has the right to participate voluntarily and purposively in transactions in which he is involved is that he is a prospective agent who wants to

fulfill his purposes" ("The Justification of Egalitarian Justice," in Flathman, *Concepts in Social and Political Philosophy,* p. 362).
30. Williams, "The Idea of Equality," p. 129.
31. Ibid., pp. 129–30. Cf. Peters, *Ethics and Education,* pp. 23–88, 291–319.
32. See Williams, "The Idea of Equality," p. 130:
   This notion is introduced into political discussion when there is a question of the access to certain goods which, first, even if they are not desired by everyone in society, are desired by large numbers of people in all sections of society (either for themselves, or, as in the case of education, for their children), or would be desired by people in all sections of society if they knew about the goods in question and thought it possible for them to attain them; second, are goods *which people may be said to earn or achieve;* and third, are goods which not all the people who desire them can have.
33. That is, unless one rejects the notion of desert as a moral term. As a moral term, desert implies that individuals have acted freely, responsibly, or deliberately to develop talents relevant to a certain social reward. Using desert as a nonmoral term, we might stipulate certain purely external, behavioral criteria as sufficient evidence that a person deserves, or more commonly merits, certain social rewards. Equality of opportunity often is justified on such "meritocratic" grounds – but it is not clear what would constitute the *justification* of those unequal rewards if merit is a nonmoral concept.
34. Williams, "The Idea of Equality," p. 133.
35. Ibid., pp. 133–34.
36. This assessment is presented in the section of Chapter 6 entitled "Distribution according to desert rejected."
37. Williams, "The Idea of Equality," p. 135.
38. Michael Young, *The Rise of the Meritocracy* (Baltimore, 1961), p. 105.
39. Ibid., p. 106.
40. Ibid., p. 108.
41. Williams, "The Idea of Equality, p. 136.
42. This notion of desert as contribution to social value is most explicitly developed in F. A. Hayek, *The Constitution of Liberty* (Chicago: 1960), pp. 85–102. There Hayek defends the free-market system as one that effects a distribution of economic rewards in (rough) proportion to each person's contribution to social value (generally defined as the store of socially valued goods and services).
43. Walzer, "In Defense of Equality," pp. 400–1.
44. See Hayek, *The Constitution of Liberty,* for the most consistent statement of this position; and Irving Kristol, "About Equality," *Commentary* 54 (November 1972):41–7, for the explicit target of Walzer's attack.
45. Young never makes clear precisely how or why production becomes the standard of reward in the meritocracy.
46. Walzer's arguments here recall the "Chelsea Manifesto" of the Technicians' Party in Young's story:
   The classless society would be one which both possessed and acted upon *plural values.* Were we to evaluate people, not only according to their intelligence and their education, their occupation, and

their power, but according to their kindliness and their courage, their imagination and sensitivity, their sympathy and generosity, there could be no classes . . . The classless society would also be the tolerant society, in which individual differences were actively encouraged as well as passively tolerated, in which full meaning was at last given to the dignity of man. Every human being would then have equal opportunity, not to rise up in the world in the light of any mathematical measure, but to develop his own special capacities for leading a rich life. [Young, *Rise of the Meritocracy*, p. 169. Emphasis added.]

47. Rather than rejecting meritocracy, Walzer could be interpreted as broadening the notion of what constitutes a just meritocracy by extending the range of qualities that merit recognition within a just society. However, Walzer makes no claims of close correspondence between social recognition and merit within a pluralist society. One might still say that the opportunities for merit winning out in an egalitarian society are greater than in an inegalitarian society. But the institutional purpose of redistribution is to end the tyranny of money, rather than to establish the reign of merit.

48. Walzer, "In Defense of Equality," p. 404.

49. See Karl Marx, *Early Writings*, ed. T. B. Bottomore (New York, 1964), p. 191.

50. Walzer, "In Defense of Equality," p. 403.

51. I use "just" loosely here, because it is not at all clear that Marx has a theory of *justice* in an ideal society. Insofar as he uses the term "justice" at all, it seems to refer to the "fittingness" or propriety of transactions within decidedly imperfect or nonideal societies. I take his vision of communist society to be one in which social justice in a nonjuridical sense would be realized, although he himself never considered justice a nonjuridical notion. Rather than speak of Marx's conception of ideal justice, we might speak of his conception of the nature of human relationships (and their mediation by social objects) within a communist society. The comparison with liberal egalitarianism still holds. The contrast between their ideal visions may be more striking (but less understandable) once one focuses upon the linguistic gaps between the liberal and Marxist conceptions. For more extensive discussions of this issue see Allen W. Wood, "The Marxian Critique of Justice," *Philosophy and Public Affairs* 1 (Spring 1972):244–82; and Tucker, *The Marxian Revolutionary Idea*, pp. 42—53.

52. Marx, *Early Writings*, pp. 193–4.

53. Walzer, "In Defense of Equality," p. 403.

54. Marx, *Early Writings*, p. 403.

55. See Marx, "Free Human Production," in *Writings of the Young Marx on Philosophy and Society*, ed. Lloyd D. Easton and Kurt H. Guddat (Garden City, N.Y., 1967), p. 281.

56. The most striking contrast to Marx's vision is Erving Goffman's. Goffman leads us to question whether we can now trust *any* "normal" appearances. See esp. "Normal Appearances," in Goffman's *Relations in Public* (New York, 1971), pp. 238–333. One would expect a liberal egalitarian society to be closer to Marx's than to Goffman's in the convergence it effects between personal appearances and reality.

57. One should take care here not to conflate "desert" with "entitlement." Liberal egalitarians can consistently deny that people "deserve" differential rewards while affirming their "entitlement" to
those same differentials insofar as they accrue to people in accordance with just distributive principles. Joel Feinberg carefully distinguishes between the two concepts; my discussion builds upon his
distinctions. In the discussion of the role of desert arguments in
egalitarian theory, I consider two concepts of desert. One, a strict
sense of moral desert, can be defined as follows: A is said to be
deserving of x in virtue of some prior action (y), where y is appropriate to x and is performed deliberately, responsibly, and inten-
tionally. The second, a looser form that I call social desert, accords
with Hayek's concept of social value: A is said to be deserving of x if
A has contributed to the social welfare by virtue of performing y,
and y is appropriate to x. See Joel Feinberg, *Doing and Deserving*
(Princeton, 1970), pp. 55–94, for a more extended discussion of the
concept of desert. See also Gregory Vlastos, "Justice and Equality,"
in Richard B. Brandt, ed., *Social Justice* (Englewood Cliffs, N.J.,
1962), pp. 42–3.
58. Walzer, "In Defense of Equality," p. 405.
59. Rousseau of course believed that social life itself provided the incentive for people to dissemble. The idea of a social order where people
freely reveal their true natures appears hopeless from Rousseau's
point of view. See Rousseau, *On the Origin of Inequality*, pt. II. See
also Judith N. Shklar's commentary, *Men and Citizens* (Cambridge,
1969), pp. 184–97, 211–14.
60. Walzer, "In Defense of Inequality," p. 404.
61. Ibid., p. 405.
62. Ibid.
63. If, on the other hand, there are no alternative justifications of inequality once merit is excluded, Walzer's suggestion of an equal distribution would be a forceful one. See, e.g., G. B. Shaw's defense of
equal shares, which accompanies his criticism of the use of money as
an incentive, in *The Road to Equality*, chaps. 8, 9. Cf. F. A.
Hayek's defense of distributive justice as a game of "catallaxy" in
Law, Legislation and Liberty, vol. II (Chicago, 1976), pp. 115–20. Also
see David Miller's discussion of alternative bases of distribution,
esp. that of "rights," in *Social Justice*, pp. 52–82. Taken by itself,
Miller's discussion begs the question what "rights" are to be recognized and why.
64. However, this objection holds only if the enterprise of attempting to
integrate potentially conflicting values is itself a valid one. Williams
and other theorists of the linguistic school often deny the validity of
this enterprise and hence the validity of political theorizing (as
Plato, Locke, Kant, Bentham, and Mill pursued it) as a systematizing
endeavor. Williams may ultimately be correct, insofar as a complete
integration of values is (at least humanly) impossible. Nevertheless,
the pursuit of an integrated theory of justice is a worthy one insofar
as failure will leave us no worse off in the end than does Williams's
position in the beginning, and even partial success will help us resolve some important moral conflicts that we face in political life. Cf.
Williams's position in "Political Philosophy and the Analytical Tra-

dition" (paper presented at the Annual International Meeting of the Conference for the Study of Political Thought, New York, March 20–23, 1975). See also Joel Feinberg, "Rawls and Intuitionism," in Norman Daniels, ed., *Reading Rawls: Critical Studies of "A Theory of Justice"* (New York, 1975), pp. 108–24. The position taken in the rest of this book does not touch Feinberg's claims for intuitionism with respect to questions of nonideal justice or of individual obligation.

CHAPTER 5. JOHN RAWLS AND DISTRIBUTIVE EQUALITY

1. The coherence and comprehensiveness of Rawls's theory account for Robert Nozick's acknowledgment of its beauty: see *Anarchy, State and Utopia*, p. 183.
2. See Rawls, *A Theory of Justice*, pp. 17–22. For development of this idea in the earlier stages of Rawls's thought, see Robert Paul Wolff, *Understanding Rawls: A Reconstruction and Critique of "A Theory of Justice"* (Princeton, 1977), pp. 25–98.
3. For a useful commentary, see Gerald Dworkin, "Non-neutral Principles," *Journal of Philosophy* 71 (August 15, 1974):501–6 (reprinted in Norman Daniels, ed., *Reading Rawls: Critical Studies of "A Theory of Justice"* (New York, 1975), pp. 135–40). Cf. Thomas Nagel, "Rawls on Justice," *Philosophical Review* 82 (April 1973):220–34 (reprinted in Daniels, *Reading Rawls*, pp. 1–16); Adina Schwartz, "Moral Neutrality and Primary Goods," *Ethics* 83 (July 1973):294–307; and Ronald Dworkin, "The Original Position," *University of Chicago Law Review* 40, (Spring 1973):500–33 (reprinted in Daniels, *Reading Rawls*, pp. 16–53).
4. John Rawls, "Fairness to Goodness," *Philosophical Review* 84 (October 1975):539. See also *A Theory of Justice*, p. 505.
5. See Rawls's explicit discussion of his Kantianism: "A Kantian Interpretation of Equality," *Cambridge Review*, February 1975, pp. 94–9.
6. See Rawls, "Fairness to Goodness," pp. 537–8.
7. Ibid., p. 538.
8. A radically egalitarian situation may or may not differ significantly from a situation in which an impartial spectator or ideal observer renders decisions, depending upon the way in which the spectator takes account of people's desires or interests. Cf. Brian Barry, *The Liberal Theory of Justice* (London, 1973), pp. 13–14.
9. I shall not consider at greater length the question whether Rawls's theory is "truly" Kantian. Clearly, the theories differ concerning the relationship between phenomenal and noumenal existence and the substance of categorical imperatives. However, Rawls does build upon – while revising – the Kantian notion of people as equal and autonomous self-legislators. For a discussion of the relationship between the two theories, see Bernard H. Baumrin, "Autonomy in Rawls and Kant," *Midwest Studies in Philosophy* 1 (1976):pp. 55–57. See also Oliver Johnson, "The Kantian Interpretation," *Ethics* 85 (October 1974):58–66; H. E. Mason, "On the Kantian Interpretation of Rawls' Theory," *Midwest Studies in Philosophy* 1 (1976):47–55;

Stephen L. Darwall, "A Defense of the Kantian Interpretation," *Ethics* 86 (January 1976):164–70; and Oliver Johnson, "Autonomy in Kant and Rawls: A Reply," *Ethics* 87 (April 1977):251–4.

10. Rawls, *A Theory of Justice*, pp. 62, 92. For a concise challenge to Rawls's claims regarding primary goods, see Michael Teitelman, "The Limits of Individualism," *Journal of Philosophy* 69 (October 5, 1972):549–51. I shall return to consider Teitelman's challenge in the concluding chapter.

11. The judgment whether this division violates the essential terms of Kant's theory accounts for much of the debate concerning Rawls's Kantianism.

12. In "Fairness to Goodness," p. 539, and *A Theory of Justice*, p. 579, Rawls admits that it is not.

13. For Rawls's account of those attributes of persons that are "arbitrary from a moral point of view," see *A Theory of Justice*, pp. 102–4, and "Fairness to Goodness," p. 537.

14. Rawls, "Fairness to Goodness," p. 539.

15. See Kant, *Groundwork*, 418–19, pp. 85–7.

16. Rawls's critics tend to concede this point but go on to deny that the similarities so arrived at can provide a sufficient basis for a theory of justice. See Teitelman, "The Limits of Individualism," p. 551.

17. For this criticism, see ibid., p. 548; and Wolff, *Understanding Rawls*, pp. 123–9.

18. See Rawls, *A Theory of Justice*, pp. 60–4, 542–3.

19. John Rawls, "Reply to Lyons and Teitelman," *Journal of Philosophy*, 69 (October 15, 1972):557.

20. Rawls, *A Theory of Justice*, p. 61.

21. Ibid.

22. See ibid., pp. 152, 244–50. Compare Mill, *On Liberty*, Introductory, par. 10.

23. Rawls, *A Theory of Justice*, p. 225.

24. Ibid., pp. 204–5.

25. Ibid., p. 275.

26. My own account following here is indebted to Frank Michelman's instructive discussion of the potential role of self-respect in Rawls's theory. See "Constitutional Welfare Rights and *A Theory of Justice*," in Daniels, *Reading Rawls*, pp. 340–7.

27. See Rawls, *A Theory of Justice*, pp. 107–8, for Rawls's discussion. He explicitly considers only those eugenic arguments that propose to *reduce* the talents of some people in the name of equality. I have here suggested grounds for his objection to the more difficult cases of genetic manipulations designed to increase people's capacities – although I do not want to suggest that the latter possibility presents an easy case for any moral theory (or for our intuitive capacities to judge). Were it possible to eliminate certain forms of genetic defects at birth, it might be rational from the perspective of the original position to devise a principle permitting parents or the state to make such changes, so long as involuntary changes operating against the interests and identities of self-conscious individuals could be ruled out. I am indebted to Huntington Terrill for suggesting this distinction.

28. Rawls, *A Theory of Justice*, pp. 301, 511–12.
29. Ibid., p. 60. See also ibid., p. 302, for its final form.
30. This is of course not to say that needs even in the cases of medical and legal care can be determined simply.
31. See similar arguments put forward by Barry, *Liberal Theory of Justice*, pp. 78–9; Norman Daniels, "Equal Liberty and Unequal Worth of Liberty," in Daniels, *Reading Rawls*, pp. 278–81; Michelman, "Constitutional Welfare Rights and *A Theory of Justice*," pp. 319–47; and Henry Shue, "Liberty and Self-Respect," *Ethics* 85 (April 1975):201–2.
32. Here I am indebted to Brian Barry's discussion of effective liberty in *The Liberal Theory of Justice*, pp. 76–80.
33. See n. 31 to this chapter.
34. My suggestion, discussed later, is that these uncertainties within the principles and application of distributive justice often leave open important realms for democratic participation and decision making.
35. My reasoning here parallels Rawls's defense of the maximin criterion. See John Rawls, "Some Reasons for the Maximin Criterion," *American Economic Review* 64 (May 1974):141–6.
36. See Mark Kelman, "The Social Costs of Inequality," *Dissent*, Summer 1973, pp. 291–8.
37. See Rawls, *A Theory of Justice*, pp. 180–3.
38. See, e.g., Russell Keat and David Miller, "Understanding Justice," *Political Theory* 2 (February 1974):16–18; Barry, *Liberal Theory of Justice*, p. 141; Lester C. Thurow, "Toward a Definition of Economic Justice," *Public Interest* 31 (Spring 1973):62; and Derek L. Phillips, "The Equality Debate: What Does Justice Require?" *Theory and Society* 4 (1977):260–2.
39. This point is made by T. M. Scanlon in "Rawls' Theory of Justice," in Daniels, *Reading Rawls*, p. 200.
40. However, there may be a principle (or principles) closer to that of absolute equality that cannot be justified by reference to individuals who have an interest in maximizing their individual life prospects. That is, by postulating individuals who have a primary moral interest in living within a society patterned by equality, one might sanction a more equal distribution of goods than would be effected by the difference principle. For a similar suggestion, see Scanlon, "Rawls' Theory of Justice," p. 200, esp. n. 17. See also David Miller's discussion of Kropotkin's theory of justice in *Social Justice*, pp. 230–44.
41. This is Rawls's most general answer to the trade-off between equality and efficiency posed by economists. For a succinct account of this potential trade-off, see Arthur M. Okun, *Equality and Efficiency: The Big Trade-off* (Washington, D.C., 1975), passim.
42. Rawls, *A Theory of Justice*, p. 94.
43. Thurow, "Toward a Definition of Economic Justice," p. 62.
44. Rawls, *A Theory of Justice*, p. 157.
45. Richard Miller, "Rawls and Marxism," *Philosophy and Public Affairs* 3 (Winter 1974):187–8.
46. Cf. Bell, "On Meritocracy and Equality," p. 65. For a discussion of a reorganization of the medical profession in a much less developed country along some of the same lines as might be suggested here,

see Victor Sidel and Ruth Sidel, *Serve the People: Observations on Medicine in the People's Republic of China* (Boston, 1973). Unlike contemporary China, a well-ordered and economically developed Rawlsian society would of course grant equal civil and political liberties to all its citizens.

47. Lester Thurow, *Generating Inequality: Mechanisms of Distribution in the U.S. Economy* (New York, 1975), pp. 170–7.
48. Ibid., pp. 205–6.
49. Thurow, "Toward a Definition of Economic Justice," p. 78.
50. Ibid., p. 76. See also Daniel Holland, "The Effects of Taxation on Effort," *Proceedings of the Sixty-second National Tax Association Conference*, October 1969, pp. 425–524; and George F. Break, "Income Taxes and Incentives to Work," *American Economic Review* 47 (September 1967):529–49.
51. Subcommittee on Fiscal Policy of the Joint Economic Committee of the U.S. Congress, *How Income Supplements Can Affect Work Behavior*, Studies of Public Welfare, Paper 13 (Washington, 1974); Harold Watts and Glen Cain, "Basic Labor Responses from the Urban Experiment," *Journal of Human Resources* 9 (Spring 1974):156–278; Glen Cain and Harold Watts, eds., *Income Maintenance and Labor Supply: Econometric Studies* (Chicago, 1973); and Robert Hall, "Effects of the Experimental Negative Income Tax on Labor Supply," in Joseph Pechman and P. Michael Timpane, eds., *Work Incentives and Income Guarantees: The New Jersey Negative Income Tax Experiment* (Washington, D.C., 1975), pp. 115–56. But cf. Henry J. Aaron, "Cautionary Notes on the Experiment," in ibid., pp. 88–114.
52. See David Macarov, *Incentives to Work* (San Francisco, 1970), esp. pp. 137–53.
53. See Thurow, *Generating Inequality*, pp. 142–52.
54. See Burton Malkiel, *A Random Walk down Wall Street* (New York, 1973), pp. 167–9; and Thurow, *Generating Equality*, p. 201. This claim must be qualified by the argument that those entrepreneurs in a position to take advantage of the disequilibrium in real capital markets are, for structural reasons, most likely to gain. Those who are wealthy by virtue of owning their own large enterprises predictably stand to gain most from market investments. Another question then arises: Did these favored investors gain their original fortunes through luck or through expertise? Because many of today's favored investors are not the original accumulators of their family fortunes, a new form of "luck" enters into the explanation, that of birth. Even if the question whether the original accumulators achieved their fortunes through luck or through skill remains unanswered, Thurow's arguments, coupled with Malkiel's analysis, still go a long way toward dispelling the illusion that present returns on investment reflect business expertise or even some purely psychological propensity for risk.
55. Thurow, *Generating Inequality*, p. 201.
56. Ibid., p. 202.
57. For an important step in the latter direction, see Charles E. Lindblom, *Politics and Markets: The World's Political–Economic Systems* (New York, 1977), esp. pts. VI and VII.
58. Rawls, *A Theory of Justice*, p. 440. Emphasis added.

59. Runciman, *Relative Deprivation and Social Justice*, pt. III, pp. 179–288.
60. Rawls, *A Theory of Justice*, pp. 106–7.
61. Ibid., p. 225.
62. Ibid., p. 226.
63. This claim is widely made, but I shall concentrate here on the arguments set forth by Macpherson in *Democratic Theory*, essays I-IV, pp. 3–94.
64. Rawls himself suggests taxation and other adjustments in the rights of property as a potential means of "equalizing the value of liberty." See *A Theory of Justice*, pp. 276–8.
65. See ibid., p. 204.
66. For a comparison of James Mill's arguments for political liberty with those of his son, see Ryan, "Two Concepts of Politics and Democracy," pp. 99–111 and passim.
67. Rawls, *A Theory of Justice*, pp. 225–6.
68. Ibid., p. 226.
69. Ibid., p. 522.
70. See Rawls's discussion of the advantages of his theory over classical utilitarianism in *A Theory of Justice*, pp. 183–92. Cf. A. K. Sen, "Rawls versus Bentham: An Axiomatic Examination of the Pure Distribution Problem," in Daniels, *Reading Rawls*, pp. 283–92; and Kenneth J. Arrow, "Some Ordinalist-Utilitarian Notes on Rawls' Theory of Justice," *Journal of Philosophy* 70 (May 10, 1973):257.
71. See Rawls, *A Theory of Justice*, pp. 232–4.
72. For an extensive critique of the utilitarian foundations of welfare economics, including a critique of the unreality of the basic assumptions, see I. M. D. Little, *Critique of Welfare Economics*, 2nd ed. (Oxford, 1957). See also Martin Hollis and Edward J. Nell, *Rational Economic Man: A Philosophical Critique of Neo-Classical Economics* (Cambridge, 1975), pp. 47–64, 205–32.
73. A similar shift in the utilitarian basis of making interpersonal comparisons is evident in Kenneth J. Arrow's "Extended Sympathy and the Possibility of Social Choice," *Proceedings of the American Economic Association 67*, no. 1 (February 1977):219–25. Arrow suggests that individuals might agree upon a preference ordering of social goods by including in the set of goods to be ordered not only those that society might distribute to them but also everything that would determine their satisfaction with those goods: "Not only the wine but the ability to enjoy and discriminate are included among the goods" (ibid., p. 224). Although Arrow admits uneasiness with this hypothetical choice assumption, he also suggests that this shift to Co-ordinal Invariance is fueled by a desire to seek a consistent utilitarian basis for a theory of justice (ibid., p. 225).
74. See Rawls's discussion in *A Theory of Justice*, pp. 161–75. This need not always be an advantage of his theory. It seems intuitively wrong to insist that no decrease in the welfare of the least advantaged, however small, can be offset by an increase in social welfare, however large. See Arrow, "Extended Sympathy and the Possibility of Social Choice," p. 223. Arrow claims that revising the maximin rule to include a continuity requirement "is a small step in the direction of

utilitarian ethics" (ibid.). True, so long as emphasis is put on the *small*, because Rawls's theory still does not shift to a preference- or utility-based standard of welfare.

75. For a recognition of the "practical similarity" of utilitarianism and Rawls's theory, see Arrow, "Some Ordinalist–Utilitarian Notes on Rawls' Theory of Justice," pp. 255–7; David Braybrooke, "Utilitarianism with a Difference: Rawls' Position in Ethics," *Canadian Journal of Philosophy* 3 (December 1973):304–8; and David Lyons, "Rawls versus Utilitarianism," *Journal of Philosophy* 18 (October 5, 1972):esp. pp. 541–2. Lyons emphasizes the point that under similar and familiar socioeconomic situations, Rawls's theory and utilitarian-ism will support the same principles. However, one might still ask which theory provides more plausible reasons for the principles it endorses.

CHAPTER 6. CONTEMPORARY CRITICS OF LIBERAL EGALITARIANISM

1. See David Hume, *A Treatise of Human Nature*, ed. L. A. Selby-Bigge (Oxford, 1888), bk. III, pt. II, sec. 2; and David Hume, *An Enquiry Concerning the Principles of Morals* (London, 1777), sec. III, pt. I. For a more recent discussion of these constraints rooted in a view of human imperfection, see Lucas, *The Principles of Politics*, pp. 1–10.

2. Nozick, *Anarchy, State and Utopia*, p. 198.

3. I shall draw directly upon the criticisms of "revisionist liberalism" Macpherson presents in *Democratic Theory*, pp. 77–94, and in "Rawls' Models of Man and Society," *Philosophy of Social Science* 3 (1973):341–7. For the development of Macpherson's perspective on liberalism, see also his *Political Theory of Possessive Individualism* (Oxford, 1962); *The Real World of Democracy* (Oxford, 1966); and his most recent work, *The Life and Times of Liberal Democracy* (Oxford, 1977). In two of his recent essays, Macpherson's position is explicitly one of a liberal democratic critic, an acknowledgment that reinforces my interpretation of his critique of liberal theory as an internal one: see "Human Rights as Property Rights," *Dissent*, Winter 1977, pp. 72–7, and "Who Needs a Theory of the State?" (paper delivered at the 1977 annual meeting of the American Political Science Association, Washington, D.C., September 1–4, 1977).

4. The cited works of the following theorists include those arguments that I take to be basic to the libertarian critique of liberal egalitarianism: Hayek, *The Constitution of Liberty*, and *Law, Legislation and Liberty*; Ludwig von Mises, *Human Action* (New Haven, 1963); *Planning for Freedom* (South Holland, Ill., 1952), *Socialism* (New Haven, 1951), and *The Anti-Capitalist Mentality* (Princeton, 1956); Nozick, *Anarchy, State and Utopia*; Ayn Rand, *Atlas Shrugged* (New York, 1975), and *Capitalism: The Unknown Ideal* (New York, 1966); and Murray Rothbard, *Man, Economy, and the State* (Princeton, 1962), and *For a New Liberty* (New York, 1973). In *Capitalism and Freedom*, Milton Friedman presents many of the libertarian arguments, yet several of Friedman's policy recommendations are un-

characteristic of libertarianism: see, e.g., his argument for an educational voucher plan, pp. 85–107. Cf. Rothbard, *For a New Liberty*, pp. 151–2.

5. Macpherson, *Democratic Theory*, p. 88.

6. Ibid., pp. 89–90.

7. Macpherson clearly means to use class in the strict sense of a group defined by its relation to the means of production. Throughout his critique, he is objecting to those inequalities remaining between the bourgeoisie who own the means of production and the proletariat who, however affluent, do not. Macpherson's argument suggests therefore that inequalities of income and wealth existing among a group of people similarly situated with respect to the production process would be less problematic than those between classes. The significant variable is the power relationship between capitalist and worker, the nature of which, Macpherson seems to suggest, is ultimately independent of factors such as relative income level, degree of economic competition, the structure of work, the level of employment opportunities, and other (democratic) state regulations over industry.

8. See Macpherson, *Democratic Theory*, p. 90; Miller, "Rawls and Marxism," pp. 187–8.

9. See, however, J. Champlin's categorization, "On the Study of Power," *Politics and Society* 1 (November 1970):91–111. For another informative discussion of the modes and meaning of power, from a radical perspective, see Steven Lukes, *Power: A Radical View* (London, 1974).

10. The two modes of power discussed are close to the Power I and Power III of Champlin's categorization in "On the Study of Power."

11. See Robert Nozick's attempt at specific criteria for coercion in "Coercion" in Sidney Morgenbesser, P. Suppes, and M. White, eds., *Philosophy, Science and Method* (New York, 1969), pp. 440–72. For purposes of the argument here, coercion is too narrow a concept; we must instead assess the distribution and nature of social power.

12. See Macpherson, "Rawls' Models of Man and Society," p. 341; and Macpherson, *Democratic Theory*, pp. 43–4, 64–7.

13. This explains why most Marxist analyses of exploitation focus upon the institutional structure of class societies rather than upon power relationships between individual capitalists and workers. For a thoughtful evaluation and reinterpretation of the Marxist theory of exploitation, see Anthony Giddens, *The Class Structure of the Advanced Societies* (New York, 1973), esp. pp. 82–138.

14. See, e.g., Richard Sennett and Jonathan Cobb, *The Hidden Injuries of Class* (New York, 1971).

15. See Rawls's discussion *A Theory of Justice*, pp. 265–72, and 280. The potentially just economic system that Rawls discusses is very similar to the "property-owning democracy" considered by J. E. Meade in *Efficiency, Equality and the Ownership of Property* (Cambridge, Mass., 1965), pp. 40–65. See also ibid., pp. 66–74, for Meade's discussion of a socialist state.

16. Macpherson, *Democratic Theory*, p. 90. See also ibid., p. 93.

17. See Mill, *Principles of Political Economy*, bk. II, chap. 1, sec. 3, pp. 210–14.

18. For two cogent attempts to integrate liberal and socialist perspectives concerning freedom and the market, see William E. Connolly, "A Note on Freedom under Socialism," *Political Theory* 5 (November 1977):461–72; and David Miller, "Socialism and the Market," *Political Theory* 5 (November 1977):473–90. Connolly's and Miller's discussions suggest that the basic ideals of both liberals and socialists will be compromised if they are inexorably wedded to the support of either a thoroughgoing free-market, private-enterprise economy or a fully centralized state-ownership system.
19. Macpherson, *Democratic Theory*, p. 42.
20. Ibid., pp. 51–2.
21. Once one imagines the Humean constraints of justice lifted, radical, liberal egalitarian, and perfectionist views all merge in at least one respect. Each will support a distribution of goods that gives people equal opportunities to develop their human capacities. However, return any of the constraints to the hypothesized social situation and these views will diverge. For example, perfectionists will claim that injustice is inherent in any society in which scarcity exists, because our entitlement to live our lives up to the limits of our innate potentiality is in each case absolute. Radical theorists will argue that those constraints are "artificially" created by an exploitative institutional structure of the economy. Liberal egalitarians, on the other hand, will tend to accept the constraint of scarcity as one relatively "natural" to the human social condition. For a lucid contemporary account of the perfectionist point of view, see David L. Norton, *Personal Destinies: A Philosophy of Ethical Individualism* (Princeton, 1976), esp. pp. 210–353.
22. See Macpherson, *Democratic Theory*, pp. 36–8, 61–3.
23. See Mill, *Principles of Political Economy*, bk. IV chap. 6, sec. 9, pp. 752–7.
24. I mean utopian here in the sense of an unrealizable vision of a completely harmonious society. This vision need not be a Marxist one. A perfectionist vision of justice could fit this extra-Humean description as well, yet might include a significantly antiegalitarian view of what constitutes a just distribution of human capacities. See, e.g., Norton's *Personal Destinies*, pp. 328 ff. Note that Norton's theory is directly applicable only to personal ethics, not to the basic political structure of distributive justice within a society.
25. Macpherson, *Democratic Theory*, p. 54.
26. Ibid., pp. 52–3.
27. The extra rewards of the difference principle may encourage people to develop those talents or to engage in those pursuits that benefit others. But certainly in any just society there will be significant noneconomic rewards for possessing "essentially human qualities."
28. See Macpherson, *Democratic Theory*, Essay III, pp. 39–76; and Macpherson, *Life and Times of Liberal Democracy*, pp. 93–115.
29. Macpherson, *Democratic Theory*, p. 55.
30. Ibid., pp. 54–5.
31. Mill's defense of free speech rests in part upon the argument that the wisest of rulers – Marcus Aurelius, for example – can be expected to commit intellectual errors. Even were we to discount falli-

bility, Mill's case for free speech could rest upon his argument concerning the way in which progressive beings must learn and know the truth (through unencumbered intellectual battle with falsehoods). This Millean argument is significant in that it suggests that the liberal argument for free speech is compatible with a vision of human beings attaining intellectual perfection. See Mill, *On Liberty*, chaps. 2, 3, pp. 228–75.

32. Robert C. Tucker's interpretation of Marx accords with this formulation: see *The Marxian Revolutionary Idea*, pp. 3–53.

33. There is an intimate relationship in Macpherson's argument between the elimination of scarcity and altering the means of production. Capitalism produces false needs and a corresponding consumer ethos among citizens, which aggravates the situation of scarcity from the demand side. Here Macpherson comes very close to endorsing Marcuse's analysis of the pervasiveness of false consciousness under capitalism. The significant difference between Marcuse's and Macpherson's arguments is that Macpherson appears more optimistic that there exists a way out of this circle of false consciousness created by the "liberal-democratic capitalist-welfare state." Why is Macpherson more optimistic than Marcuse? One plausible reason is that Macpherson views human beings as basically rational (holding, e.g., that increased consumption is a rational response to the prevailing economic structure of society); whereas Marcuse borrows, albeit with substantial revisions, a Freudian view of individuals unconsciously *driven* by psychic and/ or social forces beyond their (perhaps even collective) control.

34. Compare Joel Feinberg, "Non-comparative Justice," *Philosophical Review* 83 (July 1974):322–3; and Giddens, *Class Structure of the Advanced Societies*, pp. 130–1.

35. To the question "Who needs a theory of the state?" Macpherson's reply is that liberal democrats need one, but more pointedly they need to learn a lesson from neo-Marxist theories of the state concerning the incompatibility between maximizing human development and maintaining any form of private ownership of the means of production. See Macpherson, "Who Needs a Theory of the State?" pp. 19–20, 28–9. Macpherson sees the possibility of convergence of Marxist and liberal democratic theories of the state on the grounds that neo-Marxists are beginning to doubt the "classical Marxian revolutionary prescription" (ibid., p. 30). However, it is not at all clear that adherence to a revolutionary vision is incompatible with liberal egalitarian theories of justice. The more problematic grounds for separation still appear to be the question just discussed: whether any form of private ownership of means of production can be rendered compatible with free human development. A negative reply to this question is implicit in most contemporary Marxist critiques of advanced capitalist democracies. See, e.g., Jürgen Habermas, *Legitimation Crisis* (Boston, 1975), pp. 75–92 and passim; Ernest Mandel, *Late Capitalism* (London, 1975), pp. 523–61; Harry Braverman, *Labor and Monopoly Capital: The Degradation of Work in the Twentieth Century* (New York, 1974), passim; and James O'Connor, *The Fiscal Crisis of the State* (New York, 1973), pp. 221–60.

36. Macpherson, "Who Needs a Theory of the State?" pp. 29–30.
37. For the beginnings of such questioning, see Ralph Miliband, *Marxism and Politics* (Oxford, 1977), pp. 154–90; and Giddens, *Class Structure of the Advanced Societies*, pp. 282–94 and passim.
38. Rawls concurs on the need for a political sociology in *A Theory of Justice*, pp. 226–7.
39. See Miller, "Rawls and Marxism," pp. 167–91.
40. Ibid., pp. 181–4.
41. Ibid., pp. 175–80.
42. But, as I have noted, Miller concedes that were a communist society realized, a just distribution would probably approximate that required by Rawls's difference principle (ibid., pp. 187–8).
43. I am indebted to Dennis Thompson for clarification of this point.
44. See Marx's discussion of the Ten Hour's Bill in his "Inaugural Address of the Working Men's International Association," in *On the First International*, ed. Saul Padover, Karl Marx Library, vol. III (New York, 1973), pp. 9–10.
45. For a discussion of the possibilities in Marx's theory of a nonviolent transition to socialism within Anglo-American societies, see Shlomo Avineri, *The Social and Political Thought of Karl Marx* (Cambridge, 1968), pp. 202–39.
46. My definition of the right here is peculiarly American; in this chapter I shall be speaking exclusively of the libertarian right.
47. Nozick, *Anarchy, State and Utopia*, p. ix.
48. For this definition, see Max Weber, "Politics as a Vocation," in *From Max Weber: Essays in Sociology*, trans. and ed. H. H. Gerth and C. Wright Mills (New York, 1958), p. 78. For a similar definition of the state rendered on historical grounds and raising the substantive question whether the state's use of force is legitimate, see Franz Oppenheimer, *The State* (New York, 1926), esp. pp. 15–27.
49. John Hospers, "What Libertarianism Is," in Tibor R. Machan, ed., *The Libertarian Alternative* (Chicago, 1974). p. 4.
50. For another attempt to derive property rights from a general right to freedom see Eric Mack, "Individualism, Rights, and the Open Society," in Machan, *The Libertarian Alternative*, pp. 21–37.
51. See, e.g., Hospers, "What Libertarianism Is," p. 8; and Friedman, *Capitalism and Freedom*, pp. 7–10.
52. I do not think that the libertarian commitment to a view of individuals as free and equal moral persons should be doubted. Yet it might be argued that the conclusions libertarians reach are more consistent with an assumption of basic human inequality. For an explicit statement of the libertarian commitment to a view of human equality, see Tibor R. Machan, "On Reclaiming America's Unique Political Tradition," in Machan, *The Libertarian Alternative*, pp. 495–501.
53. Hospers, "What Libertarianism Is," p. 3.
54. See, e.g., ibid., pp. 3–6; and Nozick, *Anarchy, State and Utopia*, p. 172.
55. For a more extensive discussion of the problems of marginal price theory applied to the "real world," see Little, *Critique of Welfare Economics*, esp. pp. 121–79; William J. Baumol, *Welfare Economics and the Theory of the State* (Cambridge, Mass., 1969), pp. 24–45,

204–7; and James M. Buchanan, *The Demand and Supply of Public Goods* (Chicago, 1968), esp. pp. 49–99, 127–49, and 171–90. See also Hobhouse, *Liberalism*, pp. 98–101.

56. See Nozick, *Anarchy, State and Utopia*, p. 169; and Hospers, "What Libertarianism Is," p. 3.

57. Nozick, *Anarchy, State and Utopia*, p. 169.

58. Ibid., p. 160. See also ibid., p. 219.

59. See Locke, *Second Treatise of Government*, chap. 11, sec. 140, p. 408.

60. Macpherson, "Human Rights as Property Rights," pp. 72–7.

61. Or, to use Macpherson's alternative formulation, one might divide property rights into "exclusive" and "inclusive" rights: rights to exclude other people from one's own personal property and rights not to be excluded from the use of some things (namely, the means of life and of labor) by others. See ibid., pp. 74–5. By either formulation, the right to property is not a simple or minimally restricted right; it must either effectively serve or be constrained by the prior rights to a decent life, and by the needs of equal moral persons.

62. Compare T. H. Marshall's account of the development of "social rights" in England in *Citizenship and Social Class and Other Essays*, pp. 10–74.

63. Nozick reinterprets the meaning of the Lockean proviso so as to stipulate that private appropriation does not worsen the situation of others by making them unable to use freely (rather than to own) what they otherwise could. We might ask whether this standard is practically applicable. We might also wonder how mere "use" could satisfy a Nozickean individual to whom property appears as an appendage of himself. On libertarian grounds, use certainly cannot be considered as good as *free* use. Therefore, by the terms of the proviso, free use by private appropriation may be guaranteed either to all or to none. On the other hand, if use does not seem an inferior alternative to appropriation, an equitable interpretation of the proviso might underwrite the *equally shared* use of property. The precise contours of a just interpretation of Nozick's proviso still escape me, but these do appear to be some plausible nonlibertarian implications of the original spirit of the Lockean proviso. See Nozick, *Anarchy, State and Utopia*, pp. 174–82.

64. John Hospers, for example, defends "first come, first served" as appropriate in the case of homesteading in the American West and in the contemporary case of selling air waves. Here he follows Ayn Rand's argument in "The Property Status of Airwaves," in *Capitalism: The Unknown Ideal*, pp. 122–9. See Hospers, *Libertarianism: A Political Philosophy for Tomorrow* (Los Angeles, 1971), pp. 72–3. For two classical philosophical positions supporting the first-come, first-served, principle, see Kant, *Justice*, 246–308, pp. 51–72; and Hegel, *Philosophy of Right*, pars. 40–71, pp. 38–57. For a succinct criticism of both Kant's and Hegel's claims, see Lawrence C. Becker, *Property Rights: Philosophic Foundations* (London, 1977), pp. 29–30. Becker makes the point that the "liberty right" to appropriate does not necessarily entail the "claim right" to keep in perpetuity, as both Kant and Hegel seem to assume.

65. See Bernard Williams, "The Minimal State," *Times Literary Supplement*, January 17, 1975, pp. 46–7.
66. See Nozick's very tentative suggestion, *Anarchy, State and Utopia*, p. 231.
67. Ibid., pp. 160–2.
68. For an interesting examination of the ways in which conceptions of distributive justice can be based upon desert, see Miller, *Social Justice*, pp. 83–121. See also Michael A. Slote, "Desert, Consent, and Justice," *Philosophy and Public Affairs* 2 (Summer 1973):323–47. My argument suggests that both Miller and Slote neglect some important logical problems entailed in attempts to base institutions of distributive justice upon desert.
69. Nozick, *Anarchy, State and Utopia*, pp. 162–3.
70. Nozick might have told us a very different story from Wilt Chamberlain's with the same libertarian moral. A sports trainer and aspiring agent notices that the eldest son of a very poor family has great potential for basketball. Offering him the opportunity to travel and to be properly clothed and fed, the trainer encourages the man, on his coming of age, to sell himself into slavery for life. The player agrees, calculating that no more attractive alternative will arise. The trainer consequently makes $240,000 a season from his slave. Nothing in Nozick's theory suggests that this scenario would be morally problematic. (See Nozick, *Anarchy, State and Utopia*, p. 331, for his support of "voluntary" slave contracts.) Nor would Nozick have an easy time arguing that such a scenario would be unlikely in his libertarian state.
71. See Miller, *Social Justice*, p. 196. I am generally indebted to Miller for his insightful, extended discussion of Spencer's theory of social justice, in ibid., pp. 180–208. For Spencer's desert argument, see *The Principles of Ethics* (London, 1893), II, 17, and *The Principles of Sociology* (London, 1896), III, 563–4.
72. See Nozick, *Anarchy, State and Utopia*, pp. 155–60; Hayek, *The Constitution of Liberty*, pp. 85–102; and Irving Kristol, "'When Virtue Loses all Her Loveliness': Some Reflections on Capitalism and 'The Free Society,'" *Public Interest*, no. 21 (Fall 1970), pp. 3–15. See also Nozick's comments on Hayek in *Anarchy, State and Utopia*, pp. 158–9.
73. See Nozick, *Anarchy, State and Utopia*, pp. 213–16. For a suggestion of a logical form for a desert argument, see Becker, *Property Rights*, pp. 48–56. The objections to desert arguments that I cite shortly imply that Becker's desert argument – which recognizes that rewards must be appropriate both to the acts performed and to the value contributed – would not justify a free-market system of property transfers or a first-come, first-served, principle of property acquisition. Becker leaves as an open question whether any political institutionalization of the desert argument with respect to distributive justice is possible. He does, however, point to an often ignored aspect of such desert arguments: the suggestion that penalties be imposed on people for the disutility their productions create for the rest of society.

74. On the problems externalities and collective goods create for the free-market mechanism, see works cited in n. 55 to this chapter. See also John G. Head, "Public Goods and Public Policy," *Public Finance* 17 (1962):197–219; and Richard A. Musgrave, *The Theory of Public Finance* (New York, 1959). For an excellent summary of the economics of externalities, including a useful bibliography, see E. J. Mishan, "The Postwar Literature on Externalities: An Interpretative Essay," *Journal of Economic Literature* 9, no. 1 (March 1971):1–28.

75. Rawls, *A Theory of Justice*, pp. 311–12.

76. Nozick, *Anarchy, State and Utopia*, p. 214.

77. For a more detailed account of the concept of desert, as distinct from that of entitlement, see Feinberg, *Doing and Deserving*, pp. 55–94. I am assuming here the view that a theory of justice should at least be able to *account* for and be rendered *consistent* with our intuitive moral notions. However, our moral values need not all be realizable by the distributive institutions of a just society.

78. See Rawls, *A Theory of Justice*, pp. 104, 311–12.

79. Nozick, *Anarchy, State and Utopia*, p. 214.

80. For a more extensive discussion of the possible legitimate role of "praise according to merit" in a liberal egalitarian society, see Vlastos, "Justice and Equality," pp. 63–72. This interpretation coheres with Rawls's argument that the two principles of justice can be expected to apply only to the basic structure of a society. Distinct principles may apply to individual ethics and to actions and events not capable of being controlled by institutions of justice. See John Rawls, "The Basic Structure as Subject," *American Philosophical Quarterly* 14 (April 1977):159–65.

81. See Rawls, *A Theory of Justice*, p. 312. Rawls also points to the implausibility of arguing that what a person deserves should change as the number of people supplying or demanding his goods changes. This argument assumes, of course, that desert is not measured simply in terms of economic value.

82. Rawls appears to support this argument in saying that "there seems to be no way to discount for their greater good fortune." See *A Theory of Justice*, p. 312.

83. Differential-desert arguments include arguments that take the desert base to be some unequally distributed human characteristic and stipulate that rewards should be distributed in accordance with the distribution of that trait. One can thereby distinguish such arguments from possible "egalitarian-desert" arguments, one of which I mention later: arguments that take the desert base to be some equally distributed or minimal and therefore quasi-universal human characteristic and sanction equal treatment of people on the basis of their relatively equal desert. An egalitarian-desert argument of this sort is suggested by Alan Zaitchik, "On Deserving to Deserve," *Philosophy and Public Affairs* 6 (Summer 1977):370–88.

84. See Nozick, *Anarchy, State and Utopia*, p. 160.

85. See ibid., p. 215.

86. Ibid., pp. 224–7.

87. Rawls, *A Theory of Justice*, p. 19.

88. See ibid., p. 505. Vlastos suggests a similar criterion for according individuals equal rights, in "Justice and Equality," pp. 45–6.

89. Because many libertarians accept this basis of equality, it is possible to challenge the internal consistency of their arguments for (almost) absolute property rights. If property rights are derivative from the right to liberty, then they can rightly be constrained when they conflict with rendering individual liberty universally effective. (See Becker, *Property Rights*, p. 39.) If property rights are not considered derivative from the right to liberty, the rationale for the libertarian's particular stipulation of rights is called into question. For a challenge to Nozick's libertarianism on this basis, see Samuel Scheffler, "Natural Rights, Equality, and the Minimal State," *Canadian Journal of Philosophy* 6 (March 1976):59–76.

90. Compare Michael Teitelman's critique of Rawls on this point in "The Limits of Individualism," pp. 553–4. The argument presented here seems to meet Teitelman's objections.

91. For a sense closely related to the one I describe, see Zaitchik, "On Deserving to Deserve," pp. 385–8.

92. Hayek, *The Constitution of Liberty*, p. 101.

93. I am adopting here the notion of effective liberty put forth by Brian Barry in *Liberal Theory of Justice*, pp. 76–8; and by Norman Daniels in "Equal Liberty and Unequal Worth of Liberty," pp. 253–81. Note, however, that the principles of justice aim directly at *maximizing* the effective liberty of the least advantaged rather than at *equalizing* effective liberty.

94. Rawls has been criticized on many fronts for this circularity in his argument. However, none of his critics makes clear whether any theory of justice can avoid this problem or a similar sort of inconclusiveness. Thomas Nagel's critique is the most measured: that the original position serves to model rather than to justify the resulting conception of justice. One might accept this form of modeling, I think, as the best that can be accomplished by any such theory. See Nagel, "Rawls on Justice," pp. 233–4.

95. Rawls, *A Theory of Justice*, pp. 19–20.

96. One may wonder here why most libertarian theorists do not adopt this justification criterion. Nozick seems to suggest that such a view is merely intellectually comfortable. But it is not clear to me that we have any reasonable alternative to this form of intellectual comfort. See *Anarchy, State and Utopia*, pp. ix–xi.

97. Rawls, *A Theory of Justice*, pp. 578–9.

98. Ibid., p. 21. For an elaboration of the supporting methodological arguments, see Israel Scheffler, *Science and Subjectivity* (New York, 1967), chap. 5; and Nicholas Rescher, *The Coherence Theory of Truth* (Oxford, 1973).

99. Rawls, *A Theory of Justice*, p. 581.

100. See Charles R. Beitz, "Justice and International Relations," *Philosophy and Public Affairs* 4 (Summer 1975):360–89, esp. sec. 3.

101. For this argument and for a more extensive discussion of the alternative means of achieving an egalitarian world order, and their political implications, see Charles Beitz, "Global Egalitarianism: Can We Make Out a Case?" *Dissent*, Winter 1979, pp. 59–68.

CHAPTER 7. PARTICIPATORY AND DISTRIBUTIVE EQUALITY REINTEGRATED

1. Rousseau, *The Social Contract*, bk. IV, chap. 2, p. 106.
2. E.g., ibid., bk II, chap. 2, pp. 49–52.
3. See Nozick's discussion in *Anarchy, State and Utopia*, pp. 280–92.
4. For a distinct approach to the limitations of obligations to majority will, see Michael Walzer, *Obligations: Essays on Disobedience, War, and Citizenship* (Cambridge, Mass., 1970). For a broader discussion than I undertake here of the problems of classical consent theories, see Pitkin, "Obligation and Consent: I," pp. 990–9.
5. However, one might consistently justify a nondemocratic transition to a democratic society, were democratic means unavailable or very unlikely to succeed.
6. See the discussion later in this chapter, at the end of the section on community control of schools.
7. Rawls, *A Theory of Justice*, p. 222.
8. For Rawls's discussion of the meaning of political liberty, see ibid., pp. 221–8.
9. Rawls does mention noninstrumental grounds for self-government but does not pursue the implications any further. See ibid., pp. 233–4.
10. Again, as a reminder: For want of a clearer term, I shall use "distributive ideal" to refer to the principle(s) that govern the distribution of material goods – income, wealth, health care, housing, legal aid, etc. – within an ideal society, as distinguished from the "participatory ideal" governing the distribution of participatory opportunities. Clearly, "distributive" could be used to describe both ideals, and Aristotle does use it so: see *Politics*, trans. Rackham, 1280a8–37, pp. 211–15.
11. For a more extensive discussion of this paradox, see Richard Wollheim, "A Paradox in the Theory of Democracy," in Peter Laslett and W. G. Runciman, eds., *Philosophy, Politics and Society*, 2d ser. (Oxford, 1962), pp. 71–87; D. Goldstick, "An Alleged Paradox in the Theory of Democracy," *Philosophy and Public Affairs* 2 (Winter 1973):187–9; Marvin Schiller, "On the Logic of Being a Democrat," *Philosophy* 44 (1969):46–56; Ross Harrison, "No Paradox in Democracy," *Political Studies* 18 (1970):515–17; and Ted Honderich, "A Difficulty with Democracy," *Philosophy and Public Affairs* 3 (Winter 1974):221–6. My discussion follows Honderich's resolution most closely, taking seriously his concluding observation that a citizen's commitment to democracy must be conditional upon what it is that the majority decides. See also the distinction among democratic problems made by J. Roland Pennock in "Democracy is *not* Paradoxical: Comment," *Political Theory* 2, no. 1 (February 1974):88–93.
12. This, I think, is a plausible interpretation of Locke's argument for majority rule; it avoids assuming that Locke sanctioned the moral tyranny of the majority despite his emphasis upon the natural rights of individuals. This interpretation depends upon the assumption that majority rule is the safest way to govern the whole. Several interpretations support this view. See, e.g., Macpherson,

Political Theory of Possessive Individualism, chap. 5, pp. 252–7; and C. B. Macpherson, "The Social Bearing of Locke's Political Theory," *Western Political Quarterly 7* (1954):20–2. Cf. Alan Ryan, "Locke and the Dictatorship of the Bourgeoisie," *Political Studies* 13 (1965):219–30. The latter two essays are reprinted in Gordon Schochet, ed., *Life, Liberty, and Property* (Belmont, Calif., 1971), pp. 60–85, 86–106.

One remaining problem within this interpretation is Locke's argument that express consent perpetually binds individuals to their community, if not to their government. If the majority is the source of tyranny, why must one be obligated to obey it, even if one has previously expressly consented to a government constituted by that majority? See *Second Treatise of Government,* chap. 8, par. 121, and chap. 19, par. 243, for the source of this problem.

13. As I have already suggested, one would expect liberal societies – particularly inegalitarian liberal societies – to place great emphasis upon educational institutions to equalize opportunity among political citizens. Recently, however, sociologists have recognized the inadequacy of schools as equalizing institutions. My analysis of the necessary economic preconditions for equalizing educational opportunity coheres with this recognition. See Christopher Jencks et al., *Inequality: A Reassessment of the Effect of Family and Schooling in America* (New York, 1972); and the qualifications concerning its conclusions in *Harvard Educational Review* 43 (February 1973):37–164.

14. Robert Dahl presents the case closest to my own for how and why liberal theory must accommodate the traditionally Marxist or radical case for industrial democracy. However, I diverge from Dahl in placing emphasis upon the educational and self-development as well as on the protective aspects of participation. See Dahl, *After the Revolution?* (New Haven, 1970), pp. 115–40.

15. I shall not discuss the question of how much power bureaucracies actually do wield compared to other political institutions. Regardless of how much, bureaucratic power is considerable enough to warrant concern for its limitation within a liberal egalitarian society, a society that may necessitate the creation of more bureaucratic structures. For a major expression of the importance of bureaucracies as the locus of decision making in contemporary society, see James Burnham, *The Managerial Revolution* (New York, 1941). See also Robert V. Presthus, *The Organizational Society* (New York, 1962); Milovan Djilas, *The New Class* (London, 1957); and Ludwig von Mises, *Bureaucracy* (New Haven, 1944), for critical commentary specifically directed toward the bureaucratic expansion of the welfare state.

16. See *The Federalist Papers,* ed. Clinton Rossiter (New York, 1961), no. 10 and no. 51. For a more recent limited pluralist defense of participation in American political science, see Robert Dahl, *A Preface to Democratic Theory* (Chicago, 1954), chap. 5. Note, however, that pluralists would have much more to say were they to broaden their understanding of political power to include the economic sphere. This criticism, internal to the democratic pluralist case, has been voiced by Grant McConnell, *Private Power and American Democracy* (New York, 1966). pp. 119–54, 336–8; and Robert Paul Wolff, *The*

Poverty of Liberalism (Boston, 1968), pp. 108–12. Robert Dahl himself has demonstrated the possibility of extending pluralism to account for a broader view of the political realm in *After the Revolution?*, pp. 115–40.

17. See Mill, *Principles of Political Economy*, bk. V, chap. 11; and Dennis F. Thompson's commentary on Mill's limited use of this rationale in *John Stuart Mill and Representative Government*, pp. 20–1.

18. See Aristotle's *Politics*, trans. Rackham 1281b23–2a24, pp. 223–7; A. D. Lindsay, *The Modern Democratic State* (New York, 1962), pp. 269–71; and Harold J. Laski, *The Limitations of the Expert* (London, 1931), pp. 12–13.

19. Mill, *Principles of Political Economy*, bk. V, chap. 11, sec. 6.

20. For a contemporary advocacy of this view, see Peter Bachrach, "Interest, Participation, and Democratic Theory," in J. Roland Pennock and John W. Chapman, eds., *Nomos XVI: Participation in Politics* (New York, 1975), pp. 49–51. Bachrach puts forth his argument as one against liberal rationales for participation based upon a "static conception of political interest" (p. 50), yet Mill's argument for participation is largely based upon his belief in man's capacity for self-development through participation. Bachrach may diverge from liberal egalitarianism in his occasional refusal to ground the value of participation in interests of the self, rather than of the community. However, his argument on this point is not developed; moral obligation to the community may also be derived from interests of the self, once all citizens recognize each other as equals. See my discussion of voting later in this chapter.

   For other explications of the enlightened individualist rationale, see Pateman, *Participation and Democratic Theory*, p. 27; "The Port Huron Statement" in Paul Jacobs and Saul Landau, eds., *The New Radicals* (New York, 1966), p. 154; and Graeme Duncan and Steven Lukes, "The New Democracy," *Political Studies* 11 (June 1963):175–7.

   For a critical but undeveloped statement of the social costs of increasing participation in accordance with this rationale, see Lester W. Milbrath, *Political Participation* (Chicago, 1972), p. 147.

21. The justification for communal loyalty within liberal egalitarianism is thus directly tied to the interests of individuals within the community. This contrasts both with those who argue against expanding participation because of its potential negative effects upon social stability and with those who argue for more extensive participation regardless of its benefits to the individual. For the first sort of argument, see Bernard R. Berelson, Paul F. Lazarsfeld, and William N. McPhee, *Voting* (Chicago, 1954), pp. 314–16; and Gabriel Almond and Sidney Verba, *The Civic Culture: Political Attitudes and Democracy in Five Nations* (Boston, 1965), pp. 346–65. Compare the latter work with Sidney Verba and Norman N. Nie, *Participation in America* (New York, 1972), pp. 3–5. For the second sort of noninstrumentalist argument, see Hannah Arendt, *The Human Condition* (Garden City, N.Y., 1959), p. 135; and Donald W. Keim, "Participation in Contemporary Democratic Theories," in Pennock and Chapman, *Nomos XVI: Participation in Politics*, pp. 25–

7. See also David Braybrooke, "The Meaning of Participation and of Demands for It: A Preliminary Survey of the Conceptual Issues," in ibid., pp. 83–5; and Lawrence A. Scaff, *Participation in the Western Political Tradition: A Study of Theory and Practice* (Tucson, Ariz., 1975), pp. 81–90.

22. For an account of this tension within Rousseau's thought between natural man and the Spartan citizen, see Shklar, *Men and Citizens*, passim.

23. Not surprisingly, this is a rationale often overlooked by those who consider only the social functions of participation. For a recognition of the importance of this rationale for equalizing participatory opportunities, see Jane J. Mansbridge, "The Limits of Friendship," in Pennock and Chapman, *Nomos XVI: Participation in Politics*, pp. 248–51. As Mansbridge indicates, "mutual" and "equal" respect can be used interchangeably (p. 267, n. 7).

24. This possibility of historical relativity is perhaps why Rawls agrees that Mill's rationale for unequal plural voting is the right *sort* of rationale. Yet it is inconceivable to me that this rationale could rightly be applied to a society in which equality among persons was acknowledged in any political or socioeconomic realm.

25. If "friendship is equality," then justice can only be *constitutive* of civic friendship if it is based upon political equality. Other egalitarian forms of justice may be *means* to friendship among some citizens, but fraternity can be universally constituted throughout a society only by egalitarian political constitutions. See Aristotle's discussion in *The Nicomachean Ethics*, trans. Sir David Ross (London, 1954), bk. VIII, secs. 1–4, 9–11, pp. 192–7, 207–12. See also Aristotle, *Politics*, trans. Rackham, 1295b15–30, pp. 329–31. Cf. Lucas, "Against Equality," in Bedau, *Justice and Equality*, pp. 150–1. I follow Lucas in arguing that equality must not be considered in isolation from other values, such as liberty and fraternity. But I diverge from Lucas in my assessment of the extent to which equality compromises the values of liberty and fraternity.

26. For the difficulties in rule utilitarianism as an independent source of justification, see Smart and Williams, *Utilitarianism*, pp. 9–12; and McCloskey, "An Examination of Restricted Utilitarianism," pp. 231–49. Cf. John Rawls, "Two Concepts of Rules," *Philosophical Review* 64 (1955):3–32; and Richard Brandt, "Some Merits of One Form of Rule-Utilitarianism," in Thomas K. Hearn, Jr., ed., *Studies in Utilitarianism* (New York, 1971), pp. 169–99.

27. For a brief, more historical view of this tradition, see George H. Sabine, "The Two Democratic Traditions," *Philosophical Review* 61 (October 1952):463–70. Although Sabine's characterization of the two traditions differs in emphasis from my own, his concluding recommendation for integrating the two traditions is well taken.

28. One need not, in Rousseau's view, force equal participation. However, either the assumption of human equality or the view that extensive political participation is a necessary part of the good life collapses if one discovers that some people do not freely participate in a just society, whereas others do. The consistency of Rousseau's ideal vision therefore depends upon the effective socialization of

people, so that they all fly to the assemblies, or upon forcing those people who would not otherwise do so to fly. See Rousseau, *The Social Contract*, bk. III, chap. 15, p. 93. For more recent arguments for participation as a necessary part of the good life of all citizens, see Keim, "Participation in Contemporary Democratic Theories," p. 29; Arendt, *The Human Condition*, chap. 1, 2; Robert Pranger, *The Eclipse of Citizenship* (New York, 1968), pp. 54–5, 89–102; and Bernard Crick, *In Defense of Politics* (London, 1962). These arguments support either more or less egalitarian participatory results than liberal egalitarianism, depending upon whether they are based upon a view of people as equal or as unequal in their capacity for the good, participatory, life.

29. For arguments concerning the possible destabilizing effects of increased participation, see Seymour Martin Lipset, *Political Man* (Garden City, N.Y., 1963); Bernard R. Berelson, "Democratic Theory and Public Opinion," *Public Opinion Quarterly* 16 (Fall 1952):313–30; and Talcott Parsons, "Voting and the Equilibrium of the American Political System," in Eugene Burdick and Arthur J. Brodbeck, eds., *American Voting Behavior* (Glencoe, Ill., 1957), pp. 80–120. Cf. the critique of Berelson and Parsons by Duncan and Lukes, "The New Democracy," pp. 156–77; and Thompson, *The Democratic Citizen*, pp. 62–4, 67–9. I do not wish to suggest here that the conclusions drawn from the empirical studies cited are correct, but rather that the case for liberal egalitarianism is not dependent upon these empirical arguments.

30. Rousseau can be defended against this interpretation of the need for equal participation. In *The Social Contract*, he apparently also wishes to justify participation as a means (perhaps the only means) of safeguarding individual rights within a coherent whole. But those who criticize his theory for its conservative or totalitarian implications can cite the ambiguity of his priorities in support of their case. See *The Social Contract*, bk. II, chap. 4, pp. 28–32. For a critique of Rousseau along these lines, see J. L. Talmon, *The Rise of Totalitarian Democracy* (New York, 1960). Cf. C. B. Macpherson, "The Maximization of Democracy," in Peter Laslett and W. G. Runciman, eds., *Philosophy, Politics and Society*, 3d ser. (New York, 1967), pp. 83–103; and Pateman, *Participation and Democratic Theory*, pp. 22–7.

31. Neither, I would argue, did Rousseau think his ideal participatory society would function without a just foundation. However, as Rousseau himself admitted, he leaves the foundation and the principles of political right incompletely explored, opening up the possibility of labeling many stable, highly participatory societies just societies. In addition, his view of human nature gives us no reason to believe that loyalty and participation will be more easily and freely elicited from a just than from an unjust political order. For an intriguing discussion of the problem of equality in Rousseau's thought, see John Charvet, *The Social Problem in Rousseau's Philosophy* (Cambridge, 1974), esp. chap. 4 and conclusion. Cf. Shklar, *Men and Citizens*, chap. 5.

32. This view is extrapolated from Rousseau's discussion in *The Social*

Contract, esp. from bk. I, chap. 8; bk. II, chaps. 3–6; and bk. III, chap. 15. A similar view, but one lacking the egalitarian foundations of Rousseau's defense of political participation, can be found in Arendt's *The Human Condition.*

33. See, for instance, Aristotle, *Ethics,* bk. X, sec. 7–9.
34. See, e.g., Rousseau's "Discourse on the Moral Effects of the Arts and Sciences," and his "Letter to D'Alembert." Consider also the problems intellectual sophistication creates for the realization of Rousseau's ideal society in *The Social Contract.*
35. Aristotle, *Politics,* trans. Rackham, 1281a42–b10, pp. 221–3, and 1286a22–b, pp. 257–9.
36. These conditions closely correspond to those under which the logic of collective action applies. See Olson, *The Logic of Collective Action,* esp. pp. 12–16.
37. Here I follow the argument of Alan Wertheimer in "In Defense of Compulsory Voting," in Pennock and Chapman, *Nomos XVI: Participation in Politics,* pp. 276–96, although I diverge from several of Wertheimer's conclusions.
38. For the classic statement of this problem, see Anthony Downs, *An Economic Theory of Democracy* (New York, 1957). See also Brian Barry's sympathetic critique of Downs in *Sociologists, Economists and Democracy* (London, 1970), chaps. 5, 8. For empirical evidence of a duty to vote, see Orley Ashenfelter and Stanley Kelley, Jr., "Determination of Participation in Presidential Elections," *Journal of Law and Economics* 18 (December 1975):695–733.
39. See Wertheimer, "In Defense of Compulsory Voting," p. 283. Cf. W. H. Morris-Jones, "In Defense of Apathy," *Political Studies* 2 (1954):25–37; and Henry B. Mayo, "A Note on the Alleged Duty to Vote," *Journal of Politics* 21 (1959):319–23.
40. Wertheimer, "In Defense of Compulsory Voting," pp. 283–93.
41. For an empirical argument demonstrating the effect of difficult registration procedures on voter turnout in the United States, see Stanley Kelley, Jr., Richard E. Ayers, and William G. Bowen, "Registration and Voting: Putting First Things First," *American Political Science Review* 61 (June 1967):359–77; and Steven J. Rosenstone and Raymond E. Wolfinger, "The Effect of Registration Laws on Voter Turnout," *American Political Science Review* 72 (March 1978):25–45. Cf. Kevin P. Phillips and Paul H. Blackman, *Electoral Reform and Voter Participation* (Washington, D.C., 1975).
42. Wertheimer objects to the idea that voting in our society is a voluntary action, arguing that the psychic compulsion many of us feel is a product of society's determination ("In Defense of Compulsory Voting," p. 289). But he goes on to say that "what makes a desire or action involuntary is not that it is socially formed but that it is maintained only by constant reinforcement and perhaps even lies. Our society attempts to instill in the average citizen the feeling that his political actions do make a difference" (ibid., p. 290). One need not reject Wertheimer's contention that voting in our society is not voluntary to accept my argument for voluntary voting in a just egalitarian society. The crucial factor in Wertheimer's argument that voting is not now voluntary is the contention that people vote for

the *wrong* reasons, reasons that are a product of *false* socialization. The alternative to legal compulsion is not necessarily, as he contends, "a system that encourages us to be irrational, in which we systematically delude ourselves about the extent of our efficacy" (ibid.). Rather, one alternative is a system in which people accept moral obligations – particularly obligations that are very easy to fulfill – as part of what it means to act rationally.

43. I assume here that free development is compatible with socialization, as Wertheimer himself argues (ibid.). It is not compatible with political deception or with constant and costly indoctrination of citizens by the government.

44. See Aristotle's *Politics*, trans. Rackham, 1253a-b, pp. 9–13, and *Ethics*, 1160a, p. 208. For Rousseau's more explicit argument, see the ensuing note.

45. Rousseau, *Social Contract*, bk. II, chap. 3, p. 27.

46. For a contemporary application of Rousseau's theory to the dilemmas of participation within a small agrarian society see Benjamin R. Barber, *The Death of Communal Liberty* (Princeton, 1974). Rousseau's argument does alert us to the problems of size, problems that apply within industrial societies to democratic institutions that intend effectively to fulfill the values both of participation and of an equitable distribution of other goods and services. For an insightful analysis of the possible relationships among size, participation, and institutional capacity, see Robert A. Dahl and Edward R. Tufte, *Size and Democracy* (Stanford, 1973).

47. For a more thoroughgoing critique of Aristotle's and Rousseau's political theories based upon their assumption of the natural inequality between men and women, see Susan Moller Okin, *Women in Western Political Thought* (Princeton, 1979).

48. For the same conclusion reached from a more general perspective on the limits of time and the diversity of human interests, see Michael Walzer, "A Day in the Life of a Socialist Citizen," in *Obligations*, pp. 229–38. One might note here that Rousseau's vision of a society governed by the general will has also been criticized for not being participatory enough. At times in *The Social Contract*, Rousseau appears willing to settle for periodic general meetings "whose sole object is the maintenance of the social treaty." Citizens are simply asked whether they wish to preserve the present form of government and whether they are pleased with the present administration. Although this interpretation neglects the degree to which Rousseau's theory has been used to support widespread and frequent participation on substantive political issues, it nonetheless indicates a tension or at least an ambiguity in Rousseau's participatory ideal. See bk. III, chap. 18 of *The Social Contract*; and Thompson, *John Stuart Mill and Representative Government*, pp. 48–50.

49. Rawls, A Theory of Justice, p. 233.

50. Rawls appears to concur, although he does not emphasize this point. See ibid., pp. 233–4.

51. Mill himself recognized this in his discussion of women and the psychological effects of the unequal distribution of political rights in nineteenth-century Britain. See *The Subjection of Women*, pp. 7–10, 32–3, 76–81.

52. Mill notes in *Representative Government* that public opinion is unlikely to accept plural voting. Opinion may be more justly grounded here than Mill was willing to recognize. He does, though, acknowledge the difficulty in operationalizing his plural-voting principle. See ibid., chap. 8, pp. 476–7. Compare his *Autobiography*, pp. 183–4, and p. 153, where Mill appears to recognize that an effective policy of universal education would render plural voting unnecessary.
53. See, e.g., Almond and Verba, *The Civic Culture*, chap. 5.
54. See, e.g., Dahl, *After the Revolution?* pp. 130–40; and Robert E. Lane, *Political Life: Why and How People Get Involved in Politics* (Glencoe, Ill., 1959), chap. 21.
55. See Pateman's discussion in *Participation and Democratic Theory*, chaps. 2, 3; and Thompson's discussion in *The Democratic Citizen*, chap. 3.
56. Arnold S. Kaufman appears to acknowledge the need for similar constraints upon the principle of participation: see "Participatory Democracy: Ten Years Later," in William E. Connolly, ed., *The Bias of Pluralism* (New York, 1969), pp. 205–6.
57. See Mill, *Utilitarianism*, chap. 2, par. 7.
58. See Verba and Nie, *Participation in America*, for an example of the effect of group consciousness in narrowing the participation gap between the American white and black population in the sixties. Verba, Nie, and Kim's comparative study of the varying participation rates and gaps among socioeconomic groups *within* different nations provides strong support for the liberal argument that low participation rates are relative to socioeconomic situation, political structure, and other (e.g., cultural) environmental variables, rather than indicative of an inherent psychological aversion to political activity among the lower strata of society. See Sidney Verba, Norman Nie, and Jae-On Kim, *The Modes of Democratic Participation: A Cross-National Comparison*, Beverly Hills, 1971.
59. The findings of Verba, Ahmed, and Bhatt in their comparative study of Indian Harijans and American blacks support both this and my previous claim. The difference between the participation gaps of blacks (vs. whites) and Harijans (vs. caste Hindus) within their respective societies must be explained in part by their distinct *absolute* levels of education and socioeconomic status. The absolute level of socioeconomic status and education tends to be significant, particularly with respect to the more demanding modes of participation: campaigning, contacting public officials, and cooperative activities. See Sidney Verba, Bashiruddhin Ahmed, and Anil Bhatt, *Race, Caste and Politics* (Beverly Hills, 1971).
60. For a thorough argument against taking liberal social-contract theorists to be speaking of actual consent, see Pitkin, "Obligation and Consent: I," pp. 990–9.
61. Rousseau, "On the Origin of Inequality," pp. 197–99, 248–52.
62. There is of course little reason to think that the most advantaged in an unjust society will be more correct in their political positions than the least advantaged, even if they are better informed and more active in politics.
63. For the theoretical argument summarized see Thompson, *The Dem-*

ocratic Citizen, pp. 72–9, 156–79. For empirical evidence, see Verba, Nie, and Kim, *The Modes of Democratic Participation*; and Verba, Ahmed, and Bhatt, *Race, Caste and Politics*.

64. See Joseph M. Cronin, *The Control of Urban Schools* (New York, 1973), chaps. 3–7.

65. See Diane Ravitch, *The Great School Wars: New York City, 1805–1973* (New York, 1974), chap. 23; and Alan A. Altschuler, *Community Control: The Black Demand for Participation in Large American Cities* (New York, 1970), pp. 19–22.

66. See Cronin, *Control of Urban Schools*, p. 143; and Robert C. Wood, *Suburbia* (Boston, 1959), p. 60.

67. See Cronin, *Control of Urban Schools*, p. 186.

68. Mario D. Fantini, Marilyn Gittell, and Richard Magat, *Community Control and the Urban School* (New York, 1976), p. 92.

69. See the radical use made of this argument by Stokely Carmichael and Charles V. Hamilton in *Black Power* (New York, 1967), pp. 164–7.

70. See, e.g., Fantini, Gittell, and Magat, *Community Control and the Urban School*, p. 198; and Rhody A. McCoy, "The Formation of a Community-Controlled School District," in Harry M. Levin, ed., *Community Control of Schools* (New York, 1970), pp. 171–2.

71. Advocates of community control of schools almost universally put forward some form of this claim. See, e.g., Altshuler, *Community Control*, p. 23, and Philip Green, "Decentralization, Community Control and Revolution: Reflections on Ocean Hill–Brownsville," in Philip Green and Sanford Levinson, eds., *Power and Community: Dissenting Essays in Political Science* (New York, 1970), pp. 257, 273. Those who advocated black separatism also argued that community control was the only means of establishing self-respect among blacks. See Carmichael and Hamilton, *Black Power*, pp. 175–7.

72. Daniel Bell and Virginia Held, "The Community Revolution," *Public Interest*, no. 16 (Summer 1969), p. 166.

73. Irving Kristol and Paul Weaver, "Who Knows New York? and other Notes on a Mixed-up City," *Public Interest*, no. 16 (Summer 1969), p. 53.

74. See Peter Bachrach and Morton Baratz, *Power and Poverty: Theory and Practice* (New York, 1970), pp. 202–7.

75. See Carmichael and Hamilton, *Black Power*.

76. This goal was acknowledged by many advocates to be primary among the purposes of community control. See, e.g., Mario D. Fantini, "Community Control and Quality Education in Urban School Systems," in Levin, *Community Control of Schools*, p. 52: "Yet no matter how valuable the rewards of participation are to the individual nonstudent participant, the final measure of the value of public participation is the quality of education pupils receive." See also Marilyn Gittell, *Local Control in Education: Three Demonstration Districts in New York City* (New York, 1972), p. 98. Cf. Green, "Decentralization, Community Control and Revolution," pp. 269–73; Green suggests that participation in itself is a more central goal. My argument agrees with Green's insofar as the failure of decentralization to establish equality of education need not suggest that we

should return to preexisting forms or standards of public education.

77. Kenneth Clark, quoted by Walter Goodman in "Kenneth Clark's Revolutionary Slogan: Just Teach Them to Read!" *New York Times Magazine*, March 18, 1973, p. 61.

78. For a discussion of the theory behind the shoe-pinching argument, see Thompson, *John Stuart Mill and Representative Government*, p. 20.

79. See Gittell, *Local Control in Education*, pp. 50–1.

80. For voter-turnout figures in the early stages of community control, when low-income parents were probably most active, see ibid., tab. 3, pp. 48–9. Approximately 20% of eligible voters in Ocean Hill–Brownsville participated in the local school-board election in 1969. The activity in which most parents (86%) reported participating was visiting their children's school, an activity that could be facilitated without community control by administrative decentralization. See also Ravitch, *The Great School Wars*, p. 389. Ravitch points out that by 1973 voter turnout for community school-board elections throughout New York City had declined to less than 11%

81. Lawrence Bailis, "Bread or Justice: Grassroots Organizing in the Welfare Rights Movement" (Ph.D. dissertation, Harvard University, 1972). For a consistent explanation of the successes and failures of political mobilization among the poor, based upon an incentive theory, see James Q. Wilson, *Political Organizations* (New York, 1973), pp. 65–8. Wilson's incentive theory also supports the argument that a certain level of socioeconomic status is necessary to elicit widespread participation from other than strictly material motives. See ibid., pp. 340–5.

82. See, e.g., William R. Grant, "Community Control vs. School Integration in Detroit," *Public Interest*, no. 24 (Summer 1971), p. 75.

83. Verba and Nie cite evidence that "group consciousness" among the poor can help close the participation gap. But in communities in which desegregation became a hotly contended issue, white constituencies also developed group consciousness and thereby widened the participation gap even further. The results of this "reverse" mobilization were often increased pressure for segregated schools, legitimated by the doctrine of community control. A case in point was the successful opposition to busing by parents in the Canarsie (N.Y.) School District in the fall of 1972. See *New York Times*, October 30–31, 1972; and Ravitch, *The Great School Wars*, p. 389.

84. Quoted in Grant, "Community Control vs. School Integration in Detroit," p. 63.

85. This argument is supported by (although it is not dependent upon) the conclusion of the Coleman report that the achievement of black parents is strongly related to the proportion of whites in their schools. See James S. Coleman et al., *Equality of Educational Opportunity: Summary Report* (Washington, D.C., 1966); and Thomas F. Pettigrew, "Race and Equal Educational Opportunity," *Harvard Educational Review* 38 (Winter 1968):66–76, for an argument that integrated education is also a necessary precondition for the develop-

ment of egalitarian attitudes among future citizens. But note
criticisms of Coleman's conclusions: Samuel Bowles and Henry M.
Levin, "The Determinants of Scholastic Achievement: An Appraisal of Some Recent Evidence," *Journal of Human Resources* 3
(Winter 1968):3–24; and Harvard Educational Review, *Equal Educational Opportunity* (Cambridge, Mass., 1969), pp. 41–59, 80–249.
See James Coleman's "Equality of Educational Opportunity: Reply
to Bowles and Levin," *Journal of Human Resources* 3 (Spring
1968):237–45. In *Journal of Human Resources* 3 (Summer 1968), see
Marshall Smith, "Equality of Educational Opportunity: Comments
on Bowles and Levin," pp. 384–8; Glen Cain and Harold Watts,
"The Controversy about the Coleman Report: Comment," pp. 389–
92; and Samuel Bowles and Henry Levin, "More on Multicolinearity and the Effectiveness of Schools," pp. 393–400.

86. Grant, "Community Control vs School Integration in Detroit," p.
75.
87. Ibid., p. 76.
88. This argument of course is compatible with a limited form of community control of schools; not all aspects of educational policy need
or should be universalizable. But no one has suggested that the goal
of effectively equalizing educational opportunity is a parochial one.
For a challenge to the "liberal" view of universalizing educational
standards, see Leonard J. Fein, "Community Schools and Social
Theory: The Limits of Universalism," in Levin, *Community Control
of Schools*, pp. 76–99. Cf. Ravitch, *The Great School Wars*, p. 402.
89. In 1972, e.g., Canarsie parents contended that the central board had
"trammeled" the decentralization law by ordering the busing of
thirty-four black Brownsville students into the Canarsie School
District without the community school board's consent. See the
New York Times, October 31, 1972.
90. An interesting Supreme Court decision in this regard is *Wisconsin
v. Yoder*, 406 U.S. 205, 92 S. Ct. 1526 (1972). See Justice Douglas's
partial dissent.
91. Mill, *Principles of Political Economy*, pp. 313–14.
92. Here I follow Rawls's argument in *A Theory of Justice*, p. 222. Nozick suggests a similar test in *Anarchy, State and Utopia*, p. 212.
93. This is also one manner of resolving the mandate–independence
controversy of which Hannah Pitkin writes in *The Concept of Representation*, chap. 7, pp. 144–67.
94. See Edmund Burke, "Speech to the Electors of Bristol," in *Works*
(Boston, 1877), II, 89–98; and Pitkin, *The Concept of Representation*,
chap. 8.
95. Here, of course, is where the liberal idea of representation diverges
from Burke's.
96. This general framework of extensive participatory opportunities
within a framework of egalitarian distributional principles seems to
meet many critics' objections to participatory democracy without
sacrificing the major values of participation that Mill, Cole, and
Pateman endorse. Cf. Daniel C. Kramer, *Participatory Democracy:
Developing Ideas of the Political Left* (Cambridge, Mass., 1972),
pp. 207–30.

97. The community-control experiments in New York suggested that heterogeneous neighborhoods (such as Two Bridges in New York) produced more heated internal disagreements over educational policy than the more homogeneous ones (such as I.S. 201). Another covariable (such as class), of course, may render this a spurious relation. For a report of the differences among community control districts in New York see Gittell, *Local Control in Education.* See esp. tab. 15, p. 49, for a report of the varying rates of controversy among districts.

98. A recent exception has been Robert Dahl's argument that democratization of work relations may be a prerequisite to a well-functioning political democracy. See *After the Revolution?* pp. 130–40. My integration of workers' participation with the distributive ideal meets Dahl's objection to the lack of external controls over industry within guild socialist designs. See ibid., pp. 138–9.

99. See, for example, André Gorz's critique of "traditional unionism" in *Socialism and Revolution* (New York, 1973), pp. 83–4.

100. See ibid.; Stephen Marglin, "What Do Bosses Do? The Origins and Functions of Hierarchy in Capitalist Production," *Review of Radical Political Economics* 6, no. 2 (Summer 1974):33–60; and *Work in America: Report of a Special Task Force to the Secretary of Health, Education and Welfare* (Cambridge, Mass., 1972), pp. 20–3.

101. Pateman, *Participation and Democratic Theory,* chap. 2.

102. Ibid., pp. 25–6.

103. For the most powerful exposition of this argument, see Shklar, *Men and Citizens,* passim.

104. Pateman, *Participation and Democratic Theory,* p. 35.

105. Ibid., p. 36. Emphasis added.

106. G. D. H. Cole, *Guild Socialism Restated* (London, 1920).

107. G. D. H. Cole, *Social Theory* (London, 1920).

108. Cole, *Guild Socialism Restated,* p. 12.

109. Ibid., pp. 39–40, 96–110. See also Cole, *The World of Labour,* pp. 23–9, 393–412.

110. In *Self-Government in Industry,* Cole argues that sovereignty on wages, pricing, and investment policy should reside in a Joint Congress of Producers and Consumers. But again, he gives no indication that there exists a just policy or a public interest concerning any of these major issues apart from the balance of power within the congress. In *Guild Socialism Restated,* it is no longer clear how decentralized decision making will be, because disagreements among local guilds will be appealed to higher and more inclusive levels of government. For a discussion of Cole's guild socialism with respect to the case for participatory democracy, see Kramer, *Participatory Democracy,* chap. 2.

111. See Pateman, *Participation and Democratic Theory,* pp. 70–1.

112. Ibid., p. 74.

113. See Dahl, *After the Revolution?* pp. 64–7.

114. Ibid., p. 138.

115. Ibid., p. 139.

116. This satisfies Dahl's principle of affected interests, because issues of wage, price, and investment significantly affect all citizens inso-

far as they have a direct and primary interest in the justice of their society, and because the central government of a liberal egalitarian society will be democratically elected. See also the conclusion of Barry Clark and Herbert Gintis, "Rawlsian Justice and Economic Systems," *Philosophy and Public Affairs* 7, no. 4 (Summer 1978):324–5, calling for an economic bill of rights embedded in the constitution of a just society.

117. Clearly, there are many more bureaucratic problems than we shall be concerned with here. See, e.g., James Q. Wilson, "The Bureaucracy Problem," in Alan A. Altshuler and Norman C. Thomas, eds., *The Politics of the Federal Bureaucracy*, 2d ed. (New York, 1977), pp. 57–62; and Martin Albrow, *Bureaucracy* (New York, 1970). Of course one could go far beyond this discussion to consider problems endemic to bureaucratic organization. Here, James Q. Wilson's discussion of the internal dynamics of bureaucratic regulatory agencies is enlightening. Wilson, who is often mistakenly taken to be a proponent of the argument that bureaucracies are uncontrollable, suggests that the performance of regulatory bureaucracies can be improved by enforcing rule-governed rather than ad hoc regulation and by harnessing "self-interest to public purposes." Wilson also rightly warns us against needless, indeed sometimes harmful and inequitable, regulation. See Wilson's "The Dead Hand of Regulation," *Public Interest*, no. 25 (Fall 1971), pp. 39–58.

118. The definition of a bureaucratic organization followed in this discussion is a fairly minimalist one, close to that of Anthony Downs. A bureaucracy is (a) a large organization, (b) with a majority of full-time workers (c) who are hired and promoted on the basis of merit. I diverge from Downs in not adopting his fourth criterion, that a major portion of the output of bureaucratic organizations is not evaluated (directly or indirectly) by market criteria. Imperfect markets may be as incapable of evaluating the products of firms and the performance of individuals within firms as are the democratic constituencies or other bodies to which Downs's bureaucratic organizations are formally responsible. See Anthony Downs, *Inside Bureaucracy* (Boston, 1967), pp. 24–31.

119. See, e.g., Philip Selznick's account of the subversion of public goals by the TVA in *TVA and the Grass Roots: A Study in the Sociology of Formal Organization* (New York, 1966), pp. 69–74, 262–6; and in an earlier essay, "An Approach to a Theory of Bureaucracy," *American Sociological Review* 8 (1943):47–54. See also Marver Bernstein, *Regulating Business by Independent Commission* (Princeton, 1955), p. 90.

120. For a sweeping critique of this nature, see J. Sauvageot, A. Geismar, D. Cohn-Bendit, and J. P. Duteuil, *The Student Revolt* (London, 1968); and C. George Benello, "Organization, Conflict and Free Association," in C. George Benello and Dimitrios Roussopoulos, eds., *The Case for Participatory Democracy: Some Prospects for a Radical Society* (New York, 1971), pp. 196–212. For a more qualified critique, see Henry S. Kariel, *The Decline of American Pluralism* (Stanford 1961), chaps. 10, 11 and pt. III.

121. For concern with the effects of bureaucratic jobs upon human personality, see Chris Argyris, *Personality and Organization* (New York, 1957), and *Integrating the Individual and the Organization* (New York, 1964); Robert Merton, "Bureaucratic Structure and Personality," *Social Forces* 17 (1940):560–8; and William H. Whyte, Jr., *The Organization Man* (Garden City, N.Y., 1957). For a discussion of three modes of response to alienation within bureaucratic organizations, see Emmette S. Redford, *Democracy in the Administrative State* (New York, 1969), pp. 154–78.

122. See, e.g., B. Rizzi, *La Bureaucratisation du Monde* (Paris, 1939); Presthus, *The Organizational Society;* Michel Crozier, *The Bureaucratic Phenomenon* (Chicago, 1965); Burnham, *The Managerial Revolution;* and Max Schachtman, *The Bureaucratic Revolution* (New York, 1962). The modern sociological roots of this view can be found in Gaetano Mosca, *The Ruling Class* (New York, 1939); Robert Michels, *Political Parties* (New York, 1962); and to some extent the work of Max Weber. For the latter, see *From Max Weber,* pp. 196–244; and *The Theory of Social and Economic Organization,* ed. A. M. Henderson and Talcott Parsons (Glencoe, Ill., 1947), pp. 329–41.

123. See, e.g., Von Mises, *Bureaucracy.* Here again, Mosca and Michels were forebearers of this warning.

124. For an account of how citizen participation may function as a "front" for bureaucratic control, see Elliot A. Krause, "Functions of a Bureaucratic Ideology: 'Citizen Participation,' " *Social Problems* 16 (Fall 1968):136–42.

125. For a well-documented example of effective private pressure upon public organizations, see Robert Engler, *The Politics of Oil* (Chicago, 1961), esp. chaps. 5, 6, 10, 11. See also Selznick's discussion in *TVA and the Grass Roots,* pp. 85–153.

126. Cf. Von Mises, *Bureaucracy.*

127. For suggestions of the first sort, see Dwight Ink and Alan Dean, "A Concept of Decentralization," *Public Administration Review* 30 (January/February 1970):60–3. For suggestions of the second sort, see David E. Lilienthal, *TVA: Democracy on the March* (New York 1953); Marilyn Gittell, "Decentralization and Citizen Participation in Education," *Public Administration Review* 32, (October 1972):670–89; Lawrence C. Howard, "Decentralization and Citizen Participation in Health Services," *Public Administration Review* 32 (October 1972):701–18; and Altshuler, *Community Control.*

    For a critical account of the effects of decentralization, see Herbert Kaufman, "Administrative Decentralization and Political Power," *Public Administration Review* 29 (January/February 1969):3–14; and Irving Kristol, "Decentralization for What?" *Public Interest,* no. 11 (Spring 1968), pp. 17–25.

    For the distinction between "administrative" and "political" see James W. Fesler, "Centralization and Decentralization," *International Encyclopedia of the Social Sciences* (New York, 1968), II, 370–7.

128. Selznick's generalizations concerning the negative consequences of decentralization and local participation do not take into account the possible variations in those consequences were the social structure more egalitarian than the one he observed. For a critique of his

generalizations, see Alvin W. Gouldner, "Metaphysical Pathos and the Theory of Bureaucracy," *American Political Science Review* 49 (June 1955): pp. 496–507 (reprinted in Altshuler and Thomas, *Politics of the Federal Bureaucracy,* pp. 46–56).

129. For the classic statement of this view, see J. Donald Kingsley, *Representative Bureaucracy* (Yellow Springs, Ohio, 1944); for a critique of Kingsley, see Samuel Krislov, *Representative Bureaucracy* (Englewood Cliffs, N.J., 1974).

130. See Krislov's critique, ibid., pp. 13–18.

131. This, of course, still leaves room for the discretionary execution of principles governing the public interest. Presumably, one important qualification for bureaucratic and professional positions is the ability to take responsibility for executing established rules wisely in the public's interest. For the need for discretion even within police bureaucracies, see James Q. Wilson, *Varieties of Police Behavior: The Management of Law and Order in Eight Communities* (New York 1973), pp. 293–5.

132. In his study of local police departments, Wilson gives some indication of the different "styles" appropriate to different local situations while remaining aware of the need for bureaucratic regularity demanded by equity. One must keep in mind, of course, that communities in an egalitarian society would not differ in the same ways as do the cities Wilson examines. See *Varieties of Police Behavior,* chap. 9. For a discussion of participatory rights of the clientele of public-service organizations, as distinct from those of employees and the local community as a whole, see Elliott Jacques, *A General Theory of Bureaucracy* (New York, 1976), pp. 219–20.

133. "To whom is accountability owed?" and "How can it best be effected?" will be the most relevant questions.

134. See Pranger, *The Eclipse of Citizenship.* For a general discussion of participation as an educative process, see Pateman, *Participation and Democratic Theory,* pp. 42–4.

135. Mill considered bureaucracies a form of government, although his argument for the educative effects of participation can be extended to the problem of bureaucracies within government. For an instructive discussion of his position on the trade-off between competent administration and participation see Thompson, *John Stuart Mill and Representative Government,* pp. 63–90.

136. The protective function of the central government is discussed by Mill in *Representative Government,* chap. 15.

137. See Thompson, *John Stuart Mill and Representative Government,* pp. 197–201, for the development of this argument.

138. A case in point would be community control of total school finances and curriculum. Though a local community would not be entitled to determine these policies, one might still want to hold local school administrations and teachers partially *accountable* to the local community.

139. The quotation is taken from Lewis C. Mainzer, who also suggests the need for federal control of conservation programs in *Political Bureaucracy* (Glenview, Ill., 1973), p. 148. See Altshuler, *Community Control,* p. 44, for the example of control over police departments.

140. For an extended discussion of a similar point, see Carl J. Friedrich, "Participation without Responsibility: Codetermination in Industry and University," in Pennock and Chapman, *Nomos XVI: Participation in Politics*, pp. 195–212. On the limits of the legitimate domain of professional decision making see Stephen Wexler, "Expert and Lay Participation in Decision Making," in ibid., pp. 186–94.

141. On professionalism and civic responsibility, see David G. Smith, "Professional Responsibility and Political Participation," in ibid., pp. 213–32.

142. See V. I. U. Lenin, *The State and Revolution* (New York, 1932), chap. 3, sec. 3, pp. 43–4.

143. For an extended model of bureaucratic organization that supports this point, see Jacques, *General Theory of Bureaucracy*, pp. 181–205.

144. Compare Alvin W. Gouldner, *Patterns of Industrial Bureaucracy* (New York, 1954), and Downs, *Inside Bureaucracy*. For a discussion of alternative concepts of bureaucracy, see Albrow, *Bureaucracy*, pp. 85–105.

145. Dahl also suggests the possibility of extending the ideal of workers' participation beyond industry to white-collar employment in *After the Revolution?* p. 136.

146. See, e.g., Magali Sarfatti Larson, *The Rise of Professionalism: A Sociological Analysis* (Berkeley, 1977), pp. 232–44; and Corinne Lathrop Gilb, *Hidden Hierarchies: The Professions and Government* (New York, 1966). For a broad attack upon professionalism placed in the context of the evolution of American legalism, see Sanford Levinson, "The Rediscovery of Law," *Soundings* 57 (Fall 1974):318–37. For the criteria of professionalism, see Wilbert E. Moore, *The Professions: Roles and Rules* (New York, 1970), chap. 1; and M. L. Cogan, "Toward a Definition of Profession," *Harvard Educational Review* 23 (1953):33–50.

147. E.g., David Smith's description of professional activity emphasizes its unalienating characteristics: "Professional Responsibility and Political Participation," pp. 216–17.

148. For this empirical argument from a different normative perspective, see Lipset, *Political Man*, chap. 4; for a similar argument from a closer normative perspective, see Lane, *Political Life*, chaps. 21–2, pp. 321–57.

149. See Almond and Verba, *The Civic Culture*, chap. 11; Pateman, *Participation and Democratic Theory*, chap. 3; Robert Blauner, *Alienation and Freedom* (Chicago, 1964), passim; and Paul Blumberg, *Industrial Democracy* (London, 1968), chap. 3.

150. Rawls, *A Theory of Justice*, p. 222.

CONCLUSION

1. This distinction between the new and the old egalitarianism, with criticism of the new egalitarianism, is made most frequently by a group of writers known as "neo-conservatives." See, e.g., Kristol, "About Equality," pp. 41–7; Charles Frankel, "The New Egalitarianism and the Old," *Commentary* 56 (September 1973):54–61; Robert

Nisbet, "The Pursuit of Equality," *Public Interest*, no. 35 (Spring 1974), pp. 103–20; and Bell, "On Meritocracy and Equality," pp. 29–68. For a collection of criticisms of the neo-conservative thinkers, see Lewis A. Coser and Irving Howe, eds., *The New Conservatives: A Critique from the Left* (New York, 1977).

2. See Rawls, *A Theory of Justice*, pp. 83–90, 298–303. For arguments applied to educational opportunity that support an expanded conception of the background conditions necessary for equal opportunity, see Jencks et al., *Inequality*, esp. chaps. 1, 9; Christopher Jencks, "*Inequality* in Retrospect," *Harvard Educational Review* 43 (February 1973):138–64; James S. Coleman, "The Concept of Equality of Educational Opportunity," in Harvard Educational Review, *Equal Educational Opportunity* (Cambridge, Mass., 1969), pp. 9–24; and James S. Coleman, "Equality of Opportunity and Equality of Results," *Harvard Educational Review* 43 (February 1973):129–37.

3. See the first section of Chapter 7.

4. An alternative reading of Rousseau would stress the way in which Rousseau's notion of the general will provides a solution to the collective-goods problem and a potential coherent definition of the common good based upon individual interests, rightly understood and constrained. Though I find this reading of Rousseau more consistent than others with my own understanding, there is no doubt that Rousseau has been widely interpreted, as Barry puts it, "through Hegelian spectacles." For an alternative to the radical egalitarian reading of Rousseau, see Brian Barry, "The Public Interest," in William E. Connolly, ed., *The Bias of Pluralism* (Chicago, 1969), pp. 159–77. See also Marshall Berman's interpretation of Rousseau as a "radical liberal" in *The Politics of Authenticity: Radical Individualism and the Emergence of Modern Society* (New York, 1970), pp. 203–24. Compare Shklar, *Men and Citizens*, pp. 57–74, 204–14.

5. Thus radical egalitarian arguments are not based upon a form of methodological individualism. Owen Fiss's argument for a group-rights interpretation of the equal-protection clause of the Fourteenth Amendment shares this characteristic with radical egalitarianism, but his argument is potentially less egalitarian for individuals than either liberal egalitarianism or the form of radical egalitarianism considered here. See Fiss, "Groups and the ·Equal Protection Clause," *Philosophy and Public Affairs* 5 (Winter 1967):107–77.

6. See, e.g., Evan Simpson, "Socialist Justice," *Ethics* 87 (October 1976):13–14.

7. Note here that the understanding of how an individual's interests are constituted (by the community) does not suffice to define radical *egalitarianism*. The good society must be defined as an egalitarian one (socially, politically, and economically). When critics neglect the criterion of equality, charges of totalitarianism often result. See. J. L. Talmon, *The Rise of Totalitarian Democracy* (Boston, 1952), pp. 38–49, for such an indictment of Rousseau.

8. See Barry, "The Public Interest," pp. 168–72.

9. See Rousseau, *The Social Contract*, bk. I, chap. 8, pp. 18–19.

10. Ibid., bk. I, chap. 9, p. 22; bk. II, chap. 10, p. 50; bk. III, chap. 4, p. 66, chap. 15, p. 94.

11. See Rousseau's description of the effects of inequalities once people enter into society. (*On the Origin of Inequality*, pp. 241–2).
12. See an illuminating discussion of the corresponding limits to Rousseau's ideal with reference to New England town meetings by Jane Mansbridge: "The Limits of Friendship," pp. 246–75.
13. Rousseau, *The Social Contract*, bk. III, chap. 4, p. 66. See also Benjamin Barber's account, *The Death of Communal Liberty*.
14. See Simpson, "Socialist Justice," pp. 14–17. For a contemporary emphasis upon participatory equality, see Keim, "Participation in Contemporary Democratic Theories," pp. 25–7.
15. See Henry David Rempel, "On Forcing People to Be Free," *Ethics* 87 (October 1976):27–34.
16. For a variety of such criticisms, see Barry, *Liberal Theory of Justice*, pp. 166–8; Lukes, *Individualism*, p. 139, n. 3; Macpherson, "Rawls' Models of Man and Society," pp. 341–7; Benjamin R. Barber, "Justifying Justice: Problems of Psychology, Measurement, and Politics in Rawls," *American Political Science Review* 69 (June 1975):663–74 (reprinted in Norman Daniels, ed., *Reading Rawls: Critical Studies of "A Theory of Justice"* (New York, 1975), pp. 292–318); Nagel, "Rawls on Justice," pp. 220–34 (reprinted in Daniels, *Reading Rawls*, pp. 1–16; see esp. pp. 9–10 of *Reading Rawls*); Wolff, *Understanding Rawls*, pp. 123–9; and Teitelman, "The Limits of Individualism," pp. 546–56.
17. See Teitelman, "The Limits of Individualism," pp. 547, 555 (see esp. n. 2, p. 547).
18. Ibid., p. 548. See also Wolff, *Understanding Rawls*, pp. 123–9.
19. See Macpherson, "Rawls' Models of Man and Society," p. 342; Macpherson, *Democratic Theory*, pp. 54–6; and Clark and Gintis, "Rawlsian Justice and Economic Systems," pp. 317–25.
20. Rawls, "Reply to Lyons and Teitelman," p. 557.
21. Nozick recognizes this aspect of Rawls's theory and criticizes it as not individualistic enough. See Nozick's discussion in *Anarchy, State and Utopia*, pp. 213–31.
22. Although Rawls's method of constructing the principles of justice is based upon a consideration of the rational interests of (equally situated) individuals, a well-ordered Rawlsian society will presuppose a good deal of nonegoistic motivation and behavior among citizens. For an argument supporting the possibility of such motivation, see Thomas Nagel, *The Possibility of Altruism* (Oxford, 1970), passim. For a perception of the difficulties this starting point may create for use as a partial compliance theory, see Virginia Held, "On Rawls and Self-Interest," *Midwest Studies in Philosophy* 1 (1976):58–9.
23. One might rightly claim that Rawls's theory is not ahistorical in that it quite explicitly recognizes two distinct sets of principles, a general and a special conception of justice, applicable to less and more economically developed societies respectively. In addition, Rawls argues that in the legislative state of decision making, "it is permissable . . . to take into account the interests and needs of the persons in [a] particular society. This does not violate the idea of an Archimedean point, nor does it reverse the proper relation between harmony and justice . . . because the principles of justice are already on hand, and these set limits on what a just harmony can be" ("Reply to

Lyons and Teitelman," p. 557). His answer, however, goes only a small part of the way toward meeting Teitelman's criticism, because it is the very possibility that the principles of justice can be available at the legislative state, before the particular needs and interests of individuals within a society are known, that inspires the charge of ahistoricity in the first place.

24. See Rawls, *A Theory of Justice*, sec. 44, pp. 284–93. A plausible solution to the more specific contemporary problem of limits to growth is suggested by F. Patrick Hubbard, "Justice, Limits to Growth, and an Equilibrium State," *Philosophy and Public Affairs* 7, no. 4 (Summer 1978):326–45. Hubbard admits that we presently lack the ability to predict future growth reliably.

25. Tocqueville, *Democracy in America*, vol. II, pt. II, bk. I, chap. 16, p. 74. One might note that if Tocqueville heeded his own warning, it was not by omitting the use of abstract terms from his vocabulary.

26. Consider here the radically different conception of self that many anthropologists – following Durkheim – cite as constitutive of tribal and other societies held together by what Durkheim calls mechanical solidarity. See Durkheim, *Division of Labor in Society*, chap. 2, and *The Elementary Forms of Religious Life*, trans. Joseph Ward Swain (New York, 1965), bk. III, chap. 1 (see esp. p. 355). See also Schaar, "Some Ways of Thinking about Equality," p. 881: "It is doubtful that . . . the 'desire for self-respect' is a universal characteristic of man . . . The formulation [of Bernard Williams's essay] sounds more like an echo of Western bourgeois individualism than like the voice of science announcing a universal empirical discovery."

27. The conception of primary goods therefore may vary significantly with the level of development of society. Rawls might leave the specific content of primary goods open until the constitution-making stage. The alternative, of stipulating a fixed package of primary goods for all times, creates the same sorts of problems created by attempts to stipulate a universal content to human rights. All contemporary Americans may have rights to free legal defense and perhaps even to paid vacations, but to claim that these rights apply retrospectively to all societies would be meaningless or absurd. Relativizing the content of human rights or primary goods means that one can make a philosophical argument for specific human rights or primary goods only after the material development and/or consciousness of a particular society has reached a certain level. One need not be a Hegelian, however, to accept this modest limit to political philosophy.

28. See Teitelman, "The Limits of Individualism," pp. 553–55.

29. See Michelman, "Constitutional Welfare Rights and *A Theory of Justice*," pp. 340–3.

30. See Frankel, "The New Egalitarianism and the Old," p. 56.

31. Ibid.

32. See Hume, *Treatise of Human Nature*, bk. III, pt. II, sec. 2, and *Enquiry concerning the Principles of Morals*, bk. III, pt. I. Compare Macpherson, *Democratic Theory*, pp. 52–7, 61–3.

33. For the view that socialist justice does not conflict with, but only

moves a step beyond, liberal justice, see Simpson, "Socialist Justice," p. 6.

34. See Barry, *Liberal Theory of Justice*, pp. 162, 167–8.
35. See Nagel, *The Possibility of Altruism*, passim; and Richard Titmuss, *The Gift Relationship: From Human Blood to Social Policy* (London, 1970), pp. 195–246. Nathan Glazer voices several reservations similar to those cited here in his otherwise sympathetic review of Titmuss. See Glazer's "Blood," *Public Interest*, no. 24 (Summer 1971), pp. 86–94. However, the meaning of Glazer's concluding expression of the need for authority (in addition to community) remains unclear. I think Glazer is wrong if he means to imply that a liberal egalitarian society – in which governmental authority is derived from and consistent with the autonomy of every individual – cannot constitute a community or elicit altruistic behavior from its members.
36. See Kenneth Arrow, "Gifts and Exchanges," *Philosophy and Public Affairs* 1 (Summer 1972):343–62, for a more extended critical examination of Titmuss's argument. I do not want to suggest here that we cannot expect more altruistic behavior from people than that which they now display, but merely that we cannot extrapolate from Titmuss's study to an argument for the possibility of constructing a well-ordered society with distributive institutions relying fundamentally upon altruistic rather than market behavior. But we might also consider the possibility of restructuring job opportunities so that attractive work would serve as an incentive for production, an incentive at least partially substitutable for income. Thus we need not look only to more altruistically motivated behavior to create a more economically egalitarian society. For a suggestion of the need to restructure job opportunities to permit greater personal satisfaction in work, see Barry, *Liberal Theory of Justice*, pp. 162–5.
37. I am indebted to Michael Walzer for clarification of this point.
38. For the definition of self-esteem, see *Oxford Universal Dictionary of Historical Principles* (Oxford, 1955), p. 1835.
39. Ibid., p. 1836.
40. For the problems internal to a Rousseauean ideal of equality, stemming from Rousseau's psychological premises and goals, see Shklar, *Men and Citizens*, pp. 57–74, 127–64; John Charvet, "The Idea of Equality as a Substantive Principle of Society," *Political Studies* 17 (March 1969):6–13; and Charvet, *Social Problem in Rousseau's Philosophy*, pp. 118–46 and passim.
41. See Chap. 5, n. 50, 51.
42. Cf. Edgar K. Browning, "How Much More Equality Can We Afford?" *Public Interest*, no. 43 (Spring 1976), pp. 90–110; and Irving Kristol, "Taxes, Poverty, and Equality," *Public Interest*, no. 37 (Fall 1974), pp. 3–28.
43. See Friedrich Nietzsche, *On the Genealogy of Morals*, trans. Walter Kaufman (New York, 1967), Essays I and II, pp. 24–96.
44. See Henry Sidgwick, *The Methods of Ethics*, 7th ed. (London, 1907), bk III, chap. 5, sec. 3, pp. 271–4, and sec. 7, pp. 293–4.
45. Feinberg concisely states the paradox in "Duty and Obligation in the Non-Ideal World," *Journal of Philosophy* 70 (May 10, 1973):268:

"Every reform of an imperfect practice or institution is likely to be unfair to someone or other. To change the rules in the middle of the game, even when those rules were not altogether fair, will disappoint the honest expectations of those whose prior commitments and life plans were made in genuine reliance on the continuance of the old rules."

46. Perhaps this is the essential difference between the "intuitions" of liberal egalitarians and Marxists concerning the potential of human nature. See Robert L. Heilbroner's concluding comments in "Inescapable Marx," *New York Review of Books* 25 (June 29, 1978):36–7.

47. Nozick, *Anarchy, State and Utopia*, p. 243.

Bibliography

Only works cited in the notes are listed below. Bracketed dates appearing at the end of entries indicate the year of original publication.

Aaron, Henry J. "Cautionary Notes on the Experiment," in Joseph Pechman and P. Michael Timpane, eds., *Work Incentives and Income Guarantees: The New Jersey Negative Income Tax Experiment*, pp. 88–114. Washington, D.C., 1975.

Aaron, Richard I. *John Locke*. 2d ed. Oxford, 1955.

Ake, Christopher. "Justice as Equality." *Philosophy and Public Affairs* 5 (Fall 1975):68–89.

Albrow, Martin. *Bureaucracy*. New York, 1970.

Alker, Hayward R., Jr., and Bruce M. Russett. "Indices for Comparing Inequality," in Richard Merritt, ed., *Comparing Nations*, pp. 349–72. New Haven, 1966.

Almond, Gabriel and Sidney Verba. *The Civic Culture: Political Attitudes and Democracy in Five Nations*. Boston, 1965.

Altshuler, Alan A. *Community Control: The Black Demand for Participation in Large American Cities*. New York, 1970.

Annan, Noel. "John Stuart Mill," in Hugh Sykes Davies and George Watson, eds., *The English Mind*, pp. 219–39. Cambridge, 1964.

Arendt, Hannah. *The Human Condition*. Garden City, N.Y., 1959.

Argyris, Chris. *Integrating the Individual and the Organization*. New York, 1964.

Personality and Organization. New York, 1975.

Aristotle. *The Nicomachaen Ethics*. Trans. by Sir David Ross. London, 1954.

Politics. Trans. by H. Rackham. Cambridge, Mass., 1972.

The Politics of Aristotle. Trans. by Ernest Barker. Oxford, 1958.

Arnold Matthew. "Equality," in *The Works of Matthew Arnold: Mixed Essays*, X, 46–93. London, 1904.

Arrow, Kenneth J. "Extended Sympathy and the Possibility of Social Choice." *Proceedings of the American Economic Association* 67, no. 1 (February 1977):219–25.

"Gifts and Exchanges." *Philosophy and Public Affairs* 1 (Summer 1972):343–62.

"Some Ordinalist–Utilitarian Notes on Rawls' Theory of Justice." *Journal of Philosophy* 70 (May 10, 1973):245–63.

Ashenfelter, Orley and Stanley Kelley, Jr. "Determination of Participation in Presidential Elections." *Journal of Law and Economics* 18 (December 1975):695–733.

Avineri, Shlomo. *The Social and Political Thought of Karl Marx*. Cambridge, 1968.

Bachrach, Peter. "Interest, Participation, and Democratic Theory," in J. Roland Pennock and John W. Chapman, eds., *Nomos XVI: Participation in Politics*, pp. 39–55. New York, 1975.

Bachrach, Peter and Morton Baratz. *Power and Poverty: Theory and Practice*. New York, 1970.

Bailis, Lawrence. "Bread or Justice: Grassroots Organizing in the Welfare Rights Movement." Unpublished Ph.D. dissertation, Harvard University, 1972.

Barber, Benjamin R. *The Death of Communal Liberty*. Princeton, 1974.

"Justifying Justice: Problems of Psychology, Measurement, and Politics in Rawls," *American Political Science Review* 69 (June 1975):663–74. Reprinted in Norman Daniels, ed., *Reading Rawls: Critical Studies of "A Theory of Justice,"* pp. 292–318. New York, 1975.

Barry, Brian. *The Liberal Theory of Justice*. London, 1973.

Political Argument. London, 1965.

"The Public Interest," in William E. Connolly, ed., *The Bias of Pluralism*, pp. 159–77. Chicago, 1969.

Sociologists, Economists and Democracy. London, 1970.

Baumol, William J. *Welfare Economics and the Theory of the State*. Cambridge, Mass., 1969.

Baumrin, Bernard H. "Autonomy in Rawls and Kant." *Midwest Studies in Philosophy* 1 (1976):55–7.

Beardsley, Monroe. "Equality and Obedience to Law," in Sidney Hook, ed., *Law and Philosophy*, pp. 35–42. New York, 1964.

Beauvoir, Simone de. *The Second Sex*. New York, 1953.

Becker, Lawrence C. *Property Rights: Philosophic Foundations*. London, 1977.

Bedau, Hugo A. "Egalitarianism and the Idea of Equality," in J. Roland Pennock and John W. Chapman, eds., *Nomos IX: Equality*, pp. 3–27. New York, 1967.

Beitz, Charles R. "Global Egalitarianism: Can We Make Out a Case?" *Dissent*, Winter 1979, pp. 59–68.

"Justice and International Relations." *Philosophy and Public Affairs* 4 (Summer 1975):360–89.

Bell, Daniel. "On Meritocracy and Equality." *Public Interest*, no. 29 (Fall 1972), pp. 29–68.

Bell, Daniel and Virginia Held. "The Community Revolution." *Public Interest*, no. 16 (Summer 1969), pp. 142–77.

Benello, C. George. "Organization, Conflict and Free Association," in C. George Benello and Dimitrios Roussopoulos, eds., *The Case for Participatory Democracy: Some Prospects for a Radical Society*, pp. 196–212. New York, 1971.

Benn, Stanley I. "Egalitarianism and the Equal Consideration of Interests," in J. Roland Pennock and John W. Chapman, eds., *Nomos IX: Equality*, pp. 61–78. New York, 1967.

Benn, S. I. and R. S. Peters. *The Principles of Political Thought: Social Foundations of the Democratic State*. New York, 1965 [1959].

Bibliography

Bentham, Jeremy. *The Book of Fallacies,* in *The Works of Jeremy Bentham,* ed. by John Bowring, II, 375–487. Edinburgh, 1843 [1824].

Constitutional Code, in *Works,* ed. by John Bowring, IX, 1–662. Edinburgh, 1843 [1830].

Introduction to Principles of Morals and Legislation, in *Works,* ed. by John Bowring, vol. I. Edinburgh, 1843 [1789].

Berelson, Bernard R. "Democratic Theory and Public Opinion." *Public Opinion Quarterly* 16 (Fall 1952):313–30.

Berelson, Bernard R., Paul F. Lazarsfeld, and William N. McPhee. *Voting.* Chicago, 1954.

Berlin, Isaiah. "Equality." *Proceedings of the Aristotelian Society* 56 (1955–56):301–26.

"Two Concepts of Liberty," in *Four Essays on Liberty,* pp. 118–72. New York, 1969.

Berman, Marshall. *The Politics of Authenticity: Radical Individualism and the Emergence of Modern Society.* New York, 1970.

Bernstein, Marver. *Regulating Business by Independent Commission.* Princeton, 1955.

Blackstone, W. T. "On the Meaning and Justification of the Equality Principle." *Ethics* 77 (July 1967):239–53.

Blauner, Robert. *Alienation and Freedom.* Chicago, 1964.

Block, N. J. and Gerald Dworkin, "IQ: Heritability and Inequality, Pt I." *Philosophy and Public Affairs* 3, no. 4 (Summer 1974): 331–409.

"IQ: Heritability and Inequality, Pt. II." *Philosophy and Public Affairs* 4, no. 1 (Fall 1974):40–99.

Blumberg, Paul. *Industrial Democracy.* London, 1968.

Bowie, Norman E. *Towards a New Theory of Distributive Justice.* Amherst, Mass., 1971.

Bowles, Samuel and Henry M. Levin. "The Determinants of Scholastic Achievement: An Appraisal of Some Recent Evidence." *Journal of Human Resources* 3 (Winter 1968):3–24.

"More on Multicolinearity and the Effectiveness of Schools." *Journal of Human Resources* 3 (Summer 1968):393–400.

Brandt, Richard. "Some Merits of One Form of Rule-Utilitarianism," in Thomas K. Hearn, Jr., ed. *Studies in Utilitarianism,* pp. 169–99. New York, 1971.

Braverman, Harry. *Labor and Monopoly Capital: The Degradation of Work in the Twentieth Century.* New York, 1974.

Braybrooke, David. "The Meaning of Participation and of Demands for It: A Preliminary Survey of the Conceptual Issues," in J. Roland Pennock and John W. Chapman, eds., *Nomos XVI: Participation in Politics,* pp. 56–88. New York, 1976.

"Utilitarianism with a Difference: Rawls' Position in Ethics." *Canadian Journal of Philosophy* 3 (December 1973):303–31.

Break, George F. "Income Taxes and Incentives to Work." *American Economic Review* 47 (September 1967):529–49.

Browning, Edgar K. "How Much More Equality Can We Afford?" *Public Interest,* no. 43 (Spring 1976), pp. 90–110.

Buchanan, James M. *The Demand and Supply of Public Goods.* Chicago, 1968.

Bibliography

Burke, Edmund. "An Appeal from the New to the Old Whigs," in *Works*, IV, 57–215. Boston, 1877 [1791].

Reflections on the Revolution in France, and on the Proceedings in Certain Societies in London Relative to That Event. London, 1790.

"Speech on the Petition of the Unitarians," in *Works*, vol. VI. London, 1900–1 [1792].

"Speech on the Plan for Economical Reform," in *Works*, II, 265–364. Boston, 1877 [1780].

"Speech to the Electors of Bristol," in *Works*, II, 89–98. Boston, 1877 [1774].

Burnham, James. *The Managerial Revolution*. New York, 1941.

Cain, Glen and Harold Watts. "The Controversy about the Coleman Report: Comment." *Journal of Human Resources* 3 (Summer 1968):389–92.

Cain, Glen and Harold Watts, eds. *Income Maintenance and Labor Supply: Econometric Studies*. Chicago, 1973.

Calabresi, Guido and Philip Bobbitt. *Tragic Choices*. New York, 1978.

Carmichael, Stokely and Charles V. Hamilton. *Black Power*. New York 1967.

Carritt, E. F. "Liberty and Equality." *Law Quarterly Review* 56 (1940):61–74. Reprinted in Anthony Quinton, ed., *Political Philosophy*, pp. 127–40. New York, 1967.

Catlin, George E. G. "Equality and What We Mean by It," in J. Roland Pennock and John W. Chapman, eds., *Nomos IX: Equality*, pp. 99–111. New York, 1967.

Champlin, J. "On the Study of Power." *Politics and Society* 1 (November 1970):91–111.

Charvet, John. "The Idea of Equality as a Substantive Principle of Society." *Political Studies* 17 (March 1969):1–13.

The Social Problem in Rousseau's Philosophy. Cambridge, 1974.

Clark, Barry and Herbert Gintis. "Rawlsian Justice and Economic Systems." *Philosophy and Public Affairs* 7, no. 4 (Summer 1978): 303–25.

Cogan, M. L. "Toward a Definition of Profession." *Harvard Educational Review* 23 (1953):33–50.

Cole, G. D. H. *Guild Socialism Restated*. London, 1920.

Self-Government in Industry. London 1917. Reprint ed. London, 1972.

Social Theory. London, 1920.

Some Relations between Political and Economic Theory. London, 1934.

The World of Labour. London, 1913.

Cole, Margaret. *The Story of Fabian Socialism*. Stanford, 1961.

Coleman, James S. "The Concept of Equality of Educational Opportunity," in Harvard Educational Review, *Equal Educational Opportunity*, pp. 9–24. Cambridge, Mass., 1969.

"Equality of Educational Opportunity: Reply to Bowles and Levin." *Journal of Human Resources* 3 (Spring 1968):237–45.

"Equality of Opportunity and Equality of Results." *Harvard Educational Review* 43 (February 1973):129–37.

Coleman, James S. et al. *Equality of Educational Opportunity: Summary Report*. Washington, D.C., 1966.

Comte, Auguste. *Cours de philosophie positive*. Paris, 1877.

Bibliography

Connolly, William E. "A Note on Freedom under Socialism." *Political Theory* 5 (November 1977):461–72.
Coser, Lewis A. and Irving Howe, eds. *The New Conservatives: A Critique from the Left.* New York, 1977.
Crick, Bernard. *In Defense of Politics.* London, 1962.
Cronin, Joseph M. *The Control of Urban Schools.* New York, 1973.
Crosland, C. A. R. *The Future of Socialism.* London, 1956. Rev. ed. New York, 1963.
Crossman, Richard H. S. Fabian Tract no. 286, *Socialist Values in a Changing Civilization.* London, 1950.
Crossman, Richard H. S. *Planning for Freedom.* London, 1965 [1956].
Crossman, Richard H. S., ed. *New Fabian Essays.* London, 1970 [1952].
Crozier, Michel. *The Bureaucratic Phenomenon.* Chicago, 1965.
Dahl, Robert. *After the Revolution?* New Haven, 1970.
A Preface to Democratic Theory. Chicago, 1954.
Who Governs? New Haven, 1961.
Dahl, Robert and Edward R. Tufte. *Size and Democracy.* Stanford, 1973.
Daniels, Norman. "Equal Liberty and Unequal Worth of Liberty," in Norman Daniels, ed. *Reading Rawls: Critical Studies of "A Theory of Justice,"* pp. 253–81. New York, 1975.
Darwall, Stephen L. "A Defense of the Kantian Interpretation." *Ethics* 86 (January 1976):164–70.
Djilas, Milovan. *The New Class.* London, 1957.
Downs, Anthony. *An Economic Theory of Democracy.* New York, 1957.
Inside Bureaucracy. Boston, 1967.
Dumont, Louis. *Homo Hierarchicus: The Caste System and Its Implications.* Trans. by Mark Sainsbury. Chicago, 1970.
Duncan, Graeme. *Marx and Mill.* Cambridge, 1973.
Duncan, Graeme and Steven Lukes. "The New Democracy." *Political Studies* 11 (June 1963):156–77.
Dunn, John. *The Political Thought of John Locke.* London, 1969.
Durkheim, Emile. "The Determination of Moral Facts," in *Sociology and Philosophy,* trans. by D. F. Pocock, pp. 35–62. London, 1953 [1924].
The Division of Labor in Society. Trans. by George Simpson. New York, 1964 [1893].
The Elementary Forms of Religious Life. Trans. by Joseph Ward Swain. New York, 1965 [1912].
Moral Education. Trans. by Everett K. Wilson and Herman Schnurer. Glencoe, Ill., 1961 [1925].
On Morality and Society. Ed. by Robert N. Bellah. Chicago, 1973.
Dworkin, Gerald. "Non-neutral Principles." *Journal of Philosophy* 71 (August 15, 1974):491–506. Reprinted in Norman Daniels, ed., *Reading Rawls: Critical Studies of "A Theory of Justice,"* pp. 124–40. New York, 1975.
"Paternalism," in Richard H. Wasserstrom, ed., *Morality and the Law,* pp. 107–26. Belmont, Calif., 1971.
Dworkin, Ronald. "The Original Position." *University of Chicago Law Review* 40 (Spring 1973):500–33. Reprinted in Norman Daniels, ed., *Reading Rawls: Critical Studies of "A Theory of Justice,"* pp. 16–53. New York, 1975.
Taking Rights Seriously. Cambridge, Mass., 1977.

Bibliography

Engler, Robert. *The Politics of Oil.* Chicago, 1961.

Fabian Tract no. 4, *What Socialism Is.* London, 1886.

Fabian Tract no. 17, *The Reform of the Poor Law.* London, 1890.

Fantini, Mario D. "Community Control and Quality Education in Urban School Systems," in Henry M. Levin, ed., *Community Control of Schools,* pp. 76–99. New York, 1970.

Fantini, Mario D., Marilyn Gittell, and Richard Magat. *Community Control and the Urban School.* New York, 1976.

The Federalist Papers. Ed. by Clinton Rossiter. New York, 1961.

Fein, Leonard J. "Community Schools and Social Theory: The Limits of Universalism," in Henry M. Levin, ed., *Community Control of Schools,* pp. 76–99. New York, 1970.

Feinberg, Joel. *Doing and Deserving.* Princeton, 1970.

"Duty and Obligation in the Non-Ideal World." *Journal of Philosophy* 70 (May 10, 1973):263–75.

"Non-comparative Justice." *Philosophical Review* 83 (July 1974):297–338.

"Rawls and Intuitionism," in Norman Daniels, ed., *Reading Rawls: Critical Studies of "A Theory of Justice,"* pp. 108–24. New York, 1975.

Fesler, James W. "Centralization and Decentralization." *International Encyclopedia of the Social Sciences,* II, 370–7. New York, 1968.

Fiss, Owen. "Groups and the Equal Protection Clause." *Philosophy and Public Affairs* 5 (Winter 1967):107–77.

Flathman, Richard E. "Equality and Generalization: A Formal Analysis," in J. Roland Pennock and John W. Chapman, eds., *Nomos IX: Equality,* pp. 38–60. New York, 1967.

Frankel, Charles. "The New Egalitarianism and the Old." *Commentary* 56 (September 1973):54–61.

Frankena, William K. "The Concept of Social Justice," in Richard B. Brandt, ed., *Social Justice,* pp. 1–29. Englewood Cliffs, N.J., 1962.

Friedman, Milton. *Capitalism and Freedom.* Chicago, 1962.

Friedrich, Carl J. "Participation without Responsibility: Codetermination in Industry and University," in J. Roland Pennock and John W. Chapman, eds., *Nomos XVI: Participation in Politics,* pp. 195–212. New York, 1976.

Galbraith, John Kenneth. *The Affluent Society.* New York, 1958.

Fabian Tract no. 405, *The American Left and Some British Comparisons,* London, 1971.

The New Industrial State. New York, 1968.

Garvey, G. "Inequality of Income: Causes and Measurement," in National Bureau of Economic Research, *Studies in Income and Wealth,* XV, 25–47. New York, 1952.

Gewirth, Alan. "The 'Is-Ought' Problem Resolved." *Proceedings and Addresses of the American Philosophical Association* 47 (1974):34–61.

"The Justification of Egalitarian Justice." *American Philosophical Quarterly* 8 (October 1971):331–41. Reprinted in Richard E. Flathman, ed., *Concepts in Social and Political Philosophy,* pp. 352–65. New York, 1973.

Giddens, Anthony. *The Class Structure of the Advanced Societies.* New York, 1973.

Gilb, Corinne Lathrop. *Hidden Hierarchies: The Professions and Government.* New York, 1966.

Bibliography

Ginsberg, Morris. *On Justice in Society*. London, 1965.

Gittell, Marilyn. "Decentralization and Citizen Participation in Education." *Public Administration Review* 32 (October 1972):670–89.

Local Control in Education: Three Demonstration Districts in New York City. New York, 1972.

Glazer, Nathan. "Blood." *Public Interest*, no. 24 (Summer 1971), pp. 86–94.

Godwin, William. *Enquiry concerning Political Justice*. Ed. by G. G. Robinson and J. Robinson. 3d ed., corr. London, 1798 [1793].

Thoughts on Man. New York, 1969 [1821].

Goffman, Erving. *Relations in Public*. New York, 1971.

Goldstick, D. "An Alleged Paradox in the Theory of Democracy." *Philosophy and Public Affairs* 2 (Winter 1973):187–9.

Goodman, Walter. "Kenneth Clark's Revolutionary Slogan: Just Teach Them to Read!" *New York Times Magazine*, March 18, 1973, pp. 14 ff.

Gorz, André. *Socialism and Revolution*. New York, 1973.

Gouldner, Alvin W. "Metaphysical Pathos and the Theory of Bureaucracy." *American Political Science Review* 49 (June 1955):496–507. Reprinted in Alan A. Altshuler and Norman C. Thomas, eds., *The Politics of the Federal Bureaucracy*, 2d ed., pp. 46–56. New York, 1977.

Patterns of Industrial Bureaucracy. New York, 1954.

Grant, William R. "Community Control vs. School Integration in Detroit." *Public Interest*, no. 24 (Summer 1971):62–79.

Green, Philip. "Decentralization, Community Control and Revolution: Reflections on Ocean Hill–Brownsville," in Philip Green and Sanford Levinson, eds., *Power and Community: Dissenting Essays in Political Science*, pp. 247–75. New York, 1970.

"IQ and the Future of Equality." *Dissent*, Fall 1976, pp. 398–414.

"The Pseudoscience of Arthur Jensen." *Dissent*, Summer 1976, pp. 284–97.

"Race and IQ: Fallacy of Heritability," *Dissent*, Spring 1976, pp. 181–96.

Habermas, Jürgen. *Legitimation Crisis*. Boston, 1975.

Halbwachs, M. *L'Evolution des besoins dans les classes ouvrières*. Paris, 1933.

Halévy, Elie. *The Growth of Philosophical Radicalism*. Trans. by M. Morris. London, 1934.

Hall, Everett W. "The 'Proof' of Utility in Bentham and Mill." *Ethics* 60 (October 1949):1–18.

Hall, Robert. "Effects of the Experimental Negative Income Tax on Labor Supply," in Joseph Pechman and P. Michael Timpane, eds., *Work Incentives and Income Guarantees: The New Jersey Income Tax Experiment*, pp. 115–56. Washington, D.C., 1975.

Harrison, Ross. "No Paradox in Democracy." *Political Studies* 18 (1970):515–17.

Hart, H. L. A. "Are There Any Natural Rights?" *Philosophical Review* 64 (1955):175–91. Reprinted in F. A. Olafson, ed., *Society, Law and Morality*, pp. 173–86. Englewood Cliffs, N.J., 1961.

Harvard Educational Review, *Equal Educational Opportunity*. Cambridge, Mass., 1969.

Hawkins, David. *The Science and Ethics of Equality*. New York, 1977.

Hayek, F. A. *The Constitution of Liberty*. Chicago, 1960.

Law, Legislation and Liberty, 3 vols. Chicago, 1973, 1976, 1979.

"The Principles of a Liberal Social Order," in *Studies in Philosophy, Politics and Economics*, pp. 160–77. New York, 1969.

Head, John G. "Public Goods and Public Policy." *Public Finance* 17 (1962):197–219.

Hegel, G. W. F. *The Philosophy of Right*. Trans. by T. M. Knox. Oxford, 1942 [1821].

Heilbroner, Robert L. "Inescapable Marx." *New York Review of Books* 25 (June 29, 1978):33–7.

Held, Virginia. "Egalitarianism and Relevance." *Ethics* 81 (April 1971):259.

"On Rawls and Self-Interest." *Midwest Studies in Philosophy* 1 (1976):57–9.

Helvetius. *De l'Esprit*, in *Oeuvres*, vols. I and II. Paris, 1795 [1758].

Hernstein, Richard. "I.Q." *Atlantic Monthly* 228 (September 1971):43–64. *IQ in the Meritocracy*. Boston, 1974.

Himmelfarb, Gertrude. *On Liberty and Liberalism: The Case of John Stuart Mill*. New York, 1974.

Hobbes, Thomas. *De Cive; or, The Citizen*. Ed. by Sterling Lamprecht. New York, 1949 [1642].

Elements of Law, Natural and Politic. Ed. by F. Tönnies. Cambridge, 1928 [1650].

Leviathan, in *The English Works of Thomas Hobbes of Malmesbury*, ed. by Sir William Molesworth, vol. III. London, 1839–45 [1651].

Hobhouse, L. T. *The Elements of Social Justice*. London, 1922.

Liberalism. New York, 1964 [1911].

Holland, Daniel. "The Effects of Taxation on Effort." *Proceedings of the Sixty-second National Tax Association Conference*, October 1969, pp. 425–524.

Hollis, Martin and Edward J. Nell. *Rational Economic Man: A Philosophical Critique of Neo-Classical Economics*. Cambridge, 1975.

Honderich, Ted. "A Difficulty with Democracy." *Philosophy and Public Affairs* 3 (Winter 1974):221–6.

Hospers, John. *Libertarianism: A Political Philosophy for Tomorrow*. Los Angeles, 1971.

"What Libertarianism Is," in Tibor R. Machan, ed., *The Libertarian Alternative*, pp. 3–20. Chicago, 1974.

Howard, Lawrence C. "Decentralization and Citizen Participation in Health Services." *Public Administration Review* 32 (October 1972):701–18.

Hubbard, F. Patrick. "Justice, Limits to Growth, and an Equilibrium State." *Philosophy and Public Affairs* 7, no. 4 (Summer 1978):326–45.

Hume, David. *An Enquiry concerning the Principles of Morals*. London, 1777 [1751].

A Treatise of Human Nature. Ed. by L. A. Selby-Bigge. Oxford, 1888 [1739].

Ink, Dwight and Alan Dean. "A Concept of Decentralization." *Public Administration Review* 30 (January/February 1970):60–3.

Jacobs, Paul and Saul Landau, eds. *The New Radicals*. New York, 1966.

Jacques, Elliott. *A General Theory of Bureaucracy*. New York, 1976.

Jencks, Christopher. "*Inequality* in Retrospect." *Harvard Educational Review* 43 (February 1973):138–64.

Bibliography

Jencks, Christopher et al. *Inequality: A Reassessment of the Effect of Family and Schooling in America.* New York, 1972.

Jensen, Arthur. *Educability and Group Differences.* New York, 1973.

"How Much Can We Boost IQ and Scholastic Achievement?" *Harvard Educational Review* 39 (Winter 1969):1–23.

Johnson, Oliver. "Autonomy in Kant and Rawls: A Reply." *Ethics* 87 (April 1977):251–4.

"The Kantian Interpretation." *Ethics* 85 (October 1974):58–66.

Kamin, Leon. *The Science and Politics of IQ.* New York, 1974.

Kandor, Yaakov. "Value Judgments Implied by the Use of Various Measures of Income Inequality." *Review of Income and Wealth* 21 (1975):309–21.

Kant, Immanuel. *Groundwork of the Metaphysics of Morals.* Trans. by H. J. Paton. New York, 1964 [1785–6].

The Metaphysical Elements of Justice. Trans. by John Ladd. Indianapolis, 1965 [1797].

On the Old Saw: That May Be Right in Theory but It Won't Work in Practice. Trans. by E. B. Ashton. Philadelphia, 1974 [1793].

Perpetual Peace, in *On History,* ed. by Lewis White Beck, pp. 85–135. Indianapolis, 1963 [1795].

The Philosophy of Kant. Ed. by Carl J. Friedrich. New York, 1949.

Kariel, Henry S. *The Decline of American Pluralism.* Stanford, 1961.

Katz, J. and A. M. Capron. *Catastrophic Diseases: Who Decides What?* New York, 1975.

Kaufman, Arnold S. "Participatory Democracy: Ten Years Later," in William E. Connolly, ed., *The Bias of Pluralism,* pp. 201–12. New York, 1969.

Kaufman, Herbert. "Administrative Decentralization and Political Power." *Public Administration Review* 29 (January/February 1969):3–14.

Keat, Russell and David Miller. "Understanding Justice." *Political Theory* 2 (February 1974):3–31.

Keim, Donald W. "Participation in Contemporary Democratic Theories," in J. Roland Pennock and John W. Chapman, eds., *Nomos XVI: Participation in Politics,* pp. 1–38. New York, 1975.

Kelley, Stanley, Jr., Richard E. Ayers, and William G. Bowen. "Registration and Voting: Putting First Things First." *American Political Science Review* 61 (June 1967):359–77.

Kelman, Mark. "The Social Costs of Inequality." *Dissent,* Summer 1973, pp. 291–8.

Kendall, Willmoore. *John Locke and the Doctrine of Majority Rule.* Urbana, Ill., 1959.

Kingsley, J. Donald. *Representative Bureaucracy.* Yellow Springs, Ohio, 1944.

Kolko, Gabriel. *Wealth and Power in America: An Analysis of Social Class and Income Distribution.* New York, 1962.

Kramer, Daniel C. *Participatory Democracy: Developing Ideas of the Political Left.* Cambridge, Mass., 1972.

Krause, Elliot A. "Functions of a Bureaucratic Ideology: 'Citizen Participation.'" *Social Problems* 16 (Fall 1968):136–42.

Kretschmann, Philip. "An Exposition of Kant's Philosophy of Law," in

Bibliography

George Tapley Whitney, ed., *The Heritage of Kant*, pp. 245–76. Princeton, 1939.

Kretzmann, Norman. "Desire as Proof of Desirability." *Philosophical Quarterly* 8 (1958):246–58.

Krislov, Samuel. *Representative Bureaucracy*. Englewood Cliffs, N.J., 1974.

Kristol, Irving. "About Equality." *Commentary* 54 (November 1972):41–7.

———. "Decentralization for What?" *Public Interest*, no. 11 (Spring 1968), pp. 17–25.

———. "Taxes, Poverty, and Equality." *Public Interest*, no. 37 (Fall 1974), pp. 3–28.

——— "'When Virtue Loses All Her Loveliness': Some Reflections on Capitalism and 'The Free Society.' " *Public Interest*, no. 21 (Fall 1970), pp. 3–15.

Kristol, Irving, and Paul Weaver. "Who Knows New York? and Other Notes on a Mixed-up City." *Public Interest*, no. 16 (Summer 1969), pp. 41–63.

Lakoff, Sanford A. *Equality in Political Philosophy*. Cambridge, Mass., 1964.

Lampman, Robert J. "Recent Thought on Egalitarianism." *Quarterly Journal of Sociology* 71 (May 1957):234–66.

Lane, Robert E. *Political Life: Why and How People Get Involved in Politics*. Glencoe, Ill., 1959.

Larson, Magali Sarfatti. *The Rise of Professionalism: A Sociological Analysis*. Berkeley, 1977.

Laski, Harold J. *The Limitations of the Expert*. London, 1931.

Lenin, V. I. U. *The State and Revolution*. New York, 1932 [1917, 1918].

Letwin, Shirley Robin. *The Pursuit of Certainty*. Cambridge, 1965.

Levinson, Sanford. "The Rediscovery of Law." *Soundings* 57 (Fall 1974):318–37.

Leyden, W. von. "On Justifying Inequality." *Political Studies* 11 (February 1963):56–70.

Lilienthal, David E. *TVA: Democracy on the March*. New York, 1953.

Lindblom, Charles E. *Politics and Markets: The World's Political–Economic Systems*. New York, 1977.

Lindsay, A. D. *The Modern Democratic State*. New York, 1962.

Lipset, Seymour Martin. *Political Man*. Garden City, N.Y., 1963.

Little, I. M. D. *Critique of Welfare Economics*, 2d ed. Oxford, 1957.

Locke, John. *Essay concerning Human Understanding*, in *Works*, ed. by J. A. St. John, vol. II. London, 1889 [1690].

———. *Essays on the Law of Nature*. Trans. and ed. by W. von Leyden, Oxford, 1954.

———. *The Second Treatise of Government*, in *Two Treatises of Government*, ed. by Peter Laslett, pp. 305–477. Cambridge, 1963 [1690].

Lovejoy, Arthur O. *The Great Chain of Being*. Cambridge, Mass., 1964.

Lucas, J. R. "Against Equality." *Philosophy* 40 (October 1965):296–307. Reprinted in Hugo A. Bedau, ed. *Justice and Equality*, pp. 138–51. Englewood Cliffs, N.J., 1971.

———. *The Principles of Politics*. Oxford, 1966.

Lukes, Steven. "Alienation and Anomie," in Peter Laslett and W. G. Runciman, eds., *Philosophy, Politics and Society*, 3rd ser., pp. 134–56. Oxford, 1967.

Individualism. New York, 1973.

Power: A Radical View. London, 1974.

"Socialism and Equality," in Leszek Kolakowski and Stuart Hampshire, eds., *The Socialist Idea: A Reappraisal,* pp. 74–95. New York, 1974.

Lyons, David. "Rawls versus Utilitarianism." *Journal of Philosophy* 18 (October 5, 1972):535–45.

Macarov, David. *Incentives to Work.* San Francisco, 1970.

MacCallum, Gerald C., Jr. "Negative and Positive Freedom." *Philosophical Review* 76 (1967):312–34. Reprinted in Richard E. Flathman, ed., *Concepts in Social and Political Philosophy,* pp. 294–308. New York, 1973.

McCloskey, H. J. "An Examination of Restricted Utilitarianism," in Thomas K. Hearn, Jr., ed. *Studies in Utilitarianism,* pp. 231–49. New York, 1971.

"A Right to Equality? Re-Examining the Case for a Right to Equality." *Canadian Journal of Philosophy* 6 (December 1976):625–42.

McConnell, Grant. *Private Power and American Democracy.* New York, 1966.

McCoy, Rhody A. "The Formation of a Community-Controlled School District," in Henry M. Levin, ed., *Community Control of Schools,* pp. 169–90. New York, 1970.

MacDonald, Margaret. "Natural Rights," in Peter Laslett, ed., *Philosophy, Politics and Society,* 1st ser., pp. 35–55. Oxford, 1956.

Machan, Tibor R. "On Reclaiming America's Unique Political Tradition," in Tibor R. Machan, ed., *The Libertarian Alternative,* pp. 495–501. Chicago, 1974.

MacIntyre, Alisdair. *A Short History of Ethics.* New York, 1966.

Mack, Eric. "Individualism, Rights, and the Open Society," in Tibor R. Machan, ed., *The Libertarian Alternative,* pp. 21–37. Chicago, 1974.

Macpherson, C. B. *Democratic Theory: Essays in Retrieval.* Oxford, 1973.

"Human Rights as Property Rights." *Dissent,* Winter 1977, pp. 72–7.

The Life and Times of Liberal Democracy. Oxford, 1977.

"The Maximization of Democracy," in Peter Laslett and W. G. Runciman, eds., *Philosophy, Politics and Society,* 3d ser., pp. 83–103. New York, 1967.

The Political Theory of Possessive Individualism. Oxford, 1962.

"Rawls' Models of Man and Society." *Philosophy of Social Science* 3 (1973):341–7.

The Real World of Democracy. Oxford, 1966.

"The Social Bearing of Locke's Political Theory." *Western Political Quarterly* 7 (1954):1–22. Reprinted in Gordon Schochet, ed., *Life, Liberty, and Property,* pp. 60–85. Belmont, Calif., 1971.

"Who Needs a Theory of the State?" Paper delivered at the 1977 annual meeting of the American Political Science Association, Washington, D.C., September 1–4, 1977.

Mainzer, Lewis C. *Political Bureaucracy.* Glenview, Ill., 1973.

Malkiel, Burton. *A Random Walk down Wall Street.* New York, 1973.

Mandel, Ernest. *Late Capitalism.* London, 1975.

Mansbridge, Jane J. "The Limits of Friendship," in J. Roland Pennock and John W. Chapman, eds., *Nomos XVI: Participation in Politics,* pp. 246–75. New York, 1975.

Bibliography

Marcuse, Herbert. *One-Dimensional Man.* Boston, 1964.

Studies in Critical Philosophy. Boston, 1973.

Marglin, Stephen. "What Do Bosses Do? The Origins and Functions of Hierarchy in Capitalist Production." *Review of Radical Political Economics* 6, no. 2 (Summer 1974):33–60.

Marsden, Dennis. Fabian Tract no. 411, *Politicians, Equality and Comprehensives.* London, 1971.

Marshall, T. H. *Citizenship and Social Class and Other Essays.* Cambridge, 1950.

Marx, Karl. *Early Writings.* Ed. by T. B. Bottomore. New York, 1964.

"Inaugural Address of the Working Men's International Association," in *On the First International,* ed. by Saul Padover, Karl Marx Library, III, 9–10. New York, 1973.

Writings of the Young Marx on Philosophy and Society. Ed. by Lloyd D. Easton and Kurt H. Guddat. Garden City, N.Y., 1967 [1835, 1847].

Mason, H. E. "On the Kantian Interpretation of Rawls' Theory." *Midwest Studies in Philosophy* 1 (1976):47–55.

Masters, Roger D. "Is Contract an Adequate Basis for Medical Ethics?" *Hastings Center Report* 5 (December 1975):24–8.

Mayo, Henry B. "A Note on the Alleged Duty to Vote." *Journal of Politics* 21 (1959):319–23.

Mazlish, Bruce. *James and John Stuart Mill.* New York, 1975.

Meade, J. E. *Efficiency, Equality and the Ownership of Property.* Cambridge, Mass., 1965.

Melden, A. I. "The Concept of Universal Human Rights." *Proceedings of the American Philosophical Association: Eastern Division* 1 (1952):167–88.

Merton, Robert. "Bureaucratic Structure and Personality." *Social Forces* 17 (1940):560–8.

Michelman, Frank. "Constitutional Welfare Rights and *A Theory of Justice,*" in Norman Daniels, ed., *Reading Rawls: Critical Studies of "A Theory of Justice,"* pp. 319–47. New York, 1975.

Michels, Robert. *Political Parties.* New York, 1962 [1911].

Milbrath, Lester W. *Political Participation.* Chicago, 1972.

Miliband, Ralph. *Marxism and Politics.* Oxford, 1977.

Mill, James. *Essay on Government.* Indianapolis, 1955 [1820].

Mill, John Stuart. "Auguste Comte and Positivism," in *Collected Works,* ed. by J. M. Robson, X, 260–368. Toronto, 1969 [1865].

Autobiography and Other Writings. Ed. by Jack Stillinger. Boston, 1969 [1873].

"Chapters on Socialism," in *Collected Works,* ed. by J. M. Robson, V, 703–53. Toronto, 1967 [1879].

Considerations on Representative Government, in *Collected Works,* ed. by J. M. Robson, XIX, 371–577. Toronto, 1977 [1861].

"Grote's Aristotle," in *Dissertations and Discussions,* V, 169–215. New York, 1875 [1873].

"M. de Tocqueville on Democracy in America," in *Collected Works,* ed. by J. M. Robson, XVIII, 191–204. Toronto, 1977 [1840].

On Liberty, in *Collected Works,* ed. by J. M. Robson, XVIII, 213–310. Toronto, 1977 [1854].

Bibliography

Principles of Political Economy, in *Collected Works,* ed. by J. M. Robson, vol. III. Toronto, 1965 [1848, 1871].

The Subjection of Women. London, 1869.

A System of Logic, in *Collected Works,* ed. by J. M. Robson, vol. VIII. Toronto, 1974. [1843, 1872].

Utilitarianism, in *Collected Works,* ed. by J. M. Robson, X, 203–59. Toronto, 1969 [1861].

Miller, David. "Socialism and the Market." *Political Theory* 5 (November 1977):473–90.

Social Justice. Oxford, 1976.

Miller, Richard. "Rawls and Marxism." *Philosophy and Public Affairs* 3 (Winter 1974):167–91.

Mises, Ludwig von. *The Anti-Capitalist Mentality.* Princeton, 1956.

Bureaucracy. New Haven, 1944.

Human Action. New Haven, 1963.

Planning for Freedom. South Holland, Ill., 1952.

Socialism. New Haven, 1951.

Mishan, E. J. "The Postwar Literature on Externalities: An Interpretative Essay." *Journal of Economic Literature* 9, no. 1 (March 1971):1–28.

Mitchell, Juliet. *Woman's Estate.* London, 1971.

Moore, G. E. *Principia Ethica.* Cambridge, 1903.

Moore, Wilbert E. *The Professions: Roles and Rules.* New York, 1970.

Morris-Jones, W. H. "In Defense of Apathy." *Political Studies* 2 (1954):25–37.

Mosca, Gaetano. *The Ruling Class.* New York, 1939 [1895, 1923].

Musgrave, Richard A. *The Theory of Public Finance.* New York, 1959.

Nagel, Thomas. *The Possibility of Altruism.* Oxford, 1970.

"Rawls on Justice." *Philosophical Review* 82 (April 1973):220–34. Reprinted in Norman Daniels, ed., *Reading Rawls: Critical Studies of "A Theory of Justice,"* pp. 1–16. New York, 1975.

Nell, Onora. *Acting on Principle: An Essay on Kantian Ethics.* New York, 1975.

New York Times, October 30–31, 1972.

Nietzsche, Friedrich. *On the Genealogy of Morals.* Trans. by Walter Kaufman. New York, 1967.

Nisbet, Robert. "The Pursuit of Equality." *Public Interest,* no. 35 (Spring 1974), pp. 103–20.

Norton, David L. *Personal Destinies: A Philosophy of Ethical Individualism.* Princeton, 1976.

Nozick, Robert. *Anarchy, State and Utopia.* New York, 1974.

"Coercion," in Sidney Morgenbesser, P. Suppes, and M. White, eds., *Philosophy, Science and Method,* pp. 440–72. New York, 1969.

O'Connor, James. *The Fiscal Crisis of the State.* New York, 1973.

Okin, Susan Moller. *Women in Western Political Thought.* Princeton, 1979.

Okun, Arthur M. *Equality and Efficiency: The Big Trade-Off.* Washington, D.C., 1975.

Olivecrona, Karl. "Locke's Theory of Appropriation." *Philosophical Quarterly* 24 (September 1974):220–34.

Olson, Mancur, Jr. *The Logic of Collective Action.* Cambridge, Mass., 1965.

Oppenheim, Felix E. "Egalitarianism as a Descriptive Concept." *American Philosophical Quarterly* 7 (April 1970):143–52.

Oppenheimer, Franz. *The State.* New York, 1926.

Bibliography

Parekh, Bhikhu. "Bentham's Theory of Equality." *Political Studies* 18 (December 1970):478–95.

Parsons, Talcott. "Voting and the Equilibrium of the American Political System," in Eugene Burdick and Arthur J. Brodbeck, eds., *American Voting Behavior*, pp. 80–120. Glencoe, Ill., 1957.

Pateman, Carole. *Participation and Democratic Theory*. Cambridge, 1970.

Pennock, J. Roland. "Democracy is *not* Paradoxical: Comment." *Political Theory* 2, no. 1 (February 1974):88–93.

Liberal Democracy: Its Merits and Prospects. New York, 1950.

Pennock, J. Roland and John W. Chapman, eds. *Nomos IX: Equality*. New York, 1967.

Nomos XVI: Participation in Politics. New York, 1975.

Peters, Richard S. *Ethics and Education*. London, 1966.

Hobbes. Baltimore, 1956.

Pettigrew, Thomas F. "Race and Equal Educational Opportunity." *Harvard Educational Review* 38 (Winter 1968):66–76.

Phillips, Derek L. "The Equality Debate: What Does Justice Require?" *Theory and Society* 4 (1977):247–72.

Phillips, Kevin P. and Paul H. Blackman. *Electoral Reform and Voter Participation*. Washington, D.C., 1975.

Pitkin, Hannah Fenichel. *The Concept of Representation*. Berkeley, 1972.

"Obligation and Consent: I." *American Political Science Review* 59 (December 1965):990–9.

"Obligation and Consent: II." *American Political Science Review* 60 (March 1966):39–52.

Wittgenstein and Justice. Berkeley, 1972.

Plamenatz, John. "Diversity of Rights and Kinds of Equality," in J. Roland Pennock and John W. Chapman, eds., *Nomos IX: Equality*, pp. 79–98. New York, 1967.

Plato. *The Republic of Plato*. Trans. by Allan Bloom. New York, 1968.

Pranger, Robert. *The Eclipse of Citizenship*. New York, 1968.

Presthus, Robert V. *The Organizational Society*. New York, 1962.

Rand, Ayn. *Atlas Shrugged*. New York, 1957.

Capitalism: The Unknown Ideal. New York, 1966.

Ravitch, Diane. *The Great School Wars: New York City, 1805–1973*. New York, 1974.

Rawls, John. "The Basic Structure as Subject," *American Philosophical Quarterly* 14 (April 1977):159–65.

"Fairness to Goodness." *Philosophical Review* 84 (October 1975):536–54.

"A Kantian Interpretation of Equality." *Cambridge Review*, February 1975, pp. 94–9.

"Reply to Lyons and Teitelman." *Journal of Philosophy* 69 (October 15, 1972):556–7.

"Some Reasons for the Maximin Criterion." *American Economic Review* 64 (May 1974):141–6.

A Theory of Justice. Cambridge, Mass., 1971.

"Two Concepts of Rules." *Philosophical Review* 64 (1955):3–32.

Redford, Emmette S. *Democracy in the Administrative State*. New York, 1969.

Rees, John. *Equality*. London, 1971.

Bibliography

Rempel, Henry David. "On Forcing People to Be Free." *Ethics* 87 (October 1976):27–34.

Rescher, Nicholas. *The Coherence Theory of Truth*. Oxford, 1973.

Rizzi, B. *La Bureaucratisation du Monde*. Paris, 1939.

Rosenstone, Steven J. and Raymond E. Wolfinger. "The Effect of Registration Laws on Voter Turnout." *American Political Science Review* 72 (March 1978):22–45.

Rothbard, Murray. *For a New Liberty*. New York, 1973.

Man, Economy, and the State. Princeton, 1962.

Rousseau, Jean-Jacques. "A Discourse on the Moral Effects of the Arts and Sciences," in *The Social Contract and Discourses*, trans. by G. D. H. Cole, pp. 143–74. New York, 1950 [1750].

A Discourse on Political Economy, in *The Social Contract and Discourses*, trans. by G. D. H. Cole, pp. 285–330. New York, 1950 [1755].

"Letter to M. D'Alembert on the Theatre," in *Politics and the Arts*, trans. by Allan Bloom, pp. 1–137. New York, 1960 [1758].

On the Origin of Inequality, in *The Social Contract and Discourses*, trans. by G. D. H. Cole, pp. 175–282. New York, 1950 [1755].

The Social Contract, in *The Social Contract and Discourses*, trans. by G. D. H. Cole, pp. 1–141. New York, 1950 [1762].

Runciman, W. G. *Relative Deprivation and Social Justice*. London, 1972.

Ryan, Alan. "Locke and the Dictatorship of the Bourgeoisie." *Political Studies* 13 (1965):219–30. Reprinted in Gordon Schochet, ed., *Life, Liberty, and Property*, pp. 86–106. Belmont, Calif. 1971.

"Two Concepts of Politics and Democracy: James and John Stuart Mill," in Martin Fleisher, ed., *Machiavelli and the Nature of Political Thought*, pp. 76–113. New York, 1972.

Sabine, George H. "The Two Democratic Traditions." *Philosophical Review* 61 (October 1952):451–74.

Sabine, George H. and Thomas L. Thorson. *A History of Political Theory*. Hinsdale, Ill., 1973.

Saint-Simon, Claude-Henri. *The Doctrine of Saint-Simon: An Exposition, First Year, 1828–9*. Trans. by G. Iggers. Boston, 1958.

Sauvageot, J., A. Geismar, D. Cohn-Bendit, and J. P. Duteuil. *The Student Revolt*. London, 1968.

Scaff, Lawrence A. *Participation in the Western Political Tradition: A Study of Theory and Practice*. Tucson, Ariz., 1975.

Scanlon, T. M. "Rawls' Theory of Justice," in Norman Daniels, ed., *Reading Rawls: Critical Studies of "A Theory of Justice,"* pp. 169–205. New York, 1975.

Schaar, John H. "Some Ways of Thinking about Equality." *Journal of Politics* 26 (1964):867–95.

Schachtman, Max. *The Bureaucratic Revolution*. New York, 1962.

Scheffler, Israel. *Science and Subjectivity*. New York, 1967.

Scheffler, Samuel. "Natural Rights, Equality, and the Minimal State." *Canadian Journal of Philosophy* 6 (March 1976):59–76.

Schiller, Marvin. "On the Logic of Being a Democrat." *Philosophy* 44 (1969):46–56.

Schwartz, Adina. "Moral Neutrality and Primary Goods." *Ethics* 83 (July 1973):294–307.

Bibliography

Schwartz, Pedro. *The New Political Economy of John Stuart Mill.* London, 1968.

Seliger, M. *The Liberal Politics of John Locke.* London, 1968.

Selznick, Philip. "An Approach to a Theory of Bureaucracy." *American Sociological Review* 8 (1943):47–54.

TVA and the Grass Roots: A Study in the Sociology of Formal Organization. New York, 1966.

Sen, A. K. "Rawls versus Bentham: An Axiomatic Examination of the Pure Distribution Problem," in Norman Daniels, ed., *Reading Rawls: Critical Studies of "A Theory of Justice,"* pp. 283–92. New York, 1975.

Sennett, Richard and Jonathan Cobb. *The Hidden Injuries of Class.* New York, 1971.

Shaw, George Bernard. *The Road to Equality: Ten Unpublished Letters and Essays.* Ed. by Louis Crompton. Boston, 1971.

Shaw, George Bernard, ed. *Fabian Essays in Socialism.* Gloucester, Mass., 1967 [1889].

Shklar, Judith N. *Men and Citizens.* Cambridge, 1969.

Shue, Henry. "Liberty and Self-Respect." *Ethics* 85 (April 1975):195–203.

Sidel, Victor and Ruth Sidel. *Serve the People: Observations on Medicine in the People's Republic of China.* Boston, 1973.

Sidgwick, Henry. *The Methods of Ethics.* 7th ed. London, 1907.

Simpson, Evan. "Socialist Justice." *Ethics* 87 (October 1976):1–17.

Skinner, Quentin. *The Foundations of Modern Political Thought.* Cambridge, 1978. Vol. II, *The Age of Reformation.*

Slote, Michael A. "Desert, Consent, and Justice." *Philosophy and Public Affairs* 2 (Summer 1973):323–47.

Smart, J. J. C. and Bernard Williams. *Utilitarianism: For and Against.* London, 1973.

Smith, David G. "Professional Responsibility and Political Participation," in J. Roland Pennock and John W. Chapman, eds., *Nomos XVI: Participation in Politics,* pp. 213–32. New York, 1976.

Smith, Marshall. "Equality of Educational Opportunity: Comments on Bowles and Levin," *Journal of Human Resources* 3 (Summer 1968):384–8.

Spencer, Herbert. *The Man versus the State.* New York, 1884.

The Principles of Ethics. Vol. II. London, 1893.

The Principles of Sociology. Vol. III. London, 1896.

Spiegelberg, Herbert. "A Defense of Human Equality." *Philosophical Review* 53 (March 1944):101–24.

Stephen, James Fitzjames. *Liberty, Equality, Fraternity.* Ed. by R. J. White. Cambridge, 1967 [1874].

Strauss, Leo. *Natural Right and History.* Chicago, 1953.

Subcommittee on Fiscal Policy of the Joint Economic Committee of the U.S. Congress. *How Income Supplements Can Affect Work Behavior.* Studies in Public Welfare, Paper 13. Washington, D.C. 1974.

Talmon, J. L. *The Rise of Totalitarian Democracy.* Boston, 1952.

Tawney, R. H. *The Acquisitive Society.* New York, 1921.

The Agrarian Problem in the Sixteenth Century. New York, 1967.

Equality. 4th rev. ed. London, 1952.

The Radical Tradition. London, 1966.

Bibliography

Teitelman, Michael. "The Limits of Individualism." *Journal of Philosophy* 69 (October 5, 1972):545–56.

Terrill, Ross. *R. H. Tawney and His Times*. Cambridge, Mass., 1973.

Thompson, Dennis F. *The Democratic Citizen: Social Science and Democratic Theory in the Twentieth Century*. Cambridge, 1970.

John Stuart Mill and Representative Government. Princeton, 1976.

Thomson, David. *Equality*. Cambridge, 1949.

Thurow, Lester C. *Generating Inequality: Mechanisms of Distribution in the U.S. Economy*. New York, 1975.

"Toward a Definition of Economic Justice." *Public Interest*, no. 31 (Spring 1973), pp. 58–80.

Titmuss, Richard. *The Gift Relationship: From Human Blood to Social Policy*. London, 1970.

Tocqueville, Alexis de. *Democracy in America*. Ed. by Phillips Bradley. New York, 1945 [1835].

Troeltsch, Ernst. *The Social Teaching of the Christian Churches*. Trans. by Olive Wyon. Vol. I. London, 1931.

Tucker, Robert C. *The Marxian Revolutionary Idea*. London, 1970.

Unger, Roberto Mangabeira. *Knowledge and Politics*. New York, 1975.

Upton, Letitia. *Basic Facts: Distribution of Personal Income and Wealth in the U.S.* Cambridge, Mass., 1972.

Verba, Sidney, Bashiruddhin Ahmed, and Anil Bhatt. *Race, Caste and Politics*. Beverly Hills, 1971.

Verba, Sidney and Norman N. Nie. *Participation in America*. New York, 1972.

Verba, Sidney, Norman N. Nie, and Jae-On Kim. *The Modes of Democratic Participation: A Cross-National Comparison*. Beverly Hills, 1971.

Vlastos, Gregory. "Justice and Equality," in Richard B. Brandt, ed., *Social Justice*, pp. 31–72. Englewood Cliffs, N.J., 1962.

Voltaire, François-Marie Arouet de. "Letter to Crown Prince Frederick," in *Voltaire's Correspondence*, ed. by Theodore Besterman, VI, 230–1. Geneva, 1954 [October 1737].

Wallwork, Ernest. *Durkheim: Morality and Milieu*. Cambridge, Mass., 1972.

Walzer, Michael. "In Defense of Equality." *Dissent*, Fall 1973, pp. 399–408.

Obligations: Essays on Disobedience, War, and Citizenship. Cambridge, Mass., 1970.

Watts, Harold and Glen Cain. "Basic Labor Responses from the Urban Experiment." *Journal of Human Resources* 9 (Spring 1974):156–278.

Weale, Albert. "Paternalism and Social Policy." *Journal of Society and Politics* 7, no. 2 (April 1978):157–72.

Webb, Sidney. *The Basis and Policy of Socialism*. London, 1908.

Webb, Sidney. Fabian Tract no. 69, *The Difficulties of Individualism*. London, 1896.

Webb, Sidney and Beatrice Webb. *The Consumer Co-Operative Movement*. London, 1921.

Industrial Democracy. London, 1902.

The Prevention of Destitution. London, 1911.

Weber, Max. *From Max Weber: Essays in Sociology*. Trans. and ed. by H. H. Gerth and C. Wright Mills. New York, 1958.

Bibliography

The Protestant Ethic and the Spirit of Capitalism. Trans. by Talcott Parsons. New York, 1958 [1904, 1920].

The Theory of Social and Economic Organization. Ed. by A. M. Henderson and Talcott Parsons. Glencoe, Ill., 1947.

Weldon, T. D. *The Vocabulary of Politics.* London, 1953.

Wertheimer, Alan. "In Defense of Compulsory Voting," in J. Roland Pennock and John W. Chapman, eds., *Nomos XVI: Participation in Politics,* pp. 276–96. New York, 1975.

Wexler, Stephen. "Expert and Lay Participation in Decision Making," in J. Roland Pennock and John W. Chapman, eds., *Nomos XVI: Participation in Politics,* pp. 186–94. New York, 1976.

White, Stephen W. "The Equality Principle: Is It Linguistically Justifiable?" *Personalist* 55 (1974):53–60.

Whyte, William H., Jr. *The Organization Man.* Garden City, N.Y., 1957.

Wilensky, Harold L. *The Welfare State and Equality: Structural and Ideological Roots of Public Expenditures.* Berkeley, 1974.

Williams, B. A. O. "The Idea of Equality," in Peter Laslett and W. G. Runciman, eds., *Philosophy, Politics and Society,* 2d ser., pp. 110–31. Oxford, 1962. Reprinted in Hugo A. Bedau, ed., *Justice and Equality,* pp. 116–37. Englewood Cliffs, N.J., 1971.

"The Minimal State." *Times Literary Supplement,* January 17, 1975, pp. 46–7.

"Political Philosophy and the Analytical Tradition." Paper presented at the annual international meeting of the Conference for the Study of Political Thought, New York, March 20–23, 1975.

Wilson, James Q. "The Bureaucracy Problem," in Alan A. Altshuler and Norman C. Thomas, eds., *The Politics of the Federal Bureaucracy,* 2d ed., pp. 57–62. New York, 1977.

"The Dead Hand of Regulation." *Public Interest,* no. 25 (Fall 1971), pp. 39–58.

Political Organizations. New York, 1973.

Varieties of Police Behavior: The Management of Law and Order in Eight Communities. New York, 1973.

Wilson, John. *Equality.* New York, 1966.

Wisconsin v. Yoder, 406 U.S. 205, 92 S. Ct. 1526 (1972).

Wolff, Robert Paul. *The Poverty of Liberalism.* Boston, 1968.

Understanding Rawls: A Reconstruction and Critique of "A Theory of Justice." Princeton, 1977.

Wolin, Sheldon S. *Politics and Vision.* Boston, 1960.

Wollheim, Richard. "A Paradox in the Theory of Democracy," in Peter Laslett and W. G. Runciman, eds., *Philosophy, Politics and Society,* 2d ser., pp. 71–87. Oxford, 1962.

Wood, Allen W. "The Marxian Critique of Justice." *Philosophy and Public Affairs* 1 (Spring 1972):244–82.

Wood, Robert C. *Suburbia.* Boston, 1959.

Work in America: Report of a Special Task Force to the Secretary of Health Education and Welfare. Cambridge, Mass., 1972.

Wyman v. James. 91 S. Ct. 381 (1971).

Young, Michael. *The Rise of the Meritocracy.* Baltimore, 1961.

Zaitchik, Alan. "On Deserving to Deserve." *Philosophy and Public Affairs* 6 (Summer 1977):370–88.

Index

Index

Index

Hook, Sidney, 248
Hospers, John, 157, 158, 263, 264
housing, 99, 100, 126
Howard, Lawrence C., 281
Howe, Irving, 284
Hubbard, F. Patrick, 286
human dignity, *see* dignity (human)
human nature
    Durkheim and Kant on, 5
    Kant's dualistic view of, 33
    Macpherson on, 151
    J. S. Mill on, 49, 51, 57, 58, 66
    Rawls's difference principle and, 130
    Rousseau on, 183, 204, 223, 272
Hume, David, 286
Humean conditions of justice, 145,
    151–2, 261

idealism, 41–2
income and wealth distribution
    in Crosland, 88
    democratic participation and, 190–1,
      196, 199, 200
    industrial democracy and, 203
    Macpherson on, 150–1, 260
    Rawls on, 125, 126, 131–40
    Tawney on, 79, 80–2
    Walzer on, 113, 117–18
individualism
    argument against, in Sidney Webb,
      73–4
    belief in human equality and, 18, 234
    Burke on, 18
    G. D. H. Cole on, 76
    as criticism of liberal egalitarianism,
      220–1
    implicatons of Hobbes's, 23
    methodological, and liberal theory, 3
    Saint-Simonian socialists on, 18
    in Spencer, 73
Ink, Dwight, 281
interest (communal)
    Mill on, 179–80
    Rousseau on, 182, 219
    Tawney on, 79–82, 84, 93
interests (individual)
    classical utilitarians on, 3–4, 21–2
    Durkheim on, 4, 232
    Hobbes on, 4
    Kant on, 4, 34
    liberal egalitarianism on, 202, 220–1,
      223–4, 226–7
    liberal rights theorists on, 3
    in a liberal theory of justice, 3–4
    Locke on, 7–9, 30
    J. S. Mill on, 4, 55, 59, 142–3, 179–80
    radical egalitarians on, 220–1, 284

Rawls on, 142–3, 218, 221
    Webbs on, 73
    see also conflict (social); self-interest
international egalitarianism, 170–2, 228
investment, 61–2, 134–5, 148, 257

Jacobs, Paul, 270
Jacques, Elliott, 282, 283
Jencks, Christopher, 269, 284
Jenkins, Roy, 92, 94
Jensen, Arthur, 45, 240
Johnson, Oliver, 254, 255
justice, *see* distributive justice

Kamin, Leon, 240
Kandor, Yaakov, 231
Kant, Immanuel, 1, 19–20, 27–8, 33–41,
    42, 120–2, 234, 237–41, 253, 254,
    255, 264
Kantianism, in Rawls, 120–2, 254, 255
Kariel, Henry S., 280
Katz, J., 250
Kaufman, Arnold S., 275
Kaufman, Herbert, 281
Keat, Russell, 256
Keim, Donald, W., 270, 272, 285
Kelley, Stanley, Jr., 273
Kelman, Mark, 256
Kendall, Willmoore, 236
Kim, Jae-On, 275, 276
kingdom of ends, 34, 35
Kingsley, J. Donald, 282
Kolakowski, Leszek, 232
Kolko, Gabriel, 231
Kramer, Daniel C., 278, 279
Krause, Elliot A., 281
Kretschmann, Philip, 238
Kretzmann, Norman, 240
Krislov, Samuel, 282
Kristol, Irving, 193, 251, 265, 276, 281,
    283, 287
Kropotkin, Peter, 256

Labour Party, 94
laissez-faire
    Fabians on, 71, 73–74, 77
    J. S. Mill on, 13, 58–63, 65–8, 243
    Tawney on, 78, 85–6
    see also capitalism; free market
Lakoff, Sanford A., 232
Lampman, Richard J., 232
Landau, Saul, 270
Lane, Robert E., 275, 283
Larson, Magali Sarfatti, 283
Laski, Harold J., 270
Laslett, Peter, 233, 240, 248, 268, 272
law (civil), 35, 36, 37

311

Index

Index

Index

Rousseau, Jean-Jacques, 6, 23, 36, 79, 83, 190, 204, 219–20, 223, 235, 238, 239, 245, 253, 268, 271–5, 284, 285, 287
Roussopoulos, Dimitrios, 280
Runciman, W. G., 89–90, 138, 233, 240, 247, 258, 268, 272
Russett, Bruce M., 231
Ryan, Alan, 241, 242, 258, 269

Sabine, George H., 234, 271
Saint-Simon, Claude-Henri, 234
Sauvageot, J., 280
Scaff, Lawrence A., 271
Scanlon, T. M., 256
Schaar, John H., 239, 240–1, 286
Schachtman, Max, 281
Scheffler, Israel, 267
Scheffler, Samuel, 267
Schiller, Marvin, 268
Schochet, Gordon, 269
schools, 191–7
    accountability and, 282
    conflict between distribution and participation and, 177–8, 191–7, 276, 277, 278
    in Detroit, 192–5
    in liberal egalitarian society, 201–2
    in New York, 192–5, 277, 278, 279
    rationales for participation and, 192–3, 276
    see also segregation, school
Schwartz, Adina, 254
Schwartz, Pedro, 243
segregation, school, 192, 194–5, 197, 277
self-development
    as argument for equalizing participation, 179–80, 188, 193, 194
    G. D. H. Cole on, 76–7, 206
    Macpherson on, 146, 150, 152
    Marx on, 150
    J. S. Mill on, 13, 53, 59, 63, 64, 68, 149, 150, 179–80, 198
    Pateman on, 206
    Rawls on, 149
self-esteem, 224–5, 230
self-interest
    Bentham on, 21
    Hobbes on, 21
    and Lockean self-ownership, 32
    James Mill on, 21, 22–5
    in the original position, 120, 140, 141, 142–3
    Spencer on, 73
self-ownership, 30–3, 157–9
self-protection, 178–9, 192

self-respect
    desert arguments and, 166
    Charles Frankel on, 223
    liberal egalitarianism on, 222–3, 224–5
    Macpherson and Marxists on, 147, 204
    Rawls on, 124–5, 126, 131, 136–8, 166, 222–3, 246, 255
    Rousseau on, 204
    Tawney on, 79, 81–2
    Michael Teitelman on, 222
    voting rights and, 187
    Walzer on, 112–3
Seliger, Martin, 29, 41–2, 236, 239
Selznick, Philip, 210, 280, 281–2
Sen, A. K., 258
Sennett, Richard, 260
separation of powers, 37
Shaw, G. B., 71, 244, 245, 253
Shklar, Judith, 253, 271, 272, 279, 284, 287
shoe pinching, 179, 193, 194
Shue, Henry, 256
Sidel, Ruth, 257
Sidel, Victor, 257
Sidgwick, Henry, 228, 287
Simpson, Evan, 284, 285, 287
Skinner, Quentin, 232, 234
Slote, Michael A., 265
Smart, J. J. C., 235, 271
Smith, David G., 283
Smith, Marshall, 278
social contract, 39, 204
    see also original position
socialism
    Fabians on, 69–70, 74–5, 86–7
    liberal egalitarianism on, 149
    J. S. Mill on, 66–7, 148
    new Fabians on, 87–90, 92
    Tawney on, 82, 83
    see also capitalism
social pluralism, 178, 269
social services, 70, 73, 77, 79, 91, 118, 126, 127
    see also employment; housing; legal services; medical services; rights (welfare); welfare state
Spencer, Herbert, 73–4, 161, 245, 265
Spiegelberg, Herbert, 240
state
    Burke on, 4, 18
    classical utilitarians on, 21–2
    Crosland on, 214
    Fabians on, 91
    Hobbes on, 5, 11, 19, 234, 235

DATE DUE

DEMCO 38-297